FRAGMENTS FROM
HELLENISTIC JEWISH AUTHORS

Society of Biblical Literature

SBL TEXTS AND TRANSLATIONS
PSEUDEPIGRAPHA SERIES

Harold W. Attridge, Editor

Texts and Translations Number 20
Pseudepigrapha Number 10

*FRAGMENTS FROM HELLENISTIC
JEWISH AUTHORS*

Volume I: *Historians*

by
Carl R. Holladay

FRAGMENTS FROM HELLENISTIC JEWISH AUTHORS

Volume I: Historians

Carl R. Holladay

Scholars Press
Chico, California

FRAGMENTS FROM HELLENISTIC JEWISH AUTHORS
Volume I: *Historians*

by
Carl R. Holladay

Cover photo reproduced from Eusebius, *Praeparatio Evangelica*, vol. I, E. H. Gifford, Oxford University Press, 1903.

©1983
Society of Biblical Literature

Library of Congress Cataloging in Publication Data
Main entry under title:

Fragments from Hellenistic Jewish authors.

(Pseudepigrapha series ; 10 ISSN 0145–3238) (Texts and translations ; no. 20) (ISSN 0145-3203)
English and Greek.
Bibliography: p.
Includes index.
1. Bible. O.T.—History of Biblical events— Addresses, essays, lectures. 2. Greek literature—Jewish authors. 3. Greek literature—Translations into English. 4. English literature—Translations from Greek. I. Holladay, Carl R. II. Series. III. Series: Society of Biblical literature. Texts and translations ; 20.
BS1197.F68 1980   221.9'5   79–18090
ISBN 0–89130–349–9

Printed in the United States of America

For DJ

TABLE OF CONTENTS

PREFACE

For some time there has existed the need for a comprehensive collection of the extant fragments from
Hellenistic Jewish authors. This was recognized as early
as the turn of this century when W. N. Stearns published
a collection entitled Fragments from Graeco-Jewish Writers
(1908). Prior to this time, these fragments were not
easily available, and even then were most often to be
found within larger collections of fragmentary sources
from antiquity, or within critical editions of individual
authors by whom they were quoted.

The major exception, of course, was J. Freudenthal's
pioneering work Hellenistische Studien: Alexander Polyhistor und die von ihm erhaltenen Reste judäischer und
samaritanischer Geschichtswerke (1875), still unsurpassed
in many respects and the starting point for any serious
work on these fragments. For the first time, Freudenthal
critically researched those Jewish historians preserved
by Alexander Polyhistor, and made a serious effort to
determine their authorship/pseudonymity, and to examine
historical, literary, and textual problems. Appended to
his highly informed and imaginative research were the
texts with limited critical apparatus embodying his many
text-critical suggestions. Still, Freudenthal limited his
investigation to those "Jewish and Samaritan historical
works" preserved by Alexander Polyhistor. Left untreated
were such authors as Ezekiel the Tragedian, Philo Epicus,
Theodotus, and Aristobulus.

Apart from Freudenthal, in the 19th century the
standard resource was C. Müller's monumental Fragmenta
Historicorum Graecorum, a five-volume work published

between 1841 and 1872. In the 20th century, Müller's collection was superseded by F. Jacoby's equally monumental collection, if not literary tour de force, Die Fragmente der griechischen Historiker, begun in 1923 and stretching though sixteen separate volumes until his death in 1959 halted its completion. Jacoby's work marked a significant advance. Whereas Müller had collected the texts, provided a Latin translation, and included limited, though valuable historical and critical notes, Jacoby not only included the texts but provided an apparatus criticus, and until near the end of the project wrote extensive and richly detailed commentaries on the fragments in accompanying volumes. He did not, however, include a translation. Both Müller and Jacoby included primarily "historical texts," which automatically excluded certain Hellenistic Jewish authors, such as the dramatic poet Ezekiel (though, oddly enough, Jacoby included Philo Epicus and Theodotus) and the philosopher Aristobulus.

In 1970, in response to the same need, there appeared A.-M. Denis' collection, Fragmenta pseudepigraphorum quae supersunt Graeca una cum historicorum et auctorum Judaeorum hellenistarum fragmentis. For the first time, all these important Hellenistic Jewish texts were conveniently collected in a single volume. The value of Denis' collection was considerably enhanced by his companion volume, Introduction aux Pseudepigraphes Grecs d'Ancient Testament (1970), which provided the necessary introductory material to each author. Yet, Denis' collection failed to provide an apparatus criticus or translation.

Apart from these collections of the Greek texts, these authors were mainly available in separate editions of the authors in whom they were preserved, most notably the standard editions of Eusebius' Praeparatio Evangelica. For the 19th century, this meant Heinichen, Gaisford, Migne, and Dindorf; for the 20th, Gifford and Mras.

In translation, these texts were most readily available collectively in P. Riessler's Altjüdisches Schrifttum
ausserhalb der Bibel (1927), which included brief annotations along with the translated texts. The next major
advance in this regard occurred with the beginning of the
series edited by W. G. Kümmel, Jüdische Schriften aus
hellenistisch-römischer Zeit. Responsible for most of the
Hellenistic Jewish fragmentary texts was N. Walter who had
devoted extensive research to them in his Habilitations-
schrift at Halle, entitled Untersuchungen zu den Fragmenten
der jüdisch-hellenistischen Historiker (1967-68).
Walter's translation significantly advanced Riessler's work
not only in its quality, but also because it took into
account extensive research on the fragments undertaken
within the last half-century. In addition, the format
followed by Jüdische Schriften was distinctly superior
to that used by Riessler, since it treated as a unit
the introductory material to each author, the translation
and annotations. Walter's bibliography is also quite
useful, though intentionally selective. His work is also
valuable because of the critical notes based on his use
of a critical text.

     The other major collection of these texts is that of
J. H. Charlesworth (ed.), Old Testament Pseudepigrapha
(1983-), which provides a long awaited up-to-date English
translation of these fragments along with other Jewish
pseudepigraphical texts. Also very useful, and to be
used in conjunction with this work, is Charlesworth's
bibliographical work, The Pseudepigrapha and Modern
Research with a Supplement (1981). Fortunately, most of
the assignments on these authors in Charlesworth's collection of the pseudepigrapha fell to John Strugnell's
students, many of whom participated in the 1970 Harvard
New Testament Seminar devoted exclusively to these
fragments. Charlesworth's edition marks the first time
the Hellenistic Jewish authors are conveniently collected
into English, and the work is rendered even more useful

because of the special Appendix containing an introduction
to the fragmentary authors written by Strugnell, and
detailed critical notes on these particular fragments
written by their translators.

The other form in which these authors were available
in translation were the translation of the individual
authors in whom they were preserved. The single most
important and widely used work in this regard was Gifford's
edition of the Praeparatio Evangelica, which contained
not only a critical text, but an English translation, and
a separate volume of critical notes. Most of the critical
work on the fragments lay embedded in this, and similar
editions. Especially useful, and a mine of information
for all subsequent scholars, were Seguier's annotations
which were included in the Migne edition of the Praeparatio
(PG, 21). Another valuable resource, both for translation
and critical notes, is the edition of the Praeparatio
in Sources chrétiennes, although the volume devoted to
Book 9, which contains most of the fragments, has not
yet appeared.

This collection of Fragments from Hellenistic Jewish
Authors has been conceived and prepared for scholars and
students who wish to work closely with these texts. It
has grown out of my own need for a collection which provides
in accessible form the Greek text, critical apparatus,
English translation, introductory material to each author,
including bibliography, and annotations to the translation.
It was not originally conceived as, nor should it be used
as, an editio maior, for I have only consulted and worked
with the editions prepared by others. I have examined
none of the manuscripts themselves, and consequently in
the apparatus criticus I have attempted mainly to collect,
and present accurately, the work of my predecessors.

In preparing this volume, I have accumulated many
debts to students and colleagues at Yale and Emory who
have participated in seminars and conversations about
these texts. Among the research assistants to whom I owe

a special word of thanks are Katherine Cunningham and
Melinda Reagor at Yale, and Allen Black, Steve Pattison,
and John York at Emory, especially for their assistance
with bibliographical matters, but other details as well.
John Strugnell was especially gracious, at an early stage,
in making available to me the seminar papers from the 1970
Harvard New Testament Seminar which have proved invaluable
in the formation of my own opinions about these authors
and in the preparation of my own text and notes. Harold
Attridge, the general editor of the SBL Texts and Translations Series (Pseudepigrapha), has saved me from numerous
errors while being abidingly patient and unfailingly prompt
in returning materials. He, and Robert Doran, were also
very generous in making available pertinent materials,
including their own published work on these authors. I
should also like to thank the staffs of Yale Divinity
School Library and Pitts Theology Library of the Candler
School of Theology at Emory for their very kind assistance,
especially to Sara Mobley, Reference Librarian at Pitts.
The completion of this work was made possible through
a sabbatical leave from Candler School of Theology in
1982-83, and to Dean Jim Waits I am especially grateful
for this.

Atlanta
June 1, 1983

INTRODUCTION

The importance of the Hellenistic Jewish authors whose works exist in fragmentary form is being recognized increasingly. They are the first named Jewish authors from the Hellenistic period known to have written in Greek. Their provenance was the eastern Mediterranean, most likely Palestine and Egypt, although it is difficult to be certain in each case. What distinguishes them, in particular, is that they are the first clear examples of Jewish authors self-consciously writing in explicitly Greek literary modes.

Still, their continuity with the biblical tradition is manifest, even though they appropriate it in a fascinating variety of ways. They belong to what appears to have been an embryonic period in that stage of the development of Judaism when Jews and pagans were becoming more fully aware of each other's existence and traditions. Accordingly, they exhibit intriguing configurations where Jewish and pagan religious traditions have become intermixed and fused. They display many of the features and much of the spirit of the Hellenistic era, and for this reason scholars have been interested in them because of the examples they afford of the Hellenization of Judaism. They have also engaged the attention of scholars because of how they illuminate the social process through which a minority ethnic group accommodates and adapts to the larger, dominant culture in which it lives. Research on these fragments, as has happened in other areas of Judaism in the Graeco-Roman world, has served to alter many previously held scholarly conceptions about the nature and shape of Jewish religiosity in the Hellenistic-Roman period.

At one time, an author as seemingly open to Hellenis-
tic-Egyptian influence as Artapanus was inexplicable, and
could only be seen as a pagan, an apostate Jew, or perhaps
a Samaritan. Now, however, after decades of research on
the complexion of Judaism during the period of the Second
Temple, the sometimes bewildering variety and complexity
of the forms of Jewish religiosity are more fully recognized,
although scholarly debate still seeks fuller understanding
of this phenomenon and its historical and sociological
implications. Long gone is the positing of a "normative
Judaism" over against which every other expression of the
Jewish faith is measured and assessed as an nth degree
removed from the "center" toward some hypothetical
periphery. Now, both the "center" and the "periphery" are
seen to be historical constructs, and historians of religion have begun to reformulate the questions, and have
asked, for example, about modes of self-definition as they
seek to understand how particular persons or groups of
persons understood their own religious experience and
traditions, and how they interpreted them in their historical and social setting.

The fragmentary Hellenistic Jewish authors continue to
intrigue many scholars, not only because they document
many of the less familiar, and less well-known, aspects
of the life and thought of Greek-speaking Jews, living in
both Palestine and the Diaspora during the Hellenistic-
Roman period, but also because they are early representatives of traditions whose later forms and proponents are
far better known. The roots of the historiographical tradition as it is embodied in Josephus, long seen in continuity with 1 & 2 Maccabees, can be explored much more
fully in the fragmentary remains of earlier exponents of
this tradition, such as Demetrius the Chronographer and
Eupolemus. That Philo of Alexandria stands within a
hermeneutical tradition much earlier reflected in Aristobulus has long been known. In a word, these authors have
become valuable evidence in exploring and reconstructing

the history of traditions within Hellenistic Judaism
during one of its most shadowy periods where the sources
still remain scant.

Although the success of these authors' attempts to
write history, poetry, and philosophy in a Greek mode
must be judged partial, at best, they are nonetheless
valuable testimonies for our understanding of Judaism
during the Hellenistic-Roman period. At many points,
they exhibit interaction with a tradition of the Greek
Bible, and thus become invaluable resources for uncovering
the early history of the Septuagint. In some instances,
they may even provide examples of Greek translations of
the Bible independent of the Septuagint tradition. As in
much writing of this period, anachronism abounds, and
while they may attempt to describe an earlier era, their
value to us is often in what they tell us about the
history of the Jews in the Hellenistic-Roman period.
The Maccabean period is especially illuminated by some
of these authors. Because they stand in continuity with
the biblical tradition, they are often important examples
of midrashic interpretations, and they continue to raise
questions about the relationship between modes of biblical
interpretation in Palestine vis-à-vis those used in
Diaspora settings. Also significant about these authors
is the degree of self-consciousness in their literary
endeavors. The mere fact that they have chosen what at
the time must have been novel genres in which to reflect
and write about their Jewish heritage is itself significant, for it shows that they had entered a new literary
arena, and were expecting their efforts to be judged in a
much broader setting. It also reflects a confident position vis-à-vis the culture in which they lived. That they
were doing so in behalf of their faith is almost unexcep-
tionally true, and in this sense they are engaged in
religious propaganda. They have long been seen and
interpreted as standing within the tradition of Jewish
apologetic, a tradition deeply indebted to pagan apologetic

and highly influential on later Christian apologetic.

The authors included here are generally treated as
belonging to a distinct group. They are all named
authors, though in some cases pseudonymous, from the
Hellenistic-Roman period writing in distinctively Greek
genres: history, ethnography, poetry, and philosophy.
This in itself distinguishes them from most all the other
authors/texts generally included among the apocrypha and
pseudepigrapha, and certainly suggests a level of
participation in Hellenistic culture which would otherwise
be little known to us from other sources.

They are arranged here in probable chronological
order. The earliest of them appears to have been Demetrius
the Chronographer who flourished in Alexandria perhaps
as early as the mid-third century B.C.E. Eupolemus is
dated with relative certainty in the mid-second century
B.C.E., and confidently located in Palestine. Placed
after him is the anonymous Samaritan author, Pseudo-
Eupolemus, who also appears to belong to the early to mid-
second century B.C.E., and reflects a Samaritan provenance.
Artapanus is confidently located in Egypt and most likely
flourished during the reign of Ptolemy VI Philometor
(180-145 B.C.E.). Cleodemus Malchus, perhaps a Samaritan
author, is reasonably dated in the mid-second century
B.C.E., and Aristeas "the exegete," who is difficult to
locate, at least antedated Alexander Polyhistor (mid-
first century B.C.E.), and may be placed sometime in the
second century B.C.E. The dating of Pseudo-Hecataeus
is complicated by the question of the authenticity of the
various fragments attributed to Hecataeus, but the Jewish
author who wrote in the name of Hecataeus, however extensively, can be dated as early as the mid-second century
B.C.E. Theophilus antedated Alexander Polyhistor (mid-
first century B.C.E.), and this is all that can be said
with certainty. Thallus likely flourished in the mid- to
late first century C.E. The latest Hellenistic Jewish
author whose works survive in fragmentary form is Justus

of Tiberias who flourished in Palestine in the last
quarter of the first century C.E., and perhaps even
into the second century C.E.

A word should be said about the principle of inclusion.
This collection attempts to bring together all those
Greek-speaking Jewish authors whose works have survived
in fragmentary form, but the list is not at all easy to
construct. From the above list, Pseudo-Hecataeus,
Theophilus, and Thallus are the clearest borderline cases.
Nevertheless, in the history of Hellenistic Jewish
scholarship, plausible cases have been argued for their
Jewish identity and it seemed appropriate to include them
here.

Authors included by Jacoby in the "Juden" section of
FGrH 3C, who wrote about the Jews and whose works exist
in fragmentary form, but who were clearly pagan are not
included here. These include Apollonius Molon (No. 728 =
Stern, GLAJJ 1.148-56, Nos. 46-50), Alexander Polyhistor
(after No. 729 = No. 273 = Stern, GLAJJ 1.157-63, Nos. 51-
53), Teucer of Cyzicus (after No. 729 = No. 274, T 1 =
Stern, GLAJJ 1.165-66, No. 54), Damocritus (No. 730 =
Stern, GLAJJ 1.530-31, No. 247), Apion (after No. 730 =
No. 616, T 11 = Stern, GLAJJ 1.389-416, Nos. 163-77),
Nicharchus, the son of Ammonius (No. 731 = Stern, GLAJJ
1.532-33, No. 248), Antonius Julianus (No. 735 = Stern,
GLAJJ 1.458-61, No. 201), Philo of Byblos (after No. 735 =
No. 790, Frgs. 9-11 = Stern, GLAJJ 2.138-45, Nos. 323-39),
and Ptolemy (after No. 736 = No. 199 = Stern, GLAJJ 1.355-
56, No. 146).

In addition to these, there are those Hellenistic
Jewish authors known to have written historical works
but of which there are no extant fragments. These
include the following:

(1) One such author appears to have been Judas
(FGrH 261), mentioned by Eusebius, H.E. 6.6.7, as having
composed a "written discourse on the seventy weeks in
the book of Daniel." The name suggests that he was Jewish,

but in what sense, if any, his was an historical work, is unclear. It apparently dealt with chronological matters, and may well have been an apocalyptic work.

(2) Jacoby also includes John Hyrcanus I (No. 736) whose achievements were recorded "in the chronicles of his high priesthood" (1 Macc 16:23-24), but no fragments of this work are extant.

(3) In this same category belongs "Philo the Elder" who is said by Clement to have treated the Jewish kings differently from Demetrius the Chronographer (Strom. 1.21.141.3). He is apparently the same Philo whom Josephus regards as a pagan author and includes with Demetrius of Phalerum and Eupolemus as "exceptional in their approximation to the truth" (Ag.Ap. 1.218). Clement seems to imply that this Philo wrote a separate work on the Jewish kings, but no fragments from the work exist. Though he is sometimes treated as a separate author (e.g., Walter, JSHRZ (1,2) 112-14), he has been identified with Philo Epicus who will be treated in the second volume. Further discussion of his "historical work" will be found there.

(4) Pseudo-Hystaspes should also be mentioned here. A Greek work attributed to Hystaspes, the father of King Darius, is mentioned by Justin (Apol. 1.20.1), Clement (Strom. 6.5.43.1-2), and Lactantius (Div. Inst. 7.15.19; 18.2-3). The work was apparently apocalyptic in nature, containing predictions of the destruction of the world and a reference to the Messianic Son of God. The work is certainly Jewish, and arguably Christian. No fragments have survived (Cf. Denis, Introduction, 268-69; Schürer, Literature, 292-94).

Still another category exists which includes two authors:

(1) The memoirs (ὑπομνήματα) of Herod the Great are cited by Josephus as the source of his account of the execution of Hyrcanus (cf. Ant. 15.164-68, esp. 174). It is likely that he knew them only indirectly through

Nicolaus of Damascus, Herod's secretary. They are
mentioned in Jacoby's listing after No. 736, and excerpted
in No. 236. Though they deal with historical matters,
as "memoirs" they are generally excluded from the category
of Hellenistic Jewish historians, and consequently are
not included in this collection.

(2) It is well known that Jason of Cyrene (mentioned
by Jacoby after No. 735 = No. 182) devoted a five-volume
work to the Maccabean period, and that 2 Maccabees is an
epitome of this earlier work, written ca. 160 B.C.E.
(cf. 2 Macc 2:19-32). While extensive efforts have been
made to reconstruct the original work, or to attribute
certain parts of 2 Macc to Jason through literary
analysis, because no other fragments from the work exist
apart from 2 Macc, he is not included here, but is best
dealt with in connection with 2 Macc., concerning which
there is abundant scholarly literature.

Finally, Aristo of Pella, mentioned by Jacoby after
No. 735, but excerpted in No. 236, was a Christian
apologist (cf. Eusebius, H.E. 4.6.4, on which cf.
Lawlor-Oulton, 2.122-23; ODCC 82-83).

In a separate volume are included those authors
generally designated poets--Ezekiel the Tragedian,
Philo Epicus (FGrH No. 729), and Theodotus (FGrH No. 732),
along with Aristobulus and Pseudo-Phocylides.

The Transmission of the Texts

With few exceptions, the authors included here were
preserved by Eusebius in the Praeparatio Evangelica. He
had not read them directly, however, but excerpted them
from Alexander Polyhistor's work Concerning the Jews.
Accordingly, Alexander Polyhistor and Eusebius will be
treated as the primary tradents. Second in importance to
Eusebius in this respect is Clement of Alexandria
Stromata in which some of the fragments were first
preserved. Because of the overriding importance of the
Eusebius tradition, however, it will be treated in detail.

(i) <u>Alexander Polyhistor</u>.   The majority of these
texts were first preserved by L. Cornelius Alexander,
more familiarly known as Alexander Polyhistor, who was
born at Miletus in Asia Minor ca. 105 B.C.E.   Taken
prisoner by Sulla in his war against Mithridates VI, he
was brought to Rome where he was freed ca. 80 B.C.E.   In
Rome he became an influential teacher and counted among
his students Julius Hyginus.   He was accidentally burned
to death at Laurentum near Rome ca. 35 B.C.E.

Writing at Rome in the mid-first century B.C.E.,
Alexander Polyhistor was mainly an epitomist who excerpted
ethnographical materials on various places (e.g., Delphi
and Rome) and peoples (e.g., the Jews), and collected
a variety of other materials ranging from popular miracle
stories to philosophy and literary criticism.   He is quite
unoriginal in his treatment of the materials he collected,
but valuable to us precisely for this reason, for this
increases the likelihood that the excerpts he preserved
were relatively accurate.   The very fact that a pagan
writing in Rome in the mid-first century B.C.E. both knew
and used Jewish sources is itself significant, and too
seldom recognized in reconstructions of Judaism in the
Hellenistic-Roman period.   Unfortunately, only scattered
fragments from Alexander Polyhistor's vast literary output
have survived, but they have been conveniently collected
by Jacoby in <u>FGrH</u> 273, and even more comprehensively by
Müller in <u>FHG</u> 3.206-44.   The fragments excerpted from
Jewish authors are most likely from a separate ethnographic
work, Περὶ ʼΙουδαίων (cf. Clement, <u>Strom</u>. 1.21.130.3;
Eusebius, <u>P.E.</u> 9.17.1), devoted entirely to Judaica.

(ii) <u>Eusebius</u>. Alexander Polyhistor became a
primary source for Eusebius in his apologetic work the
<u>Praeparatio Evangelica</u>, written after his celebrated
<u>Historica Ecclesiastica</u>, and conceived as a prolegomenon
to the <u>Demonstratio Evangelica</u>.   The fragments are cited
by Eusebius primarily because they are preserved by a

pagan author who became a valuable witness to the antiquity
of Judaism, and by extension, to the credibility of
Christianity. The former, of course, was to become a
major theme in both Jewish and Christian apologetic.

With few exceptions, most of the Jewish authors
are excerpted in Book 9 of P.E., although some occur in
Book 10 (Pseudo-Hecataeus) and Book 13 (Aristobulus).

The Textual History of the Praeparatio Evangelica.

The textual history of P.E. is most thoroughly treated by
K. Mras, Die Praeparatio Evangelica (GCS, 43,1), vol. 1,
pp. xiii-liv. The earlier work by I. A. Heikel, De
Praeparationis Evangelicae Eusebii edendae ratione (1888)
is also valuable, but was taken into full account by
Mras. P. Henry's Recherches sur la Préparation Évangélique
d'Eusèbe et l'édition perdue des oeuvres de Plotin publiée
par Eustochius (Bibl. de l'École des Hautes-Études,
Sc. rel. 50, 1935) was not taken into account by Mras,
but does inform the brief survey of the textual tradition
of P.E. by E. des Places in La préparation évangélique
(Sources chrétiennes, 206; 1975), vol. 1, pp. 55-58.

There is a broad consensus among textual critics who
have dealt with the manuscript tradition of P.E. that the
MS evidence can be divided into two major families with
one MS (I) occupying a mediating position. The first
family has as its chief representative A, the oldest extant
MS of P.E., dated in 914 C.E. It contains the writings
of several authors, including Eusebius, but only Books
1-5 of P.E. Since none of our fragments derives from
this section of P.E., as a witness it is irrelevant for
our purposes. The other chief witness of this family is
H, an eleventh century MS, but it too contains only Books
1-5, and is clearly dependent directly on A. Thus, neither
is of any value for this collection. In this family,
des Places also includes S, a tenth century parchment
MS of minor importance.

The second family constitutes a definable text type
whose chief representatives are BO(G)VND, all of which
contain Books 1-15. The principal representative of this
family is O, a paper MS copied at the end of the thirteenth
century by a scribe named Nicephorus, whom Mras designated
O^1. Because the ink used by O^1 was fading, chapters 1-8
were recopied about fifty years later (but prior to 1344)
by a scribe designated O^y. A third hand, O^z, made some
corrections after the work of O^1, but before O^y. G, a
paper MS dated in 1344, has been copied from O^y. This is
now well established and widely accepted. It is therefore
only subsidiary to O, but useful enough to be mentioned
separately because it fills in several places where O is
hard to read. Two other MSS, F and C, are directly copied
from G, and thus of no direct value in preparing a
textual edition.

The other major representatives of the second family
are of unequal value. The earliest is B, a thirteenth
century paper MS, copied primarily by a single scribe,
Longinus, who worked very carelessly. He simplified forms
and omitted lines, sections and chapters. He even left
out the entire twelfth book! Because of his carelessness,
approximately one-third of P.E. has been omitted in B.
However, according to Mras, the Vorlage he used was of
good quality. The few places where his text is longer
than the other MSS are likely to be genuine and should be
given careful consideration. Not surprisingly, the work
of several correctors can be detected in B. Not only did
B^1 (Longinus) correct many mistakes himself, but other
correctors whom Mras designates as B^2, B^x, and B^4 worked
to improve his MS. B^y is the siglum used by Mras to
indicate that he cannot identify the hand of a corrector
with certainty, and thus a reading so designated cannot
be clearly assigned to B^2, B^x, or B^4.

V, a paper MS from the beginning of the fourteenth
century (1335), written by a single copyist, is well
preserved and of high literary quality. It is an excellent

representative of the second family, but provides nothing
really new when compared with other witnesses.

N, a well preserved fifteenth century paper MS, was
written by a single copyist, though a few corrections stem
from a second hand. Although Heikel believed that N
derived from O, Mras regards N as an independent representative of the second family because in many instances
it has preserved, over against O, the genuine reading of
that family. However, kinship between N and O is
especially prominent in Books 1-9 and in the last two
books. N is even more closely related to D and comes
from the same Vorlage used by D, except in Book 9 (see
comments on D).

D, a sixteenth century paper MS, is written by two
hands, the first of whom is designated as Damaskenos,
who wrote the majority of the MS. Book 9, however, was
written by a second hand, D^2 (my designation). Mras
establishes that D^2 copied Book 9 from I or j (see
comments on I and j). As mentioned in the previous
paragraph, apart from Book 9, D is the twin of N, stemming
from the same Vorlage. Two other copyists -- D^x and D^4 --
made corrections and additions (using I or j).

Representing a mediating position between these two
families is another witness, I, a fifteenth century MS,
written by two copyists, designated by Mras as I^a and I^b.
Book 9 is part of the work of I^a. Generally, I depends
on two sources: (1) B, in Books 1-3.1.5, and in Book
15.17.1-15.62.18, and (2) a Vorlage (now lost) belonging
primarily to family one, but influenced by MSS from the
other family. Overall, I is an excellent text, though
unreliable in orthographical matters. It is an important
MS primarily because it represents a mediating position
between the two families (except in Books 1, 2, and 15,
where it is directly dependent on B). It is also
important because it is the MS translated into Latin
by George Trapezunt, the first Latin translation of P.E.
I also contains corrections from three other hands:

I^x, I^y, and I^z.

Another witness, related to I, is j, a fifteenth
century MS written in Rome by Kosmas, a monk, for
Bessarion, bishop of Rome. Though disputed, its direct
dependence on I has been established by Mras who found
the same peculiarities in j as in I and gives convincing
examples proving direct dependence. It is important for
establishing the chronology of I. Since j copied from I,
and since j is firmly dated in 1470, this provides a
terminus ante quem for I. E, a paper MS of the sixteenth
century, was copied from j.

At the conclusion of his description of the major
MSS, Mras sketches their relationship as follows:

$$A(H) \mid I \mid\mid BO(G)VND$$

This formula indicates that there are two basic families,
A(H) and BO(G)VND, with I occupying a mediating position
which is closer to the A family. The parentheses around
H and G indicate that they are copies of A and O respec-
tively and are thus only valuable for supplementing A and
O. Mras omits j and E as copies of I.

Since A and H do not contain Book 9, and since in
Book 9, D was copied from I and j, the relationship of the
MSS in Book 9 may be represented as follows:

$$I(j,D) \mid BO(G)VN$$

In this case, j and D are probably of negligible value.

The general principles guiding Mras in the preparation
of his text are as follows: in Books 6-15, I is preferred
when it is more detailed and complete than the other MSS.
When this is not the case, a decision has been made based
on the individual merits of the reading. Generally, a
reading is regarded as correct (1) in Books 1-5 when A and
I agree, and (2) in Books 6-15 when B and I agree. It
should be noted that this procedure seems questionable

for chapter 15.17.1-15.62.18 where I copied from B. Mras
has also made a few conjectures. He is very cautious in
this respect and is critical of previous editors, who
in his opinion made too many conjectures.

A word should also be said about the chapter headings
which appear throughout the work, and which occur frequently in the fragments. Mras convincingly demonstrated
that they, along with the table of contents for each
book were prepared by Eusebius himself. Later editors
often omitted them, but Bidez rightly questioned their
omission by Gifford in his edition. Their authenticity
can be established by conclusive proofs, e.g., the titles
often presuppose the contents of the chapters and vice
versa. They should be regarded as an intrinsic part of
the work. Numerous examples are cited by Mras (viii-ix).

Preparation of the Text and Apparatus

In the fragments preserved by Eusebius, I have used
the text of K. Mras, _Die Praeparatio Evangelica_, Bd. 8,
Eusebius Werke (_GCS_, 43; Berlin: Akademie Verlag, 1954-56),
with the kind permission of the Akademie Verlag. The
apparatus criticus for each of these fragments has been
prepared, based primarily on Mras' apparatus, but always
in close consultation with Jacoby, _FGrH_ 3C, Nos. 722-37.
It should be noted here that in constructing his apparatus,
Jacoby consistently omitted references to MS N, probably
because of Heikel's contention that N was derived from O.
Moreover, Mras' apparatus proved to be constructed with
far greater care and accuracy than Jacoby's, and thus
provided a far superior basis for constructing my
apparatus.

In supplying Mras' text, I have retained his
punctuation, paragraph divisions, format of indentations,
and numbering system. I have also retained his practice
of supplying the paragraph division numbers of Viger in
the margin, with a vertical line (|) within the text
marking the page divisions, although I have checked each

of these in Viger independently. Only in the form of the
chapter headings have I altered the form of Mras' text.

   In constructing the apparatus criticus, I have
sought to include all of Mras' variants, but have supplemented them when necessary from other editions, mostly
from Jacoby. Not all of Mras' variants have been included.
Some minor orthographical variants, insignificant numerical
variants, and other minor grammatical variants have in
some cases been omitted. In selecting the variants to be
included, I have followed this principle: once the decision has been made to include a "variation unit," all of
the MS evidence adduced by Mras has been transmitted to
my apparatus, and I have sought to do so with as much
clarity and exacting detail as Mras did. Because he had
examined the manuscripts with such painstaking care,
recording his findings with such lucidity and accuracy,
this has not always been possible to the same degree.
Parallel references, explanatory comments, and other
information provided by Mras within his apparatus which
is not directly related to the manuscript tradition, I have
not included in my apparatus, but have sought to incorpo-
rate within the annotations at the end of each section.
I have taken an additional liberty: because of the
peculiar tendencies of B, I have been more generous in
including variants from B in the apparatus, thus allowing
the interested reader to follow the tendencies of B with
some consistency.

   I have also followed Mras' practice of listing in
the register directly above the apparatus the pertinent
MSS for a particular fragment. It may be assumed that
these are the MSS in which a given fragment is located.
In most instances, this has meant BION, but there are
some exceptions. In those cases, the relationship between
the MSS can be clarified by the discussion in the above
section, or by consulting Mras directly.

This is also the appropriate place to note an
important difference between Mras' and Freudenthal's
textual critical work on these authors. Whereas Mras
was only interested in reconstructing the original text
of Eusebius, Freudenthal (and later Jacoby) sought to
reconstruct the original text of the Jewish authors
themselves. Accordingly, Freudenthal proposes conjectures
far more often than does Mras, who, after all, had little
need to do so, given the nature of his work. For this
reason, internal contradictions within the text remain
in Mras' edition of Eusebius, whereas Freudenthal, on
the other hand, sought to reconcile such problems when
he encountered them.

In preparing the text and the apparatus criticus, I
have used M. L. West, Textual Criticism and Editorial
Technique (Stuttgart: B. G. Teubner, 1973), as the
fundamental guide. The form of the apparatus conforms
to his suggestions, and the changes in the editorial
sigla from those used by Mras are thereby explained.
Since it has been impossible to reproduce Mras' apparatus
exactly, I have sought to retain the exactness and preci-
sion he achieved but in the form suggested by West. I
have followed West's suggestions as rigorously as possible,
except when I thought the nature of this collection
demanded otherwise. For example, West recommends that
"the statement of sources of a transmitted reading
should not be augmented by names of editors or critics
who have approved it" and that" with conjectures, only
the original propounder should be named" (p. 90, n. 19).
I have followed this advice in most cases, but in those
instances where the crucial role played by editors in
reconstructing and interpreting these texts has figured
prominently in the scholarly debate, I have included more
than the "original propounder."

In the case of those fragments not preserved in
Eusebius, P.E., but in his H.E., or in other sources,
I have followed the same practice: to use the apparatus
from the critical edition from which the text is cited
as the basis of my apparatus, but supplemented with
information from other relevant editions or sources, but
placed in the form suggested by West. Thus, I have
sought to achieve uniformity in the use of sigla, abbreviations, and format throughout the work, in spite of the
great variety in the editions from which the fragments
are taken.

Manuscripts

In this listing of the MSS, to assist the reader in
the use of the apparatus criticus, I have included the MSS
from the various primary sources from which the fragments
are taken. The following are the most frequently used
sources for the fragments, with P.E. by far the most
important single source, and Stromata the second:
Eusebius, P.E., Clement, Strom., and Josephus, Ag.Ap.
The following sources supply only a few of the fragments,
in most cases, only one fragment: Eusebius, H.E.
(Aristobulus, Frg. 1); Josephus, Ant. (Cleodemus Malchus,
Frg. 1); Life (Justus of Tiberias, Frgs. 4 & 5), Epiphanius,
Panarion (Ezekiel the Tragedian, Frg. 4); Syncellus
(Thallus, Frgs. 1 & 5; Justus of Tiberias, Frgs. 2 & 3),
Theophilus, Ad Autolycum (Thallus, Frg. 2), Diogenes
Laertius (Justus of Tiberias, Frg. 1).

For ease of reference, the sources are listed below
in alphabetical order (by author).

Manuscripts (cont.)

1. Clement, Stromata

    L   Laurentianus V 3, 11th cent.

          L^1 The original scribe who corrected many
                         mistakes

          L^2-L^3 Two younger hands who corrected many
                         mistakes

    Ath   Cod. Athous (Codex Lawra B 113), 11th cent.

    (Cf. Stählin-Früchtel, GCS (52[15]), vol. 2, pp.
    vii-xv and xvii.)

2. Epiphanius, Panarion

    V   Vaticanus 503

    M   Marcianus 125

    U   Urbinas 17/18

    (Cf. K. Holl, GCS (31), vol. 2, p. v.)

3. Eusebius, Historia Ecclesiastica

    A   Paris, Bibliothèque Nationale 1430

          a   Rome, Vaticanus 399, copy of A

    B   Paris, Bibliothèque Nationale 1431

          b   Venice, Marcianus 339, copy of B

          β   Paris, Bibliothèque Nationale 1432, copy
                  of B

    D   Paris, Bibliothèque Nationale 1433

    E   Florence, Laurentianus 70, 20

    M   Venice, Marcianus 338

    R   Moscow, Library of H. Synod 50

    T   Florence, Laurentianus 70,7

3.   Eusebius, <u>Historia Ecclesiastica</u>

      Π   Text of Greek MSS

            1   First hand

            c   Older corrector distinguishable from the
                      original author

            r   More recent corrector

            m   In the margin

      Σ   Syriac translation (Wright and M'Lean, <u>The
            Ecclesiastical History of Eusebius in Syriac</u>
            [Cambridge, 1898]; German translation by Nestle
            <u>TU</u> N.F. 6.2 [Leipzig, 1901])

            Σ^t Chapter headings within the text

            Σ^a MS in Petersburg

            Σ^b London, British Museum Add. 14639

            Σ^{arm} Armenian translation of Syriac trans-
                      lation, Venice, 1877.

            Σ^e Excerpts, e.g., Wright and M'Lean, p.
                      vii.

            [ɡ̌]   Agreement of a biblical citation in Σ
                      with the Syriac translation of the Bible

      Manuscripts of Rufinus:

      F   München 6375 (Freisingen)

      N   Paris, Bibliothèque Nationale 18282

      O   Paris, Bibliothèque Nationale 5500

      P   Rome, Vaticanus Palatinus 822

      Λ   = Rufinus

      (Cf. Schwartz/Mommsen, <u>GCS</u> (9.1), p. 1.)

4.   Eusebius, _Praeparatio Evangelica_

A   Codex Parisinus graecus 451, 914 C.E.

B   Codex Parisinus graecus 465, 13th century
       (3rd quarter)

C   Codex Parisinus graecus 466, 16th century

D   Codex Parisinus graecus 467, 16th century
       (older than E)

E   Codex Parisinus graecus 468, 16th century

F   Codex Laurentianus Plut. VI 6, 15th century

G   Codex Laurentianus VI 9, 1344 C.E.

H   Codex Marcianus graecus 343, 11th century

I   Codex Marcianus graecus 341, 15th century

j   Codex Marcianus graecus 342, 1470 C.E.

N   Neapolitanus graecus II AA 16, 15th century

O   Codex Bononiensis Univ. 3643, end of 13th century

V   Codex Batopedianus 180, 1335 C.E.

(Cf. Mras, _GCS_ (43.1 [8]), vol. 1, pp. XIII-LVIII,
esp. p. LIX.)

5.   Josephus, _Against Apion_

L   Codex Laurentianus, Plut. 69.22, 11th cent.

Lat. Old Latin version commissioned by Cassiodorus

(Cf. H. St. J. Thackeray, _LCL_, vol. 1, pp. xviii-xix.)

6.   Josephus, _Antiquities_

       Whenever possible, fragments which first appear
in Josephus have been taken from Niese's _editio_ _maior_.
For the _Antiquities_, a thorough discussion of the
textual tradition underlying Niese's text may be
found in vol. 1, pp. v-lxxx. The textual authorities
cited by Niese (summarized by Thackeray in _LCL_, vol.
4, pp. xvii-xviii) are as follows:

6.   Josephus, Antiquities (cont.)

E   Epitome antiquitatum. Epitome used by Zonaras
     and conjectured by Niese to have been made in
     the 10th or 11th century. Written in good
     Attic Greek and omits Vita.

L   Codex Laurentianus, plut. 69.20, 14th century

M   Codex Marcianus (Venice), Gr. no. 381, 13th
     century

O   Codex Oxoniensis (Bodleianus), miscell. gr.
     186, 15th century

P   Codex Parisinus Gr. 1419, 11th century

R   Codex Regius Parisinus Gr. 1421, 14th century

S   Codex Vindobonensis II. A 19, histor. Gr. 2,
     11th century

V   Codex Vaticanus, Gr. no. 147, 14th century

Lat. Latin version made by order of Cassiodorus,
     5th or 6th century

Zon. Chronicon of J. Zonaras, 12th century

Exc. Excerpta Peiresciana. Excerpts made by order of
     Constantine VII Porphyrogenitus, 10th century

Other witnesses cited from the fathers cited in the
upper register of the apparatus criticus are self-
explanatory.

Note: In the apparatus criticus of Niese's edition
the asterisk (*) preceding a word for which variants
are provided indicates that the word/words in the
manuscript(s) cited agree with the epitome of the
manuscript(s) so cited. The asterisk has not been
included in my apparatus criticus.

7.   Josephus, Life

A   Codex Ambrosianus (Mediolanensis) F. 128,
     11th century

P   Codex Palatinus (Vaticanus) Graecus 14,
     9th or 10th century

7.   Josephus, _Life_ (cont.)

    R   Codex Regius (Parisinus) Gr. 1423, 14th century

    M   Codex Mediceo-Laurentianus, Plut. 69, cod. 10,
        15th century

    W   Codex Vaticanus Gr. 984, 1354 C.E.

    (Cf. H. St. J. Thackeray, _LCL_, vol. 1, p. xvii.)

8.   Syncellus

    A   Paris 1711, 1021 C.E., used by Scaliger and
        Goar, the first two editors. Editions: Paris,
        1652; Venice, 1729.

    B   Paris 1764, superior to A.

    (Cf. Dindorf, Syncellus (_CSHB_), preface; W. G. Waddell,
    Manetho (_LCL_; Cambridge: Mass.: Harvard University
    Press/London: Heinemann, 1940), p. xxx.

9.   Theophilus, _Ad Autolycum_

    B   Codex Bodleianus Auct. E I.II, 16th century

    P   Codex Parisinus graecus 887, 1540 C.E.

    V   Codex Marcianus (Venetus graecus) 496,
        11th century

    V^2 Corrector of Marcianus 496, 15th century

    (Cf. R. M. Grant, _Theophilus of Antioch: Ad Autolycum_
    [Oxford: Clarendon Press, 1970], pp. xix-xx and
    xxix.)

Symbols Used in Apparatus Criticus

< >   Conjectural addition (omitted in all MSS)

{ }   Conjectural deletion

[ ]   Lacuna(e) resulting from physical damage (full stops may be used to represent letter-spaces)

⟦ ⟧   Scribal deletion or erasure

`   '   Scribal correction

⌞ ⌟   Non-conjectural lacuna(e), that is, lacuna(e) whose content is known or can be supplied from another source (full stops may be used to represent letter-spaces)

†   Editorial indication of corruption in the text (corrupt phrase enclosed by †   †; corrupt word preceded immediately by †)

αβγ   Letters deciphered with uncertainty

x/×   Stands in letter-space left by erasure

:   Separates variants within a variation unit

| Separates variation units

?   Indicates editorial uncertainty

(!)   = (sic)

( )   Encloses parenthetical remarks

1 2 3   Designates first, second, third correctors (i.e., B^1, B^2 = B corrected by the original scribe, by the second hand, etc.

.   Letter absent in MS(S)

*   Beside MS = original MS or MS before correction

Γ^ρ In the MSS, Γ with ρ inserted = γράφεται, to introduce a variant (Cf. Mras, GCS (43,1) 8.1, p. LX.)

(Cf. M. L. West, Textual Criticism and Editorial Technique [Stuttgart: Teubner, 1973] 80-81.)

Abbreviations Used in Apparatus Criticus

abbrev.	=	*abbreviavit*
ac	=	*ante correctionem*
add.	=	*addidit*
aspir.	=	*aspiritus*
cf.	=	*confer*
cj.	=	*conjecit*
corr.	=	*correxit*
del.	=	*delevit*
ditt.	=	dittography
ed(d.)	=	*editio/-nes; editor/-es*
emend.	=	*emendavit*
et al.	=	*et alii*
fort.	=	*fortasse*
frg(s).	=	fragment(s)
κ.τ.λ.	=	καὶ τὰ λοιπά
lac.	=	*lacuna*
lin.	=	line(s)
mg/marg.	=	*in margine*
MS(S)	=	manuscript(s)
mut.	=	*mutavit* or *mutilatus*
n/not.	=	note(s)
om.	=	*omisit*
p(p).	=	page(s)
par.	=	paragraph(s)
pc	=	*post correctionem*

Abbreviations Used in Apparatus Criticus (cont.)

rest.	=	*restituit*
sq(q).	=	*sequens(-entis)*
superscr.	=	*superscripsit*
transp.	=	*transposuit*
x/×	=	*rasura*
v. l.	=	*varia lectio*

Cf. Association Internationale des Études Byzantines, Bulletin d'Information et de Coordination 4 (1968) 24-31; also, K. Aland, et al. Novum Testamentum Graece (26th ed.; Stuttgart: Deutsche Bibelstiftung, 1979) 776-79; also H. P. Rüger, An English Key to the Latin Words and Abbreviations and the Symbols of BIBLIA HEBRAICA STUTTGARTENSIA (Stuttgart: German Bible Society, 1981).

BIBLIOGRAPHY

Sources for Hellenistic Jewish Fragments

I. Collections of the Fragments.

    A. Texts.

        Müller, C. Fragmenta Historicorum Graecorum
           collegit, disposuit, notis et prolegomenis
           illustravit, indicibus instruxit. Paris,
           1841-72. 5 vols. (= Müll., FHG)

           Fragments of Alexander Polyhistor contained
           in vol. 3 (1849), pp. 206-44. Fragments
           "concerning the Jews," Nos. 3-24, arranged
           in order in which they occur in P. E., Bk.
           9. Reprints Greek text and Latin translation
           from Gaisford.

        Freudenthal, J. Hellenistische Studien.
           Alexander Polyhistor und die von ihm
           erhaltenen Reste jüdischer und samaritanischer
           Geschichtswerke. Breslau, 1874-75. 2 vols.
           (= Freu.)

           Bulk of the work (vol. 2) devoted to detailed
           analysis and discussion based on Freudenthal's
           pioneering research on these authors. Miscel-
           laneous notes, especially text critical, pp.
           199-218. Freudenthal's text, with critical
           apparatus, contained in pp. 219-36.

        Stearns, W. N. Fragments from Graeco-Jewish
           Writers. Chicago, 1908. (= Stearns)

           Includes texts of most of the authors;
           reprints Heinichen's text; no translation.
           Introduction and fairly extensive notes
           of limited value.

        Jacoby, F. Die Fragmente der griechischen
           Historiker. Leiden, 1954-69. 3 vols. in
           16 parts. (= Jac., FGrH)

           The Jewish "historical texts" are contained in
           Teil III C, Band 2 (1958, repr. 1969), Nos.
           722-737, pp. 666-713. Extensive critical
           apparatus at bottom of each page. For texts
           taken from P. E., Jacoby uses Mras's text as a
           basis, but makes a few changes based primarily
           on Freudenthal.

I.   Collections of the Fragments.

   A.   Texts.

        Denis, A. M. Fragmenta pseudepigraphorum quae
          supersunt Graeca una cum historicorum et
          auctorum Judaeorum hellenistarum fragmentis
          (published with M. Black, Apocalypsis
          Henochi Graece). Leiden, 1970.
          (= Denis, Frag.)

          The most comprehensive collection of frag-
          mentary Hellenistic Jewish authors to date.
          Useful introduction, texts (pp. 61-228),
          minimal critical apparatus, indices of
          biblical references, ancient and modern
          authors. Useful introductory material and
          extensive bibliography of each author
          provided in Denis, Introduction aux pseude-
          pigraphes grecs d'ancien testament (Leiden,
          1970) (= Denis, Intro.).

   B.   Translations.

       English:

       Charlesworth, J. H. (ed.). The Old Testament
          Pseudepigrapha. 2 vols. Garden City, NY:
          Doubleday, 1983- . (= Charlesworth, OTP)

       German:

       Riessler, P. Altjüdisches Schrifttum ausserhalb
          der Bibel. Heidelberg, 1927. 2. Aufl., 1966.
          (= Riessler)

          First comprehensive collection of pseudepigrapha
          in German. Arranged alphabetically by author
          and/or title. Notes, pp. 1266-1339.

       Walter, N. Jüdische Schriften aus hellenistisch-
          Römischer Zeit. Ed. W. G. Kümmel, et al.
          Gütersloh, 1976 - . (= Walter, JS).

       "Fragmente jüdisch-hellenistischer Historiker,"
       in Bd. 1, Lfg. 2: Historische und legendarische
       Erzählungen, 1976; pp. 91-163.

          Eupolemus, Theophilus, Philo the Elder,
          Cleodemus Malchus, Artapanus, Pseudo-
          Eupolemus, Pseudo-Hecataeus I & II.

       "Fragmente jüdisch-hellenistischer Exegeten,"
       in Bd. 3, Lfg. 2: Unterweisung in lehrhafter
       Form, 1975; pp. 257-99.

                                                  (cont.)

I. Collections of the Fragments (cont.)

    B. Translations. (cont.)

       <u>German</u>:

       Walter (cont.)

          "Fragmente jüdisch-hellenistischer Exegeten"

             Aristobulus, Demetrius, Aristeas.

          "Poetische Schriften," in Bd. 4 (forthcoming)

             Ezekiel the Tragedian, Philo the Epic Poet, Theodotus.

II. Individual Authors.

    A. Eusebius, <u>Praeparatio Evangelica</u>.

       Texts.

       Stephanus, R. <u>Eusebii Pamphili Evangelicae
          Praeparationis libri XV</u>. Paris, 1544.
          (= Estienne, Étienne, Stephens, Steph.)

          The earliest edition of the Greek text of
          <u>P. E.</u> Based on MSS D & E. The page
          numbers of this edition appear in the
          margins of some subsequent editions.

       Vigerus, F. <u>Eusebii Pamphili Caesareae
          Palaestinae episcopi Praeparatio Evangelica</u>.
          Paris, 1628. (= Viger, Vigier, Viguier,
          Vig.)

          Contains text expertly revised by Viger,
          also his fresh Latin translation and
          annotations. His re-division of the
          chapters was adopted by later editions,
          especially Mras. The page numbers of this
          edition, with the additional a-d division,
          appeared in the margins of most subsequent
          editions, and became the most widely used
          system of reference.

       Heinichen, F. A. <u>Eusebii Pamphili Praepara-
          tionis Evangelicae libri XV</u>. Leipzig,
          1842-43. 2 vols. (= Hein.)

          Reprints Greek text based on Stephanus and
          Viger. Underneath the text are critical
          notes including textual notes, parallel
          references, explanations. Indices of authors,
          topics, and Greek words.

II.   Individual Authors.

   A.   Eusebius, Praeparatio Evangelica.

        Texts.   (cont.)

        Gaisford, T.   Eusebii Pamphili Evangelicae
        Praeparationis Libri XV.   Oxford, 1843.
        4 vols.   (= Gais.)

           Contains text revised by Gaisford, with
           full critical apparatus and Viger's
           Latin translation on each page.   Vol. 4
           contains Viger's notes (pp. 148-338),
           two appendices, one on Aristobulus by
           L. C. Valckenaer (pp. 339-451), another on
           the Orphic fragments by P. Wesselingii
           (pp. 452-58), as well as indices of authors,
           biblical passages, names and subjects.

        Migne, J. P.   Patrologia Graeca (21):
        Eusebius Pamphili Caesariensis Episcopus (3):
        Praeparatio Evangelica.   Paris, 1857.   (= PG)

           Prints Viger's Greek Text, notes, and Latin
           translation on each page.   Greek and Latin
           in parallel columns.   Appendices (cols.
           1457-1666) contain notes by Seguier whose
           French translation of P. E. appeared in
           1846.   Indices of authors, names, and subjects.

        Dindorf, W.   Eusebii Caesariensis Opera.
        [Teubner]   Leipzig, 1867.   2 vols.
        (= Dind.)

           Greek text based on previous editions, but
           advances earlier work.   No critical apparatus
           and no annotations as announced in preface
           (pp. iv and xxivf.).   Indices of authors,
           biblical passages, and Viger's index of
           names and subjects.

        Gifford, E. H.   Eusebii Pamphili Evangelicae
        Praeparationes.   Libri XV.   Oxford, 1903.
        4 vols, in 5 parts.   (= Giff.)

           Greek text based on entirely new collation
           of MSS; used MS O for the first time.   Sig-
           nificant advance over previous work.   Vols.
           1 & 2 contain Greek text with critical appa-
           ratus at bottom of each page; vol. 2 contains
           index of authors, biblical references, names
           and subjects based on Greek text.   Vol. 3
           (in two parts) contains English translation.
           Part 2 contains index based on English
           translation.   Vol. 4 contains notes in English
           and index of Greek words.

II.   Individual Authors.

    A.   Eusebius, Praeparatio Evangelica.

       Texts.

          Mras, K. Die Praeparatio Evangelica. Bd. 8,
            Eusebius Werke [Griechischen christlichen
            Schriftsteller (=GCS), 43]. Berlin, 1954-
            56. 2 vols. (= Mras).

            Standard Greek text of P. E. now in use.
            Based on collation of all available MSS
            and takes into account all previous editions.
            Corrects previous work. Introduction in
            vol. 1 (pp. xiii - lx) provides description
            of textual history, manuscript witnesses,
            editions, and introductory material to P. E.
            Extensive critical apparatus at bottom of
            each page. Extensive indices, including
            biblical passages, Christian and non-
            Christian authors, other works of Eusebius,
            names and subjects. Especially helpful
            Greek index including Greek terms as well
            as matters of Greek grammar and style.

          des Places, E., J. Sirinelli, G. Schroeder,
            et al. Eusèbe de Césarée. La Préparation
            évangélique. [Sources chrétiennes (= SC),
            ed. C. Mondésert] Paris, 1974 -.

            Only 5 volumes have appeared to date:
            Book 1 (No. 206), Books 2-3 (No. 228),
            Books 4-5.17 (No. 262), Books 5.18-6
            (No. 266), and Book 7 (No. 215).
            Various translators and contributors.
            Reprints Mras's text with facing French
            translation. Abbreviated critical apparatus
            at bottom of each page prepared by des
            Places. Vol. 1 contains useful introduction
            to P. E. and extensive commentary on Book 1
            (pp. 212-323). Other volumes contain
            introductory material and notes.

       Translations.

       English:

          Gifford, E. H. Eusebii Pamphili Evangelicae
            Praeparationes. Oxford, 1903. Vol. 3
            (Parts 1 & 2). Cf. entry above.

II. Individual Authors.

    A. Eusebius, Praeparatio Evangelica.

        Translations.

        French:

        Seguier de Saint-Brisson (Marquis Nicolas-
           Maximilien-Sidoine). Eusèbe Pamphile.
           La préparation évangélique ... avec des
           notes critiques, historiques, et philo-
           logiques. Paris, 1846. 2 vols.

        des Places, E., et al. Eusèbe de Césarée.
           La préparation évangélique. [Sources
           chrétiennes, 206, 215, 228, 262, and 266] Paris
           1974 - . Books 1-7. Cf. entry above.

        Latin:

        Trapezunt, G. von. Eusebium Pamphili de
           evangelica praeparatione latinum ex graeco
           beatissime pater iussu tuo effecti ...
           Venice, 1470. Subsequent editions in
           1473, 1480, 1497, 1500, 1501, 1522.
           (= George of Trebizond/Trepizond).

           The first Latin translation of P. E.,
           based primarily on MS I.

        Vigerus, F. Eusebii Pamphili Caesareae
           Palaestinae episcopi Praeparatio Evangelica.
           Paris, 1628. Cf. entry above.

           Viger's Latin translation appears in
           Gaisford, Müller, FHG, and Migne (PG).

II.   Individual Authors.

   B.   Eusebius, Historia Ecclesiastica.

      Texts.

      Stephanus, R. Ecclesiasticae historiae
        Eusebii Pamphili libri X. Eiusdem de
        Vita Constantini libri V. Socratis
        libri VII. Theodoriti episcopi Cyrensis
        libri V. Collectaneorum ex Historia
        eccles. Theodori Lectoris libri II.
        Hermii Sozomeni libri IX. Evagrii
        libri VI. Paris, 1544.

      Valesius, Henricus, Eusebii Pamphili
        Ecclesiasticae historiae libri decem.
        Eiusdem de Vita imp. Constantini libri
        IV, quibus subjicitur Oratio Constan-
        tini ad sanctos et Panegyricus Eusebii.
        Henricus Valesius graecum textum
        collatis IV mss. codicibus emendavit,
        latine vertit et adnotationibus illu-
        stravit. Paris, 1659. (= Henri de Valois)

        Subsequent editions of Valesius' edition of
        Eusebius, Historia were published in 1672 and
        1677, but the most notable in Cambridge in
        1720; also contained his edition of Socrates,
        Sozomen, and the other Greek historians.

      Heinichen, F. A. Eusebii Pamphili Historiae
        ecclesiasticae libri x, ex nova recognitione
        cum aliorum ac suis prolegomenis, integro
        Henrici Valesii commentario, selectis
        Readingi, Strothii aliorumque virorum
        doctissimorum observationibus edidit,
        suas animadversiones et excursus, indices
        ... Leipzig, 1827-28. 3 vols.

      Burton, Edward. Eusebii Pamphili Historiae
        ecclesiasticae libri decem, ad codices
        manuscriptos recensuit Eduardus Burton
        ... Oxford, 1838. 2 vols.

      Migne, J. P. Patrologia Graeca (20):
        Eusebius Pamphili Caesariensis Episcopus
        Historia Ecclesiastica. Paris, 1857.
        cols. 45-906.

        Reprints Valesius' 1720 edition.

II.   Individual Authors.

    B.   Eusebius, Historia Ecclesiastica.

        Texts. (cont.)

            Schwartz, E. Eusebius Werke, Bd. 9:
               Die Kirchengeschichte. [Griechischen
               christlichen Schriftsteller, 9]
               Leipzig, 1903-1909. 3 vols.
               Vol. 1 & 2: texts; Vol. 3: introductions
               and indices.

               Also contains Latin translation of Rufinus,
               edited by T. Mommsen.

            Schwartz, E. Eusebius Kirchengeschichte.
               Kleine Ausgabe. 5. Aufl., unveränderter
               Nachdruck der 2. durchgesehenen Aufl.
               Leipzig, 1955.

            Grapin, E. Eusèbe de Césarée. Histoire
               ecclésiastique. Texte grec et trad.
               française. Paris, 1905-13. 3 vols.

            Lake, K. Eusebius. The Ecclesiastical History.
               [Loeb Classical Library (= LCL)] London, 1926,
               1932. 2 vols. Reprints GCS text.

            Bardy, G. Eusèbe de Césarée. Histoire
               ecclésastique. [Sources chrétiennes,
               31 (1952), 41 (1955), 55 (1958)]
               Paris, 1952-58. 3 vols.

        Translations.

        English:

        Cruse, C. F. The Ecclesiastical History of
           Eusebius Pamphilus. Translated from Greek with
           notes selected from the edition of Valesius.
           London, 1889.

        McGiffert, A. C. Later Post-Nicene Fathers.
           [Series 2] London, 1890; 1. 73-387.

        Lawlor, H. J. and J. E. L. Oulton. Eusebius.
           The Ecclesiastical History. London,
           1927-28. 2 vols.

        Lake, K. Eusebius. The Ecclesiastical History.
           [LCL] London, 1926, 1932. 2 vols.

           Vol. 2 reprints Oulton's translation.

II.   Individual Authors.

    B.   Eusebius, Historia Ecclesiastica.

       Translations.

       French:

       Seissel, C. L'histoire ecclesiastique.
         Paris, 1532.

       Grapin, E. Eusèbe de Césarée. Histoire
         ecclésiastique. Paris, 1905-1913.
         3 vols. Cf. entry above.

       Bardy, G. Eusèbe de Césarée. Histoire
         ecclésiastique. [Sources chrétiennes,
         31, 41, 55] Paris, 1952, 1955, 1958.
         3 vols. Cf. entry above.

       German:

       Hedio, Caspar. Chronica, das ist:
         wahrhaftige Beschreibunge aller alten
         Christlichen Kirchen; zum ersten, die
         hist. eccles. Eusebii Pamphili Caesar-
         iensis, Eilff Bücher; et al. Frankfort-
         Main, 1582.

       Stigloher, M. Des Eusebius Pamphili zehn Bücher
         der Kirchengeschichte, nach dem Urtexte
         übersetzt. [Texte und Untersuchungen, Bd.
         21, Hft. 2] Leipzig, 1901.

       Häuser, P. Des Eusebius Pamphili ...
         Kirchengeschichte Aus dem Griechischen
         übersetzt. [BKV^2, 1] München, 1932.

       Latin:

       Rufinus, Tyrannius. Ecclesiastica historia.

         According to Fabricius, Rufinus' Latin trans-
         lation was first printed in 1476 at Rome.
         Bibliothèque Nationale, however, lists other
         editions: Strassburg, ca. 1475-80; also
         Utrecht, 1474; Rome, 1476; Mantua, 1479;
         Strassburg, 1500.

II.   Individual Authors

B.   Eusebius, Historia Ecclesiastica.

   Translations.

   Latin: (cont.)

   Valesius, Henricus. Eusebii Pamphili
   Ecclesiasticae historiae libri decem.
   . . . Paris, 1659. Cf. entry above.

   Important subsequent edition in 1720.

   Mommsen, T. Eusebius Pamphili. Werke,
   Bd. 9: Die Kirchengeschichte. Die
   latinische Übersetzung des Rufinus.
   Leipzig, 1903-1909. 3 vols.
   Vol. 1 & 2: text; Vol. 3: introductions
   and indices.

C.   Clement of Alexandria, Protrepticus, Paedagogus,
   and Stromata.

   Texts.

   Migne, J. P. Patrologia Graeca: Clemens
   Alexandrinus (8-9). Paris, 1857.
   Protrepticus, 1.49-246; Paedagogus, 1.247-
   684; Stromata I-IV, 1.685-1382; Stromata
   V-VIII, 2.9-602.

   Dindorf, W. Clementis Alexandrini Opera.
   Oxford, 1869. 4 vols. Protrepticus, 1.1-123;
   Paedagogus, 1.124-409; Stromata I-IV, 2.1-417;
   Stromata V-VIII, 3.1-378; Annotations, 4.1-461.

   Stählin, O., L. Früchtel, & U. Treu. Clemens
   Alexandrinus [GCS] 3 Bde. Berlin, 1909-72.
   (Bd. I: GCS 12 (=56), 3. Aufl., hrsg. U. Treu,
   1972; Bd. II: GCS 15 (=52), 3. Aufl., hrsg.
   L. Früchtel, 1960; Bd. III: GCS 17 (=17^2),
   2. Aufl., hrsg. L. Früchtel & U. Treu, 1970).
   Protrepticus, 1.3-86; Paedagogus, 1.90-292;
   Stromata I-VI, 2.3-518; Stromata VII-VIII,
   3.3-102.

   Mondésert, C., et al. Clément d'Alexandrie [SC]
   7 vols. Paris, 1944-81. C. Mondésert & A.
   Plassart, Protreptique (No. 2, 2e ed., 1944);
   C. Mondésert & M. Caster, Les Stromates I
   (No. 30, 1951); P. T. Camelot & C. Mondésert,
   Les Stromates II (No. 38, 1954); H. I. Marrou
   & M. Harl, Le Pédagogue I (No. 70, 1960);
   C. Mondésert & H. I. Marrou, Le Pédagogue II
   (No. 108, 1965); A. Le Boulluec & P. Voulet,
   Les Stromates V (et commentaire) (Nos. 278-79,
   1981).

II.   Individual Authors.

   C.   Clement of Alexandria (cont.)

      Translations.

      English:

      Wilson, William. Ante-Nicene Fathers. Edinburgh,
         1867-97. American edition: Grand Rapids, 1962
         (repr.) 2.165-605.

      French:

      Mondésert, C., et al. Clément d'Alexandrie [SC].
         Cf. entry above.

      German:

      Stählin, O. Des Clemens von Alexandreia Ausge-
         wählte Schriften aus dem Griechischen Übersetzt
         [Bibliothek der Kirchenväter, 2. Reihe, Nos.
         7, 18, 17, 19, 20] München, 1934-38. 5 Bde.

   D.   Josephus.

      Texts.

      Niese, B. Flavii Josephi Opera. Editio
         maior. Berlin, 1885-95. 7 vols. in 5.

      Naber, S. A. Flavii Josephi Opera Omnia.
         [Teubner] Leipzig, 1888-96. 6 vols.

      Thackeray, H. St. J., R. Marcus, W. Wikgren
         and L. Feldman. Josephus, with an English
         translation. [LCL]. London, 1926-65.
         9 vols.

      Translations.

      English:

      Whiston, William. The Genuine Works of Flavius
         Josephus the Jewish Historian. London, 1737-.

      Thackeray, H. St. J., et al. Josephus. [LCL]
         Cf. above entry.

      French:

      Reinach, Th. Oeuvres complètes de Flavius
         Josèphe. Paris, 1900-32. 7 vols.

II.   Individual Authors

   D. Josephus.

      Translations.

      German:

      Martin, R. Die jüdischen Alterthümer des
         Flavius Josephus übersetzt und mit Anmerk-
         ungen versehen. Köln, 1852. 2 vols.

      Clementz, Heinrich. Antiquitates judaicae.
         Des Flavius Josephus jüdische Altertümer,
         übersetzt und mit Einleitung und Anmerkungen
         versehen von H. Clementz. Berlin/Vienna,
         1923. 2 vols.

   E. Epiphanius.

      Texts.

      D. Epiphanii episcopi Constantiae Cypri, Contra
         octoaginta haereses opus, Panarium, sive
         arcula, art capsula, medica appelatum,
         continens libros tres, & tomos sive sectiones
         ex toto septem: Iano Cornario interprete.
         Item eiusdem D. Epiphanii Epistola sive Liber
         ancoratus appellatus, docens de vera side
         Christiana. Eiusdem D. Epiphanii Anacephaeolis,
         sive summa totius opera Panari; appellati
         & contra octoaginta haereses conscripti,
         Eiusdem D. Epiphanii Libellos de mensuris
         ac ponderibus ... Basel, 1542.

      ... contra octoginta haereses opus, Panarium,
         sive Arcula, aut capsula medica appelatum,
         continens libros tres, & tomos sive sectiones
         ex toto septem. Iano cornario interprete.
         Una cum aliis eiusdem De Epiphanii operibus,
         partim nunc demum ultra superiorem editionem
         adiectis, partim etiam multo quam antea
         emendatioribus ... Paris, 1564.

      Opera omnia [Greek and Latin] Dion Petavius
         recensuit ... ed. Nova juxta Parisinam 1622
         ... qui accessit vita D. Petavii ... et
         appendices. Coloneae, 1682.

      Dindorf, W. Epiphanii episcopi Constantiae
         Opera. [Bibliotheca patrum graecorum et
         latinorum] Leipzig, 1859-62. 5 vols, in 3.
         Vols, 1 & 2 contain Panarion.

II.   Individual Authors.

    E.   Epiphanius.

        Texts.

        Oehler, Franciscus. Panaria eormque Ana-
          cephalaeois, Ad veteres libros recensuit
          et cum latina Dion. Petavii interpretatione
          et integris eius Animadversionibus, ed.
          Franciscus Oehler. Berlin, 1859-61.
          4 vols. in 2 (Corporis haeresologici
          t. 2-3). vol. 2, pt. 2: Panarion.

        Holl, Karl. Epiphanius Werke. Ancoratus
          und Panarion. [GCS]. Berlin, 1915-33.
          3 vols.

            Vol. 1: Ancoratus und Panarion haer. 1-33
            Vol. 2: Panarion haer. 34-64.
            Vol. 3: Panarion haer. 65-80. De fide.
              (ed. H. Lietzmann).

        Translations.

        English:

        Williams, Frank. Translation of Panarion in
          preparation.

        German:

        Wolfsgruber, C. Ausgewählte Schriften des
          heiligen Epiphanius, Erzbischofs von Salamis
          und Kirchenlehrers aus dem Urtexte übersetzt
          von Dr. Cölestin Wolfsgruber. [BKV, 64]
          Kempten, 1880.

        Hörmann, Joseph. Das heiligen Epiphanius von
          Salamis Ausgewählte Schriften, aus dem
          griechischen übersetzt von dr. Joseph
          Hörmann. [BKV, 38] Kempten/München, 1919.

    F.   Theophilus of Antioch, Ad Autolycum, Syncellus,
        John Malala, Tertullian, Diogenes Laertius --
        Cf. Index to Editions and Translations in each
        section.

BIBLIOGRAPHY

General

Adler, W. George Syncellus and His Predecessors: Ante-
    Diluvian History in the Chronicle of Syncellus and
    His Acknowledged Authorities. Unpublished Ph.D.
    Dissertation. University of Pennsylvania, 1982.
    (= Adler, Syncellus).

Baron, S. W. A Social and Religious History of the Jews.
    2nd ed., revised and enlarged. 2 vols. Philadelphia:
    Jewish Publication Society of America, 1952.
    (= Baron, History).

Beloch, K. J. Griechische Geschichte. 4 vols. in 8.
    2nd ed. Strassburg: K. J. Trübner, 1912-27.
    (= Beloch, Geschichte).

Bernfeld, S. Bibel, Apokryphen und jüdisch-hellenistisches
    Schrifttum. Berlin: Jüdischer Verlag, 1921.
    (= Bernfeld, Bibel).

Bernhardy, G. Grundriss der griechischen Litteratur mit
    einem vergleichenden Ueberblick der Römischen.
    3 parts in 2 vols. 2nd and 3rd ed. Halle: E. Anton,
    1856-61. (Vol. 1, 3rd ed., 1861; Vol. 2.1, 2nd ed.,
    1856; Vol. 2.2, 2nd ed., 1859) 1.485-561.
    (= Bernhardy, Grundriss).

Bousset, W. and Gressmann, H. Die Religion des Judentums
    in späthellenistischen Zeitalter. 4th ed. Handbuch
    zum Neuen Testament, 21. Tübingen: J. C. B. Mohr
    (Paul Siebeck), 1966.
    (= Bousset-Gressmann, RJ).

Braun, M. History and Romance in Graeco-Oriental Literature.
    Oxford: Basil Blackwell, 1938.
    (= Braun, History and Romance).

Cardauns, B. "Juden und Spartaner, Zur hellenistisch-
    jüdischer Literatur," Hermes 95 (1967) 317-24.
    (= Cardauns, "Juden und Spartaner").

Charlesworth, J. H. (ed.). The Old Testament Pseudepigrapha.
    2 vols. Garden City, New York: Doubleday, 1983-.
    (= Charlesworth, OTP).

_____. The Pseudepigrapha and Modern Research. Septua-
    gint and Cognate Studies, 7. Missoula: Scholars Press,
    1976. With a Supplement. Septuagint and Cognate
    Studies, 7S. Chico, CA: Scholars Press, 1981.
    (= Charlesworth, PAMR and PAMRS).

Collins, J. J. Between Athens and Jerusalem. Jewish
    Identity in the Hellenistic Diaspora. New York:
    Crossroad, 1983.
    (= Collins, Athens and Jerusalem).

Conzelmann, H. Heiden, Juden, Christen: Auseinandersetz-
ungen in der Literatur der hellenistisch-römischen
Zeit. Beiträge zur historischen Theologie, 62.
Tübingen: J. C. B. Mohr (Paul Siebeck) 1981.
(= Conzelmann, HJC).

Dähne, A. F. Geschichtliche Darstellung der jüdisch-
alexandrinischen Religionsphilosophie. 2 vols.
Halle: Buchhandlung des Waisenhauses, 1834. 1.1-15.
(= Dähne, Geschichtliche).

Dalbert, P. Die Theologie der hellenistisch-jüdischen
Missionsliteratur unter Ausschluss von Philo und
Josephus. Hamburg-Volksdorf: Herbert Reich, 1954.
(= Dalbert, Missionsliteratur).

Delling, G. (ed.). Bibliographie zur jüdisch-hellenistischen
und intertestamentarischen Literatur, 1900-1970.
2nd ed. Texte und Untersuchungen, 106². Berlin:
Akademie Verlag, 1975.
(= Delling, Bibliographie).

_____. "Perspektiven der Erforschung des hellenistischen
Judentums," HUCA 45 (1974) 133-89.
(= Delling, "Perspektiven").

Denis, A.-M. Introduction aux Pseudépigraphes Grecs
d'Ancien Testament. Studia in Veteris Testamenti
Pseudepigrapha, vol. 1. Leiden: Brill, 1970.
(= Denis, Introduction).

Dihle, A. Griechische Literaturgeschichte. Stuttgart:
Kröner, 1967. 410-19.
(= Dihle, Griechische).

Ewald, H. The History of Israel. 3rd ed. 8 vols.
London: Longmans, Green, and Co., 1876-86. 5.223-492.
(= Ewald, History).

Fraser, P. M. Ptolemaic Alexandria. 3 vols. Oxford:
Oxford University Press, 1972. 1.52-87, 280-301,
674-716.
(= Fraser, Ptolemaic Alexandria).

Freudenthal, J. Alexander Polyhistor und die von ihm
erhaltenen Reste judäischer und samaritanischer
Geschichtswerke. Hellenistische Studien, Heft 1 & 2.
Breslau: H. Skutsch Verlag, 1875.
(= Freu./Freudenthal, Alexander Polyhistor).

Friedländer, M. Geschichte der jüdischen Apologetik als
Vorgeschichte des Christentums. Zurich: C. Schmidt,
1903.
(= Friedländer, Geschichte).

Gager, J.   Moses in Greco-Roman Paganism. JBL Monograph
    Series, No. 16.   New York: Abingdon Press, 1972.
    (= Gager, Moses).

Geffcken, J.   Zwei griechische Apologeten. Sammlung
    wissenschaftlicher Kommentare zu griechischen und
    römischen Schriftstellern. Leipzig/Berlin: Teubner,
    1907. Repr. Hildesheim/New York: G. Olms, 1974.
    (= Geffcken, Apologeten).

Gelzer, H. Sextus Julius Africanus und die byzantinische
    Chronographie. 2 vols. (Vol. 1: Die Chronographie
    des Julius Africanus; Vol. 2: Nachfolger des Julius
    Africanus). Leipzig: B. G. Teubner, 1880-85.
    (= Gelzer, Sextus).

Georgi, D.   Die Gegner des Paulus im 2. Korintherbrief.
    Studien zur religiösen Propaganda in der Spätantike.
    Wissenschaftliche Monographien zum Alten und Neuen
    Testament, No. 11. Neukirchen-Vluyn: Neukirchener
    Verlag, 1964.
    (= Georgi, Gegner).

Ginzberg, L.   The Legends of the Jews. 7 vols. Philadelphia:
    The Jewish Publication Society of America, 1913-38.
    (= Ginzberg, Legends).

Goodenough, E. R.   Jewish Symbols in the Greco-Roman World.
    13 vols. New York: Bollingen Foundation, 1953-68.
    (= Goodenough, Jewish Symbols).

Gordon, C. H.   "Homer and the Bible: The Origin and Char-
    acter of East Mediterranean Literature," HUCA
    26 (1955) 43-108.
    (= Gordon, "Homer and Bible").

Graetz, H.   Geschichte der Juden von den ältesten Zeiten
    bis auf die Gegenwart. Vol. 3: Geschichte der Judäer
    von dem Tode Juda Makkabi's bis zum Untergange des
    judäischen Staates. 3rd ed. Leipzig: O. Leiner,
    1878. Esp. 26-54, 390-451, 621-34.
    (= Graetz, Geschichte).

Gutman, Y.   The Beginnings of Jewish-Hellenistic Literature
    (in Hebrew). 2 vols. Jerusalem: Mosad Bialik, 1958-63.
    (= Gutman, Beginnings).

Gutschmid, A.   Kleine Schriften. Edited by F. Rühl. 5 vols.
    Leipzig: B. G. Teubner, 1889-94.
    (= Gutschmid, Kleine Schriften).

Hadas, M. Hellenistic Culture: Fusion and Diffusion.
    New York: Norton, 1959.
    (= Hadas, Hellenistic Culture).

Harnack, A. The Mission and Expansion of Christianity
     in the First Three Centuries. New York: Harper
     Torchbooks, 1962.
     (= Harnack, Mission).

Hegermann, H. "Das hellenistische Judentum." In Umwelt
     des Urchristentums. 3 vols. Edited by J. Leipoldt
     and W. Grundmann. Berlin: Evangelische Verlags-
     anstalt, 1967-72. 1.292-345.
     (= Hegermann, Umwelt).

Hengel, M. "Anonymität, Pseudepigraphie und 'Literarische
     Fälschung' in der jüdisch-hellenistischen Literatur,"
     Pseudepigrapha I. Entretiens su L'Antiquité Classique,
     18. Vandoeuvres-Génève: Fondation Hardt, 1972. 231-329.
     (= Hengel, "Anonymität).

_____. Jews, Greeks, and Barbarians. Aspects of the
     Hellenization of Judaism in the Pre-Christian Period.
     Philadelphia: Fortress Press, 1980.
     (= Hengel, Aspects).

_____. Judaism and Hellenism: Studies in Their Encounter
     in Palestine During the Early Hellenistic Period.
     2 vols. Philadelphia: Fortress Press, 1974.
     (= Hengel, Judaism and Hellenism).

Herzfeld, L. Geschichte des Volkes Israel von der
     Zerstörung des ersten Tempels bis zur Einsetzung des
     Mackabäers Schimon zum hohen Priester und Fürsten.
     3 vols. Braunschweig: G. Westermann, 1847-57.
     3.425-579.
     (= Herzfeld, Geschichte).

Hody, H. Die Bibliorum Textibus Originalibus, Versionibus
     Graecis, & Latina Vulgata. Libri IV. Oxford, 1705.
     97-110.
     (= Hody, Bibliorum).

Holladay, C. R. THEIOS ANER in Hellenistic Judaism. A
     Critique of the Use of This Category in New Testament
     Christology. SBL Dissertation Series, 40. Missoula:
     Scholars Press, 1977.
     (= Holladay, THEIOS ANER).

Jackson, F. J. Foakes and Lake, K. The Beginnings of
     Christianity. 5 vols. London: Macmillan, 1920-33.
     (= Jackson-Lake, Beginnings).

Jeremias, J. Jerusalem in the Time of Jesus: An Investiga-
     tion into Economic and Social Conditions During the
     New Testament Period. London: SCM, 1969.
     (= Jeremias, Jerusalem).

Jones, A. H. M. The Cities of the Eastern Roman Provinces.
    2nd ed. Oxford: The Clarendon Press, 1971.
    (= Jones, Cities).

Juster, J. Les Juifs dans l'empire romain, leur condition
    juridique, économique et sociale. 2 vols. Paris:
    P. Geuthner, 1914.
    (= Juster, Juifs).

Karpeles, G. Geschichte der jüdischen Literatur. 4th ed.
    2 vols. (Repr. of 3rd ed. Berlin: M Poppelauer,
    1920-21). Graz-Austria: Akademische Druck - U.
    Verlagsanstalt, 1963. 1.109-204.
    (= Karpeles, Geschichte).

Kirk, G. S. and Raven, J. E. The Presocratic Philosophers:
    A Critical History with A Selection of Texts.
    Cambridge: Cambridge University Press, 1969.
    (= Kirk and Raven, Presocratic).

Knaack, G. "Alexandrinischer Litteratur," PW 1 (1894)
    cols. 1399-1407.
    (= Knaack, "Alexandrinischer Litteratur").

Laqueur, R. "Griechische Urkunden in der jüdisch-
    hellenistischen Literatur," Historische Zeitschrift
    136 (1927) 228-52.
    (= Laqueur, "Urkunden").

Lesky, A. A History of Greek Literature. New York:
    Thomas Y. Crowell Co., 1966. 799-806.
    (= Lesky, History).

Lieberman, S. Hellenism in Jewish Palestine. Texts and
    Studies of the Jewish Theological Seminary, 18.
    New York: Jewish Theological Seminary, 1962.
    (= Lieberman, Hellenism).

Lumbroso, G. L'Egitto dei Greci e dei Romani. 2nd ed.
    Rome: Ermanno Loescher, 1895.
    (= Lumbroso, L'Egitto).

Mahaffy, J. P. Greek Life and Thought from the Age of
    Alexander to the Roman Conquest. 2nd ed. New York:
    Macmillan, 1896. Repr. New York: Arno Press, 1976.
    (= Mahaffy, Greek Life).

Marcus, R. "Hellenistic Jewish Literature." In The Jewish
    People - Past and Present. Edited by S. W. Baron,
    et al. 4 vols. New York: Jewish Encyclopedia Hand-
    books-Central Yiddish Culture Organization, 1946-55
    (Vol. 3: 1952) 3.40-53.
    (= Marcus, "Hellenistic Jewish Literature (1952)").

_____. "Hellenistic Jewish Literature." In The Jews:
Their History, Culture, and Religion. 3rd ed.
2 vols. Edited by L. Finkelstein. New York:
Harper, 1960. 2.1077-1115.
(= Marcus, "Hellenistic Jewish Literature (1960)").

Meeks, W. A. The Prophet-King: Moses Traditions and the
Jonannine Christology. Supplements to Novum
Testamentum, 14. Leiden: Brill, 1965.
(= Meeks, Prophet-King).

Momigliano, A. Alien Wisdom: The Limits of Hellenization.
Cambridge: Cambridge University Press, 1975.
(= Momigliano, Alien Wisdom).

Nicholai, R. Geschichte der neugriechischen Literatur.
Leipzig: Brockhaus, 1876.
(= Nicholai, Geschichte).

_____. Griechische Literaturgeschichte in neuer Bear-
beitung. 3 vols. Magdeburg: Heinrichshofensche
Buchhandlung, 1873-78. 2.80-81.
(= Nicholai, Griechische).

Nock, A. D. Essays on Religion and the Ancient World.
2 vols. Edited by Z. Stewart. Cambridge, Mass.:
Harvard University Press, 1972.
(= Nock, Essays)

Pfeiffer, R. H. History of New Testament Times With an
Introduction to the Apocrypha. London: A. & C.
Black, 1963. 197-230.
(= Pfeiffer, History).

Reinach, T. Textes d'auteurs grecs et romains relatifs
au judaïsme. Publications de la société des études
juives. Paris: Ernest Leroux, 1895.
(= Reinach, Textes).

Routh, M. J. Reliquiae Sacrae: sive Auctorum Fere jam
Perditorum Secundi Tertiique Saeculi Post Christum
Natum Quae Supersunt. 5 vols. Oxford: University
Press, 1846-48.
(= Routh, Reliquiae Sacrae).

Safrai, S. and Stern, M. with D. Flusser and W. C. van
Unnik. The Jewish People in the First Century:
Historical Geography, Political History, Social,
Cultural and Religious Life and Institutions.
2 vols. Assen: Van Gorcum, 1974.
(= Safrai and Stern, Jewish People).

Schalit, A. (ed.). The World History of the Jewish People.
    First Series. Ancient Times. Vol. VI: The Hellenistic
    Age: Political History of Jewish Palestine from 332
    B.C.E. to 67 B.C.E. New Brunswick: Rutgers, 1972.
    (= Schalit, Hellenistic Age).

Schlatter, A. Geschichte Israels von Alexander des
    Grossen bis Hadrian. 3rd ed. Stuttgart: Calwer
    Verlag, 1925. Repr. Darmstadt: Wissenschaftliche
    Buchgesellschaft, 1972.
    (= Schlatter, Geschichte).

Schmid, W. and Stählin, O. Geschichte der griechischen
    Literatur. Handbuch der Altertumswissenschaft,
    7.2.1; 6th ed. München: C. H. Beck, 1920; repr. 1959.
    (= Schmid-Stählin, Geschichte).

Schürer, E. Geschichte des jüdischen Volkes im Zeitalter
    Jesu Christi. 3 vols. Hildesheim: G. Olms, 1960.
    Repr. of Vol. 1: 1901 (3rd and 4th ed.); Vol. 2:
    1907 (4th ed.); Vol. 3: 1909 (4th ed.).
    (= Schürer, Geschichte).

_____. The Literature of the Jewish People in the Time
    of Jesus. New York: Schocken Books, 1972.
    (= Schürer, Literature).

Siegfried, C. "Der jüdische Hellenismus: Ein Rückblick auf
    seine geschichtliche Entwickelung mit Beziehung auf
    die neuesten Forschungen innerhalb seines Gebietes,"
    Zeitschrift für wissenschaftliche Theologie 18 (1875)
    465-89.
    (= Siegfried, "Der jüdische Hellenismus").

Smallwood, E. M. The Jews Under Roman Rule from Pompey
    to Diocletian. Leiden: Brill, 1976.
    (= Smallwood, Jews).

Smyth, H. W. Greek Grammar. Cambridge, Mass.: Harvard
    University Press, 1956.
    (= Smyth, Greek Grammar).

Stählin, O. "Die hellenistisch-jüdische Litteratur."
    In Geschichte der griechischen Literatur. 6th ed.
    2 vols. Edited by W. Schmid and O. Stählin. München:
    Verlag C. H. Beck, 1959. 2,1.535-656.
    (= Schmid-Stählin, Geschichte).

Stearns, W. N. Fragments from Graeco-Jewish Writers.
    Chicago: The University of Chicago Press, 1908.
    (= Stearns, Fragments).

Stein, E. "Alttestamentliche Bibelkritik in der späthelle-
    nistischen Literatur," Collectanea Theologica
    16 (1935) 38-83.
    (= Stein, "Bibelkritik").

Stern, M. Greek and Latin Authors on Jews and Judaism.
    2 vols. available; vol. 3 (with remaining authors
    and indices forthcoming). Vol. 1: From Herodotus to
    Plutarch; Vol. 2: From Tacitus to Simplicius.
    Jerusalem: The Israel Academy of Sciences and
    Humanities, 1974-.
    (= Stern, Greek and Latin Authors, or GLAJJ).

Susemihl, F. Geschichte der griechischen Litteratur in
    der Alexandrinerzeit. 2 vols. Leipzig: B. G. Teubner,
    1891-92.
    (= Susemihl, Geschichte).

Swete, H. B. Introduction to the Old Testament in Greek.
    Cambridge: Cambridge University Press, 1902.
    Repr. New York: KTAV, 1968.
    (= Swete, Introduction).

Tcherikover, V. Hellenistic Civilization and the Jews.
    Philadelphia: The Jewish Publication Society,   1966.
    (= Tcherikover, Hellenistic Civilization).

_____. "Jewish Apologetic Literature Reconsidered,"
    Eos 48 (1956) 169-93.
    (= Tcherikover, "Jewish Apologetic Literature").

Thraede, K. "Erfinder II (geistesgeschichtlich),"
    RAC 5 (1962) 1191-1278.
    (= Thraede, "Erfinder").

_____. "Das Lob des Erfinders. Bemerkungen zur Analyse
    der Heuremata-Kataloge." Rheinisches Museum für
    Philologie, N.F. 105 (1962) 158-86.
    (= Thraede, "Das Lob").

Tiede, D. L. The Charismatic Figure As Miracle Worker.
    SBL Dissertation Series, 1. Missoula: Scholars
    Press, 1972.
    (= Tiede, Charismatic Figure).

Vaillant, V. De historiciis qui ante Josephum Judaicas
    res scripsere, nempe Aristea, Demetrio, Hecataeo
    Abderita, Cleodemo, Artapano, Justo Tiberiensi,
    Cornelio Alexandro Polhistore, disputationem propone-
    bat facultati litterorum Pariensi. Paris: Firmin
    Didot Fratres, 1851.
    (= Vaillant, Historiciis).

Valckenaer, L. C. Diatribe de Aristobulo Judaeo, Alexan-
    drino Judaeo, Scriptore Commentarii in Legem Moysis
    (Lugduni Batavorum, 1806); repr. in T. Gaisford,
    Eusebii Pamphili Evangelicae Praeparationis Libri XV
    (Oxford, 1843) 4.148-338 (with original pagination
    in margin).
    (= Valckenaer, Aristobulo or Diatribe de Aristobulo).

Volkmann, R. "Alexandriner," PW 1 (1842-64) 743-53.
    (= Volkmann, "Alexandriner").

Wacholder, B. Z. "Biblical Chronology in the Hellenistic
    World Chronicles," HTR 61 (1968) 451-81.
    (= Wacholder, "Biblical Chronology").

_____. Eupolemus. A Study of Judaeo-Greek Literature.
    Monographs of the Hebrew Union College, 3. Cincinnati
    and New York: Hebrew Union College and Jewish
    Institute of Religion, 1974.
    (= Wacholder, Eupolemus).

_____. "How Long Did Abram Stay in Egypt? A Study in
    Hellenistic, Qumran, and Rabbinic Chronography,"
    HUCA 35 (1964) 43-56.

_____. "Pseudo-Eupolemus' Two Greek Fragments on the
    Life of Abraham," HUCA 34 (1963) 83-113.
    (= Wacholder, "Pseudo-Eupolemus' Two Greek Fragments").

Walter, N. Der Thoraausleger Aristobulos. Untersuchungen
    zu seinen Fragmenten und zu pseudepigraphischen Resten
    der jüdisch-hellenistischen Literatur. Texte und
    Untersuchungen, 86. Berlin: Akademie Verlag, 1964.
    (= Walter, Aristobulos).

_____. Untersuchungen zu den Fragmenten der jüdisch-
    hellenistischen Historiker. Unpublished Habilitations-
    schrift, Halle, 1967-68.
    (= Walter, Untersuchungen).

Wendland, P. Die hellenistisch-römische Kultur in ihren
    Beziehungen zum Judentum und Christentum. 4th ed.
    Tübingen: J. C. B. Mohr (Paul Siebeck) 1972.
    (= Wendland, HRK).

Willrich, H. Judaica. Forschungen zur hellenistisch-
    jüdischen Geschichte und Litteratur. Göttingen:
    Vandenhoeck and Ruprecht, 1900.
    (= Willrich, Judaica).

_____. Juden und Griechen vor der makkabäischen Erhebung.
    Göttingen: Vandenhoeck and Ruprecht, 1895.
    (= Willrich, Juden und Griechen).

_____. Urkundenfälschung in der hellenistisch-jüdischen
    Literatur. Forschungen zur Religion und Literatur des
    Alten und Neuen Testaments, 21. Göttingen: Vanden-
    hoeck and Ruprecht, 1924.
    (= Willrich, Urkundenfälschung).

Bibliography

Abbreviations

ANET   J. B. Pritchard, ed., Ancient Near Eastern
          Texts

ANF   The Ante-Nicene Fathers

APOT   R. H. Charles, ed., Apocrypha and Pseude-
          pigrapha of the Old Testament

BAG   Bauer-Arndt-Gingrich, A Greek-English
          Lexicon of the New Testament and Other
          Early Christian Literature

BDB   Brown-Driver-Briggs, Hebrew and English
          Lexicon of the Old Testament

BHH   B. Reicke and L. Rost, eds., Biblisch-
          Historisches Handwörterbuch

BJRL   Bulletin of the John Rylands Library

BK   Bibliothek der Kirchenväter

CAH   Cambridge Ancient History

CPJ   V. Tcherikover and A. Fuks, Corpus
          Papyrorum Judaicarum

CSHB   Corpus Scriptorum Historiae Byzantinae

DB   Dictionnaire de la Bible

EHBS   Ἐπετηρὶς τῆς Ἑταιρείας Βυζαντινῶν
          Σπουδαιῶν = Annuaire de l'Association
          d'Etudes Byzantines

EncJud   Encyclopaedia Judaica

ETL   Ephemerides theologicae Lovanienses

FGrH   F. Jacoby, Die Fragmente der griechischer
          Historiker

FHG   C. Müller, Fragmenta Historicorum Graecorum

GCS   Griechische christliche Schriftsteller

GLAJJ   M. Stern, Greek and Latin Authors on Jews
          and Judaism

HAW   Handbuch der klassischen Altertums-wissen-
          schaft in systematischer Darstellung

Abbreviations (cont.)

HDB	J. Hastings, ed., Dictionary of the Bible
HERE	J. Hastings, ed., Encyclopaedia of Religion and Ethics
HJC	H. Conzelmann, Heiden, Juden, Christen
HRK	P. Wendland, Die hellenistische-römische Kultur in inhren Beziehungen zum Judentum und Christentum
HUCA	Hebrew Union College Annual
IDB	Interpreter's Dictionary of the Bible
JAOS	Journal of the American Oriental Society
JE	Jewish Encyclopedia
JEA	Journal of Egyptian Archaeology
JS	W. G. Kümmel, et al., eds., Jüdische Schriften aus hellenistisch-römischer Zeit
JSHRZ	W. G. Kümmel, et al., eds., Jüdische Schriften aus hellenistisch-römischer Zeit
JSJ	Journal for the Study of Judaism in the Persian, Hellenistic, and Roman Period
JTS	Journal of Theological Studies
KP	Kleine Pauly
LCL	Loeb Classical Library
LSJ	Liddell-Scott-Jones, A Greek-English Lexicon With Supplement
LTK	Lexikon für Theologie und Kirche
MGWJ	Monatsschrift für Geschichte und Wissenschaft des Judentums
OCD	Oxford Classical Dictionary
ODCC	Oxford Dictionary of the Christian Church
OGIS	W. Dittenberger, ed., Orientis Graeci Inscriptiones Selectae

Abbreviations (cont.)

OTP	J. H. Charlesworth, ed., Old Testament Pseudepigrapha
PAMR/ PAMRS	J. H. Charlesworth, The Pseudepigrapha and Modern Research (1976) with Supplement (1981)
PG	J. Migne, Patrologia Graeca
PL	J. Migne, Patrologia Latina
PW	Pauly-Wissowa, Real-Encyclopädie der classischen Altertumswissenschaft
RAC	Reallexikon für Antike und Christentum
RGG	Religion in Geschichte und Gegenwart
RHR	Revue de l'histoire des religions
RJ	W. Bousset and H. Gressmann, Die Religion des Judentums in späthellenistischen Zeitalter
SC	Sources chrétiennes
SEG	Supplementum Epigraphicum Graecum
SIG	W. Dittenberger, ed., Sylloge Inscriptionum Graecarum
TDNT	G. Kittel and G. Friedrich, eds., Theological Dictionary of the New Testament
ThEE	A. Martinos, ed., Thrēskeutikē kai Ēthikē Enkuklopaideia. 12 vols. Athens. 1962-68.
TU	Texte und Untersuchungen
VT	Vetus Testamentum
ZNW	Zeitschrift für die neutestamentliche Wissenschaft

Other Abbreviations

Abbreviations throughout the work, for the most part, conform to those suggested in the Journal of Biblical Literature "Instructions for Contributors." (Cf. Society of Biblical Literature Member's Handbook, 1980.) The major difference is that I have chosen to underline the names of series. For the classical authors and sources, abbreviations in Liddell-Scott-Jones, A Greek-English Lexicon with Supplement (Oxford: Clarendon, 1968) and Lewis and Short, A Latin Dictionary (Oxford: Clarendon, 1879; repr. 1969) have been used, with some minor modifications for the sake of clarity. The most frequently cited sources are abbreviated as follows:

Ag.Ap.	Josephus, Against Apion
Ant.	Josephus, Antiquities
H.E. or Hist. eccl.	Eusebius, Historia Ecclesiastica
J.W.	Josephus, Jewish War
P.E.	Eusebius, Praeparatio Evangelica
Strom.	Clement of Alexandria, Stromata

The names of persons frequently referred to, usually editors, are abbreviated as follows:

Denis	A.-M. Denis
Dind.	Dindorf (of whom there are several; cf. Bibliography of Sources for the Collection.)
Freu.	J. Freudenthal
Gais.	T. Gaisford
Giff.	E. H. Gifford
Hein.	F. A. Heinichen
Jac.	F. Jacoby
Müll.	C. Müller (= K. Müller)
Riessler	P. Riessler
Stearns	W. N. Stearns
Steph.	R. Stephanus/Estienne/Etienne/ Stephens/Stephani
Walter	N. Walter
Vig.	F. Viger/Vigerus/Vigier/Viguier

DEMETRIUS

Six fragments from the writings of Demetrius have been identified with relative certainty.[1] The first five fragments deal with events recorded in Genesis and Exodus, while the sixth is a chronological summary of a later period of Israel's history based on material from 2 Kings. Possibly, the fragments derive from separate works since the title given to Demetrius' work by Clement of Alexandria-- Concerning the Kings in Judaea --[2] does not appropriately describe the contents of the first five fragments. But if all six fragments derive from a single work, this chronicle of Jewish history was probably comprehensive in scope, extending from the period of the patriarchs until the time of the fall of Judah.

Although the literary remains of Demetrius' work are not extensive, the text is corrupt in a number of places. This is probably because the bulk of them were originally preserved by Alexander Polyhistor, a non-Jew who most likely was recording material unfamiliar to him, and later were excerpted from Polyhistor by Eusebius for inclusion in Book IX of his Praeparatio Evangelica. Either Eusebius, or a later editor, may have attempted to correct the textual difficulties transmitted by Polyhistor.

Date and Provenance. The major clue to the date and provenance of Demetrius is provided in Fragment 6 where the reign of Ptolemy IV (Philopator, ca. 222-205 B.C.E.)[3] is given as the terminus ad quem of his chronological summary. Assuming that he would extend his chronology to the time in which he wrote, this suggests that he flourished in the last quarter of the third century B.C.E. Moreover, this datum provides one of the major reasons for suggesting an Alexandrian provenance, since it is likewise assumed that one who uses the reign of a Ptolemy to establish chronology would be living under Ptolemaic rule, notably in Egypt.[4] Thus, the emerging scholarly consensus

is that Demetrius flourished in Alexandria during the last
half of the third century B.C.E.

The work. The genre of Demetrius' work seems to have
resembled a chronicle more than anything else; hence the
designation Demetrius the Chronographer.[5] To be sure, the
chronology of the biblical narrative is one of his most
persistent preoccupations. The biblical narrative interests
him not for its religious or moralistic value, but for its
historical worth in documenting birthdates, genealogies,
and other matters of chronological interest. Important
biblical stories are omitted, abbreviated, or mentioned
only casually. He stands in sharp contrast to later Jewish
historians in several respects. Important figures in
Jewish history do not loom larger than life in his account;
they are not re-portrayed in the image of popular ideals
and heroes current in the Hellenistic age. His work remains
unembellished, free of legend and mythology. Stylistically,
it is simple, unadorned, totally without literary preten-
tion. He seeks neither to explain the actions of characters nor to interpret the significance of events within
the biblical narrative.

He is clearly influenced by Greek literary models, yet
shows no direct dependence on them. At the time he wrote,
Alexandria was experiencing a renewed interest in historiography; not only was the method for doing history being
refined, chronography in particular had become established
as a respectable intellectual discipline in its own right.[6]
Hellanicus, Eratosthenes, Hecataeus of Abdera, Manetho,
Berossus, and Fabius Pictor form the intellectual horizon
within which Demetrius should be viewed. Yet he also provides an interesting contrast to Jewish works possessing
demonstrable interests in matters of chronology, notably
the Book of Jubilees, the Genesis Apocryphon, and Seder
Olam Rabbah.

Perhaps the most notable characteristic of Demetrius'
work is its biblicism. The LXX serves as his only source,[7]
and his knowledge of its contents is detailed and exact.

Knowledge of Hebrew or familiarity with the Hebrew text
would have saved him from some simple mistakes. Although
he closely adheres to the biblical story line, he does not
read it uncritically. Indeed, his chief task is to reconcile difficulties which the biblical text itself presents
upon a close reading--not only chronological difficulties,
but moral and logical inconsistencies as well: How could
twelve children have been born to Jacob within the space
of seven years?[8] How could Moses have married Zipporah,
separated as they are by three generations?[9] Why did
Joseph remain in Egypt nine years -- flourishing -- and
not report his whereabouts to his aged father in Canaan?[10]
Why did Joseph show partiality to Benjamin and thereby
slight his other brothers?[11] How did the Israelites who
left Egypt unarmed manage to obtain weapons with which
they fought after crossing the Red Sea?[12] Why is the
sinew of the thigh of cattle not eaten by Jews?[13] Thus,
while his preoccupation with chronology is a distinctive
feature of his work, it appears to be part of a larger
concern. Demetrius is perhaps the first Jewish author who
systematically engages in biblical criticism.

What prompted him to this critical reading of the text
presents one of the major problems in assessing Demetrius.
Whether he does so as an apologist,[14] an exegete,[15] or
as an historian[16] is still debated, and no clear consensus has yet been reached.

Importance. Although his work made no lasting
impression on Greek historiography, he is an important
figure nevertheless. He is the earliest known independent
Jewish author (excepting the LXX translators, of course)
to have written in Greek, and thus is the first representative of Greek-speaking Judaism. He is the earliest
witness for a Greek version of the Pentateuch, and thus is
an important source for locating the origins of the LXX and
assessing its initial impact upon Greek-speaking Judaism in
Alexandria. He is an important source for examining the
relationship between Palestinian and Alexandrian methods of

exegesis. He is perhaps the first Jewish author whose
work reflects an awareness--and understanding--of Greek
historiography, and is thus an important source for examining the roots of Hellenization among Jews in the Diaspora.
Depending upon how one assesses the work the Chronicler,[17] Demetrius may be said to stand at the dawn of
Jewish historiography.

NOTES

1. Testimonia: Josephus, Ag.Ap. 1. 218 (although
Josephus confuses him with Demetrius of Phalerum);
Clement of Alexandria, Strom. 1.21.141.1; Eusebius, Hist.
eccl. 6.13.7; P.E. 9.42.3. (also, cf. individual references in fragments); Jerome, De viris illustribus 38.

The system of numeration and identification of the
fragments used in this translation is that originally
employed by Freudenthal, and adopted by Denis and Walter.
This scheme is now widely accepted and used rather than
the modified scheme employed by Jacoby in FGrH, No. 722.
Yet another scheme is devised by Riessler, 241-245.

2. Cf. Frg. 6.

3. Because the dates of the reign of Ptolemy IV Philopator
conflict with other calculations made by Demetrius, various
emendations have been suggested. The most plausible suggestion was that of Freudenthal who emended the text to read
Ptolemy III (Euergetes, ca. 247-221 B.C.E.). Cf.
Gutschmid, "Zeit und Zeitrechnung," 186-91.

4. The weight of this observation is diminished by the
fact that the extent of Ptolemaic rule fluctuated frequently and considerably during the Hellenistic era, especially during the five Syrian wars (cf. W. W. Tarn, "The
Struggle of Egypt Against Syria and Macedonia," in CAH,
7. 699-731.; also Hengel, Judaism and Hellenism, 1. 6-12.
Generally speaking, however, Ptolemaic rule encompassed
Syria (including Palestine) during the third century B.C.E.,
but after the battle of Paneion in 200 B.C.E. Palestine
was under Seleucid control. Thus, prior to 200 B.C.E. it
is conceivable that Demetrius lived in either Palestine or
Egypt. After 200 B.C.E., however, the likelihood of a
Palestine provenance is slim. Other considerations also
point to an Egyptian provenance, e.g., that Demetrius
knows only the Greek version of the Bible; he apparently
knew no Hebrew whatever, an unlikely possibility for some-
one living in Palestine. Thus he is entering the same
literary arena with the likes of Hellanicus and Eratosthenes and this would suggest the intellectual environment
of Alexandria.

5. The designation is used by Freudenthal, 35; cf. also
p. 37.

6. Cf. Wacholder, "Biblical Chronology," 451-81; now in
expanded form in Eupolemus 97-128. Also, Hengel,
"Anonymität," 236.

7.   The orthography of proper names in Demetrius corre-
sponds to that of the Greek Bible, for the most part. Also,
the calculations which he uses to compute the lengths of
the generations presupposes the ages of the patriarchs
given in the Greek Bible rather than the Hebrew Bible.
There are also specific instances where his misunderstanding of the biblical narrative stems from his use of a
Greek version of the Bible. Cf., for example, Frg. 2,
par. 10 and Frg 5; also cf. Freudenthal, 390-40.

8.   Frg. 2, par. 3-5.

9.   Frg. 3, par. 1-3.

10.   Frg. 2, par. 13.

11.   Frg. 2, par. 14-15.

12.   Frg. 5.

13.   Frg. 2, par. 7.

14.   So Dalbert, Missionsliteratur, 29; also Hengel,
Judaism and Hellenism, 1. 69; cf. Jerome, De viris
illustribus 38.

15.   According to Freudenthal, p. 67, Demetrius is primarily engaging in hellenistic midrash, and does so as a
member of an established midrashic school of exegesis within Alexandria but not uninfluenced by Palestinian modes of
exegesis. Also, cf. Schlatter, Geschichte, 74-75; Walter,
JS (3.2), 287; Denis, Introd., 251; Wacholder, Eupolemus,
99.

16.   Fraser, Ptolemaic Alexandria, 1. 690, calls Demetrius
"much less of an apologist than a historian";also, 1. 713,
"an academic writer with little interest in apologetic or
propaganda."

17.   Cf. Bickerman, "Demetrios," 78.

Bibliography

Bickerman, E. J. "The Jewish Historian Demetrios." In
    Christianity, Judaism, and Other Greco-Roman Cults.
    5 vols. Edited by J. Neusner. Studies in Judaism in
    Late Antiquity, 12. Leiden: Brill, 1975. 3.72-84.

Bloch, H. Die Quellen des Flavius Josephus in seiner
    Archäologie. Leipzig: B. G. Teubner, 1879. 56-58.

Broydé, I. "Demetrius," JE 4 (1903) 512-13.

Charlesworth, PAMRS, 93-94, 277.

Collins, Athens and Jerusalem, 27-30.

Conzelmann, HJC, 141-42.

Dalbert, Missionsliteratur, 27-32.

Denis, Introduction, 248-51.

Ewald, History, 1.212; 2.90; 4.206; 8.62.

Fiebig, P. "Demetrius (1)," RGG² 1 (1927) 1823.

Fraser, Ptolemaic Alexandria, 1.510, 690-94.

Freudenthal, Alexander Polyhistor, 35-82, 205-207.

Gaster, M. "Demetrius und Seder Olam. Ein Problem der
    hellenistischen Literatur." In Festskrift in anledning
    af professor David Simonsens 70-aarige fødselsdag.
    Copenhagen, 1923. 243-52. Reprinted in Studies and
    Texts in Folklore, Magic, Mediaeval Romance, Hebrew
    Apocrypha, and Samaritan Archaeology. 3 vols.
    London: Maggs Bros., 1925-28. 2.650-59.

Gelzer, Sextus, 1.52-118, esp. 87-89.

Graetz, H. "Die Chronologie des Demetrios," Monatsschrift
    für Geschichte und Wissenschaft des Judentums
    26 (1877) 68-72.

_____, Geschichte, 3.623-35.

Gutman, Beginnings, 1.132-39.

Gutschmid, A. "Zeit und Zeitrechnung der jüdischen
    Historiker Demetrios und Eupolemos." In Kleine
    Schriften. 5 vols. Edited by F. Rühl. Leipzig:
    B. G. Teubner, 1890. 2.186-91.

Hadas, Hellenistic Culture, 94-95.

Hanson, J. S. "Demetrius the Chronographer," in Charles-
    worth, OTP.

Hegermann, Umwelt, 1.318-19.

Hengel, Judaism and Hellenism, 1.69.

_____, "Anonymität," 235-37.

Herzfeld, Geschichte, 3.486-87.

Hoenig, S. B. "Demetrius (5)," IDB 1 (1962) 816.

Holladay, C. R. "Demetrius the Chronographer as Historian
    and Apologist." In Christian Teaching: Studies in
    Honor of Lemoine G. Lewis. Abilene, TX: Abilene
    Christian University, 1981. 117-29.

Karpeles, Geschichte, 1.174-75.

Lewy, H. "Demetrius," EncJud 5 (1930) 930.

Lohse, E. "Demetrius," RGG^3 2 (1958) 75-76.

Miller, J. and J. Hanson. "Demetrius Historicus,"
    Unpublished seminar paper. Harvard New Testament
    Seminar. March 9, 1970. 33 pp.

Pfeiffer, History, 200.

Schlatter, Geschichte, 72-77.

Schmid-Stählin, Geschichte, 2,1. 583-89.

Schürer, Geschichte, 3.472-74.

Schwartz, E. "Demetrios (79)," PW 4 (1901) 2813-14.

Susemihl, Geschichte, 2.647-48.

Swete, Introduction, 17-18, 369-70.

Vaillant, Historicis, 45-52.

Wacholder, "Biblical Chronology," 451-81, esp. 452-58.

_____, "Demetrius," EncJud 5 (1971) 1490-91.

_____, Eupolemus, 54-56, 66-67, 98-104, 247, 280-82.

_____, "How Long," 43-56.

Walter, Aristobulos, 41-51, 97-99.

_____, Untersuchungen, 15-36, 141-55.

Index to Editions and Translations

Fragment One

Source: Eusebius, P.E. 9.19.4.

Reference Number in P.E.:   Steph., 246; Vig., 421b.

Greek Text Used: Mras, GCS (43,1) 8.1, p. 505,
    lines 18-23.

Editions: Steph., 246; Vig., 421b; Hein., 2.22;
    Gais., 2.375-76; Müll., FHG 3. (om.); Migne,
    PG (21), col. 712B; Dind., 1.487-88; Freu.,
    219 (= No. 1); Giff., 1.531 (notes, 4.303);
    Stearns (om.); Mras, GCS (43,1) 8.1, 505;
    Jac., FGrH 3.671 (= No. 722, Frg. *7);
    Denis, 175 (= Frg. 1).

Translations:

English: Giff., 3.452-53.

French:

German: Riessler (om.); Walter (JS, 3.2),
    284 (= Frg. 1).

Fragment Two

Source: Eusebius, P.E. 9.21.1-19.

Reference Number in P.E.:   Steph., 247-49;
    Vig., 422d-426a.

Greek Text Used: Mras, GCS (43,1) 8.1, p. 508,
    line 4 - p. 512, line 10.

Editions: Steph., 247-49; Vig., 422d-426a; Hein.,
    2.24-28; Gais., 2.378-85; Müll., FHG 3.214
    (= No. 8); Migne, PG (21), cols. 713B-721A
    (notes, cols. 1569-72); Dind., 1.489-93;
    Freu., 219-22 (= Frg. 2); Giff., 1.532-36
    (notes, 4.304-307); Stearns, 18-25 (= Frg. 1);
    Mras, GCS (43,1) 8.1, 508-12; Jac., FGrH
    3.666-70 (= No. 722, Frg. 1); Denis, 175-78
    (= Frg. 2).

Translations:

English: Giff., 3.454-57.

French:

German: Riessler, 241-44; notes, 1281 (Riessler's
    Frg. 1, chap. 1 = Frg. 2:1-11; Frg. 1,
    chap. 2 = Frg. 2:12-19); Walter
    (JS, 3.2), 284-90 (= Frg. 2).

Fragment Three

Source: Eusebius, P.E. 9.29.1-3.

Reference Number in P.E.: Steph., 257; Vig., 439 b-d.

Greek Text Used: Mras, GCS (43,1) 8.1, p. 528,
lines 1-18.

Editions: Steph., 257; Vig., 439b-d; Hein., 2.42;
Gais., 2.409-10; Müll., FHG 3.224 (= No. 16);
Migne, PG (21), cols. 737 D - 740 B (notes,
cols. 1575-77); Dind., 1.507-508; Freu., 222
(= Frg. 3); Giff., 1.550 (notes, 4.315-16);
Stearns, 25-27 (= Frg. 2); Mras, GCS (43,1) 8.1,
528; Jac., FGrH 3.670 (= No. 722, Frg. 2); Denis,
178 (= Frg. 3).

Translations:

English: Giff., 3.469-70.

French:

German: Riessler, 245; notes, 1281 (= Frg. 2);
Walter (JS, 3.2), 290-91 (= Frg. 3).

Fragment Four

Source: Eusebius, P.E. 9.29.15.

Reference Number in P.E.: Steph, 262; Vig., 445d.

Greek Text Used: Mras, GCS (43, 1) 8.1, p. 536,
lines 21-26.

Editions: Steph., 262; Vig., 445d; Hein., 2.48;
Gais., 2.421; Müll., FHG 3. (om.) Migne, PG
(21), col. 745 C; Dind., 1.514; Freu., 223
(= Frg. 4); Giff., 1.556-57; Stearns, 27
(= Frg. 3); Mras, GCS (43,1) 8.1, 536; Jac.,
FGrH 3.670 (= No. 722, Frg. 4); Denis, 178-79
(= Frg. 4).

Translations:

English: Giff., 3.474.

French:

German: Riessler, (om.); Walter (JS, 3.2),
291 (= Frg. 4).

Fragment Five

Source: Eusebius, P.E. 9.29.16.

Reference Number in P.E.: Steph., 262; Vig., 446d

Greek Text Used: Mras, GCS (43,1) 8.1, p. 538,
    lines 7-10.

Editions: Steph., 262; Vig., 446d; Hein., 2.49;
    Gais., 2.423; Müll., FHG 3. (om.); Migne, PG
    (21), col. 748 A; Dind., 1.515; Freu., 223
    (= Frg. 5); Giff., 1.558; Stearns, (om.); Mras,
    GCS (43,1) 8.1, 538; Jac., FGrH 3.670-71
    (= No. 722, Frg. 5); Denis, 179 (= Frg. 5).

Translations:

English: Giff., 3.475.

French:

German: Riessler, (om.); Walter (JS, 3.2),
    291-92 (= Frg. 5).

Fragment Six

Source: Clement of Alexandria, Stromata 1.21.141.1-2.

Greek Text Used: Stahlin- Früchtel, GCS (52 [15]) 2,
    p. 87, lines 17-24.

Editions: Müll., FHG 3.208; Dind., 2.114; Freu., 223
    (= Frg. 6); Migne, PG (8), cols. 887 A-B;
    Stearns, 27-28 (= Frg. 4); Stählin-Früchtel,
    GCS (52) 2.87; Jac., FGrH 3.671 (= No. 722, Frg.
    6); Denis, 179 (= Frg. 6).

Translations:

English: Wilson (ANF), 2.332.

French: M. Caster, (SC 30), 1.147.

German: Riessler, 245, (= Frg. 3); Stählin
    (BK), 3.119; Walter (JS, 3.2), 292
    (= Frg. 6).

FRAGMENT ONE (Eusebius, P.E. 9.19.4)

(4) Τοσαῦτα ὁ Πολυΐστωρ· οἷς μεθ'   (4)
ἕτερα ἐπιφέρει λέγων·   421b

"Μετ' οὐ πολὺν δὲ χρόνον τὸν θεὸν τῷ Ἀβραὰμ
προστάξαι Ἰσαὰκ τὸν υἱὸν ὁλοκαρπῶσαι αὐτῷ. τὸν
5 δὲ ἀναγαγόντα τὸν παῖδα ἐπὶ τὸ ὄρος πυρὰν νῆσαι
καὶ ἐπιθεῖναι τὸν Ἰσαάκ· σφάζειν δὲ μέλλοντα
κωλυθῆναι ὑπὸ ἀγγέλου, κριὸν αὐτῷ πρὸς τὴν κάρ-
πωσιν παραστήσαντος· τὸν δὲ Ἀβραὰμ τὸν μὲν παῖδα
καθελεῖν ἀπὸ τῆς πυρᾶς, τὸν δὲ κριὸν καρπῶσαι."

FRAGMENT TWO (Eusebius, P.E. 9.21.1-19)

10   (1) Ἀπίωμεν δὲ πάλιν ἐπὶ τὸν Πολυΐστορα·   (1)

         ΔΗΜΗΤΡΙΟΥ ΠΕΡΙ ΤΟΥ ΙΑΚΩΒ· ΑΠΟ ΤΗΣ ΑΥΤΗΣ   422d
              ΤΟΥ ΠΟΛΥΙΣΤΟΡΟΣ ΓΡΑΦΗΣ

         "Δημήτριός φησι τὸν Ἰακὼβ γενόμενον ἐτῶν
ἑβδομήκοντα πέντε φυγεῖν εἰς Χαρρὰν τῆς Μεσοπο-
15 ταμίας, ἀποσταλέντα ὑπὸ τῶν γονέων διὰ τὴν πρὸς
τὸν ἀδελφὸν κρυφίαν ἔχθραν Ἡσαῦ, διὰ τὸ εὐλογῆ-
σαι αὐτὸν τὸν πατέρα δοκοῦντα εἶναι τὸν Ἡσαῦ,
καὶ ὅπως λάβῃ ἐκεῖθεν γυναῖκα. (2) ἀφορμῆσαι   (2)
οὖν τὸν Ἰακὼβ εἰς Χαρρὰν τῆς Μεσοποταμίας,
20 τὸν μὲν πατέρα καταλιπόντα Ἰσαὰκ ἐτῶν ἑκατὸν

BION

1 ὁ Πολ.: οὗτος Β | 1-9 οἷς -- καρπ. om. Β |
10 πάλιν om. Β | 11-12 ΔΗΜ. -- ΓΡΑΦ. ΒΟΝ: om. I |
14 ἑβδομ. πέν.: οε' ΟΝ: ἑβδομ. ἑπτά Vig. |
17 δοκοῦντα εἶναι τὸν: ὡς Β | 18-19 ἀφορμ. -- Μεσοπ.
om. Β | 20 καταλιπεῖν Β | ἐτῶν ὄντα Β |

FRAGMENT ONE[1]

(4)   (19.4) Thus says Polyhistor, to which he adds
the following, after some other remarks:

"Not long after, God commanded Abraham to offer
his son Isaac as a whole burnt offering to him.[2] And
he led his son up to the mountain, heaped up a pile
of wood for an altar, and placed Isaac on it. When
he was about to kill him, he was prevented by an
angel who provided him a ram for the sacrifice. And
Abraham took the lad down from the altar and sacri-
ficed the ram."

FRAGMENT TWO [3]

(1)   (21.1) Now let us turn again to Polyhistor:
Demetrius' Remarks Concerning Jacob --- From
The Same Book of Polyhistor

"Demetrius says that Jacob was seventy-five [4]
years old when he fled to Haran in Mesopotamia. He
was sent by his parents because of the hidden
resentment which Esau had for his brother (this
because his father had bestowed the blessing upon him
thinking he was Esau) and so that he might obtain a
(2) wife while there.[5] (2) Thus Jacob set out for Haran
in Mesopotamia, leaving behind his father Isaac

τριάκοντα ἑπτά, αὐτὸν δὲ ὄντα ἐτῶν ἑβδομήκοντα
ἑπτά. (3) διατρίψαντα οὖν αὐτὸν ἐκεῖ ἑπτὰ ἔτη|
Λάβαν τοῦ μητρῴου δύο θυγατέρας γῆμαι, Λείαν καὶ
῾Ραχήλ, ὄντα ἐτῶν ὀγδοήκοντα τεσσάρων·καὶ γενέσ-
5 θαι ἐν ἑπτὰ ἔτεσιν ἄλλοις αὐτῷ παιδία ιβ'· ὀγδόῳ
μὲν ἔτει μηνὶ δεκάτῳ ῾Ρουβίν· καὶ τῷ ἔτει δὲ τῷ
ἐνάτῳ μηνὶ ὀγδόῳ Συμεών· καὶ τῷ ἔτει δὲ τῷ δεκάτῳ μηνὶ ἕκτῳ Λευίν· τῷ δὲ ἑνδεκάτῳ ἔτει μηνὶ
τετάρτῳ ᾽Ιούδαν. ῾Ραχήλ τε μὴ τίκτουσαν ζηλῶσαι
10 τὴν ἀδελφὴν καὶ παρακοιμίσαι τῷ ᾽Ιακὼβ τὴν ἑαυτῆς
παιδίσκην Ζελφάν, τῷ αὐτῷ χρόνῳ ᾧ καὶ Βάλλαν
συλλαβεῖν τὸν Νεφθαλείμ, τῷ ἑνδεκάτῳ ἔτει μηνὶ
πέμπτῳ, καὶ τεκεῖν τῷ δωδεκάτῳ ἔτει μηνὶ δευτέρῳ
υἱόν, ὃν ὑπὸ Λείας Γὰδ ὀνομασθῆναι· καὶ ἐκ τῆς
15 αὐτῆς τοῦ αὐτοῦ ἔτους καὶ μηνὸς δωδεκάτου ἕτερον
τεκεῖν, ὃν καὶ αὐτὸν προσαγορευθῆναι ὑπὸ Λείας
᾽Ασήρ. (4) καὶ Λείαν πάλιν ἀντὶ τῶν μήλων τῶν
μανδραγόρου, ἃ ῾Ρουβὴλ εἰσενεγκεῖν παρὰ ῾Ραχήλ,
συλλαβεῖν καὶ τὴν παιδίσκην Ζελφάν τῷ αὐτῷ χρόνῳ,
20 τῷ δωδεκάτῳ ἔτει μηνὶ τρίτῳ, καὶ τεκεῖν τοῦ αὐτοῦ
ἔτους μηνὸς δωδεκάτου υἱὸν καὶ ὄνομα αὐτῷ θέσθαι
᾽Ισσάχαρ. (5) καὶ πάλιν Λείαν τῷ τρισκαιδεκάτῳ
ἔτει μηνὶ δεκάτῳ υἱὸν ἄλλον τεκεῖν, ᾧ ὄνομα
Ζαβουλών, καὶ τὴν αὐτὴν τῷ τεσσαρεσκαιδεκάτῳ ἔτει
25 μηνὶ ὀγδόῳ τεκεῖν υἱὸν ὄνομα Δάν. ἐν ᾧ καὶ ῾Ραχὴλ
λαβεῖν ἐν γαστρὶ τῷ αὐτῷ χρόνῳ, ᾧ καὶ Λείαν

(3)
423a

423b

(4)

423c

(5)

BION

1 ὄντα om. B | 1-2 ἑβδομ. ἑπτά: o͞ζ BON | 11 παιδίσκην
<Βαλλάν, ἣν τεκεῖν τῷ ἑνδεκάτῳ ἔτει. μηνὶ τετάρτῳ Δάν
καὶ τῷ δωδεκάτῳ ἔτει μηνὶ δευτέρῳ Νεφθαλείμ. Λείαν δὲ
καὶ αὐτὴν παρακοιμίσαι τῷ ᾽Ιακὼβ τὴν ἑαυτῆς παιδίσκην>
Freu. | 13 δευτέρῳ: υ͞ι (!) B | 18 ἃ ῾Ρουβὴλ Giff.:
ἀρουβὴλ BION: ἃ ῾Ρουβίν Steph. | 19 συλλαβεῖν I:
συλλαβεῖν (σ. τε B) ἐν γαστρὶ BON | καὶ I: om. BON |
τὴν -- χρόνῳ I: τῷ α. χρ. καὶ τὴν παιδ. αὐτῆς Z. BON:
τῷ α. χρ. <ᾧ> {καὶ} τὴν παιδ. Z. Freu.: (τῷ α. χρ. καὶ
τὴν παιδ. αὐτῆς Z.) Giff. (not.): {τῷ α. χρ. καὶ τὴν
παιδ. αὐτῆς Z.} ? Jac. | 25 υἱὸν ὄνομα Δάν: θυγατέρα
ὄνομα Δείναν Freu. |

(3)

who was 137 years old, whereas he himself was
seventy-seven years old.[6] (3) Thus, after he
had spent seven years there, he married Leah and
Rachel, the two daughters of Laban his maternal
uncle. At that time he was eighty-four years old.
Now in the next seven years twelve children were
born to him: in the eighth year and tenth month,
Reuben; and in the ninth year and eighth month
Simeon; and in the tenth year and sixth month
Levi; in the eleventh year and fourth month Judah.
Now because Rachel was not bearing children, she
became jealous of her sister and made her own
handmaid Zilpah[7] lie with Jacob. This was at the
time that Bilhah also became pregnant with Naphtali, that is, in the eleventh year and fifth
month, and in the twelfth year and second month
she[8] gave birth to a son whom Leah named Gad.
And in the same year and twelfth month by the
same woman he[9] fathered another son, Asher, who

(4)

was also named by Leah. (4) And Leah, in return
for the fruit of the mandrakes which Reuben
brought into Rachel, once again became pregnant
at the same time as her handmaid Zilpah, that is,
in the twelfth year and third month; and, in the
same year and twelfth month she gave birth to a

(5)

son and gave him the name Issachar. (5) And once
more Leah, in the thirteenth year and tenth month,
gave birth to another son whose name was Zebulun;
and in the fourteenth year and eighth month the
same Leah gave birth to a son by the name of Dan.[10]
At the same time that Rachel became pregnant, Leah

τεκεῖν θυγατέρα Δείναν, καὶ τεκεῖν τῷ τεσσαρεσκαιδεκάτῳ ἔτει μηνὶ ὀγδόῳ υἱόν, ὃν ὀνομασθῆναι
'Ιωσήφ, ὥστε γεγονέναι ἐν τοῖς ἑπτὰ ἔτεσι τοῖς
παρὰ Λάβαν δώδεκα παιδία. (6) θέλοντα δὲ τὸν   (6)
5 'Ιακὼβ πρὸς τὸν πατέρα εἰς Χαναὰν ἀπιέναι, ἀξιω-   423d
θέντα ὑπὸ Λάβαν ἄλλα ἔτη ἓξ μεῖναι, ὥστε τὰ πάντα
αὐτὸν μεῖναι ἐν Χαρρὰν παρὰ Λάβαν ἔτη εἴκοσι.
(7) πορευομένῳ δ' αὐτῷ εἰς Χαναὰν ἄγγελον τοῦ   (7)
θεοῦ παλαῖσαι καὶ ἅψασθαι τοῦ πλάτους τοῦ μηροῦ
10 τοῦ 'Ιακώβ, τὸν δὲ ναρκήσαντα ἐπισκάζειν· ὅθεν
οὐκ ἐσθίεσθαι τῶν κτηνῶν τὸ ἐν τοῖς μηροῖς νεῦρον.
καὶ φάναι αὐτῷ τὸν ἄγγελον ἀπὸ τοῦδε μηκέτι
'Ιακώβ, ἀλλ' 'Ισραὴλ ὀνομασθήσεσθαι. (8) καὶ   (8)
ἐλθεῖν αὐτὸν τῆς Χαναὰν γῆς εἰς ἑτέραν πόλιν
15 Σικίμων, ἔχοντα παιδία 'Ρουβὶμ ἐτῶν δώδεκα μηνῶν
δυοῖν, Συμεῶνα ἐτῶν ἕνδεκα μηνῶν τεσσάρων, Λευὶν
ἐτῶν δέκα μηνῶν ἕξ, 'Ιούδαν ἐτῶν ἐννέα μηνῶν
ὀκτώ, Νεφθαλείμ | ἐτῶν ὀκτὼ μηνῶν δέκα, Γὰδ ἐτῶν   424a
ὀκτὼ μηνῶν δέκα, 'Ασὴρ ἐτῶν ὀκτώ, 'Ισσάχαρ ἐτῶν
20 ὀκτώ, Ζαβουλὼν ἐτῶν ἑπτὰ μηνῶν δυοῖν, Δείναν
ἐτῶν ἓξ μηνῶν τεσσάρων, 'Ιωσὴφ ἐτῶν ἓξ μηνῶν
τεσσάρων. (9) παροικῆσαι δὲ 'Ισραὴλ παρὰ 'Εμμὼρ   (9)
ἔτη δέκα, καὶ φθαρῆναι τὴν 'Ισραὴλ θυγατέρα Δείναν
ὑπὸ Συχὲμ τοῦ 'Εμμὼρ υἱοῦ, ἐτῶν οὖσαν δεκαὲξ
25 μηνῶν τεσσάρων. ἐξαλλομένους δὲ τοὺς 'Ισραὴλ

ΒΙΟΝ

1 Δεινάν Ν: Δίναν Β | 2 ὧ ὄνομα θέσθαι Β | 5 Χαναὰν:
Χαρρὰν ΟΝ | 8 sq. περὶ τῆς 'Ιακὼβ πάλης Ι^mg | 9 παλ-
λεῦσαι Ι | 10 sq. διατί τὸ ἐν τοῖς μηροῖς 'Εβραῖοι οὐκ
ἐσθίουσι νεῦρον Ι^mg | 11 οὐκ ἐσθίεσθαι ΒΟΝ: οὐ καθί-
εσθαι Ι | τῶν κτηνῶν post μηροῖς transp. Β |
13 ὀνομασθῆναι Β | 14 τῆς Χαναὰν γῆς om. Β | ἑτέραν
om. Β | πόλιν om. Ι | 16-p. 68,5 Συμεῶνα -- ἑπτὰ
om. Β | 16 ἕνδεκα: ια ΟΝ: δώδεκα Ι | 17 δέκα:
ι ΟΝ: δώδεκα Ι | 18 ὀκτώ¹ <Δὰν ἐτῶν ἐννέα μηνῶν ὀκτώ,>
Freu. | δέκα Ι: Γ ΟΝ | 20 Δείναν: Δὰν Mras |
25 ἐφαλλομένους Freu. |

also gave birth to a daughter Dinah. And in the
fourteenth year and eighth month Rachel gave birth
to a son who was named Joseph. Thus it is seen
how in the seven years spent with Laban twelve
(6)   children were born. (6) Although Jacob wished to
return to his father in Canaan, he was asked by
Laban to remain six additional years, so that in
all he remained with Laban in Haran for twenty
(7)   years.[11] (7) While he was on the way to Canaan,[12]
an angel of God wrestled with him and struck the
broad part of Jacob's thigh; it became stiff and
he limped on it. It is for this reason that the
tendon in the thigh of animals is not eaten. And
the angel said to him that from then on he would
(8)   no longer be called Jacob but Israel. (8) Then
he came into Shechem,[13] another city in the land
of Canaan, accompanied by his children -- Reuben
whose age was twelve years and two months, Simeon
eleven years and four months,[14] Levi ten years and
six months,[15] Judah nine years and eight months,[16]
Naphtali eight years and ten months, Gad eight
years and ten months, Asher eight years, Issachar
eight years, Zebulun seven years and two months,
Dinah[17] six years and four months, and Joseph six
(9)   years and four months. (9) Now Israel had dwelt
near Hamor ten years when Dinah, the daughter of
Israel, was raped by Shechem, Hamor's son; at this
time she was sixteen years and four months old.
And Israel's sons Simeon (who was twenty-one years

υἱούς, Συμεῶνα μὲν ὄντα ἐτῶν εἴκοσιενὸς μηνῶν
τεσσάρων, Λευὶν δὲ ἐτῶν εἴκοσι μηνῶν ἕξ, ἀποκτεῖ-
ναι τόν τε Ἐμμὼρ καὶ Συχὲμ τὸν υἱὸν αὐτοῦ καὶ   424b
πάντας τοὺς ἄρσενας διὰ τὴν Δείνας φθοράν· Ἰακὼβ
5   δὲ τότε εἶναι ἐτῶν ἑκατὸν ἑπτά. (10) ἐλθόντα τε   (10)
οὖν αὐτὸν εἰς Λουζὰ τῆς Βαιθήλ, φάναι τὸν θεὸν
μηκέτι Ἰακώβ, ἀλλ᾽ Ἰσραὴλ ὀνομάζεσθαι.
ἐκεῖθεν δὲ ἐλθεῖν εἰς Χαφραθά, ἔνθεν παραγενέσθαι
εἰς Ἐφραθά, ἣν εἶναι Βηθλεέμ, καὶ γεννῆσαι αὐτὸν
10   ἐκεῖ Βενιαμίν, καὶ τελευτῆσαι Ῥαχήλ, τεκοῦσαν
τὸν Βενιαμίν, συμβιῶσαι δ᾽ αὐτῇ τὸν Ἰακὼβ ἔτη
εἴκοσι τρία. (11) αὐτόθεν δὲ ἐλθεῖν τὸν Ἰακὼβ   (11)
εἰς Μαμβρὶ τῆς Χεβρὼν πρὸς Ἰσαὰκ τὸν πατέρα.   424c
εἶναι δὲ τότε Ἰωσὴφ ἐτῶν δεκαεπτά, καὶ πραθῆναι
15   αὐτὸν εἰς Αἴγυπτον καὶ ἐν τῷ δεσμωτηρίῳ μεῖναι
ἔτη δεκατρία, ὥστ᾽ εἶναι αὐτὸν ἐτῶν τριάκοντα,
Ἰακὼβ δὲ ἐτῶν ἑκατὸν εἴκοσιν, ἐν ᾧ καὶ τελευτῆσαι τὸν Ἰσαὰκ ἔτει ἑνὶ ἔμπροσθεν, ἐτῶν ὄντα
ἑκατὸν ὀγδοήκοντα. (12) κρίναντα δὲ τῷ βασιλεῖ   (12)
20   τὸν Ἰωσὴφ τὰ ἐνύπνια ἄρξαι Αἰγύπτου ἔτη ἑπτά,
ἐν οἷς καὶ συνοικῆσαι Ἀσενέθ, Πεντεφρῆ τοῦ
Ἡλιουπόλεως ἱερέως θυγατρί, καὶ γεννῆσαι Μανασ-   424d
σῆν καὶ Ἐφραΐμ· καὶ τοῦ λιμοῦ ἐπιγενέσθαι ἔτη
δύο. (13) τὸν δὲ Ἰωσὴφ ἔτη ἐννέα εὐτυχήσαντα   (13)
25   πρὸς τὸν πατέρα μὴ πέμψαι, διὰ τὸ ποιμένα αὐτὸν

BION

5 καὶ ἐλθόντα B | 5-6 τε οὖν αὐτὸν om. B |
10 τελευτῆσαι: θνῆξαι (!) B | 11 αὐτῇ om. B |
17 ἑκατὸν εἴκοσιν: ρκ BON: ἑκατὸν δέκα I |
24 sqq. ση (σημείωσαι)· διὰ τὸ ποιμένας εἶναι τὸν
πατέρα καὶ τοὺς ἀδελφοὺς οὐ μετεπέμπετο Ἰωσήφ I^mg |

and four months old) and Levi (who was twenty years
and six months old) rushed forth and killed both
Hamor and his son Shechem, and all their men-folk
because of Dinah's rape.[18]   Jacob was then 107 years
(10) old.   (10)   Therefore, when Jacob came to Luz in
Bethel,[19] God said that he was no longer to be
called Jacob but Israel.[20]   From there he went to
Chaphrath,[21]   and thereafter he went to Ephrath,
which is Bethlehem.   There he fathered Benjamin,[22]
and Rachel died while giving birth to Benjamin.
Jacob had lived with her for twenty-three years.

(11)   (11)   From there Jacob went to Mamre in Hebron to
Isaac his father.[23]   Joseph was then seventeen
years old,[24] and he was sold into Egypt, and he
remained in prison for thirteen years, so that he
was thirty years old.[25]   Jacob was 120 years old[26]
and this was one year before Isaac died at the age
(12) of 180 years.[27]   (12)   After he interpreted the
dreams to the king, Joseph ruled Egypt for seven
years.[28]   During this time he was married to
Asenath,[29] the daughter of Potiphera, priest of
Heliopolis, and he fathered Manasseh and Ephraim.[30]
(13) Two years of famine followed.[31]   (13)   But though
Joseph had good fortune for nine years, he did not
send for his father because he was a shepherd

τε καὶ τοὺς ἀδελφοὺς εἶναι· ἐπονείδιστον δὲ Αἰ-
γυπτίοις εἶναι τὸ ποιμαίνειν. ὅτι δὲ διὰ τοῦτο
οὐκ ἔπεμψεν αὐτὸν δεδηλωκέναι· ἐλθόντων γὰρ αὐτοῦ
τῶν συγγενῶν φάναι αὐτοῖς, ἐὰν κληθῶσιν ὑπὸ
5 τοῦ βασιλέως καὶ ἐρωτῶνται   τί   διαπράσσονται,
λέγειν κτηνοτρόφους αὐτοὺς εἶναι. (14) διαπο- (14)
ρεῖσθαι δὲ διὰ τί ποτε ὁ Ἰωσὴφ Βενιαμὶν ἐπὶ τοῦ
ἀρίστου πενταπλασίονα μερίδα ἔδωκε, μὴ δυναμένου
αὐτοῦ τοσαῦτα καταναλῶσαι κρέα. | τοῦτο οὖν 425a
10 αὐτὸν πεποιηκέναι διὰ τὸ ἐκ τῆς Λείας τῷ πατρὶ
αὐτοῦ γεγονέναι υἱοὺς ἑπτά, ἐκ δὲ Ῥαχὴλ τῆς
μητρὸς αὐτοῦ δύο· διὰ τοῦτο τῷ Βενιαμὶν πέντε
μερίδας παραθεῖναι καὶ αὐτὸν λαβεῖν δύο· γενέσθαι
οὖν ἑπτά, ὅσας καὶ τοὺς ἐκ τῆς Λείας υἱοὺς
15 λαβεῖν. (15) ὡσαύτως δὲ καὶ ἐπὶ τοῦ τὰς στολὰς (15)
δοῦναι ἑκάστῳ διπλᾶς, τῷ δὲ Βενιαμὶν πέντε
καὶ τριακοσίους χρυσοῦς καὶ τῷ πατρὶ δὲ ἀποστεῖλαι κατὰ ταὐτά, ὥστε τὸν οἶκον αὐτοῦ τῆς
μητρὸς εἶναι ἴσον. (16) οἰκῆσαι δὲ αὐτοὺς ἐν γῇ (16)
20 Χαναάν, ἀφ' οὗ ἐκλεγῆναι Ἀβραὰμ ἐκ τῶν ἐθνῶν καὶ 425b
μετελθεῖν εἰς Χαναάν, Ἀβραὰμ ἐτῶν εἴκοσι πέντε,
Ἰσαὰκ ἐτῶν ἐξήκοντα, Ἰακὼβ ἐτῶν ἑκατὸν
τριάκοντα· γίνεσθαι τὰ πάντα ἔτη ἐν γῇ Χαναὰν
σιε'. (17) καὶ τῷ τρίτῳ ἔτει λιμοῦ οὔσης ἐν (17)
25 Αἰγύπτῳ ἐλθεῖν εἰς Αἴγυπτον τὸν Ἰακὼβ ὄντα ἐτῶν

BION

1-2 ἐπον. -- εἶναι: δι' ὀνείδους εἶναι Αἰγ. Β |
3 γὰρ ΒΟ: δὲ (superscr. γὰρ) Ν¹: om. Ι |
6 εἶναι < > Freu. | 6 sqq. διατί Ἰωσὴφ τῶν
ἀδελφῶν αὐτοῦ συνδειπνούντων αὐτῷ, τῶν^{οῖς} μὲν ^{ἄλλοις}
ἀδελφῶν ^{οῖς} ἀνὰ μίαν μερίδα ἔδωκε, τῶ δὲ Βενιαμὶν ε' Ι¹ᵐᵍ |
11 ἑπτά: ἕξ Freu. | 13 δύο Vig. (not.): μίαν MSS |
14 ἑπτά: ἕξ Freu. | 18 ταῦτα ΟΝ | 19 εἶναι:
λαβεῖν ? Freu. | 24 οὔσης Ι: ὄντος ΒΟΝ |

as were his brothers too, and Egyptians consider
it a disgrace to be a shepherd. That this was the
reason he did not send for him, Joseph himself
declared. For when his kin did come, he told them
that if they should be summoned by the king and
were asked what they did for a living, they were
(14) to say that they were cowherds.[32]   (14) A crucial
question arises as to why Joseph gave Benjamin a
five-fold portion at the meal even though he would
not be able to consume so much meat.[33] He did this
because seven[34] sons had been born to his father
by Leah whereas only two sons had been born to
him by Rachel his mother. For this reason, he
served up five portions for Benjamin and he himself
took two.[35] Thus, there were between them seven
portions,[36] that is, as many as all the sons of
(15) Leah had taken.[37]   (15) The same explanation
applies to his giving double-folded garments to
each brother, while giving Benjamin five such garments[38] along with 300 [39] pieces of gold. He also
sent to his father the same amount so that his
(16) mother's house would be equal. (16) From the time
when Abraham was chosen from among the nations
and migrated to Canaan, they dwelt in the land of
Canaan as follows: Abraham -- twenty-five years;[40]
Isaac -- sixty years;[41] Jacob -- 130 years;[42]
in all, 215 years were spent in the land of
(17) Canaan. (17) In the third year of famine in Egypt
Jacob came into Egypt, and he was 130 years old.

ἑκατὸν τριάκοντα, ʽΡουβὶν ἐτῶν με᾽, Συμεῶνα ἐτῶν
μδ᾽, Λευὶν ἐτῶν μγ᾽, ᾽Ιούδαν ἐτῶν μβ᾽ μηνῶν δύο,
Νεφθαλεὶμ ἐτῶν μα᾽ μηνῶν ζ᾽, Γὰδ ἐτῶν μα᾽ μηνῶν 425c
γ᾽, ᾽Ασὴρ ἐτῶν μ᾽ μηνῶν ὀκτώ, Ζαβουλὼν ἐτῶν μ᾽,
5 Δείναν ἐτῶν λθ᾽, Βενιαμὶν ἐτῶν κη᾽. (18) τὸν δὲ (18)
᾽Ιωσὴφ φησι γενέσθαι ἐν Αἰγύπτῳ ἔτη λθ᾽. εἶναι
δὲ ἀπὸ τοῦ ᾽Αδὰμ ἕως τοῦ εἰσελθεῖν εἰς Αἴγυπτον
τοὺς τοῦ ᾽Ιωσὴφ συγγενεῖς ἔτη ͵γχκδ᾽. ἀπὸ δὲ τοῦ
κατακλυσμοῦ ἕως τῆς ᾽Ιακὼβ παρουσίας εἰς Αἴγυπτον
10 ἔτη ͵ατξ᾽. ἀφ᾽ οὗ δὲ ἐκλεγῆναι ᾽Αβραὰμ ἐκ τῶν
ἐθνῶν καὶ ἐλθεῖν ἐκ Χαρρὰν εἰς Χαναὰν ἕως εἰς 425d
Αἴγυπτον τοὺς περὶ ᾽Ιακὼβ ἐλθεῖν, ἔτη σιε᾽.
(19) ᾽Ιακὼβ δὲ εἰς Χαρρὰν πρὸς Λάβαν ἐλθεῖν ἐτῶν (19)
ὄντα π᾽ καὶ γεννῆσαι Λευίν· Λευὶν δὲ ἐν Αἰγύπτῳ
15 ἐπιγενέσθαι ἔτη ιζ᾽, ἀφ᾽ οὗ ἐκ Χαναὰν αὐτὸν
ἐλθεῖν εἰς Αἴγυπτον, ὥστε εἶναι αὐτὸν ἐτῶν ξ᾽,
καὶ γεννῆσαι Κλάθ, τῷ αὐτῷ δὲ ἔτει ᾧ γενέσθαι
Κλάθ, τελευτῆσαι ᾽Ιακὼβ ἐν Αἰγύπτῳ, εὐλογήσαντα
τοὺς ᾽Ιωσὴφ υἱούς, ὄντα ἐτῶν ρμζ᾽, καταλιπόντα
20 ᾽Ιωσὴφ ὄντα ἐτῶν νς᾽. Λευὶν δὲ γενόμενον ἐτῶν
ρλζ᾽ τελευτῆσαι, Κλάθ δὲ ὄντα ἐτῶν μ᾽ γεννῆσαι
᾽Αμβράμ, ὃν ἐτῶν εἶναι ιδ᾽ ἐν ᾧ τελευτῆσαι ᾽Ιωσὴφ
ἐν Αἰγύπτῳ ὄντα ρι᾽ ἐτῶν· Κλάθ δὲ γενόμενον
ἐτῶν ἑκατὸν λγ᾽ τελευτῆσαι. | ᾽Αμβρὰμ δὲ λαβεῖν 426a
25 γυναῖκα τὴν τοῦ θείου θυγατέρα ᾽Ιωχαβὲτ καὶ ὄντα

BION

1-5_ ʽΡουβὶν -- κη᾽ om. B | 2 δύο Mras: δ. (!) O
(= δ̄ GFC apud Gais.) N: δ᾽ < > Freu.: τριῶν I |
2-3 δύο <Δὰν ἐτῶν μβ᾽ μηνῶν δ᾽> Freu. (not.) (cf. Frg. 2,
par. 8) | 4 γ᾽: τριῶν Giff.: ἔξ Freu.: | ᾽Ασὴρ --
ὀκτώ ON (A. ἐ. μ̄ μην. η̄): ante 3 Νεφθ. transp. I |
ὀκτώ, <᾽Ισσαχὰρ ἐτῶν μ᾽ μηνῶν ὀκτώ,> Freu. | 5 Δείναν
(Δεῖνα N): Δὰν Mras (cf. Frg. 2, par. 8) | 6 φησι om. B|
11 ἐκ: ὑ (= ἐν ? cf. infra lin. 13) B | 13 εἰς Freu.
(p. 53): ἐν B: ἐκ ION (cf. Frg. 2, par. 1 & 2) |
17 γενέσθαι: γεννῆσαι B | 22 ᾽Αμβράμ Mras: ᾽Αμβρὰν N:
᾽Αβράμ (emend. ex ᾽Αβραάμ) O¹: ῎Αμβραν B: ᾽Αβράμ I:
᾽Αμράμ Gais. | 22-24 ὃν -- τελευτ.: ὃν ἐτῶν ρμζ κατα-
λιπόντα ἰωσὴφ ὄντα ἐτῶν νς B (ditt.?) | 24 ᾽Αμβράμ Mras:
᾽Αμβρὰν ON: ῎Αμβραν B: ᾽Αβράμ I: ᾽Αμράμ Gais. |

Reuben was forty-five years old,[43] Simeon forty-
four years old, Levi forty-three years old, Judah
forty-two years and two[44] months old,[45] Naphtali
forty-one years and seven months old, Gad forty-
one years and three[46] months old, Asher[47] forty
years and eight months old,[48] Zebulun forty years
old, Dinah[49] thirty-nine years old, Benjamin twenty-
(18) eight years old.[50] (18) Joseph, he[51] says, turned
thirty-nine while in Egypt.[52] From Adam until the
time when the brothers of Joseph came into Egypt
there were 3,624 years;[53] from the flood until
Jacob's arrival in Egypt there were 1,360 years;[54]
and from the time when Abraham was chosen from
among the nations and came from Haran into Canaan
until the time when those with him came into Egypt
(19) there were 215 years.[55] (19) Jacob came into Haran
to Laban when he was eighty years old,[56] and then
he fathered Levi.[57] From the time when Levi left
Canaan and came into Egypt, he was subsequently
in Egypt seventeen years, so that he was sixty years[58]
old when he fathered Kohath.[59] But in the same year
in which Kohath was born, Jacob died in Egypt (after
having blessed the sons of Joseph) at the age of
147 years,[60] leaving Joseph who was fifty-six years
old. Levi died at the age of 137 years, while Kohath,
at the age of forty, fathered Amram,[61] who was
fourteen years old when Joseph died in Egypt at the
age of 110 years.[62] Kohath was 133 years old when
he died. Amram took for a wife his uncle's daughter,

BION

Ἀβράμ (emended from Ἀβραάμ by first (?) copyist) O:
Ἀβραάμ Vig. Hein.: Ἄμβραν B Freu. (p. 206): Ἀβραάμ I:
Ἀμράμ Gais. Dind. Giff. Jac. | 22-24 ὃν -- τελευτ.:
ὃν ἐτῶν ρμζ καταλιπόντα ἰωσὴφ ὄντα ἐτῶν νς (all others
omit) B |

ἐνιαυτῶν οε΄ γεννῆσαι ᾿Ααρὼν {καὶ Μωσῆν}· γεννῆσαι δὲ Μωσῆν τὸν ᾿Αμβρὰμ ὄντα ἐτῶν οη΄, καὶ
γενόμενον ᾿Αμβρὰμ ἐτῶν ρλς΄ τελευτῆσαι."

    Ταῦτά μοι κείσθω ἀπὸ τῆς ᾿Αλεξάνδρου τοῦ
5 Πολυΐστορος γραφῆς.   426b

FRAGMENT THREE   (Eusebius, P.E. 9.29.1-3)

    ΔΗΜΗΤΡΙΟΥ ΠΕΡΙ ΤΟΥ ΑΥΤΟΥ ΟΜΟΙΩΣ

    (1) "Δημήτριος δὲ περὶ τῆς ἀναιρέσεως τοῦ   (1)
Αἰγυπτίου καὶ τῆς διαφορᾶς τῆς πρὸς τὸν μηνύσαντα
τὸν τελευτήσαντα ὁμοίως τῷ τὴν ἱερὰν βίβλον
10 γράψαντι ἱστόρησε· φυγεῖν μέντοι γε τὸν Μωσῆν
εἰς Μαδιὰμ καὶ συνοικῆσαι ἐκεῖ τῇ ᾿Ιοθὼρ θυγατρὶ   439c
Σεπφώρᾳ, ἣν εἶναι, ὅσα στοχάζεσθαι ἀπὸ τῶν
ὀνομάτων, τῶν γενομένων ἐκ Χεττούρας, τοῦ ᾿Αβραὰμ
γένους, ἐκ τοῦ ᾿Ιεζὰν τοῦ γενομένου ᾿Αβραὰμ ἐκ
15 Χεττούρας· ἐκ δὲ τοῦ ᾿Ιεζὰν γενέσθαι Δαδάν,
ἐκ δὲ Δαδὰν ᾿Ραγουήλ, ἐκ δὲ ᾿Ραγουὴλ ᾿Ιοθὼρ καὶ
᾿Οβάβ, ἐκ δὲ τοῦ ᾿Ιοθὼρ Σεπφώραν, ἣν γῆμαι Μωσῆν.
    (2) καὶ τὰς γενεὰς δὲ συμφωνεῖν· τὸν γὰρ Μωσῆν   (2)
εἶναι ἀπὸ ᾿Αβραὰμ ἕβδομον, τὴν δὲ Σεπφώραν ἕκτην.
20 συνοικοῦντος γὰρ ἤδη τοῦ ᾿Ισαάκ, ἀφ᾿ οὗ Μωσῆν
εἶναι, γῆμαι ᾿Αβραὰμ τὴν Χεττούραν ὄντα ἐτῶν ρμ΄
καὶ γεννῆσαι ᾿Ισαὰρ ἐξ αὐτῆς δεύτερον· τὸν δὲ   439d
᾿Ισαὰκ ὄντα ἐτῶν ἑκατὸν γεννῆσαι. ὥστε μβ΄ ἐτῶν
ὕστερον γεγονέναι τὸν ᾿Ισαάρ, ἀφ᾿ οὗ τὴν Σεπφώραν
25 γεγενεαλογῆσθαι. (3) οὐδὲν οὖν ἀντιπίπτει τὸν   (3)

BION
1-3 ἐνιαυτῶν -- ᾿Αμβρὰμ om. B | 1 {καὶ Μωσῆν} Mras |
2 ᾿Αμβρὰμ Mras: ᾿Αμβρᾶν ON: ᾿Αβραὰμ I: ᾿Αμράμ Gais. |
3 ᾿Αμβρὰμ Mras: ῎Αμβραν ON: ᾿Αβραὰμ I: ᾿Αμράμ Gais. |
τελευτῆσαι < > Freu. | 6 ΔΗΜ. -- ΟΜ. BI^mg ON |
11 Μαδιὰν Steph. | ᾿Ιοθὼρ ON: ᾿Ιοθὸρ I¹: Ιωθὼ (sine
aspir.) B | 14 ᾿Ιεζὰν I | ᾿Αβραὰμ B | 15 ᾿Ιεξὰν I |
16 ᾿Ιοθὼρ ON: ᾿Ιωθὼρ B: ᾿Ιοθὸρ I | 17 ᾿Οβάβ BON:
᾿Οβάβ I: ᾿Ιωβάβ Freu. | ᾿Ιοθὼρ BON; ᾿Ιοθὸρ I |

(cont.)

Jochebed, and at the age of seventy-five he
fathered Aaron and Moses.[63] Amram fathered Moses
when he was seventy-eight years old[64] and Amram
was 136   years old when he died."[65]

   These things I have quoted from Alexander
Polyhistor's work.

FRAGMENT THREE[66]

   Similarly, Demetrius' Remarks Concerning
   The Same Man (Moses)

(1)   (1) "With respect to his slaying the Egyptian
and his disagreement with the informant about the
dead man, Demetrius' account agrees with that of
the writer of the Sacred Book: Moses fled to
Midian[67] and there was married to Zipporah,[68] the
daughter of Jethro,[69] who was (as can be ascertained
from the names) of the descendants of Keturah,[70]
and thus of the stock of Abraham. He was descended
from Jokshan[71] who was born to Abraham by Keturah.
From Jokshan, Dedan[72] was born, and from Dedan,
Raguel.[73] From Raguel, Jethro and Hobab[74] were
born, and from Jethro, Zipporah, whom Moses
(2)   married. (2) The number of generations coincides
as well, for Moses was seventh[75] from Abraham and
Zipporah was sixth. For Isaac (from whom Moses
was descended) was already married when Abraham,
at the age of 140, wedded Keturah, and by her
he fathered a second son, Ishbak.[76] He was one
hundred years old when he fathered Isaac. Consequently, it was forty-two years later when he
fathered Ishbak,[77] from whom Zipporah has been
(3)   traced. (3) Therefore, there is nothing contradictory

19 Ἀβραάμ B | 20-25 συνοικ. -- γεγεν. om. B |
22 Ἰσαάρ: Ἰεζάν Freu. (in not.; cf. p. 206) cf. supra
lin. 14-15 | 25 τοίνυν οὐδὲν B | οὖν I: ἂν ON: om. B |

Μωσῆν καὶ τὴν Σεπφώραν κατὰ τοὺς αὐτοὺς
γεγονέναι χρόνους. κατοικεῖν δὲ αὐτοὺς Μαδιὰμ
πόλιν, ἣν ἀπὸ ἑνὸς τῶν Ἀβραὰμ παίδων ὀνομασθῆναι.
φησὶ γὰρ τὸν Ἀβραὰμ τοὺς παῖδας πρὸς ἀνατολὰς
5 ἐπὶ κατοικίαν πέμψαι· διὰ τοῦτο δὲ καὶ Ἀαρὼν
καὶ Μαριὰμ εἰπεῖν ἐν Ἀσηρὼθ Μωσῆν Αἰθιοπίδα
γῆμαι γυναῖκα."

FRAGMENT FOUR (Eusebius, P.E. 9.29.15)

   (15) καὶ πάλιν μετ' ὀλίγα·   (15)
                                                         445d
   "Ἐκεῖθεν ἦλθον ἡμέρας τρεῖς, ὡς αὐτός τε ὁ
10 Δημήτριος λέγει καὶ συμφώνως τούτῳ ἡ ἱερὰ βίβλος.
μὴ ἔχοντα δὲ ὕδωρ ἐκεῖ γλυκύ, ἀλλὰ πικρόν, τοῦ
θεοῦ εἰπόντος ξύλον τι ἐμβαλεῖν εἰς τὴν πηγὴν
καὶ γενέσθαι γλυκὺ τὸ ὕδωρ. ἐκεῖθεν δὲ εἰς
Ἐλεὶμ ἐλθεῖν καὶ εὑρεῖν ἐκεῖ δώδεκα μὲν πηγὰς
15 ὑδάτων, ἑβδομήκοντα δὲ στελέχη φοινίκων."

FRAGMENT FIVE (Eusebius, P.E. 9.29.16)

   (16) καὶ μετὰ βραχέα·   (16)
                                                         446d
   "Ἐπιζητεῖν δέ τινα πῶς οἱ Ἰσραηλῖται ὅπλα
ἔσχον ἄνοπλοι ἐξελθόντες· ἔφασαν γὰρ τριῶν ἡμερῶν
ὁδὸν ἐξελθόντες καὶ θυσιάσαντες πάλιν ἀνακάμψειν.
20 φαίνεται οὖν τοὺς μὴ κατακλυσθέντας τοῖς ἐκείνων
ὅπλοις χρήσασθαι."

BION

3 Ἀβραὰμ Β | 4 Ἀβραὰμ Β | 9 ἐκεῖθεν ἦλθον:
ἦλθεν (!) ἐκεῖθεν Β | αὐτός τε om. Β | 13 καὶ om. Β
14 Ἐλεὶμ I: Ἐλὶμ Β: Ἐλεὶν ΟΝ | 19 ἐξελθόντες καὶ
θυσιάσαντες Steph.: -θόντας κ. -σαντας MSS | 20 φαίνεται
Steph.: φαίνονται MSS |

in saying that Moses and Zipporah lived at the
same time. They lived in the city of Midian,[78]
which is named after one of the children of
Abraham. For it[79] says that Abraham sent his
sons to the East to make their home. For this
reason, too, Aaron and Miriam said at Hazeroth[80]
that Moses had married an Ethiopian woman."[81]

FRAGMENT FOUR[82]

(15)   (15) And a little further on:

          "From there they[83] traveled three days, as
Demetrius himself says -- and the Holy Book agrees
with this.[84] But finding no sweet water there,[85]
only bitter water, as God had commanded, he threw
a piece of wood into the spring and the water
became sweet. From there they came to Elim[86]
and there they found twelve springs of water
and seventy palm trees."

FRAGMENT FIVE[87]

(16)   (16) And a little further on:

          "But someone asked how the Israelites obtained
weapons, seeing that they departed from Egypt
unarmed[88] -- for they[89] said that after they had
gone a three days' journey and had offered a
sacrifice, they would return again.[90] It appears,
therefore, that those who did not drown appropriated
the weapons of those who did drown."

FRAGMENT SIX (Clement of Alex., Strom. 1.21.141.1-2)

(1) Δημήτριος δέ φησιν ἐν τῷ Περὶ τῶν ἐν τῇ   (1)
'Ιουδαίᾳ βασιλέων τὴν 'Ιούδα φυλὴν καὶ Βενιαμεὶν
καὶ Λευὶ μὴ αἰχμαλωτισθῆναι ὑπὸ τοῦ Σεναχηρείμ,
ἀλλ' εἶναι ἀπὸ τῆς αἰχμαλωσίας ταύτης   εἰς   τὴν
5   ἐσχάτην, ἣν ἐποιήσατο Ναβουχοδονόσορ ἐξ 'Ιεροσολύμων, ἔτη ἑκατὸν εἴκοσι ὀκτὼ μῆνας ἕξ. (2) ἀφ'   (2)
οὗ δὲ αἱ φυλαὶ αἱ δέκα ἐκ Σαμαρείας αἰχμάλωτοι
γεγόνασιν ἕως Πτολεμαίου τετάρτου ἔτη πεντακόσια
ἑβδομήκοντα τρία μῆνας   ἐννέα, ἀφ' οὗ δὲ ἐξ
10   'Ιεροσολύμων ἔτη τριακόσια   τριάκοντα ὀκτὼ μῆνας
τρεῖς.

L

3 Σεναχηρείμ <ἀλλὰ πολλὰ χρήματα καὶ σκεύη τοῦ ναοῦ,
μηδὲ μετ' ὀλίγον χρόνον ἐκείνας αἰχμαλώτους γενέσθαι,>
Freu. (in not.; cf. p. 59) | 6 ὀκτώ: πέντε Gutschmid
(Kleine Schriften 2.188) apud Stählin | 8 τετάρτου:
τοῦ τρίτου Freu. (in not.; cf. p. 62): ἑβδόμου Mendels-
sohn apud Jac. | πεντακόσια: τετρακόσια Reinesius apud
Stählin | 9 δὲ <αἱ> ? Mendelssohn apud Jac. |
10 τριακόσια: τετρακόσια Raška (Chronologie der Bibel,
97-8) apud Stählin | τριάκοντα: τετταράκοντα Gutschmid
(Kleine Schriften) apud Stählin |

FRAGMENT SIX[91]

(1)   (1)   In his book _Concerning the Kings in Judaea_ Demetrius says that the tribes of Judah, Benjamin, and Levi were not taken captive by Sennacherib, but[92] that between the time of this captivity and the last captivity of Jerusalem by Nebuchadnezzar there were 128 years[93] and

(2)   six months.[94]   (2)   From the time when the ten tribes were taken captive from Samaria until the time of Ptolemy the Fourth[95] there were 573 years[96] and nine months; from the time that the captivity from Jerusalem took place there were 338 years[97] and three months.

ANNOTATIONS

1. This fragment occurs in the section on Abraham (P.E.
9.16-20) in which Eusebius quotes various authors mentioned by Josephus and Alexander Polyhistor who refer to
Abraham. Previously Eusebius has excerpted authors who
discuss Abraham in Egypt and Phoenicia, his status as
wise man and astrologer, and now turns to his sons. Frg.
1 occurs between quotations from Apollonius Molon which
treats Abraham's travels and his children and Philo the
Epic Poet depicting the sacrifice of Isaac. Although
this fragment is anonymous, it is now widely attributed
to Demetrius. Cf. Freu., 14-15, 36.

2. Cf. Gen   22:1-19.

3. This fragment occurs immediately following a set of
quotations concerning Abraham and his sons, and is the
first of several quotations devoted primarily to Jacob
(P.E. 9.21-22). It is immediately followed by a fragment
from Theodotus giving further information on Shechem and
the family of Emmor.

4. Because this figure contradicts that given in the next
paragraph (Frg. 2, par. 2), Viger (PG (21) col. 713D, n.
41) proposes that πέντε be emended to ἑπτά. This emendation is adopted by Freu., 219 (full discussion, 52-53).
Actually, the text of Demetrius (i.e. Eusebius) edited by
Mras gives three different ages for Jacob when he departed
for Haran: 75 years (par. 1): 77 years (par. 2): 80 years
(par. 19). But since the calculations of Demetrius throughout are based on the figure 77, the other two figures
appear to be corruptions. Cf. Miller-Hanson, "Demetrius
Historicus," 17. Freu., 52-53, attributes the differences
to scribal errors. Cf. notes 6 and 56 below.

5. Cf. Gen 27:41-28:5.

6. According to Freu., 39, Demetrius probably arrives at
these figures in the following way. Between the time of
Jacob's death at the age of 147 (Gen 47:28) and his
departure to Haran, a total of 70 years elapsed. This is
calculated as follows: 14 years in the service of Laban
(Gen 31:41), at the end of which Joseph was born (cf.
Frg. 2, par. 5); 30 years between the time of Joseph's
birth and the time of his entry into the service of Pharaoh
(Gen 41:46); 9 years in the service of Pharaoh before the
first appearance of his brothers (Gen 45:6 -- seven years
of plenty presupposed and added to the two years of famine
before the arrival of the brothers); 17 years between the
arrival of Joseph's family and the death of Jacob (Gen 47:
28). Thus, 14+30+9+17=70 years. Since Jacob was 147 years

old when he died (Gen 47:28), he must have been 77 years
old when he left for Haran (147-70=77).

Isaac's age of 137 years is derived by simply adding
Jacob's age at the time of his departure to Haran (77
years) to Isaac's age (60 years) at the time of Jacob's
birth (Gen 25:26).

7. Zilpah, of course, was Leah's handmaid (Gen 29:24, 29;
30:1-13), not Rachel's. In Frg. 2, par. 4, Zilpah appears
to be correctly identified as Leah's handmaid, but the
syntax is unclear. An apparently simply solution would
be to emend the text by substituting Βάλλαν for Ζελφάν
(line 11), but this is impossible because the remarks
which immediately follow would not only be incorrect but
incomprehensible. Freu. suggests a more extensive emendation. Assuming that the biblicist Demetrius would not
have made such a blatant error, he suggests that homoeoteleuton occurred at some point in the transmission of the
text. He proposes the following emendation in par. 3,
line 11: παιδίσκην <Βαλλάν, ἣν τεκεῖν τῷ ἐνδεκάτῳ ἔτει.
μηνὶ τετάρτῳ Δάν καὶ τῷ δωδεκάτῳ ἔτει μηνὶ δευτέρῳ
Νεφθαλείμ· Λείαν δὲ καὶ αὐτὴν παρακοιμίσαι τῷ Ἰακώβ
τὴν ἑαυτῆς παιδίσκην> Ζελφαν. ("Rachel ... made her own
handmaid<Bilhah>to lie with Jacob,<and by her, in the
eleventh year and fourth month, he fathered Dan, and in
the twelfth year and second month Naphtali. Leah also
made her own handmaid>Zilpah<to lie with Jacob,>this at
the same time that Bilhah became pregnant with Naphtali,
that is, in the eleventh year and fifth month; and in the
twelfth year and second month he also fathered a son
(by Zilpah) whom Lean named Gad ...").

It should be noted that this emendation requires
another emendation in par. 5. Since it makes room for Dan,
placing him with his proper mother in the proper sequence,
υἱὸν ὄνομα Δάν in Frg. 2, par. 5, is emended to θυγατέρα
ὄνομα Δείναν (cf. Gen 30:21; Freu., 54-56). Walter, JS
(3,2), 285, suggests an emendation even more extensive,
but based on Freu.'s suggestion. Cf. below, notes 10, 16,
17, 45, and 49.

8. I.e., Zilpah.

9. Mras proposes Rachel as the subject of τεκεῖν (line 16).
Cf. GCS (43.1) 508, app. crit., line 22.

10. Freu., 54, suggests that in Frg. 2, par. 3, a section
which included the account of the birth of Dan was omitted
because of homoeoteleuton. In this case, υἱὸν ὄνομα Δάν
here in par. 5 would be a later editor's attempt to include
Dan's name in the list of children. The phrase is thus

bracketed in Freu.'s text, 220. The similarity between
Δεῖναν and Δάν no doubt added to the confusion, and would
have prompted attempts at correction. Cf. note 7 above.

11. Cf. Gen 31:41; also Josephus, Ant. 1.319.

12. Cf. Gen 32:25-32; also Josephus, Ant. 1.331-34.

13. The spelling is unusual. שׁכם is ordinarily rendered
Συχεμ or Σικιμα. Bickerman, apud Jacoby, app. crit.,
thus calls ἑτέραν πόλιν Σικίμων a "strange variant."
Jacoby suggests that the unusual spelling of Shechem here
might have resulted from abbreviating the LXX (Gen 33:17-
18): καὶ ᾽Ιακωβ ἀπαίρει εἰς Σκηνάς .... καὶ ἦλθεν ᾽Ιακωβ
εἰς Σαλημ πόλιν Σικίμων, ἥ ἐστιν ἐν γῆι Χανααν. Polyhistor
or, less likely, Demetrius may have taken the genitive
plural as a place name.

14. Note the discrepancy in MS I (line 16) where Simeon's
age is given as 12 years and four months.

15. Note the discrepancy in MS I (line 17) where Levi's
age is given as 12 years and 6 months. The numbers are
clearly corrupt. No corresponding variants are given by
MS I in par. 3.

16. Freu., 220, in keeping with his earlier emendation
in par. 3, line 11 (cf. note 7 above), suggests inserting
here Δάν ἐτῶν ἐννέα μηνῶν ὀκτώ ("Dan, nine years and
eight months"). He was possibly omitted because of the
similarity between his age and that of Judah. Cf. Walter,
JS (3,2) 286, n. 86.

17. Another way of including Dan in the list is to read
Δάν here instead of Δεῖναν, as Mras suggests (GCS (43.1),
509, app. crit. on line 19). But the age (six years and
four months) would have to be adjusted. To do this,
Freu.'s emendation would be required (cf. note 16 above).
Still, the order would be unusual. Cf. par. 17, note 49.

18. Cf. Gen 34.

19. The text, as it stands, implies that Bethel is the
region in which Luz is located, thus misconstruing the
LXX: εἰς Λουζα ... ἥ ἐστιν Βαιθηλ (cf. Gen 35:6; Josh
16:1; 18:13). Perhaps it is to be understood as a genitive of apposition (cf. Smyth, Greek Grammar, par. 1322),
or, more likely, a chorographic genitive (cf. Smyth,
par. 1311). As it stands, it is to be translated "to
Luz in Bethel."

20. Cf. Gen 35:10; also Frg. 2, par. 7; also Gen 32:28.

21. Demetrius, or perhaps Polyhistor, has misconstrued the LXX χαβραθα (Gen 35:16) as the name of a place, whereas it is actually a transliteration of כברת in the expression כברת־הארץ.

22. Cf. Gen 35:16-19.

23. Cf. Gen 35:27.

24. Cf. Gen 37:2.

25. Cf. Gen 41:46.

26. In MS I Jacob's age is given as 110 years. This reading is adopted by Vig. Gais. Dind. Giff. The majority of witnesses (BON) give his age as 120 years. This is adopted by Freu. Mras Jac. Freu., however, proposes a lacuna after ρκ'. Walter, JS (3.2), 287, n. 11d, proposes 121 years, based on the information given in Frg. 2, par. 2.

27. The Greek wording is puzzling, particularly the phrase "one year before" (ἔτει ἑνὶ ἔμπροσθεν). Assuming the figures given in Frg. 2, par. 2, the chronology would require Jacob to be 120 years old at the time when Isaac died at the age of 180, not one year earlier:

137 yrs.	Isaac's age when Jacob left for Haran (par. 2)
20 yrs.	Length of Jacob's stay with Laban in Haran (par.6)
10 yrs.	Length of Jacob's stay at Hamor (par. 9)
13 yrs.	Length of Jacob's stay at Mamre (par. 11)
180 yrs.	Isaac's age when he died

77 yrs.	Jacob's age when he departed for Haran (par. 2)
20 yrs.	As above
10 yrs.	As above
13 yrs.	As above
120 yrs.	Jacob's age at the time of Isaac's death

The text, as it stands, however, may presuppose another method of calculation:

77 yrs.	Jacob's age when he departed for Haran (par. 2)
7 yrs.	Length of Jacob's stay in Haran with Laban before he married Leah and Rachel (par. 3)
7 yrs.	Length of time which elapsed before the birth of Joseph (par. 5)
30 yrs.	Joseph's age at the time of his release from prison (par. 11)
121 yrs.	Jacob's age at the time of Isaac's death at age 180

If Jacob's age is calculated in this manner, then he would indeed have been 120 years old one year before Isaac died at the age of 180. Walter, JS (3,2), 287, n. 11d, thus suggests placing ἔτει ἐνὶ ἔμπροσθεν before Ἰακωβ δὲ ἐτῶν ἐκατὸν εἴκοσιν, thus reading "one year before -- when Jacob was 120 years old -- Isaac died at the age of 180."

The figures, of course, are even further skewed if Jacob's age when he departed to Haran is taken as 75 (cf. Frg. 2, par. 1); cf. also note 4. On Isaac's age at the time of his death, cf. Gen 35:28-29.

28.   Cf. Gen 41:46-57.

29.   Cf. Gen. 41:45, 50-52; also Josephus, Ant. 2.91; T. Jos. 18.

30.   Walter, JS (3,2), 287, n. 12c, suggests that the summary of Joseph's career based on Gen 41:45-49; 42:6 found in Artapanus, Frg. 2, par. 4, may originally have belonged here.

31.   Cf. Gen 45:6.

32.   Freu., 45, suggests that Alexander Polyhistor has mutilated the text by omitting the explanation offered in Gen 46:34, and thus proposes a lacuna. Cf. Walter, JS (3,2), 287, n. 13a. As the text stands, Demetrius' remarks alter the point of Gen 46:28-34. The passage does not address the question of the impropriety of Joseph's failure to send for his aged father, once he had met with good fortune in Egypt. Given Demetrius' close familiarity with the LXX, some of the fault may lie with Polyhistor.

33.   Cf. Gen 43:34.

34.   All the MSS here read "seven" (ἑπτά) as the number of Leah's sons. This reading is retained by most editors (Vig. Hein. Gais. Dind. Giff. Stearns Mras Denis). This agrees with the list in Frg. 2, par. 2-5 (though cf. note 7 above), but disagrees with the biblical account which lists only six sons by Leah (Gen 35:23). Noting how easily confused were the numbers "six" (ϛ̄) and "seven" (ζ̄), Freu., 53-54, emended ἑπτά to read ἕξ. This emendation was adopted by Jac., and also incorporated by Walter, JS (3,2) 287-88, esp. n. 14b. The reading adopted affects the rest of the arithmetical scheme in par. 14. Cf. notes 35, 36, 37, below.

35. All the MSS here read "one" (μίαν), a reading which
can be retained convincingly only if ἑπτά in line 11 is
emended to ἕξ (so Freu. Jac., followed by Walter). But,
if ἑπτά is retained, to be consistent, it is necessary to
emend μίαν to δύο (so Dind. Giff. Stearns Mras Denis).
The problem was recognized by Vig., who notes: "Sensus
et ἀκολουθία postulat δύο, alioqui sex tantum, non
septem partes habiturus erat" (PG, col. 718, n. 53).
Some editions, however, do retain the unemended text,
and read ἑπτά in lines 11 and 14, and μίαν in line 13
(so Vig., Hein., Gais.).

36. As in line 11, so here all the MSS read "seven"
(ἑπτά), which may be retained or emended, depending on
the arithmetic scheme one adopts, either 5+1 or 5+2.
Cf. notes 34 and 35 above, and note 37 below.

37. As already noted above, the text in par. 14 presents
two interrelated problems involving (1) the number of
Leah's sons, and (2) the number of portions of food
served by Joseph. For Demetrius' point to have weight,
the total number of portions of food received by Rachel's
two sons, Joseph and Benjamin, must equal the total number of portions received by all of Leah's other sons
combined. The main question is whether the total is six
or seven.

     The MS tradition contains a contradiction. In all the
MSS, the number of Leah's sons is given as "seven" (ἑπτά)
in line 11. Similarly, in all the MSS, the total number
of portions of food received by Joseph and Benjamin is
given as "seven" (ἑπτά) in line 14. But, all the MSS
also agree in stating that Joseph gave himself only "one"
portion of food (μίαν, line 13). The numbers obviously do
not tally. If Benjamin received five portions of food
(and this is the only uncontested figure given in par. 14;
cf. Gen 43:34 and 45:22), and if Joseph gave himself only
one portion, this does not equal "seven," the total number
of Leah's sons given in the MSS tradition. Thus, either
the "seven" in lines 11 and 14 is incorrect, or the "one"
in line 13 is incorrect.

     Accordingly, editors have adopted one of three
solutions, and they may be outlined as follows: (1) Retain
ἑπτά in lines 11 and 14, and emend μίαν to read δύο in
line 13, thus adopting a 5 + 2 scheme (so Dind. Giff.
Stearns Mras Denis). This has the merit of agreeing with
the earlier list of Leah's sons in Frg. 2, par. 2-5,
which attributes seven sons to Leah (though, cf. n. 7
above). (2) Retain μίαν in line 13, and emend ἑπτά in
lines 11 and 14 to read ἕξ, thus yielding a 5 + 1 scheme
(so Freu. Jac., followed by Walter). This solution is
based on the suggested emendation by Freu. noted above
in n. 34. In addition, it conforms to the list in the
biblical text (Gen 35:23). (3) Retain the contradiction

and print the unemended text which reads ἑπτά in lines
11 and 14, and μίαν in line 13   (so Vig. Hein. Gais.,
though Vig. and Gais. recognize the problem and propose
δύο in a note).

The problem and its solution obviously relate to
other textual problems noted earlier in Frg. 2, par. 2-5.
Cf. note 7 above.

38.   It should be noted that Demetrius has τὰς στολὰς ...
διπλᾶς instead of the LXX δισσὰς στολὰς (Gen 45:22).
Compare MT: חֲלִפֹת שְׂמָלֹת. The translation here takes
διπλᾶς to mean "double-folded" rather than "two" (so
Giff.); cf. Homer, Iliad 3.126; 4.133; 10.134; Odyssey
19.226 and 241.

39.   Giff. incorrectly translates τριακοσίους as "thirty."
Cf. Gen 45:22.

40.   I.e., 25 years to the death of Isaac; cf. Gen 12:4
and 21:5.

41.   I.e., to the birth of Jacob; cf. Gen 25:26.

42.   I.e., to the flight into Egypt; cf. Gen 47:9.

43.   The ages of the children in this list are rounded
off. Cf. Walter, JS (3,2), 288, notes, for details.
Also, cf. Gen 46:8-27.

44.   The MSS read "three" (I) or "four" (ON) months.
"Two" months is correctly supplied by Mras (cf. GCS (43,1)
511, app. crit. to line 13), since the age difference
between Levi and Judah was given as 10 months (cf. Frg.
2, par. 8).

45.   According to Freu., 55, Dan should be included here:
"Dan, forty-two years and four months old." Also, cf.
Frg. 2, par. 8, and notes 7, 10, 16 and 17.

46.   The ages of Naphtali and Gad should be identical;
cf. Frg. 2, par. 3, though both MSS and edd. read "seven"
and "three" months respectively.

47.   Some editors place Asher between Judah and Naphtali
(cf. app. crit.).

48.   According to Freu., 206, Issachar should be included
after Asher: Ἰσσαχὰρ ἐτῶν μ̄ μηνῶν ὀκτώ ("Issachar,
forty years and eight months old").

49.   Mras suggests reading "Dan" here rather than "Dinah"
(cf. note 17 above). Cf. Mras, GCS (43.1), 511, app. crit.
to line 15.

50.   According to Walter, <u>JS</u> (3,2), 288, n. 17i, Benjamin's
correct age is 23 years. According to Frg. 2, par. 9-10,
he was 16 1/3 - 17 years younger than Dinah. Walter
suggests that Demetrius originally wrote "22 years and
8 months."

51.   I.e., Demetrius.   (N.B., φησι om. B).

52.   Cf. Gen 37:2; 50:22.

53.   This number conforms to the LXX chronology. Cf.
Wacholder, <u>Eupolemus</u>, 97-128, esp. 102. According to the
MT chronology: 2,238 years. Cf. Walter, <u>JS</u> (3,2) 289, n.
18c.

54.   This also conforms to the LXX chronology. Cf.
Wacholder, 97-128. According to the MT chronology: 580
years. Cf. Walter, <u>JS</u> (3,2) 289, n. 18d.

55.   Here, both LXX and MT support Demetrius. Cf. Wacholder,
101, n. 8.

56.   This is one of the three ages given as the age of
Jacob at the time of his departure for Haran. Cf. Frg. 2,
par. 1, and notes 4 and 6 above.

57.   Walter, <u>JS</u> (3,2), 289, n. 19b, suggests that Polyhistor has overlooked part of Demetrius' calculations at
this point, probably because it appeared to duplicate
parts of Frg. 2, par. 17.

58.   I.e., adding 17 years to his age (43) when he entered
Egypt. Cf. Frg. 2, par. 17.

59.   It should be noted that all the MSS read Κλάθ (line
17 and following), the spelling adopted by Mras and Jac.
Compare LXX: Καάθ (Gen 46:11).

60.   Cf. Gen 47:28.

61.   The variation in spelling should be noted. Cf.
app. crit. on line 22.

62.   Cf. Gen 50:26.

63.   The words "and Moses" have been added by Mras. Cf.
app. crit. This creates an obvious difficulty within the
text: Amram is then said to be 75 and 78 years old when
he fathered Moses -- a problem Mras appears not to recognize nor address.

64.   Cf. Exod 7:7 for the differences in the ages of Moses
and Aaron.

65.   Cf. Exod 6:20. Amram's age at his death was 132
according to the LXX, 137 according to the MT.

66. This fragment occurs among the witnesses Eusebius
gives to the life of Moses. Immediately preceding this
text is a fragment from Ezekiel the Tragedian which
sketches Moses' life prior to the Exodus. Following
this fragment is another excerpt from Ezekiel the Tragedian
depicting Moses' experiences in Midian.

67. Exod 2:15.

68. Exod 2:16, 21-22.

69. The several names given to Moses' father-in-law in
the biblical account are notoriously confusing. He is
variously designated as Reuel (רעואל, Exod 2:18; Num 10:
29), Jethro (יתרו, Exod 3:1; 4:18; 18:1-27), and Hobab
(חבב, Judg 4:11; cf. Num 10:29). Of these three names,
Jethro is consistently applied only to Moses' father-in-
law, whereas the other two are not. Reuel (or Raguel)
is also used to refer to Jethro's father, thus the same
term is used to designate Zipporah's father and grand-
father (cf. Frg. 3, par. 1, lines 16 and 17). Hobab is
used both of Reuel himself (Judg 4:11) and of Reuel's
son (Num 10:29); the latter use is found in Frg. 3, par. 1
(line 16). Cf. L. Hicks, art. "Reuel," IDB 4. 54.

70. Cf. Gen 25:1-6; 1 Chr 1:32-33.

71. Cf. Gen 25:2-3.

72. Cf. Gen 25:3.

73. I.e., Reuel, altough in the biblical account (Exod
2:18; Num 10:29), Reuel is not Jethro's father, as here,
but is another name for Jethro himself. It may be a
gloss, however. Cf. Gen 25:3.

74. Cf. Num 10:29; Judg 4:11; cf. note 69 above.

75. I.e., Abraham, Isaac, Jacob, Levi, Kohath, Amram,
and Moses. Cf. Frg. 2, par. 15-19.

76. If Demetrius is following the biblical account here
(cf. Gen 25:2), this should be Jokshan rather than Ishbak
(cf. Frg. 3, par. 1, lines 14 and 15).

77. Cf. note 76 above.

78. Cf. Gen 25:2; Exod 2:15; also Josephus, Ant. 2.257.

79. I.e., "the sacred book" (cf. Frg. 3, par. 1; also
Gen 25:6).

80. Cf. Num 11:35; 12:16.

81.   Cf. Num 11:35; 12:1; also Josephus, <u>Ant</u>. 2.252-53.

82.   After Eusebius recounts Ezekiel's verses concerning
the crossing of the Red Sea, still quoting from Polyhistor,
he includes this fragment from Demetrius about Moses and
the bitter water incident. Eusebius then continues the
narrative with Ezekiel's description of Moses at Elim.

83.   I.e., the Israelites.

84.   Cf. Exod 15:22-27.

85.   I.e., at Marah; cf. Exod 15:23.

86.   LXX: Αιλιμ.   Cf. Exod 15:27; also Josephus, <u>Ant</u>.
3.9.

87.   Eusebius, still quoting from Polyhistor, places this
fragment from Demetrius after Ezekiel's description of the
Phoenix at Elim. Following this Demetrius quotation is a
fragment from Eupolemus delineating Israel's leaders from
Moses to Solomon.

88.   Demetrius here tackles a still controversial feature
of the Exodus narrative. The MT uses the rarely used term
חמשים whose meaning is uncertain (cf. Josh 1:14; 4:12;
Judg 7:11; conjectured in Num 32:17). Its similarity to
חמש, "five," no doubt accounts for the LXX rendering
πέμπτῃ γενεᾷ in Exod 13:18, i.e. "in the fifth generation,"
although according to the promise of Gen 15:16 the
Israelites were to return to the land of Canaan in the
fourth generation. Because the term is elusive, it has
been variously rendered: "in five divisions or squadrons,"
"by fifties," "marching in array," "armed," "in military
order," to mention a few. Whether the term implies
"armed" in the strict sense is debatable. A. H. McNeile,
<u>The Book of Exodus</u> (London, 1908), 81, "The word <u>hamushim</u>
appears to describe not the bearing of weapons but the
order and arrangement of a body of troops as though
divided into five parts." At the very least, it seems
to imply "in military formation." So, U. Cassuto, <u>A Commentary on the Book of Exodus</u> (Jerusalem, 1967), 156-57,
"... on the basis of the Arabic, in proper military formation [translate: 'in orderly array']. They went out
not like a mob of slaves escaping from their masters in
confusion and disorder, but well organized ..." S. R.
Driver, <u>The Book of Exodus</u> (Cambridge, 1911), 112, "It in
any case implies that the Israelites were prepared for
hostile encounters." Cf. G. Bush, <u>Notes ... Exodus</u>
(New York, n.d.), 1.162-63. More recent commentaries
(Noth, Childs) do not discuss the point. To be sure,
with the LXX alone before Demetrius, he could only con-
clude that the Israelites departed unarmed. Josephus
apparently follows Demetrius. In <u>Ant</u>. 2.321 he calls the
Israelites ἀνόπλων (cf. note in Loeb ed., ad loc, 305).

Accordingly, in _Ant_. 2.349 he (like Demetrius) attempts
to explain the _aporia_ of how an unarmed people could be
prepared to do battle with the Egyptians immediately
after the Exodus (cf. Exod 17:8). Cf. also, Freu., 46,
who refers to Wis 10:20 and Jalk. Sim. on Exod 14:30.
Also, cf. Ginsberg, _Legends_, 3.30.

89. The antecedent is unclear; presumably, the Israelites.

90. Presumably, to Egypt.

91. This fragment occurs in a chapter about the antiquity
of the Jewish laws and institutions. The immediate context is Clement's discussion of the chronology of Israel,
where he compares the duration of the periods of Israel's
history with those of other nations.

92. The second clause introduced by ἀλλά in line 4
abruptly changes the subject. Freu. suspects another
case of homoeoteleuton, and emends the text as follows:
ἀλλὰ πολλὰ χρήματα καὶ σκεύη τοῦ ναοῦ, μηδὲ μετ' ὀλίγον
χρόνον ἐκείνας αἰχμαλώτους γενέσθαι (" ... were not taken
captive by Sennacherib, but <the vessels and utensils of
the temple were taken, and that not until a short time
later were the tribes themselves (actually) taken as
captives>". Cf. app. crit., line 3; also, Freu. 58-59;
Schürer, _Gesch. Jüd_. 3.473, apud Walter, _JS_ (3,2), 292;
Walter, _Untersuchungen_, 17ff. The problem is, of course,
that in one breath Demetrius denies that there was a
"captivity" (αἰχμαλωτισθῆναι), and yet in the next breath
computes the years "from this captivity." Freu.'s suggestion is ingenious, but requires a somewhat forced meaning
of αἰχμαλωτίζω, i.e. "plundering" rather than an offical
"captivity."

93. Gutschmid, 2.188, reads "five" instead of "eight,"
i.e. 125 years instead of 128 yeras. Cf. app. crit. on
line 6.

94. Demetrius' source for this calculation is apparently
2 Kgs 18:9-13.

95. Because of the difficulties raised by Demetrius'
computations, Freu., 62, suggests that τετάρτου should
be emended to τοῦ τρίτου, thus Ptolemy the Third (ca.
245-221). For full discussion of the chronological problems raised by the text, cf. E. Bickerman, "The Jewish
Historian Demetrios," 72-84, esp. 80-84.

96. Note the variant: τετρακόσια. This suggestion is
attributed to Reinesius who thought 473 years would be
more correct in this chronological scheme.

97. Note the variant: τετρακόσια. The suggestion is
attributed to Raška by Stählin, but according to Bickerman, "Demetrios," 81, n. 35, the suggestion was originally
made by Graetz as yet another attempt to correct Demetrius.

Eupolemus[1] was a Greek-speaking Jewish historian[2] who flourished in Palestine[3] in the mid-2nd century B.C.E.[4] He is reliably identified as "Eupolemus, the son of John, the son of Accos," whom Judah Maccabee sent, along with Jason, the son of Eleazar, to negotiate a friendship alliance with Rome in 161 B.C.E.[5] As a member of the Accos family, he would have belonged to one of the leading priestly families of Jerusalem during the Maccabean period, distinguished by its long history of service and dedication to the temple, its active and influential role in foreign affairs, and its pro-Seleucid sympathies.[6]

Title. His work was most likely entitled Concerning the Kings in Judaea.[7] Although it included chronographical calculations extending from Adam until the Maccabean period (cf Frg. 5), both the title and the contents of the surviving fragments suggest that it focused mainly on the period of the united monarchy and exile. There are no clear indications of the length of the original work.

Transmission. Five fragments from the work survive,[8] all of which are attributed to Eupolemus.[9] Frgs. 1-4 were first preserved by Alexander Polyhistor in his work On the Jews (ca. mid-1st century B.C.E.). Polyhistor appears to have faithfully transmitted the content of the quotations, although he has rendered them into indirect discourse. They were later abstracted from Polyhistor by Eusebius in P.E., Book 9. Alternate versions (Frg. 1) or subsections of these four fragments (Frg. 2) were also preserved by Clement of Alexandria, who apparently also depended directly on Alexander Polyhistor. Frg. 5 was preserved only by Clement. Whether he drew directly on Polyhistor as its source or depended on another source, e.g. Ptolemy of Mendes, is disputed.[10]

Contents. Frg. 1, a very brief fragment,
describes Moses as the first wise man and cultural benefactor. A version of this fragment occurs repeatedly
through the ancient and medieval periods. Frg. 2, the longest of the five fragments, summarizes Israelite history
from Moses to David, but focuses primarily on Solomon's
achievements. It is especially remarkable for its fairly
detailed, and in many respects unique description of the
preparation and construction of the Solomonic temple.
Also remarkable is its inclusion of formal copies of the
exchange of letters between Solomon and Hiram, but also
for the apocryphal set of similar letters exchanged by
Solomon and one Vaphres, king of Egypt. Frg. 3, a fragment of only a few lines, continues the lavish description
of Solomon, also giving the length of his reign. Frg. 4,
a longer fragment, relates events from the life of
Jeremiah. It encompasses under the reign of "Jonacheim"
events from the reigns of the last three kings of Judah:
Jehoiakim, Jehoiachin, and Zedekiah, and describes the
destruction of Jerusalem by Nebuchadnezzar. Frg. 5 is a
chronographical summary calculating the number of years
from Adam, and the exodus respectively, until the reign of
Demetrius I Soter (162-150 B.C.E.)

Another fragment which Eusebius extracts from Polyhistor is also attributed to a "Eupolemus," but since
Freudenthal showed it to be from an anonymous Samaritan
author,[11] it is no longer included among the genuine fragments of Eupolemus. It, along with another anonymous fragment dealing with Abraham, is now generally designated
Pseudo-Eupolemus (cf. Introduction to Pseudo-Eupolemus).

Features of the work. Although one must always allow
for the possibility that the fragments have been altered
at the hands of Alexander Polyhistor, and even Eusebius,
as they stand, they nevertheless exhibit distinctive features.[12]

The work was originally written in Greek,
but when compared with classical Greek authors, the quality
of Greek in the fragments is inferior, displaying crude,
and sometimes unusual, constructions and stylistic features.[13]
Eupolemus is clearly dependent on both the LXX[14] and MT,[15]
indicating that he was bilingual, though Hebrew and Aramaic
were doubtless his native languages. The work also reflects
knowledge of, and perhaps direct use of Greek sources, including the works of Ctesias and Herodotus.[16]

In his use of biblical traditions, he displays great
freedom. Haggadic traditions are freely incorporated,[17]
and the biblical text is frequently altered,[18] even con-
tradicted.[19] The work most heavily depends on 2 Chr, but
displays a harmonizing tendency in its use of 1 Kgs and 2
Chr.[20]

The work belongs to a historiographical tradition well
established in the Hellenistic period, and represented by
authors such as Manetho and Berossus who sought to depict
their own national history in the Greek language.[21]
Typical of this genre are its pervasive encomiastic tendencies, through which Israel's history, heroes, and
institutions are magnified and presented in glorious terms.[22]
Also typical of this tradition is the interest displayed
in chronography[23] as a means for establishing national and
cultural respectability. The fragments are replete with
geographical,[24] chronological,[25] and grammatical[26] anachronisms, a feature not at all unusual in this genre of
encomiastic history.

The central prominence of the Solomonic temple has
been taken as an indication of its strong cultic interest,
not surprising in an author from a priestly family.
Theological tendencies are also visible, though easily
exaggerated: devotion to the temple and the cult; lack of
emphasis on the law; rationalizing tendencies in treating
theophanies, anthropomorphic language, and prophecies; lack

of eschatological   perspective.[27]   The work exudes
a strongly patriotic, even nationalistic character   in
its glorified depiction of   the Jewish nation   under
David and Solomon.[28]

Importance. Its value for reconstructing the history
of the period it describes is negligible, although it is
an important testimony to the existence of certain traditions pertaining to historical figures and institutions,
most notably Solomon and the Solomonic temple. Similar
to Jubilees in its handling of the biblical story, it
offers a useful analogue for examining and assessing
midrashic treatments of the biblical story in Hellenistic
Judaism.

It is perhaps most useful, for the purposes of historical reconstruction, for what it reveals about the
Maccabean period.[29] If the work is correctly attributed
to Eupolemus, the son of John, it is a valuable source
for understanding the impact of Hellenism on Maccabean
supporters. That it served as a source for 1 Macc has
been plausibly suggested.[30]

The fragments are certainly an early witness to the
existence of Greek translations of 1 Kgs and 2 Chr and
their use in Hellenistic Palestine. Eupolemus appears to
be the first named author who sought to harmonize 1 Kgs
and 2 Chr, and as such, he is an important witness to this
harmonistic tradition of biblical interpretation. Though
he was not essentially a chronographer, as was Demetrius,
he is an early representative in Palestine of the chronographical traditions which were to have a long history in
pagan, Jewish, and Christian circles.

He is an early witness to, and in some cases perhaps
the first instance of the following traditions: the
depiction of Moses as cultural benefactor, the reference
to Jeremiah's rescue of the sacred objects from the temple,
Solomon's gift of the golden pillar to Hiram for display

in the temple of Zeus at Tyre, and the bar mitzvah tradition where Solomon begins the building of the temple at
age thirteen symbolizing his entry to adulthood.[31]

He is the earliest Hellenistic-Jewish historian, in
the strict sense of the term, the first representative
of the tradition later to be embodied by Josephus. His
importance lies in the fact that he is an early example
of a single individual in whom the two streams of Hellenism and Judaism merged.[32] His work was apologetic in a
qualified sense.[33] While it may not have been written to
pagans primarily, the fact that it was preserved by
Alexander Polyhistor indicates that this glorified history
of the Jewish kings was known and read by pagans outside
Palestine.

NOTES

1. Testimonia: 1 Macc 8:17-20; 2 Macc 4:11 (cf. Josephus,
Ant. 12.415); Josephus, AgAp 1.218 (cf. Eusebius, P.E.
9.42.3); Eusebius, Hist. eccl. 6.13.7 (also Jerome, De
viris illustribus 38 = PL (23) 879 A and Cyril of Alexandria, Contra Julianum 7.231 E = PG (76) 853 B-C, all
dependent on Clement, Strom. 1.23.153.4, and perhaps
1.21.141.4-5). For medieval testimonia, cf. Annotations,
note 1; also Wacholder, Eupolemus, 68, n. 171.

2. Josephus, AgAp 1.218, mentions Eupolemus, along with
Demetrius Phalerum and the elder Philo, in his discussion
of Greek, i.e. pagan historians (συγγραφεῖς) who wrote
about Jewish affairs. The passage is quoted by Eusebius,
P.E. 9.42.3, without disclaimer. Yet, in Hist. eccl.
6.13.7, Eusebius includes Eupolemus with other Jewish
writers ('Ιουδαίων συγγραφέων), viz. Philo (of Alexandria ?),
Aristobulus, Josephus, and Demetrius. The quotations from
Eupolemus included by Eusebius, P.E., Book 9, are all extracted from Alexander Polyhistor, whom Eusebius is citing
as a Greek witness to the antiquity of the Jews. He does
not, however, in these instances address the question of
Eupolemus' nationality. Jerome, De viris illustribus 38,
who depends on Clement, Strom. 1.23.153.4, includes Eupolemus with Aristobulus and Demetrius as "Jewish authors who
wrote against the nations" (Judaeis ... scriptores adversus
gentes). Cyril of Alexandria, Contra Julianum 7.231 C,
also dependent on Clement, makes no reference to his nationality, but is apparently the first to designate him "the
historian" (ὁ ἱστορικός). Though Clement makes no explicit
reference to his nationality, he does mention him along
with other Greek witnesses whom he quoted, e.g. Euphorus
and Plato. Still, he apparently regarded him as Jewish
(cf. Eusebius, Hist. eccl. 6.13.7).

Since the earliest reference to an author named
Eupolemus (Josephus, AgAp 1.218) included him among pagan
authors (Wacholder, Eupolemus, 2-3, notwithstanding; N.B.
τοῖς ἡμετέροις γράμμασι), it heavily influenced those
scholars who regarded him as a pagan author (e.g. Kuhlmey
and Willrich). There were other factors, as well:
(1) those instances where he displayed an otherwise inexplicable ignorance of elementary biblical facts, e.g.
David as Solomon's son (Frg. 2b, par. 30.3), and Eli as
the high priest at Solomon's accession (Frg. 2b, par. 30.8);
(2) his free alteration of the biblical text, e.g. by
enlarging the extent of Hiram's rule to include Sidon and
Phoenicia (Frg. 2b, par. 33.1), depicting the pagan kings
Vaphres and Hiram as agreeing to build the temple in
obedience to the command of God (Frg. 2b, par. 31.1-34.3),
inventing the names of districts to assist in the building
of the temple (Frg. 2b, par. 33.1), enlarging the amounts

2. (cont.) of provisions for the temple builders (Frg. 2b,
par. 33.1), and altering the measurements of the temple
(Frg. 2b, par. 34.4); (3) his syncretistic tendencies, e.g.
his mention of breast-shaped nails (Frg. 2b, par. 34.5),
and Solomon's gift of a golden pillar to Hiram to be displayed in Tyre in the temple of Zeus (Frg. 2b, par. 34.18).
Earlier scholarship noted even more blatant syncretistic
tendencies in the work of Eupolemus (e.g. the identification of Atlas with Enoch, P.E. 9.30.1), but this fragment
is now attributed to an anonymous Samaritan author,
designated as Pseudo-Eupolemus, largely through the efforts
of Freudenthal, 105-30, also 82-103, who first convincingly established Eupolemus' status as a Jewish historian
(followed by Schürer, Jacoby, Walter, Wacholder). Among
other considerations suggesting his Jewishness are his use
of Hebraisms, his dependence on the LXX, his heroic depiction of Jewish figures (most notably Moses and Solomon),
and his cultic interest (especially his knowledge of and
devotion to the Jerusalem temple). Cf. Wacholder, Eupolemus, 1-5, for a more detailed review of the debate.

3. A Palestinian provenance is suggested by his use of
Hebrew measuring units (cors; Frg. 2b, par. 33.1), his
use of MT and pre-MT traditions (cf. below, note 12), and
his use of chronological calculations based on Seleucid
reigns in Frg. 5 (Cf. Annotations, Nos. 118 and 121. The
references to Ptolemaic and Roman rulers in this fragment
are now plausibly attributed to later redactors.)

4. He must have antedated Alexander Polyhistor (fl. mid-
1st century B.C.E.), from whom Eusebius quoted his works.
His chronographical calculations in Frg. 5 terminate ca.
158/157 B.C.E., "the fifth year of the reign of Demetrius
(I Soter)." Cf. Annotations, No. 118. Bousset/Gressmann,
20, n. 2, place him after 145 B.C.E.

5. Cf. 1 Macc 8:17-20; 2 Macc 4:11; Josephus, Ant. 12.
415. Also, Freudenthal, 127; Wacholder, Eupolemus, 4-21;
Hengel, Judaism and Hellenism, 2.63, n. 269; dissenting
view by Krauss, 269. On the historicity of this embassy,
cf. Schürer, 1.220-21; Walter, Untersuchungen, 157-58.

6. The Accos family was already an influential priestly
family in Jerusalem as early as the post-exilic period
(cf. 1 Chr 24; Ezra 2:61; Neh 3:4, 21; 7:63), and its
influence continued through the Maccabean period, perhaps
rivalling that of the Tobiads. In 198 B.C.E., Eupolemus'
father, John, successfully extracted concessions from
Antiochus III, guaranteeing Jewish civil rights following
the Seleucid conquest of Coele-Syria (2 Macc 4:11; Josephus,
Ant. 12.138-56). John was also a member of the council of
elders (gerousia) in Jerusalem, a position possibly held

6. (cont.) by Eupolemus as well. The family thus became
closely aligned with the Seleucids, exercising an influential role in foreign affairs and flourishing in a time and
place favorable to Hellenization. Cf. Wacholder, Eupolemus, 7-21.

7. This title is given only by Clement of Alexandria
(Strom. 1.23.153.4) in his version of Frg. 1, and perhaps
implied by his introductory remarks to Frg. 5 (Strom. 1.21.
141.4). Eusebius, however, in P.E. 9.30.1, introduces
Frg. 2 as deriving from a work entitled Concerning the
Prophecy of Elijah, an unusual title since Elijah is mentioned nowhere else in the fragments, although prophecy
is a recurrent motif. "Elijah" may be a corrupt reading,
or it may refer to a subsection of the larger work. Cf.
Annotations, Nos. 2 and 12. A third work, On the Jews of
Assyria, is also attributed to a Eupolemus by Eusebius,
P.E. 9.17.2, but the title is corrupt and the fragment from
this work is now attributed to Pseudo-Eupolemus. Cf.
above, note 2, and Introduction to Pseudo-Eupolemus.
Also, Freudenthal, 82-103; Wacholder, Eupolemus, 21-26.

8. For the location of the fragments, cf. Index to
Editions and Translations.

9. The authenticity of Frg. 4 has been disputed (cf.
Freudenthal, 208-209; Jacoby, FGrH 723 = *5, "Ohne Autornamen"). It is, however, attributed in all MSS to Eupolemus
in the title, on the authenticity of which, cf. Mras,
Eusebius Werke (GCS, 43.1) VIII.

10. Cf. Walter, "Überlieferung;" JS 1.94, n. 4; Wacholder,
Eupolemus, 111-14; Fallon, OTP.

11. Freudenthal, 82-103.

12. The degree of Polyhistor's fidelity to his sources
can be measured to some extent in the case of Eupolemus,
using the Solomon-Hiram correspondence as a control.
Cf. Freudenthal, 106.

13. Cf. Frg. 2b, par. 32.1: περὶ ὧν ... περὶ τῶν; Frg. 2b,
par. 34.3: καλῶς ποιήσεις + participle or infinitive;
Frg. 2b, par. 32.1: ὡς ἄν. Freudenthal, 109-110: "a Jewish
writer who breathes superficially the spirit of Greek
literature." F. Jacoby, PW 6 (1907) 1229: "His style is
miserable, his vocabulary scanty, and the sentence construction clumsy."

14. As seen by his inclusion of certain features within
the narrative, e.g. Solomon's accession to the throne at
age twelve (Frg. 2b, par. 30.8): LXX 1 Kgs 2:12 (codex A),
the form of Hiram's eulogy (Frg. 2b, par. 34.1): 2 Chr
2:11, and possibly the reference to the 48-pillared north
portico (Frg. 2b, par. 34.9): 1 Kgs 7:31 (LXX). Orthography

14. (cont.) of proper names often follows the LXX, e.g.
Σηλωμ (Frg. 2b, par. 34.14): Σηλω/Σηλωμ (1 Sam 1:3; 4:3),
'Ιησους and Ναυη (Frg. 2b, par. 30.1), Σαμουηλ (Frg. 2b,
par. 30.2), Σαουλος (Frg. 2b, par. 30.2), and possibly
'Ηλει (Frg. 2b, par. 30.8). Also, technical names for the
tabernacle (σκηνή τοῦ μαρτυρίου, Frg. 2b, par. 34.7; cf.
Exod 27:21; 29 & 30 passim), its furnishings (λουτήρ
χαλκοῦς, Frg. 2b, par. 34.9; cf. Exod 30:18), and the
temple's furnishings (e.g., ἔνδεσμος, Frg. 2b, par. 34.5;
cf. 1 Kgs 6:10). Cf. Freudenthal, 119.

15. Orthography of proper names sometimes depends on
the MT, e.g. Σουρον (Frg. 2b, par. 30.4, 33.1, & 34.1) is
based on the Hebrew (חורם) rather than the LXX (Χειραμ,
Χιραμ). Cf. Freudenthal, 108, 209, on the transliteration
from ח to Σ. Similarly, Ουφρη (Frg. 2b, par. 30.7):
MT (אופיר) -- LXX (Σουφιρ); Σιλοι (Frg. 2b, par. 30.1):
MT (שילה) -- LXX (Σηλω/Σηλωμ). Especially decisive are
those instances where Eupolemus provides an appropriate
Greek translation of a Hebrew word merely transliterated
in the LXX: e.g. 1 Kgs 6:3 -- MT: אלם; LXX: αιλαμ;
Eupolemus (Frg. 2b, par. 34.4): οἰκοδομῆς; 2 Chr 3:16 --
MT: שרשרת; LXX: σερσερωθ; Eupolemus (Frg. 2b, par. 34.11):
ἁλυσιδωτούς; 2 Chr 4:12 -- MT: גלות; LXX: γωλαθ; Eupolemus
(Frg. 2b, par. 34.11): δακτυλίους; 1 Kgs 7:17 -- MT: מכנוה;
LXX: μεχωνωθ; Eupolemus (Frg. 2b, par. 34.11): μηχανημάτων.
A similar pattern of Eupolemus' improving the LXX based
on his knowledge of the Hebrew is seen in 1 Kgs 5:22 --
MT: ארז & ברוש; LXX: κέδρος & πεύκε; Eupolemus (Frg. 2b,
par. 34.5): κέδρος & κυπαρίσσινος. The chronological
calculations in Frg. 5 are based on figures in both MT and
LXX. Cf. Annotations, No. 120. Another Hebraism preserved
in Frg. 2b, par. 34.14 is ὁλοκάρπωσιν, an indication that
Polyhistor has faithfully transmitted rather than altered
the text of Eupolemus in some instances. Cf. Freudenthal,
119-20.

16. Frg. 1, Frg. 2, par. 30.4; Frg. 4, par. 4; cf.
Wacholder, Eupolemus, 13.

17. Moses as cultural benefactor and first wise man
(Frg. 1); the appearance of an angel named Dianathan
(assuming no textual corruption) to David instructing
him to build the temple (Frg. 2b, par. 30.6); the Solomon-
Vaphres correspondence (Frg. 2a and 2b, par. 31.1-32.1);
Jeremiah's rescue of the ark and sacred vessels from the
temple (Frg. 4, par. 5).

18. E.g., the measurements of the temple (Frg. 2b, par.
34.4). Cf. note 2 above. Also, Freudenthal, 107.

19. E.g., Solomon began to build the temple in the first
year of his reign (Frg. 2, par. 34.4); cf. 1 Kgs 6:1;
2 Chr 3:2. Also, note 2 above.

20. From Kgs are drawn various details, e.g. the interior
paneling of the temple (1 Kgs 6:14-15) and the width of
the vestibule ? (1 Kgs 6:3). Chr is primarily followed,
however: the angel's signifying to David the location of
the altar (Frg. 2b, par. 30.5-6): 1 Chr 27:1 and 2 Chr
3:1; David's disqualification from building the temple
because of his "shedding much blood" (Frg. 2b, par. 30.5):
1 Chr 22:8; 28:3; the peaceful transition from David to
Solomon (Frg. 2b, par. 30.8): 1 Chr 29, against 1 Kgs 1-2;
David's preparations for the building of the temple (Frg.
2b, par. 30.6-8): 1 Chr 22 & 28; the transportation of the
building materials from Lebanon to Joppa to Jerusalem
by Solomon (Frg. 2b, par. 34.4): 2 Chr 2:16; provision of
wine for Phoenician workers (Frg. 2b, par. 33.1): 2 Chr
2:9; use of foreign workers instead of Israelites as
temple builders (Frg. 2b, par. 31.1-34.4): 2 Chr 2:17-18,
against 1 Kgs 5:13-18. The spelling of Σουρων is based
on Chr (חורם) rather than Kgs (חירם). Cf. Freudenthal,
119.

21. Cf. Introduction to Demetrius, note 6; also Freudenthal, 105; Braun, History and Romance.

22. The influence and accomplishments of Israel's heroes
are greatly magnified. Moses is depicted as cultural
benefactor, first lawgiver, and first wise man (Frg. 1).
The borders of David's realm are enlarged to encompass
regions of northernmost Syria (Commagene), extending to
the Euphrates River (though cf. 2 Sam 8:3; 1 Chr 18:3).
His influence reaches from Egypt to the Euphrates, from
northern Syria to the Gulf of Aqaba (Frg. 2b, par. 30.3-7).
Solomon's kingdom is said to have included Moab and
Ammon, both of which were independent of his rule in the
biblical account. Eupolemus also elevates him to the
status of world ruler beside whom the kings of Egypt and
Phoenicia are minor by comparison and who do his bidding.
His wealth and generosity are greatly embellished (Frg.
2b, par. 31.1-34.18).

Similar encomium occurs with respect to the temple
(Frg. 2b, par. 34.4-18). The dimensions of the Solomonic
temple are larger: a 60-cubit quadrangle rather than a
60 x 20 cubit rectangle, as given in all other accounts,
biblical and non-biblical, although Eupolemus' temple is
not 120 cubits high, as 2 Chr states. Eupolemus' temple
is far more lavishly decorated and furnished than even
the one described in 2 Chr. Especially is it more thoroughly wrought in gold. The interior, including the ceiling,
is inlaid with gold. It has a bronze tile roof. Each of
the two bronze pillars standing at the entrance is covered
with a layer of gold a finger thick. The furnishings are
more golden: there are ten lampstands made of gold, each
weighing ten talents. The doors are also covered with
gold. In all, a staggeringly fantastic 4,600,000 (assuming
no textual corruption) talents of gold was said to have

22. (cont.) been used in constructing the temple, and
some was even left over, and returned to Hiram. Cf.
Freudenthal, 106-118; Schlatter, Geschichte, 187-192;
Giblet, 548-49.

23. Cf. Frg. 5, especially, but also Frg. 2, par. 30.1-2,
34.4. Also, Wacholder, Eupolemus, 97-128.

24. Geographical divisions from the Maccabean period are
retrojected to the period of the United Monarchy and Exile:
David's kingdom encompassed Commagene and Galadene, both
of which were Hellenistic geographical divisions (Frg. 2b,
par. 30.3). David is said to have waged war with the
Nabataeans, who entered Palestine sometime prior to the
4th century B.C.E.   There is no evidence that they did so
as early as the time of David (cf. Frg. 2b, par. 30.3).
Solomon's Palestine is described with a sevenfold geographical division reflecting the Maccabean period: Galilee,
Samaria, Moab, Ammon, Gilead, Judaea, and Arabia (Frg. 2b,
par. 33.1). Samaria was not designated as a geographical
division until the time of Omri, and Arabia as a geographical division appears to be late (though cf. 1 Kgs 10:15;
2 Chr 9:14). Nebuchadrezzar is said to have conquered
Samaria, Galilee, and the city of Scythopolis, the Hellenistic name of the biblical city of Beth-shan (Frg. 4,
par. 5).

25. The Vaphres who exchanged letters with Solomon and
lent assistance in building the temple appears to have been
taken from an Egyptian king list, or is possibly based
on Jer 44:30. In either case, the only historical figure
with whom he can be identified flourished approximately
four centuries after the time of Solomon (Frg. 2a and
2b, par. 31.1-32.1). In Frg. 4, Samaria is said to have
been destroyed by Nebuchadrezzar, when 2 Kgs 17 indicates
that Samaria and the northern kingdom was conquered by
Assyria approximately 35 years before the destruction of
the temple. Some features of the temple described by
Eupolemus, e.g. the absence of the vestibule (though, cf.
Annotations, No. 71), the presence of the north portico
supported by 48 pillars (Frg. 2b, par. 34.9), the 60-cubit
wide sanctuary (Frg. 2b, par. 34.14) appear to describe
the temple of Zerubbabel. Another chronological anachronism occurs when Solomon is anointed king before Eli,
the high priest (Frg. 2b, par. 30.8), who flourished much
earlier in the time of Samuel.

26. The reference to "artabae" in Frg. 2b, par. 33.1, if
it is original with Eupolemus, and is not a gloss by Polyhistor, is anachronistic, since it was a Persian measure-
ment, though it later acquired widespread use in Egypt.
The use of ἱερόν in Frg. 2b, par. 34.14 is possibly
another anachronism. It occurs only once in 1 Kgs and 2
Chr, yet it is the preferred word for describing the temple
in 1 and 2 Macc. The tendency to derive foreign names
from Greek words (Frg. 2b, par. 34.13) was Hellenistic.

27. Cf. Dalbert, Missionsliteratur, 35-42.

28. Hengel, Judaism and Hellenism, 94, especially empha-
sizes the strong nationalistic tendency.

29. The geographical situation depicted in the fragments
presupposes a Maccabean setting (cf. note 24 above).
Broadening the extent of the Davidic and Solomonic realm
may have functioned to justify Maccabean expansionistic
policies. Similarly, the heroic depiction of David and
Solomon may reflect the kinds of monarchical propaganda
used to justify the existence and enhance the position
of the Hasmonean dynasty. The depiction of Egypt and
Phoenicia as allies of Israel certainly tells us more
about realities and hopes of Hellenistic Palestine than
about the political situation of the United Monarchy.
The depiction of the strength of Israel as requiring the
combined forces of the Babylonians and Medes to subdue it
may also point to the level of strength the Jewish state
hoped for but never achieved in the Maccabean period.

30. Cf. Walter, JS, 1.96, n. 11.

31. Wacholder, Eupolemus, 155.

32. Wacholder, Eupolemus, 11, notes that "John's choice
of the name Eupolemus for his son is the first recorded
case of a Greek name given in Jerusalem."

33. Cf. Tcherikover, "Jewish Apologetic Literature."

Bibliography

Bousset-Gressmann, RJ, 20, 494-95.

Charlesworth, PAMRS, 107-108, 283.

Collins, Athens and Jerusalem, 40-42.

Colpe, C. "Eupolemos," KP 2 (1967) 437-38.

Conzelmann, HJC, 143-44.

Dalbert, Missionsliteratur, 35-42.

Dancy, J. C. A Commentary on 1 Maccabees (Oxford:
    Blackwells, 1954) 129.

Denis, Introduction, 252-55.

Ewald, History, 1.50; 5.322; 8.63.

Fallon, F. "Eupolemus," in Charlesworth, OTP,

Fallon, F. and H. W. Attridge. "The Genuine Eupolemus."
    Unpublished seminar paper. Harvard New Testament
    Seminar. March 2, 1970. 30 pp.

Fiebig, P. "Eupolemos," RGG[2] 2 (1927) 411.

Fraser, Ptolemaic Alexandria, 1.694; extensive note,
    2.962:101.

Freudenthal, Alexander Polyhistor, 105-30; 208-15; also
    82-103.

Gelzer, Sextus, 1.96; 2.364.

[Georgoulēs, K. D.] "Eupolemus," ThEE 5 (1962-68) 1069
    (in Greek).

Giblet, J. "Eupolème et l'historiographie du judaïsme
    hellénistique," ETL 39 (1963) 539-54.

Graetz, Geschichte, 3.622-23.

Gutman, Beginnings, 2.73-94.

Gutschmid, A. "Zeit und Zeitrechnung der jüdischen
    Historiker Demetrios und Eupolemos," in Kleine
    Schriften (5 vols. Edited by F. Rühl. Leipzig:
    B. G. Teubner, 1889-94) 2.186-95, esp. 191-95.

Hadas, Hellenistic Culture, 95-96.

Hanhart, R. "Eupolemus," BHH 1 (1962-66) 448-49.

Hegermann, Umwelt, 1.319.

Hengel, Judaism and Hellenism, 1.92-95.

_____. "Anonymität," 237-38.

Jacoby, F. "Eupolemus (11)," PW 6.1 (1907) cols. 1227-29.

Karpeles, Geschichte, 1.178-80.

Krauss, S. "Eupolemus," JE 5 (1904) 269.

Kuhlmey, C. G. A. Eupolemi Fragmenta prolegomenis et
    commentario instructa. Berlin, 1840.

Lohse, E. "Eupolemos," RGG³ 2 (1957) cols. 733-34.

Meecham, H. G. The Letter of Aristeas (Manchester:
    University of Manchester Press, 1935) 327-28.

Meyer, R. "Eupolemos," Lexikon der Alten Welt (1965) 918.

Montgomery, J. A. The Samaritans. The Earliest Jewish
    Sect: Their History, Theology, and Literature.
    (Philadelphia: J. C. Winston, 1907) 284.

Movers, F. Die Phönizier (2 vols.; Bonn: E. Weber, 1841-
    56).

Schlatter, A. "Eupolemus als Chronolog und seine
    Beziehungen zu Josephus und Manetho," Theologische
    Studien und Kritiken 64 (1891) 633-703.

_____, Geschichte, 187-93.

Schürer, Geschichte, 3.474-77.

Schmid-Stählin, Geschichte, 2,1.589-90.

Schnabel, P. Berossos und die babylonische-hellenistische
    Literatur. (Leipzig/Berlin, 1923) 67-69.

Schubart, W. "Bemerkungen zum Stile hellenistischer
    Königsbriefe," Archiv für Papyrusforschung 6 (1920)
    324-47.

Simchoni, J. M. "Eupolemus," EncJud 6 (1930) 836-37.

Susemihl, Geschichte, 2.648-52.

Thraede, K. "Erfinder II (geistesgeschichtlich)," RAC
    5 (1962) cols. 1191-1278.

Tiede, Charismatic Figure, 138-40.

Turner, N. "Eupolemus," IDB 2 (1962) 181.

Unger, F. G. "Wann schrieb Alexander Polyhistor?"
    Philologus 43 (1884) 528-31.

_____. "Die Blüthezeit des Alexander Polyhistor,"
    Philologus 47 (1888) 177-83.

Vigouroux, R. "Eupolème," DB 2/2 (1926) 2050.

Wacholder, B. Z. "Biblical Chronology."

_____. Eupolemus: A Study of Judaeo-Greek Literature.
    (Monographs of the Hebrew Union College, 3; Cincinnati
    and New York: Hebrew Union College and Jewish Institute
    of Religion, 1974).

_____. "Eupolemus," EncJud 6 (1971) cols. 964-65.

_____. "Pseudo-Eupolemus' Two Fragments on the Life of
    Abraham," HUCA 34 (1963) 83-113.

Walter, N.   "Eupolemos," in JSHRZ (1,2), 93-108.

_____, "Frühe Begegnungen zwischen jüdischem Glauben
und hellenistischer Bildung in Alexandrien," in Neue
Beiträge zur Geschichte der Alten Welt (Ed. by E. C.
Welskopf; Berlin: Akademie Verlag, 1964) 1.367-78.

_____, "Zur Überlieferung einiger Reste früher jüdisch-
hellenistischer Literatur bei Josephus, Clemens, und
Eusebius," Studia Patristica 7 (TU 92; Berlin:
Akademie Verlag, 1966) 314-20.

_____, Untersuchungen, 37-56, 156-75.

Wendland, HRK, 198.

White, H. A. "Eupolemus," HDB 1 (1898) 794.

Willrich, H. Juden und Griechen vor der makkabäischen
Erhebung (Göttingen: Vandenhoeck und Ruprecht, 1895)
157-61.

_____, Judaica (Göttingen: Vandenhoeck und Ruprecht,
1900) 71-72, 111, 117.

_____. "Eupolemos (9)," PW 6 (1907) 1227.

Index to Editions and Translations

Fragment One

1a)

Source: Clement of Alexandria, Stromata 1.23.153.4.

Greek Text Used: Stählin-Früchtel, GCS (52), p. 95,
     line 20 - p. 96, line 3.

Editions: Dind., 2.123 (notes, 4.228); Freu., 225
     (= Frg. 1); Migne, PG (8), col. 900 A-B; Jac.,
     FGrH 3.672 (=No. 723, Frg. 1b); Stählin-Früchtel,
     GCS (52) 95-96; Denis, 179 (= Frg. 1).

Translations:

     English: Wilson (ANF), 2.335; Wacholder,
                Eupolemus, 308 (= Frg. 1b).

     French: Caster (SC, 30), 1.155.

     German: Stählin (BK, 17), 3.128.

1b)

Source: Eusebius, P.E. 9.26.1.

Reference Number in P.E.: Steph., 252; Vig. 431b-c.

Greek Text Used: Mras, GCS (43.1) 8.1, p. 519,
     lines 4-7.

Editions: Steph., 252; Vig.,431b-c; Hein. 2.33;
     Gais., 2.394; Müll., FHG 3.220 (= No. 13);
     Migne, PG (21), col. 728 C; Dind., 1.498;
     Freu., 225 (= Frg. 1); Giff., 1.541-42 (notes,
     4.312); Stearns, 29-30 (= Frg. 1); Mras, GCS
     (43,1) 8.1, p. 519; Jac., FGrH 3.672 (= No. 723,
     Frg. 1a); Denis, 179 (= Frg. 1).

Translations:

     English: Giff., 3.462; Wacholder, Eupolemus,
                307-308 (= Frg. 1a).

     French: Giblet, 541.

     German: Riessler, 328 (= Frg. 1); Walter
                (JS 1.2), 99 (= Frg. 1).

Fragment Two

2a)

Source: Clement of Alexandria, Stromata 1.21.130.3.

Greek Text Used: Stählin-Früchtel, GCS (52) p. 80,
     lines 23-29.

Editions: Dind., 2.105 (notes, 4.214); Freu. (om.);
     Migne, PG (8) col. 861 C; Jac., FGrH 3.672
     (= No. 723, Frg. 2a); Denis, 184 (= Frg. 2).

Translations:

     English: Wilson (ANF), 2.330; Wacholder,
                Eupolemus, 308 (= Frg. 2a).

     French: Caster (SC, 30), 1.141.

     German: Stählin (BK, 17), 3.111; Walter (JS,
                1.2), 101 (cf. n. 31, 1a).

2b)

Source: Eusebius, P.E. 9.30.1 - 34.18.

Reference Number in P.E.: Steph., 262-65; Vig.,
     447a-451d.

Greek Text Used: Mras, GCS (43,1) 8.1, p. 538,
     line 11 - p. 544, line 16.

Editions: Steph., 262-65; Vig.,447a-451d; Hein., 2.
     49-53; Gais., 2.423-43; Müller, FHG 3.225-28
     (= No. 18); Migne, PG (21) col. 748 B - 753 D
     (notes, cols. 1578-81); Dind., 1.515-21; Freu.,
     225-29 (= Frg. 2); Giff., 1.558-63 (notes, 4.
     317-21); Stearns, 30-39 (= Frg. 2-5, om. P.E.
     34.4-18); Mras, GCS (43,1) 8.1, pp. 538-44;
     Jac., FGrH 3.672-77 (= No. 723, Frg. 2b; N.B.
     altered paragraph numeration in 34.1-18); Denis,
     180-85 (= Frg. 2).

Translation:

     English: Giff., 3.475-80; Wacholder, Eupolemus,
                308-11 (= Frg. 2b).

     French: Giblet, 541-44.

     German: Riessler, 328-32 (= Frg. 2); Walter
                (JS, 1.2), 99-106 (= Frg. 2).

Fragment Three

 Source: Eusebius, P.E. 9.34.20.

 Reference Number in P.E.: Steph., 265; Vig. 452a.

 Greek Text Used: Mras, GCS (43,1) 8.1, p. 545,
   lines 1-4.

 Editions: Steph., 265; Vig., 452a; Hein., 2.53;
   Gais., 2.433; Müll., FHG 3.228 (= No. 20);
   Migne, PG (21) cols. 753 D - 756 A; Dind.,
   1.521; Freu., 229 (=Frg. 3); Giff., 1.563
   (notes, 4.321); Stearns (om.); Mras, GCS
   (43,1) 8.1, p. 545; Jac., FGrH 3.677 (= No. 723,
   Frg. 3); Denis, 185 (= Frg. 3).

 Translations:

   English: Giff., 3.480; Wacholder, Eupolemus,
      311 (= Frg. 3).

   French: Giblet, 544.

   German: Riessler (om.); Walter (JS, 1.2),
      106 (= Frg. 3).

Fragment Four

 Source: Eusebius, P.E. 9.39.1-5.

 Reference Number in P.E.: Steph., 266-67; Vig. 454b-d.

 Greek Text Used: Mras, GCS (43,1) 8.1, p. 548,
   lines 1-20.

 Editions: Steph., 266-67; Vig., 454b-d; Hein.,
   2.55-56; Gais., 2.436-37; Müll., FHG 3.229-30
   (= No. 24); Migne, PG (21) col. 757 B-D (notes,
   col. 1582); Dind., 1.523-24; Freu., 229-30
   (= Frg. 4); Giff., 1.565-66 (notes, 4.323);
   Stearns, 39-41 (= Frg. 6); Mras, GCS (43,1) 8.1,
   p. 548; Jac., FGrH 3.677-78 (= No. 723, Frg. *5,
   "Ohne Autornamen"); Denis, 185 (= Frg. 4).

 Translations:

   English: Giff., 3.482-83; Wacholder, Eupolemus,
      311-12 (= Frg. 4).

   French: Giblet, 544-45.

   German: Riessler, 332 (= Frg. 3); Walter (JS,
      1.2), 106-107 (= Frg. 4).

Fragment Five

Source: Clement of Alexandria, Stromata 1.21.141.4-5.

Greek Text Used: Stählin-Früchtel, GCS (52), p. 87,
    line 26 - p. 88, line 6.

Editions: Müll., FHG 3.208; Dind., 2.114; Freu., 230
    (= Frg. 5); Migne, PG (8) col. 877 B-C; Stearns
    (om.); Jac., FGrH 3.677 (= No. 723, Frg. 4);
    Denis, 186 (= Frg. 5).

Translations:

    English: Wilson (ANF), 2.332; Wacholder,
               Eupolemus, 312 (= Frg. 5).

    French: Caster (SC, 30), 1.147; Giblet (om.).

    German: Riessler, 332-33 (= Frg. 4); Stählin
               (BK, 17), 3.119; Walter (JS, 1.2),
               107-108 (= Frg. 5).

FRAGMENT ONE

A. Clement of Alexandria, Stromata 1.23.153.4

(4) Εὐπόλεμος δὲ ἐν τῷ περὶ τῶν ἐν τῇ   (4)
'Ιουδαίᾳ βασιλέων τὸν Μωυσῆ φησι πρῶτον σοφὸν
γενέσθαι καὶ γραμματικὴν πρῶτον τοῖς 'Ιουδαίοις
παραδοῦναι καὶ παρὰ 'Ιουδαίων Φοίνικας παραλαβεῖν,
5 ᾿Ελληνας δὲ παρὰ Φοινίκων.

B. Eusebius, P.E. 9.25.4 - 26.1

(25.4) Τοσαῦτα καὶ περὶ τούτων ὁ Πολυΐστωρ.   (4)
Καὶ περὶ Μωσέως δὲ ὁ αὐτὸς πλεῖστα παρα-
τίθεται, ὧν καὶ αὐτῶν ἐπακοῦσαι ἄξιον·

ΕΥΠΟΛΕΜΟΥ ΠΕΡΙ ΜΩΣΕΩΣ   431c

10   (26.1) "Εὐπόλεμος δέ φησι τὸν Μωσῆν πρῶτον   (1)
σοφὸν γενέσθαι καὶ γράμματα παραδοῦναι τοῖς 'Ιουδαίοις πρῶτον,   παρὰ   δὲ 'Ιουδαίων Φοίνικας
παραλαβεῖν, ᾿Ελληνας δὲ παρὰ Φοινίκων, νόμους τε
πρῶτον γράψαι Μωσῆν τοῖς 'Ιουδαίοις."

Frg. 1a   -- L

1 τῶν ἐν L¹ ᵐᵍ | 1-2 τῇ ἰουδαίᾳ L¹: τῆς ἰουδαίας Lᵃᶜ |

Frg. 1b   -- BION

6 τούτων: 'Ιὼβ B | Πολ. φησὶ B | 7-8 ὁ -- ἄξιον:
τάδε παρατίθεται B | 7 πάλιν πλεῖστα C apud Gais. |
9 ΕΥΠ. -- ΜΩΣ. BIᵐᵍON: ante 7-8 καὶ -- ἄξιον transp.
Vig.: om. Jac. | 11 σοφὸν γενέσθαι: ⌊..........⌋ N |
14 γράψ. Μωσ. I: Μωσ. γράψ. BON | τοὺς 'Ιουδαίους B |

FRAGMENT ONE

A. Clement of Alexandria, Stromata 1.23.153.4.[1]

(4)   (4) And Eupolemus says in his work Concerning the
Kings in Judaea[2] that Moses was the first wise man
and that he gave the alphabet[3] to the Jews first;
and, that the Phoenicians received it from the Jews,
and the Greeks received it from the Phoenicians.

B. Eusebius, P.E. 9.25.4 - 26.1.[4]

(4)   (25.4) So much says Polyhistor on this subject.
        And concerning Moses the same author (Polyhistor)
again quotes many things which are also worth hearing:

Eupolemus' Remarks Concerning Moses

(1)   (26.1) "Eupolemus says that Moses was the first wise
man[5] and that he gave the alphabet to the Jews first;
then the Phoenicians received it from the Jews, and
the Greeks received it from the Phoenicians.[6] Also,
Moses was the first to write down laws, and he did
so for the Jews."[7]

FRAGMENT TWO

A. Clement of Alexandria, Stromata 1.21.130.3

(3) Ἀλέξανδρος δὲ ὁ Πολυΐστωρ ἐπικληθεὶς   (3)
ἐν τῷ περὶ Ἰουδαίων   συγγράμματι   ἀνέγραψέν
τινας ἐπιστολὰς Σολομῶνος μὲν πρός τε Οὐάφρην
τὸν Αἰγύπτου βασιλέα   πρός τε   τὸν Φοινίκης
5 Τυρίων τάς τε αὐτῶν πρὸς Σολομῶντα, καθ' ἃς
δείκνυται ὁ μὲν Οὐάφρης ὀκτὼ μυριάδας ἀνδρῶν
Αἰγυπτίων ἀπεσταλκέναι αὐτῷ εἰς οἰκοδομὴν τοῦ
νεώ, ἄτερος δὲ τὰς ἴσας σὺν ἀρχιτέκτονι Τυρίῳ
ἐκ μητρὸς Ἰουδαίας ἐκ τῆς φυλῆς Δαβίδ, ὡς ἐκεῖ
10 γέγραπται, Ὑπέρων τοὔνομα.

B. Eusebius, P.E. 9.30.1 - 34.18

|ΕΥΠΟΛΕΜΟΥ ΠΕΡΙ ΔΑΒΙΔ ΚΑΙ ΣΟΛΟΜΩΝΟΣ ΟΙ   447a
ΕΒΑΣΙΛΕΥΣΑΝ ΕΒΡΑΙΩΝ ΚΑΙ ΠΕΡΙ ΙΕΡΟΣΟΛΥΜΩΝ

(30.1) "Εὐπόλεμος δέ φησιν ἔν τινι Περὶ   (1)
τῆς Ἡλίου προφητείας Μωσῆν προφητεῦσαι ἔτη μ'·
15 εἶτα Ἰησοῦν, τὸν τοῦ Ναυῆ υἱόν, ἔτη λ'· βιῶσαι
δ' αὐτὸν ἔτη ρι' πῆξαί τε τὴν ἱερὰν σκηνὴν ἐν
Σιλοῖ. (2) μετὰ δὲ ταῦτα προφήτην γενέσθαι   (2)
Σαμουήλ. εἶτα τῇ τοῦ θεοῦ βουλήσει ὑπὸ Σαμουήλ   447b
Σαοῦλον βασιλέα αἱρεθῆναι, ἄρξαντα δὲ ἔτη κα'
20 τελευτῆσαι. (3) εἶτα Δαβὶδ τὸν τούτου υἱὸν   (3)

Frg. 2a -- L
3-6 Οὐάφρην -- Οὐάφρης Syl.: οὔαφρην -- οὔαφρης L |
9 Δαβίδ: Δάν Stäh. (cf. Frg. 2b, par. 34.2) |

Frg. 2b -- BION

11 (et al.) Δαβὶδ Mras: Δᾱ̇δ (abbrev.) MSS | 11-12 ΕΥΠ. --
IEP. BI^mgON | 13-14 ἕν † τινι(libri numerus)πρὸ τῆς Ἡλεῖ
? Jac. | 14 Ἡλιοῦ ON | 16 ρι' ION: ι' πρὸς τοῖς ρ' Β |
17 Σηλοῖ I: Σηλοῖ < > Freu. (p. 121) | 19 Σαοὺλ Β |
20 υἱὸν: γαμβρὸν Β |

FRAGMENT TWO

A.   Clement of Alexandria, Stromata 1.21.130.3.[8]

(3)   (3) And Alexander (who is called Polyhistor) in his
    work Concerning the Jews recorded some letters of
    Solomon to Vaphres the king of Egypt and to the Phoe-
    nician king of the Tyrians, and also their letters
    to Solomon. These letters show that Vaphres sent
    80,000 Egyptian men to Solomon for the purpose of
    building the temple, and that the Phoenician king
    sent an equal number, along with a Tyrian whose mother
    was a Jewess of the tribe of David [9] to serve as
    director of works, and whose name, according to the
    records, was Hyperon.[10]

B.   Eusebius, P.E.   9.30.1 - 34.18.[11]

    Eupolemus' Remarks Concerning David and Solomon
    Who Ruled the Hebrews and His Remarks Concerning
    Jerusalem

(1)   (30.1) "In a certain book entitled Concerning The
    Prophecy of Elijah[12] Eupolemus says that Moses prophe-
    sied forty years;[13] then Joshua, the son of Nun,
    prophesied thirty years.[14] Joshua lived 110 years and
(2) pitched the holy tabernacle in Shiloh.[15] (2) After
    that,[16] Samuel became a prophet. Then, by the will of
    God, Saul was chosen by Samuel to be king,[17] and he
(3) died after ruling twenty-one years.[18] (3) Then David
    his son[19] ruled, and he subdued the Syrians who lived

δυναστεῦσαι, ὃν καταστρέψασθαι Σύρους τοὺς παρὰ
τὸν Εὐφράτην οἰκοῦντας ποταμὸν καὶ τὴν Κομμαγηνὴν
καὶ τοὺς ἐν Γαλαδηνῇ Ἀσσυρίους καὶ Φοίνικας.
στρατεῦσαι δ' αὐτὸν καὶ ἐπὶ Ἰδουμαίους καὶ Ἀμ-
5 μανίτας καὶ Μωαβίτας καὶ Ἰτουραίους καὶ
Ναβαταίους καὶ Ναβδαίους, (4) αὖθις δὲ   (4)
ἐπιστρατεῦσαι ἐπὶ Σούρωνα βασιλέα Τύρου καὶ
Φοινίκης· οὓς καὶ ἀναγκάσαι φόρους Ἰουδαίοις   447c
ὑποτελεῖν· πρός τε Οὐαφρῆν τὸν Αἰγύπτιον βασιλέα
10 φιλίαν συνθέσθαι.   (5) βουλόμενόν τε τὸν Δαβὶδ   (5)
οἰκοδομῆσαι ἱερὸν τῷ θεῷ ἀξιοῦν τὸν θεὸν τόπον
αὐτῷ δεῖξαι τοῦ θυσιαστηρίου. ἔνθα δὴ ἄγγελον
αὐτῷ ὀφθῆναι ἑστῶτα ἐπάνω τοῦ τόπου, οὗ τὸν
βωμὸν ἱδρῦσθαι ἐν Ἱεροσολύμοις, καὶ κελεύειν
15 αὐτὸν μὴ ἱδρύ<ε>σθαι τὸ ἱερόν, διὰ τὸ αἵματι
ἀνθρωπίνῳ πεφύρθαι καὶ πολλὰ ἔτη πεπολεμηκέναι·
(6) εἶναι δ' αὐτῷ ὄνομα Διαναθάν· προστάξαι τε   (6)
αὐτῷ τοῦτον ὅπως τῷ υἱῷ ἐπιτρέψῃ τὴν οἰκοδομίαν,   447d
αὐτὸν δὲ εὐτρεπίζειν τὰ πρὸς τὴν κατασκευὴν
20 ἀνήκοντα, χρυσίον, ἀργύριον, χαλκόν, λίθους, ξύλα
κυπαρίσσινα καὶ κέδρινα.   (7) ἀκούσαντα δὲ τὸν   (7)
Δαβὶδ πλοῖα ναυπηγήσασθαι ἐν Ἐλάνοις πόλει τῆς
Ἀραβίας καὶ πέμψαι μεταλλευτὰς εἰς τὴν Οὐφρῆ
νῆσον, κειμένην ἐν τῇ Ἐρυθρᾷ θαλάσσῃ, μέταλλα
25 χρυσικὰ ἔχουσαν· καὶ τὸ χρυσίον ἐκεῖθεν
μετακομίσαι τοὺς μεταλλευτὰς εἰς τὴν Ἰουδαίαν.

BION
2 Ἐφράτην BON | οἰκ. ποτ. om. B | 3 ἐν I: ἐν τῇ
BON | 4 Ἰδουμαίους: Ἰουδαίους B | 5 Μωαμίτας I |
9 ὑποτελεῖν I: ἐπιτελεῖν ON: τελεῖν B | Οὐαφρῆν BI[1]:
Οὐαφρήν I[ac]: Οὐααφρήν ON | Αἰγύπτιον MSS:
-ίων Steph. | 15 ἱδρύ<ε>σθαι Mras: ἱδρῦσθαι B:
ἱδρύσθαι ION: ἱδρῦσαι Freu.: ἱδρύσασθαι ? Jac. |
17-26 εἶναι -- Ἰουδαίαν om. B | 17 (εἶναι --
Διαναθάν) Freu.: ἄγγελον δ' αὐτῷ ἔπεμψε διὰ Νάθαν
Herzfeld apud Freu., p. 121 | 18 ἐπιστρέψῃ: ἐπιστρέψῃ I:
-ψει ON | 22 Ἐλάνοις: Αἰλάνοις Holsten apud Freu.,
pp. 209-10 | 23 Οὐφρῆ I: -εῖ ON: Οὐφρῆ ? Freu. |

along the Euphrates river and near Commagene, the
Assyrians in Galadene, and the Phoenicians. He also
waged war against the Idumeans, the Ammonites, the
Moabites, the Itureans, the Nabateans, and the Nab-

(4)   deans.[20]   (4) After that, he marched against Souron,[21]
king of Tyre and Phoenicia, whom he also forced to
pay tribute to the Jews.[22]   He also concluded a pact
of friendship with Vaphres,[23] the Egyptian king.

(5)   (5) Inasmuch as David desired to build a temple to
God, he entreated God to show him a place for the
altar.[24]   And so an angel appeared to him in a vision
standing over the place where the altar was to have
been located[25] in Jerusalem.[26]   The angel commanded
him not to build[27] the temple because he had been
defiled with human blood and had spent many years

(6)   fighting wars.[28]   (6) The angel's name was Dianathan.[29]
The angel commanded him to turn the construction over
to his son, but for David himself to prepare the
materials needed for construction -- gold, silver,

(7)   copper, stones, cypress and cedar wood.[30]   (7) Now
when David heard this, he commissioned ships to be
built in Elana, a city in Arabia.[31]   He also sent
miners to the island of Ophir situated in the Red Sea
and possessing gold mines.[32]   The   miners
transported   the   gold   from   there   to   Judaea.

(8) βασιλεύσαντα δὲ τὸν Δαβὶδ ἔτη μ' Σολομῶνι   (8)
τῷ υἱῷ τὴν ἀρχὴν παραδοῦναι, ὄντι ἐτῶν   ιβ',
ἐνώπιον 'Ηλεὶ τοῦ ἀρχιερέως καὶ τῶν δώδεκα
φυλάρχων καὶ παραδοῦναι αὐτῷ τόν τε χρυσὸν καὶ
5   ἄργυρον καὶ χαλκὸν καὶ λίθον καὶ ξύλα κυπαρίσσινα
καὶ κέδρινα. | καὶ αὐτὸν μὲν τελευτῆσαι, Σολο-   448a
μῶνα δὲ βασιλεύειν καὶ γράψαι πρὸς Οὐαφρῆν τὸν
Αἰγύπτου βασιλέα τὴν ὑπογεγραμμένην ἐπιστολήν."

                    ΕΠΙΣΤΟΛΗ ΣΟΛΟΜΩΝΟΣ

10 (31.1) "Βασιλεὺς Σολομῶν Οὐαφρῆ βασιλεῖ Αἰγύπτου   (1)
                  φίλῳ πατρικῷ χαίρειν
        Γίνωσκέ με παρειληφότα τὴν βασιλείαν παρὰ
Δαβὶδ τοῦ πατρὸς διὰ τοῦ θεοῦ τοῦ   μεγίστου,   448b
{καὶ} ἐπιτεταχότος μοι οἰκοδομῆσαι ἱερὸν τῷ θεῷ,
15 ὃς τὸν οὐρανὸν καὶ τὴν γῆν   ἔκτισεν, ἅμα δέ σοι
γράψαι ἀποστεῖλαί μοι τῶν παρὰ σοῦ λαῶν, οἳ
παραστήσονταί μοι μέχρι τοῦ ἐπιτελέσαι   πάντα
κατὰ τὴν χρείαν, καθότι ἐπιτέτακται."

                ΕΠΙΣΤΟΛΗ ΟΥΑΦΡΗ ΑΝΤΙΓΡΑΦΟΣ

20 (32.1) "Βασιλεὺς Οὐαφρῆς Σολομῶνι βασιλεῖ μεγάλῳ   (1)
                         χαίρειν
        "Αμα   τῷ ἀναγνῶναι   τὴν παρὰ σοῦ ἐπιστολὴν   448c

BION

3 'Ηλεὶ I (-ει rest. I¹) | 4 τόν: τάν I | 5 ἄργ. καὶ
χαλ.: τὸν ἄργ. καὶ τὸν χαλ. B | κυπαρίττινα B |
6-7 Σολ. -- γράψ.: ἐπὶ Σολομῶνι βασιλεῖ γράψαντι B |
7 Οὐαφρῆν I: Οὐάαφρῆν B: Οὐάφρην O: Οὐααφρην O¹N |
8 τήν: τήνδε τὴν B | ὑπογεγρ. om. B | 9 ΕΠ. ΣΟΛ.
BION: om. Jac. | 10 Οὐαφρῆ BI: Οὐααφρῆ ON |
13 τοῦ² om. B | 14 {καὶ} Mras | ἐπιτεταχότος: -χότι ON |
18 ἐπιτέτακται I: μοι ἐπιτ. BON | 19 'Επιστολὴ Οὐαφρῆ
ἀντίΓ I: 'Αντίγραφος ἐπιστολὴ Οὐαφρέος B: 'Αντίγραφος
ἐπιστολῆς ἣν ἔγραψεν Οὐαφρῆς ON: ΕΠ. -- ΑΝΤ. om. Jac. |
20 Οὐαφρῆς I: -ρῆν B: Οὐααφρὴς ON | μεγάλως B |
22 τῷ: τὸ I |

(8) (8) After David reigned for forty years,[33] he trans-
     ferred the rule to his son Solomon who was twelve
     years old.[34] He did this in the presence of Eli[35]
     the high priest and the heads of the twelve tribes.[36]
     He gave him the gold, silver, copper, stone, the
     cypress and cedar wood. And then he died, and Solo-
     mon ruled, and he wrote to Vaphres the king of Egypt
     the letter copied below:[37]

The Epistle of Solomon

(1) (31.1) "King Solomon to Vaphres, king of Egypt,
     friend of my father:[38] Greetings.

          Know that I have received the kingdom from
     David my father with the help of the Most High God,
     (and)[39] that he has commanded me to build a temple to
     the God who created heaven and earth. Furthermore,
     know that he commanded me to write to you asking
     you to send me some of your people to assist me
     until everything necessary has been completed,
     just as it was commanded."

The Epistle of Vaphres: A Copy

(1) (32.1) "King Vaphres to Solomon the great king:[40]
     Greetings.

          I rejoiced exceedingly as soon as I read the
     letter from you. Indeed, both I and all my realm

σφόδρα ἐχάρην καὶ λαμπρὰν ἡμέραν ἤγαγον ἐγώ τε
καὶ ἡ δύναμίς μου πᾶσα ἐπὶ τῷ παρειληφέναι σε
τὴν βασιλείαν παρὰ χρηστοῦ ἀνδρὸς καὶ δεδοκι-
μασμένου ὑπὸ τηλικούτου θεοῦ. περὶ δὲ ὧν γράφεις
5   μοι, περὶ τῶν κατὰ τοὺς λαοὺς τοὺς παρ᾿ ἡμῖν,
ἀπέσταλκά σοι μυριάδας ὀκτώ, ὧν καὶ τὰ πλήθη ἐξ
ὧν εἰσι διασεσάφηκά σοι· ἐκ μὲν τοῦ Σεβριθίτου
νομοῦ μυρίους, ἐκ δὲ τοῦ Μενδησίου καὶ Σεβεννύτου
δισμυρίους· Βουσιρίτου, Λεοντοπολίτου καὶ ᾿Αθρι-   448d
10 βίτου ἀνὰ μυρίους. φρόντισον δὲ καὶ τὰ δέοντα
αὐτοῖς καὶ τὰ ἄλλα, ὅπως εὐτακτῇ, καὶ ἵνα
ἀποκατασταθῶσιν εἰς τὴν ἰδίαν, ὡς ἂν ἀπὸ τῆς
χρείας γενόμενοι."

ΕΠΙΣΤΟΛΗ ΣΟΛΟΜΩΝΟΣ

15 (33.1) "Βασιλεὺς Σολομῶν Σούρωνι τῷ βασιλεῖ   (1)
Τύρου καὶ Σιδῶνος καὶ Φοινίκης φίλῳ πατρικῷ
χαίρειν
Γίνωσκέ με παρειληφότα τὴν βασιλείαν παρὰ
Δαβὶδ τοῦ πατρὸς διὰ τοῦ θεοῦ τοῦ μεγίστου,
20 ἐπιτετεταχότος μοι οἰκοδομῆσαι ἱερὸν τῷ θεῷ, ὃς
τὸν οὐρανὸν καὶ | τὴν γῆν ἔκτισεν, ἅμα δὲ καὶ   449a
σοὶ γράψαι ἀποστεῖλαί μοι τῶν παρὰ σοῦ λαῶν, οἳ
συμπαραστήσονται ἡμῖν μέχρι τοῦ ἐπιτελέσαι τὴν
τοῦ θεοῦ χρείαν, καθότι μοι ἐπιτέτακται. γέγραφα
25 δὲ καὶ εἰς τὴν Γαλιλαίαν καὶ Σαμαρεῖτιν καὶ

BION

4-5 γράφ. -- ἡμῖν: ἔγραψάς μοι λαῶν Β | 6 <καὶ> ἐξ ?
Mras | 7 εἰσι: εἰ σὲ Β | Συβριθίτου Β: Σεθρωίτου
Kuhlmey apud Jac. | 8 νόμου MSS | Σεβεννύτου <ἀνὰ> ?
Jac. | 9 δισμυρίους· <ἐκ δὲ τοῦ> Müll. | 9-10 ᾿Αθρι-
βίτου Holsten apud Mras: Βαθριθίτου I: βαθριοίτου O:
Βαριοίτου Ν: Βαθροιίτου Β | 11 καὶ ἵνα: ἵνα τε Β |
13 χρόιας Β | γενόμενοι Vig. (not.): -μένης MSS |
14 ΕΠ. -- ΣΟΛ. I: ᾿Επ. πρὸς Σούρωνα Σολ. Β: ῎Αλλη
ἐπιστολὴ Σούρωνι ἧς ἀντίγραφος ἐπιστολὴ Σολομῶνος ON |
19 τοῦ² om. Β | τοῦ³ om. O | μεγάλου Β | 20 καὶ
ἐπιτετα χ. N Dind. | 22 παρὰ σοὶ Β |

observed a day of celebration for your having received
the kingdom from a man both noble and approved by so
great a God. Now concerning those matters about which
you wrote to me, specifically about your request for
some of our people, I am sending you 80,000 men[41]
whose numbers as well as where they are from[42] I am
now providing you: from the Sethroite[43] nome 10,000;
from the Mendesian and Sebennyte nomes 20,000 each;
(from the)[44] Bousirite, Leontopolite, and Athribite[45]
nomes 10,000 each. Take care to provide for their
needs and anything else so that their stay might be
orderly, and so that whenever they have completed
their period of service[46] they might be returned to
their own homeland."

The Epistle of Solomon[47]

(1)   (33.1) "King Solomon to Souron, the king of Tyre,
Sidon, and Phoenicia,[48] friend of my father:[49] Greet-
ings.[50]

Know that I have received the kingdom from David
my father with the help of the Most High God,[51] that
he has commanded me to build a temple to the God who
created heaven and earth.[52] Furthermore, know that he
commanded me to write to you asking you to send me
some of your people to assist us until the task of God
has been completed, just as I have been commanded.[53]
I have   also   written   to Galilee, Samaria,

Μωαβῖτιν καὶ Ἀμμανῖτιν καὶ Γαλαδῖτιν χορηγεῖσθαι
αὐτοῖς τὰ δέοντα ἐκ τῆς χώρας, κατὰ μῆνα κόρους
σίτου μυρίους· ὁ δὲ κόρος ἐστὶν ἀρταβῶν ἕξ· καὶ
οἴνου κόρους μυρίους· ὁ δὲ κόρος τοῦ οἴνου ἐστὶ
5 μέτρα δέκα. τὸ δὲ ἔλαιον καὶ τὰ ἄλλα χορηγηθή-   449b
σεται αὐτοῖς ἐκ τῆς Ἰουδαίας, ἱερεῖα δὲ εἰς
κρεωφαγίαν ἐκ τῆς Ἀραβίας."

ΕΠΙΣΤΟΛΗ ΣΟΥΡΩΝΟΣ

(34.1) "Σούρων Σολομῶνι βασιλεῖ μεγάλῳ χαίρειν   (1)
10   Εὐλογητὸς ὁ θεός, ὃς τὸν οὐρανὸν καὶ τὴν γῆν
ἔκτισεν, ὃς εἵλετο ἄνθρωπον χρηστὸν ἐκ χρηστοῦ
ἀνδρός· ἅμα τῷ ἀναγνῶναι τὴν παρὰ σοῦ ἐπιστολὴν   449c
σφόδρα ἐχάρην καὶ εὐλόγησα τὸν θεὸν ἐπὶ τῷ
παρειληφέναι σὲ τὴν βασιλείαν. (2) περὶ δὲ ὧν   (2)
15 γράφεις μοι, περὶ τῶν κατὰ τοὺς λαοὺς τοὺς παρ'
ἡμῖν, ἀπέσταλκά σοι Τυρίων καὶ Φοινίκων ὀκτακισ-
μυρίους καὶ ἀρχιτέκτονά σοι ἀπέσταλκα ἄνθρωπον
Τύριον, ἐκ μητρὸς Ἰουδαίας, ἐκ τῆς φυλῆς τῆς
Δαβίδ. ὑπὲρ ὧν ἂν αὐτὸν ἐρωτήσῃς τῶν ὑπὸ τὸν
20 οὐρανὸν πάντων κατ' ἀρχιτεκτονίαν, ὑφηγήσεταί
σοι καὶ ποιήσει. (3) περὶ δὲ τῶν δεόντων καὶ   (3)
ἀποστελλομένων σοι παίδων καλῶς ποιήσεις ἐπι-   449d
στείλας τοῖς κατὰ τόπον ἐπάρχοις, ὅπως χορηγῆται
τὰ δέοντα.

BION

1 καὶ Γαλαδῖτιν om. B | κατὰ μῆνα κόρους BI: κατὰ
κόρους N: κατακόρους O | 6 ἐρεῖα B | 7 κρεωφαγίαν:
κρxxφαγίαν I^{ac}: κρεωφαγίαν I¹ON: κρεοφαγίαν B | 8 ΕΠ.--
ΣΟΥ. I: Ἀντίγραφος ἐπ. Σ. BON | 9 Σολομῶνι I:
Σολομῶντι BON | 10 τ. οὐρ. καὶ τ. γῆν BON: τ. γῆν
καὶ τ. οὐρ. I | 12 παρὰ: περὶ B | 18 τῆς²: τοῦ B |
19 Δαβίδ: Δάν Freu. (cf. Frg. 2a) | ἐρωτήσεις B |
20 κατ' ἀρχ. Mras: καὶ ἀρχ. MSS: <τῶν> κατὰ ἀρχ. Vig.
(marg.): {καὶ ἀρχ.} Freu. | 21 δεόντων καὶ: δεόντων
τῶν Freu. (p. 210): {δεόντων καὶ} ? Jac. | 22-23 ἐπι-
στείλας I: ἀποστείλας ON: ἀπέστειλας B |

Moab, Ammon, and Gilead to furnish their needs from
the country[54]-- every month 10,000 cors of wheat (a
cor is six artabae) and 10,000 cors of wine (a cor of
wine is ten measures).[55] The olive oil and everything
else will be furnished to them by Judaea.[56] Cattle
for meat will be supplied by Arabia."[57]

The Epistle of Souron[58]

(1) (34.1) "Souron to Solomon the great king:[59] Greet-
ings.

Blessed be the God who created heaven and earth
who chose for himself a noble man, the son of a noble
man.[60] As soon as I read the letter from you, I
rejoiced exceedingly and blessed God for your having
(2) received the Kingdom. (2) Now concerning the matters
about which you wrote me, specifically about your
request for some of our people, I am sending you
80,000 Tyrians and Phoenicians.[61] Also, I am sending
you a master builder, a man of Tyre whose mother was
a Jewess, of the tribe of David.[62] Any question under
heaven which you might ask him about architecture he
will answer, and any request you make of him he will
(3) carry out.[63] (3) Now concerning the slaves which you
need (and which I am sending you), you will do well
to enjoin the princes in that area to supply their
needs.

(4) Διελθὼν δὲ Σολομῶν, ἔχων τοὺς πατρικοὺς   (4)
φίλους, ἐπὶ τὸ ὄρος τὸ τοῦ Λιβάνου μετὰ τῶν
Σιδωνίων καὶ Τυρίων, μετήνεγκε τὰ ξύλα τὰ προκε-
κομμένα ὑπὸ τοῦ πατρὸς αὐτοῦ διὰ τῆς θαλάσσης
5 εἰς Ἰόππην, ἐκεῖθεν δὲ πεζῇ εἰς Ἱεροσόλυμα.
καὶ ἄρξασθαι οἰκοδομεῖν τὸ ἱερὸν τοῦ θεοῦ, ὄντα
ἐτῶν τρισκαίδεκα, ἐργάζεσθαι δὲ τὰ ἔθνη τὰ προ-
ειρημένα καὶ φυλὰς δώδεκα τῶν Ἰουδαίων καὶ
παρέχειν ταῖς ἑκκαίδεκα μυριάσι τὰ δέοντα πάντα,
10 κατὰ μῆνα φυλὴν μίαν. θεμελιῶσαί τε τὸν ναὸν
τοῦ θεοῦ, μῆκος πηχῶν ξ΄, πλάτος πηχῶν ξ΄, τὸ δὲ
πλάτος τῆς οἰκοδομῆς καὶ τῶν θεμελίων πηχῶν ι΄.
| οὕτω γὰρ αὐτῷ προστάξαι Νάθαν τὸν προφήτην   450a
τοῦ θεοῦ. (5) οἰκοδομεῖν δὲ ἐναλλὰξ δόμον   (5)
15 λίθινον καὶ ἔνδεσμον κυπαρίσσινον, πελεκίνοις
χαλκοῖς ταλαντιαίοις καταλαμβάνοντα{ς} τοὺς δύο
δόμους. οὕτω δ᾽ αὐτὸν οἰκοδομήσαντα ξυλῶσαι
ἔσωθεν κεδρίνοις ξύλοις καὶ κυπαρισσίνοις, ὥστε
τὴν λιθίνην οἰκοδομὴν μὴ φαίνεσθαι· χρυσῶσαί
20 τε τὸν ναὸν ἔσωθεν χωννύντα πλινθία χρυσᾶ πεντα-
πήχη καὶ προστιθέναι προσηλοῦντα ἥλοις ἀργυροῖς,
ταλαντιαίοις τὴν ὁλκήν, μαστοειδέσι τὸν ῥυθμόν,
τέσσαρσι δὲ τὸν ἀριθμόν. (6) οὕτω δ᾽ αὐτὸν   (6)
χρυσῶσαι ἀπὸ ἐδάφους ἕως τῆς ὀροφῆς τό τε ὀρόφωμα 450b
25 ποιῆσαι ἐκ φατνωμάτων χρυσῶν, τὸ δὲ δῶμα ποιῆσαι

BION
1 ante Διελθὼν titulum Σολομῶν εἰς Λίβανον ἀπελθὼν κεκό-
μικεν εἰς Ἱερουσαλὴμ τὰ ξύλα ἃ ὁ πατὴρ αὐτοῦ προέτεμεν
habet B | 8 φυλῆς I | {καὶ²} Vig. (not.) | 9 ἐξα-
καίδεκα B | 11 πλάτος πηχῶν ξ΄ I: om. BON: ὕψος π. ξ΄
vel πλάτος π. κ΄ Kuhlmey apud Freu. (p. 211) | 16 κατα-
λαμβάνοντα Freu.: -οντας MSS | 18 ἔσωθεν BON:
εὔωθεν (!) I: ἔξωθεν Steph. | ξ. κεδρ. καὶ κυπαρατ-
τίνοις B | 20 χωννύντα: χωνεύοντα Freu. (p. 211) |
21 ἥλ. ταλαντιαίοις ἀργυροῖς ON | 23 τέσσ. -- ἀριθ. IO:
om. BN |

(4)   (4) Solomon, accompanied by his father's advisors,[64] journeyed to the mountain of Lebanon with
the Sidonians and Tyrians.[65] The trees which had been
cut previously by his father he transported by sea
to Joppa and from there by land to Jerusalem.[66] He
began to build the temple of God when he was thirteen
years old.[67] The aforementioned nations supplied the
labor[68] and the twelve tribes of the Jews also supplied the 160,000 men with all the necessary provisions -- one tribe each month.[69] He laid the foundations of the temple of God sixty cubits long and sixty
cubits wide;[70] the width of the building and its
foundations was ten cubits,[71] for this is what Nathan

(5) the prophet of God commanded him.[72] (5) He proceeded
to build by alternating a course of stone and a bond-
ing of cypress wood, joining the two courses with
bronze dovetails weighing a talent each.[73] After he
finished building, he paneled the inside with cedar
and cypress wood so that the stone construction was
no longer visible.[74] Then he gilded the inside of the
sanctuary by casting[75] gold bricks five cubits long
and fastening them with four silver nails, each
weighing a talent and each having a breast-shaped

(6) head.[76] (6) In this manner he gilded the interior
from floor to ceiling. The ceiling he made of coffered
gold, but the roof he made of bronze, using bronze

χαλκοῦν ἀπὸ κεραμίδων χαλκῶν, χαλκὸν χωνεύσαντα
καὶ τοῦτον καταχέαντα. ποιῆσαι δὲ δύο στύλους
χαλκοῦς καὶ καταχρυσῶσαι αὐτοῦς χρυσίῳ ἀδόλῳ,
δακτύλου τὸ πάχος. (7) εἶναι δὲ τοὺς στύλους   (7)
5   τῷ ναῷ ἰσομεγέθεις, τὸ δὲ πλάτος κύκλῳ ἕκαστον
κίονα πηχῶν δέκα· στῆσαι δὲ αὐτοὺς τοῦ οἴκου ὅν
μὲν ἐκ δεξιῶν, ὅν δὲ ἐξ εὐωνύμων. ποιῆσαι δὲ   450c
καὶ λυχνίας χρυσᾶς <δέκα>, δέκα τάλαντα ἑκάστην
ὁλκὴν ἀγούσας, ὑπόδειγμα λαβόντα τὴν ὑπὸ Μωσέως
10 ἐν τῇ σκηνῇ τοῦ μαρτυρίου τεθεῖσαν· (8) στῆσαι   (8)
δ᾽ ἐξ ἑκατέρου μέρους τοῦ σηκοῦ τὰς μὲν ἐκ
δεξιῶν, τὰς δὲ ἐξ εὐωνύμων. ποιῆσαι δ᾽ αὐτὸν
καὶ λύχνους χρυσοῦς ο᾽, ὥστε καίεσθαι ἐφ᾽ ἑκάστης
λυχνίας ἑπτά. οἰκοδομῆσαι δὲ καὶ τὰς πύλας τοῦ
15 ἱεροῦ καὶ κατακοσμῆσαι χρυσίῳ καὶ ἀργυρίῳ· καὶ
καταστεγάσαι φατνώμασι κεδρίνοις καὶ κυπαρισσίνοις. (9) ποιῆσαι δὲ καὶ κατὰ τὸ πρὸς βορρᾶν   (9)
μέρος τοῦ ἱεροῦ στοὰν καὶ στύλους αὐτῇ ὑποστῆσαι   450d
χαλκοῦς μη᾽· κατασκευάσαι δὲ καὶ λουτῆρα χαλ-
20 κοῦν, μῆκος πηχῶν κ᾽ καὶ πλάτος πηχῶν κ᾽, τὸ δὲ
ὕψος πηχῶν ε᾽. ποιῆσαι δὲ ἐπ᾽ αὐτῷ στεφάνην
πρὸς τὴν βάσιν ἔξω ὑπερέχουσαν πῆχυν ἕνα πρὸς τὸ
τοὺς ἱερεῖς τούς τε πόδας προσκλύζεσθαι καὶ τὰς
χεῖρας νίπτεσθαι ἐπιβαίνοντας· ποιῆσαι δὲ καὶ
25 τὰς βάσεις τοῦ λουτῆρος τορευτὰς χωνευτὰς δώδεκα

ΒΙΟΝ

1 κεράμων Β | 4 δακτύλου Freu.: δακτύλῳ MSS |
5 ἰσομεγέθει Ι | 6 στῆσαι ΒΟΝ: στῆναι Ι (cf. infra
lin. 10) | τοῦ: τοὺς Β | 8 χρυσᾶς <δέκα>, δέκα
τάλαντα Seguier: χρυσᾶς, δέκα τάλαντα MSS: χρυσᾶς
δέκα, τάλαντον Freu. | 25 ταύρους χωνευτοὺς Freu.
(p. 211) |

tiles which he made by first smelting the bronze, then pouring it into molds.[77] He made two bronze pillars and gilded them with a layer of pure gold a finger

(7) thick. (7) The pillars were the same height as the temple and the circumference of each pillar was ten cubits. He set them, one on the right side and the other on the left side of the building.[78] He made ten[79] golden lampstands weighing ten talents each, using as a pattern the one placed by Moses in the tent

(8) of testimony.[80] (8) He set them in the sacred precinct, some on the right side and others on the left. He made seventy gold lamps so that seven of them might burn upon each lampstand.[81] He also built the doors of the temple and adorned them with both gold and silver and he covered them with coffered cedar and

(9) cypress.[82] (9) He also built a portico on the north side of the temple and supported it with forty-eight bronze pillars.[83] In addition, he constructed a bronze laver twenty cubits long, twenty cubits wide, and five cubits high.[84] On the laver he placed a rim one cubit wide extending away from the base the purpose of which was to provide the priests a step on which to stand to wash their feet and dip their hands into the laver.[85] He also made for the laver twelve pedestals cast of bronze and worked in relief each

καὶ τῷ ὕψει ἀνδρομήκεις καὶ στῆσαι ἐξ ὑστέρου
μέρους ὑπὸ τὸν λουτῆρα, ἐκ δεξιῶν τοῦ θυσιαστηρίου. (10) ποιῆσαι δὲ καὶ βάσιν χαλκῆν τῷ ὕψει   (10)
πηχῶν δυοῖν κατὰ τὸν λουτῆρα, ἵν' ἐφεστήκῃ ἐπ'
5 αὐτῆς ὁ βασιλεύς, ὅταν προσεύχηται, ὅπως ὁπτάνη-
ται τῷ λαῷ τῶν Ἰουδαίων. | οἰκοδομῆσαι δὲ καὶ   451a
τὸ θυσιαστήριον πηχῶν κε' ἐπὶ πήχεις κ', τὸ δὲ
ὕψος πηχῶν δώδεκα. (11) ποιῆσαι δὲ καὶ δακτυ-   (11)
λίους δύο χαλκοῦς ἀλυσιδωτοὺς καὶ στῆσαι αὐτοὺς
10 ἐπὶ μηχανημάτων ὑπερεχόντων τῷ ὕψει τὸν ναὸν
πήχεις κ' καὶ σκιάζειν ἐπάνω παντὸς τοῦ ἱεροῦ·
καὶ προσκρεμάσαι ἑκάστῃ δίκτυϊ κώδωνας χαλκοῦς
ταλαντιαίους τετρακοσίους· καὶ ποιῆσαι ὅλας τὰς
δίκτυας πρὸς τὸ ψοφεῖν τοὺς κώδωνας καὶ ἀποσοβεῖν
15 τὰ ὄρνεα, ὅπως μὴ καθίζῃ ἐπὶ τοῦ ἱεροῦ μηδὲ
νοσσεύῃ ἐπὶ τοῖς φατνώμασι τῶν πυλῶν καὶ στοῶν
καὶ μολύνῃ τοῖς ἀποπατήμασι τὸ ἱερόν. (12) περι-   (12)
βαλεῖν δὲ καὶ τὰ Ἱεροσόλυμα τὴν πόλιν τείχεσι   451b
καὶ πύργοις καὶ τάφροις· οἰκοδομῆσαι δὲ καὶ
20 βασίλεια ἑαυτῷ. (13) προσαγορευθῆναι δὲ τὸ   (13)
ἀνάκτορον πρῶτον μὲν ἱερὸν Σολομῶνος, ὕστερον δὲ
παρεφθαρμένως τὴν πόλιν ἀπὸ τοῦ ἱεροῦ Ἰερουσαλὴμ
ὀνομασθῆναι, ὑπὸ δὲ τῶν Ἑλλήνων φερωνύμως
Ἱεροσόλυμα λέγεσθαι. (14) συντελέσαντα δὲ τὸ   (14)
25 ἱερὸν καὶ τὴν πόλιν τειχίσαντα ἐλθεῖν εἰς Σηλὼμ

BION

1 {καὶ¹} Jac. | 1-20 καὶ²-- ἑαυτῷ om. B | 4 δυεῖν I |
7 κε' om. N: κ' Kuhlmey apud Freu. (p. 211) |
8-9 δακτυλίους: δίκτυα Seguier (PG (21), col. 1581) |
11 <   > καὶ σκιάζειν Freu.: ὡς σκ. ? Jac. | 13-14 ὅλας
τὰς δίκτυας I: ὅλους τοὺς δικτύους ON: κοιλὰς τὰς
δίκτυας ? Freu. | 15 καθίζῃ I: ἐπικαθίζῃ ON |
20-21 τὰ ἀνάκτορα B |21 πρῶτον μὲν post 20 δὲ transp. I |
24 λέγεσθαι om. B |

the height of a man. These he placed under the laver

(10) from the rear at the right of the altar.[86] (10) He

also made a bronze platform two cubits high to be

placed opposite the laver. This was a platform on

which the king could stand when he prayed so that he

would be seen by the Jewish people.[87] He also built

the altar twenty-five cubits long,[88] twenty cubits

(11) wide, and twelve cubits high.[89] (11) He also made

two bronze rings wrought in the shape of a chain and

placed them on supporting devices towering twenty

cubits above the temple, and they overshadowed the

entire temple. He hung on each net 400 bronze bells

each weighing a talent. He made the whole network so

that the bells would ring and frighten the birds,

preventing them from alighting on the temple and from

building their nests on the tiles of the gates and

porticoes and defiling the temple with their dropp-

(12) ings.[90] (12) He also surrounded the city of Jerusalem

with walls and towers and trenches.[91] In addition, he

(13) built a palace for himself.[92] (13) The shrine was

first called the temple of Solomon. Later the city

was incorrectly named Jerusalem (the name being de-

rived from the temple); it is called Hierosoluma by

(14) the Greeks.[93] (14) After he completed the temple and

walled the city, Solomon came to Shiloh and offered

καὶ θυσίαν τῷ θεῷ εἰς ὁλοκάρπωσιν προσαγαγεῖν
βοῦς χιλίους. λαβόντα δὲ τὴν σκηνὴν καὶ τὸ   451c
θυσιαστήριον καὶ τὰ σκεύη, ἃ ἐποίησε Μωσῆς, εἰς
Ἱεροσόλυμα ἐνεγκεῖν καὶ ἐν τῷ οἴκῳ θεῖναι.
5 (15) καὶ τὴν κιβωτὸν δὲ καὶ τὸν βωμὸν τὸν   (15)
χρυσοῦν καὶ τὴν λυχνίαν καὶ τὴν τράπεζαν καὶ τὰ
ἄλλα σκεύη ἐκεῖ καταθέσθαι, καθὼς προστάξαι αὐτῷ
τὸν προφήτην. (16) προσαγαγεῖν δὲ τῷ θεῷ   (16)
θυσίαν μυρίαν, πρόβατα δισχίλια, μόσχους τρισ-
10 χιλίους πεντακοσίους. τὸ δὲ σύμπαν χρυσίον τὸ
εἰς τοὺς δύο στύλους καὶ τὸν ναὸν καταχρησθὲν   451d
εἶναι τάλαντα μυριάδων υξ΄· εἰς δὲ τοὺς ἥλους
καὶ τὴν ἄλλην κατασκευὴν ἀργυρίου τάλαντα χίλια
διακόσια τριάκοντα δύο· χαλκοῦ δὲ εἰς τοὺς
15 κίονας καὶ τὸν λουτῆρα καὶ τὴν στοὰν τάλαντα
μύρια ὀκτακισχίλια πεντήκοντα. (17) ἀποπέμψαι   (17)
δὲ τὸν Σολομῶνα καὶ τοὺς Αἰγυπτίους καὶ τοὺς
Φοίνικας, ἑκάστους εἰς τὴν ἑαυτῶν, ἑκάστῳ χρυσοῦ
σίκλους δόντα δέκα· τὸ δὲ τάλαντον εἶναι σίκλον.
20 καὶ τῷ μὲν Αἰγύπτου βασιλεῖ Οὐαφρῇ   ἐλαίου
μετρητὰς μυρίους, φοινικοβαλάνων ἀρτάβας χιλίας,
μέλιτος δὲ ἀγγεῖνα ἑκατὸν καὶ ἀρώματα πέμψαι·
(18) τῷ δὲ Σούρωνι εἰς Τύρον πέμψαι τὸν χρυσοῦν   (18)
κίονα, τὸν ἐν Τύρῳ ἀνακείμενον ἐν τῷ ἱερῷ τοῦ
25 Διός."

BION
7 καταθέσθαι BON: κατατίθεσθαι I | προσέταξεν αὐτῷ
ὁ προφήτης B (cf. supra par. 4) | 10 τὸ²: τὸν B |
11 δύο BI: om. ON | καταχρισθὲν BON | 12 μυριάδων
υξ΄ ION: μυριάδων τετρακισμυρίων ἑξήκοντα B: μυριάδων
(μυρία καὶ ?) υξ΄ Müll.: {μυριάδων} υξ΄ Freu. |
16 μυρία (!) ὧν B | 18-19 χρυσίου σίκλας B |
20 Οὐαφρῇ I: Οὐααφρῇ ON: Οὐασφρῇ B | 22 καὶ ἀρώμ.
πέμ.: πέμψαι δὲ καὶ ἀρώμ. B |

a sacrifice to God of 1,000 oxen as a whole burnt-
offering.[94]   He then took the tabernacle, the altar,
and the vessels which Moses had made, brought them to
(15) Jerusalem, and placed them in the temple.[95]   (15) The
ark, the gold altar, the lampstand, the table, and
all the other vessels he also placed there, just as
(16) the prophet had commanded him.[96]   (16) And he offered
an immense offering to God -- 2,000 sheep and 3,500
calves.[97]   The total amount of gold used for the two
pillars and the temple was 4,600,000 talents. For
the nails and all the other furnishings he used 1,232
talents of silver. For the pillars, the laver, the
(17) portico he used 18,050 talents of bronze.[98]   (17)
Solomon returned the Egyptians and the Phoenicians
each to their own countries after having given each
man ten golden shekels (a talent is a shekel).[99]   To
Vaphres the king of Egypt he sent 10,000 measures of
olive oil, 1,000 artabae of dates, 100 vessels of
(18) honey and spices.[100]   (18) And to Souron at Tyre he
sent the golden pillar which is now set up in the
temple of Zeus in Tyre."[101]

FRAGMENT THREE (Eusebius, P.E. 9.34.20)

ΕΥΠΟΛΕΜΟΥ ΠΕΡΙ ΣΟΛΟΜΩΝΟΣ

(20) "Ποιῆσαι δέ φησιν ὁ Εὐπόλεμος τὸν   (20)
Σολομῶνα καὶ ἀσπίδας χρυσᾶς χιλίας, ὧν ἑκάστην   452a
πεντακοσίων εἶναι χρυσῶν. βιῶσαι δὲ αὐτὸν ἔτη
5 πεντήκοντα δύο, ὧν ἐν εἰρήνῃ βασιλεῦσαι ἔτη μ'."

FRAGMENT FOUR (Eusebius, P.E. 9.39.1-5)

(1) Ἐπὶ τούτοις καὶ τῆς Ἰερεμίου προφη-   (1)
τείας τοῦ Πολυΐστορος μνήμην πεποιημένου, ἡμᾶς   454b
ἀποσιωπῆσαι ταύτην πάντων ἂν εἴη παραλογώτατον.
κείσθω τοίνυν καὶ αὕτη·

10   ΕΥΠΟΛΕΜΟΥ ΠΕΡΙ ΙΕΡΕΜΙΟΥ ΤΟΥ ΠΡΟΦΗΤΟΥ ΟΜΟΙΩΣ

(2) "Εἶτα Ἰωαχείμ· ἐπὶ τούτου προφητεῦσαι   (2)
Ἰερεμίαν τὸν προφήτην. τοῦτον ὑπὸ τοῦ θεοῦ
ἀποσταλέντα καταλαβεῖν τοὺς Ἰουδαίους θυσιάζοντας
εἰδώλῳ χρυσῷ, ᾧ εἶναι ὄνομα Βάαλ. (3) τοῦτον δὲ   (3)
15 αὐτοῖς τὴν μέλλουσαν ἀτυχίαν δηλῶσαι. τὸν δὲ
Ἰωαχεὶμ ζῶντα αὐτὸν ἐπιβαλέσθαι κατακαῦσαι·
τὸν δὲ φάναι τοῖς ξύλοις τούτοις Βαβυλωνίοις   454c
ὀψοποιήσειν καὶ σκάψειν τὰς τοῦ Τίγριδος καὶ
Εὐφράτου διώρυχας αἰχμαλωτισθέντας. (4) τὸν δὲ   (4)
20 τῶν Βαβυλωνίων βασιλέα ἀκούσαντα Ναβουχοδονόσορ

BION

1 ΕΥΠ. -- ΣΟΛΟΜΩΝΟΣ   ΒΙ: ΕΥΠ. -- ΣΟΛΟΜΩΝΤΟΣ   ΟΝ |
5 ὧν I: ὃν ΒΟΝ | 6-9 ἐπὶ -- αὕτη om. Β |
9 αὕτη I: αὐτή ΟΝ | 10 ΕΥΠ. -- ΟΜ. ΙΟΝ: ΕΥΠ. --
ΠΡΟΦ. Β: ΕΥΠ. -- ΠΡΟΦ. ante 6 ἐπὶ transp. Vig. |
18 ὀψοποιῆσαι Β | 19 Ἐφράτου ΒΟΝ |

FRAGMENT THREE[102]

Eupolemus' Remarks Concerning Solomon

"And Eupolemus says that Solomon also made 1,000 gold shields each of which weighed 500 shekels of gold.[103]   And he lived fifty-two years, forty of which he reigned in peace."[104]

FRAGMENT FOUR[105]

(1)   (1) In addition to these things Polyhistor has also mentioned the prophecy of Jeremiah which it would be inexcusable for us to pass over in silence. Now let me report this.

Eupolemus' Remarks Concerning Jeremiah the Prophet -- In Similar Fashion

(2)   (2) "Then Jonacheim ruled.[106] At this time the prophet Jeremiah prophesied. Sent by God, he caught the Jews sacrificing to a golden idol whose name was

(3) Baal.[107]   (3) He declared to them the coming mis-fortune.[108]   Jonacheim attempted to burn him alive, but Jeremiah said that with that very timber they would prepare food for the Babylonians and that as captives they would dig the trenches of the Tigris

(4) and Euphrates.[109]   (4) When Nebuchadnezzar the king of the Babylonians heard what was being prophesied by

τὰ ὑπὸ τοῦ Ἱερεμίου προμαντευθέντα παρακαλέσαι
᾿Αστιβάρην τὸν Μήδων βασιλέα συστρατεύειν αὐτῷ.
(5) παραλαβόντα δὲ Βαβυλωνίους καὶ Μήδους καὶ   (5)
συναγαγόντα πεζῶν μὲν ὀκτωκαίδεκα, ἱππέων   δὲ
5 μυριάδας δώδεκα καὶ πεζῶν ἄρματα μυρία, πρῶτον
μὲν τὴν Σαμαρεῖτιν καταστρέψασθαι καὶ Γαλιλαίαν
καὶ Σκυθόπολιν καὶ τοὺς   ἐν τῇ   Γαλααδίτιδι   454d
οἰκοῦντας Ἰουδαίους· αὖθις δὲ τὰ Ἱεροσόλυμα
παραλαβεῖν καὶ τὸν Ἰουδαίων βασιλέα Ἰωναχεὶμ
10 ζωγρῆσαι· τὸν δὲ χρυσὸν τὸν ἐν τῷ ἱερῷ καὶ
ἄργυρον καὶ χαλκὸν ἐκλέξαντα εἰς   Βαβυλῶνα
ἀποστεῖλαι, χωρὶς τῆς   κιβωτοῦ καὶ τῶν ἐν αὐτῇ
πλακῶν· ταύτην δὲ τὸν Ἱερεμίαν κατασχεῖν."

FRAGMENT FIVE (Clement of Alex., Strom. 1.21.141.4-5)

(4) ἔτι δὲ καὶ Εὐπόλεμος ἐν τῇ ὁμοίᾳ πραγ-   (4)
15 ματείᾳ τὰ πάντα ἔτη φησὶν ἀπὸ ᾿Αδὰμ ἄχρι τοῦ
πέμπτου ἔτους Δημητρίου βασιλείας Πτολεμαίου τὸ
δωδέκατον βασιλεύοντος Αἰγύπτου συνάγεσθαι ἔτη
,ερμθ'. (5) ἀφ' οὗ δὲ χρόνου ἐξήγαγε Μωυσῆς   (5)
τοὺς Ἰουδαίους ἐξ Αἰγύπτου ἐπὶ τὴν προειρημένην
20 προθεσμίαν συνάγεσθαι ἔτη {δισ}χίλια πεντακόσια
ὀγδοήκοντα. ἀπὸ δὲ τοῦ χρόνου τούτου ἄχρι τῶν
ἐν Ῥώμῃ ὑπάτων Γναίου Δομετίου καὶ ᾿Ασινίου
συναθροίζεται ἔτη ἑκατὸν εἴκοσι.

Frg. 4 -- BION
5 {πεζῶν} Vig. (marg.) | 6 καταστρέφει B |
7 Γαλααδίτιδι Β: Γαλαδίτιδι Ι: Γαλατίδι ΟΝ: Γαλαατίδι
Steph. (cf. Frg. 2b, par. 30.3 et 33.1) | 10 δὲ -- ἱερῷ:
δ' ἐν τ. ἱερῷ χρυσὸν Β |11 ἐκλέξαντα Freu.: -αντας MSS |
Frg. 5 -- L
16-17 {Πτολ. -- Αἰγ.} Gutschmid apud Jac. | 20 {δισ}
Clinton (Fasti Hell. 1. 291) apud Stählin; cf. Freu.,
212-15 | 22 Γναίου Δομετίου καὶ ᾿Ασινίου Freu. (p. 214):
γαίου δομετιανοῦ κασιανοῦ L: Καίσαρος Δομετιανοῦ καὶ
Σαβίνου Syl. apud Stählin: Γναίου Δομετίου <καὶ
᾿Ασινίου ὑπὸ> Κασσιανοῦ Gutschmid (Kleine Schriften, 2.192)
apud Stählin |

Jeremiah, he called upon Astibares,[110] the king of the

(5) Medes, to join him in making war. (5) Using the

Babylonians and the Medes, after he gathered 180,000

footsoldiers, 120,000 cavalry, and 10,000 chariots

for footsoldiers,[111] he first subdued Samaria, Gali-

lee, Scythopolis, and the Jews living in Gilead.[112]

Then he took Jerusalem and captured alive Jonacheim

the king of the Jews.[113] After he had taken as tri-

bute the gold in the temple, as well as the silver and

he bronze, he transported it to Babylon without the

ark and the tablets which it contained. These Jere-

miah withheld."[114]

FRAGMENT FIVE[115]

(4)   (4) In a similar work[116] Eupolemus also says

that all the years from Adam until the fifth year of

the reign of Demetrius,[117] in the twelfth year that

Ptolemy ruled over Egypt,[118] total 5,149 years.[119]

(5) (5) And from the time when Moses led the Jews out of

Egypt to the aforesaid time was 2,580 years.[120] (And

from that time until the time of the consuls of Rome

Gnaeus Domitius and Asinius totals 120 years.)[121]

ANNOTATIONS

1. Having sought to demonstrate the antiquity of the Jews and their role as cultural benefactors to the Greeks (chs. 21 & 22), Clement launches into a panegyric on Moses (ch. 23). Following the biblical account in Exodus 2, but also depending on extrabiblical sources, e.g. Philo's Life of Moses, he rehearses the circumstances of Moses' birth and upbringing, focusing especially on his "philosophical" education. This quotation from Eupolemus occurs in the context of his description of Moses' education in Egypt where he acquired knowledge from Greeks, Egyptians, and Chaldeans. It is followed by quotations from Artapanus (= Frg. 3b) and Ezekiel the Tragedian (= parts of Frg. 1).

This quotation from Eupolemus documenting Moses' status as the first wise man became a standard feature in the Christian apologetic tradition. The following witnesses are worth noting:

Cyril of Alexandria (d. 444), Contra Julianum 7.231E = PG (76) 853 B-C:

Εὐπόλεμος γοῦν ὁ ἱστορικὸς τοὺς ἐπ' αὐτῷ λόγους συντιθείς, ἐν τῷ Περὶ τῶν ἐν τῇ Ἰουδαίᾳ βασιλέων φησὶν ἐναργῶς, Μωσέα δὴ πρῶτον γενέσθαι σοφόν, καὶ γραμματικὴν τοῖς Ἰουδαίοις παραδοῦναι, τὴν τὸ τηνικάδε τάχα που νενομισμένην· Φοίνικας δὲ παρ' αὐτῶν κατακτήσασθαί τε τὴν ἐπιστήμην, ἅτε δὴ καὶ ὁμόρους ὄντας Ἰουδαίοις· παραδοῦναι δὲ τοῖς Ἑλλήνων παισί, Κάδμου δηλονότι παρ' αὐτοῖς γεγονότος, καὶ αὐτὰ δὲ διδάξαντος τὰ πρῶτα στοιχεῖα. Ταύτης ἰδίᾳ μέμνηται τῆς ἱστορίας ἐν τοῖς Στρωματεῦσιν ὁ Κλήμης, ἀνὴρ ἐλλόγιμος καὶ φιλομαθής, καὶ ἀναγνωσμάτων Ἑλληνικῶν πολυπραγμονήσας βάθος, ὡς ὀλίγοι τάχα που τῶν πρὸ αὐτοῦ.

Chronicon Paschale (7th cent.), ed. L. Dindorf (1832) [Corpus Scriptorum Historiae Byzantinae, 16] 1.117, lin. 11-14 = PG (92) 201 A-B:

Εὐπόλεμος δέ φησι Μωϋσῆν πρῶτον σοφὸν γενέσθαι καὶ γράμματα παραδοῦναι τοῖς Ἰουδαίοις πρῶτον, Φοίνικας δὲ παρὰ Ἰουδαίων παραλαβεῖν, Ἕλληνας δὲ παρὰ Φοινίκων, νόμους δὲ πρῶτον Μωϋσέα γράψαι τοῖς Ἰουδαίοις.

Georgius Cedrenus, Compendium Historiarum (11th cent.), ed. I. Bekker (1838-39) [Corpus Scriptorum Historiae Byzantinae, 34] 1.87, lin. 8-11 = PG (121) 116 D:

Ὅτι Εὐπόλεμός φησι τὸν Μωϋσέα πρῶτον σοφὸν γενέσθαι, καὶ γράμματα παραδοῦναι Ἰουδαίοις πρῶτον, παρὰ δὲ Ἰουδαίων Φοίνικας παραλαβεῖν, Ἕλληνας δὲ παρὰ Φοινίκων· νόμους δὲ πρῶτον Μωϋσῆς γράφει τοῖς Ἰουδαίοις.

Cf. also Georgius Hamartolus, Chronicon = PG (110) 27-28;
J. A. Cramer, Anecdota Graeca (Oxford, 1837) 4.238, 245.

2. Only Clement gives this as the title of Eupolemus'
work. It is now generally accepted as accurate. Cf. Frg.
2b, par. 1, and notes 12 and 116 below. Also, Freudenthal,
208; Wacholder, Eupolemus, 21-26.

3. γραμματική, ordinarily "grammar" (Plato, Cra. 431 E;
Sph. 253 A; Aristotle, Top. 142ᵇ31), but also "alphabet"
or "script" (Strabo 3.1.6; Plutarch, Arist. 1; OGIS
56.64 ἡ ἱερὰ γ. = hieroglyphic writing). LSJ, s.v. Also,
Syrianus' commentary on Hermogenes Στάσεις: ἡ γοῦν κατὰ
Κάδμον ... γραμματική κ.τ.λ. in Walz, Rhet. Gr. 443, apud
Freudenthal, 209. It was perhaps Eupolemus' original word,
but changed by Eusebius in Frg. 2b, par. 26.1. Cf. note 6
below. Also, Wacholder, Eupolemus, 73, n. 8, and 77.

4. After citing the testimony of various authors quoted by
Alexander Polyhistor who mention the patriarchs Jacob,
Joseph, and Job, Eusebius devotes a long section to Moses
(P.E. 9.26-29). This fragment from Eupolemus, also taken
from Polyhistor, is the first of several testimonies to
Moses, followed by quotations from Artapanus (P.E. 9.27.1-
37 = Frg. 3), Ezekiel the Tragedian (P.E. 9.28.1-4 = Frg.
1), Demetrius (P.E. 9.29.1-3 = Frg. 3), Ezekiel the Trage-
dian (P.E. 9.29.4-14 = Frg. 2), Demetrius (P.E. 9.29.15a=
Frg. 4), and Ezekiel the Tragedian (P.E. 9.29.15b-16 =
Frg. 3).

5. That Moses' wisdom both preceded and exceeded that of
the Greek "sages," especially Plato, became a recurrent
theme within Hellenistic Jewish, and later, Christian apologetic. Cf. Artapanus, Frg. 3, par. 4; Aristobulus, Frg. 3,
par. 12.1; Philo, V. Mos.; Josephus, AgAp 1.1-5; 2.168;
Clement, Strom. 1.21.101; 25.165-66; 29.180-82; Eusebius,
Hist. eccl. 6.13.7; P.E. 9-11. Other Jewish "sage" traditions developed, for example, around Enoch. Cf. Jub. 4:
17-20; cf. 1 Enoch 12:3-4; 15:1. Cf. Wacholder, Eupolemus,
72-77; also Braun, History and Romance; Tiede, Charismatic
Figure.

Frg. 1b constitutes a miniature "cultural benefactor"
topos. A more fully elaborated version occurs in Artapanus,
Frg. 3. For an extended treatment of this richly diverse
literary tradition on which Eupolemus draws, cf. K. Thraede,
"Erfinder II (geistesgeschichtlich)," RAC 5 (1962) 1191-
1278; also "Das Lob des Erfinders. Bemerkungen zur Analyse
der Heuremata-Kataloge," Rheinisches Museum für Philologie
N.F. 105 (1962) 158-86. Also, A. Kleingünther, ΠΡΩΤΟΣ
ΕΥΡΕΤΗΣ, Philologus Suppl. 26.1 (1933).

6. That the Phoenicians invented the alphabet (γράμματα)
was a well-established, though not unchallenged, tradition
in antiquity. Cf. Herodotus 5.58; Athenaeus 1.28c; Pliny,
Nat. Hist. 7.192-93; Diodorus Siculus 3.67.1; 5.74.1; also
Plato, Phdr. 274 C-D; Diodorus Siculus 1.9.2; 69.5. Cf.
Artapanus, Frgs. 1, 2, and 3, par. 4; Pseudo-Eupolemus,
Frg. 1, par. 3-4; also Wacholder, Eupolemus, 77-83. On
the origin of the alphabet, cf. P. K. McCarter, The Antiquity of the Greek Alphabet and the Early Phoenician Scripts
(Harvard Semitic Monographs 9; Missoula: Scholars Press,
1975).

7. There were many candidates for the status of "first
lawgiver." Cf. Pliny, Nat. Hist. 7.191; Euripides, Supp.
352-53; Isocrates, Helen 35-37; also Diogenes Laertius
1.40. On Moses as the pre-eminent lawgiver, cf. Philo,
V. Mos. 2.1-65; Josephus, AgAp 2.154-89; also Hecataeus
of Abdera in Diodorus Siculus 1.94.1. Cf. Gager, Moses,
25-112; Wacholder, Eupolemus, 83-96. On the Christian
appropriation of this tradition, cf. W. J. Malley,
Hellenism and Christianity: The Conflict Between Hellenic
and Christian Wisdom in the CONTRA GALILAEOS of Julian the
Apostate and the CONTRA JULIANUM of St. Cyril of Alexandria
(Analecta Gregoriana. Cura Pontificae Universitatis
Gregorianae edita, Vol. 210. Series Facultatis Theologiae:
Sectio B, n. 68; Rome: Universita Gregorina Editrice, 1978)
254-58.

8. This fragment occurs in a chapter (ch. 21) where Clement
seeks to demonstrate that Jewish laws and institutions are
of far greater antiquity than the philosophy of the Greeks.
In the immediate context, he stresses that Solomon antedated the Greek sages, and cites this testimony from
Alexander Polyhistor to document Solomon's renown among
his neighboring kings in Phoenicia and Egypt.

9. 2 Chr 2:14 suggests that "Dan," not "David" must have
been read originally. Freudenthal, 55, suggests that the
similarity between the abbreviation for David (ΔΑΔ) and
Dan (ΔΑΝ) would have easily led to such a scribal error,
although the fault may have been Polyhistor's. The same
problem occurs in Frg. 2b, par. 34.1. The MSS in both
cases read "David," however.

10. Stählin, GCS (52), 80, app. crit., proposes that
Clement has derived "Hyperon" by misconstruing the words
ὑπὲρ ὧν ἂν αὐτὸν ἐρωτήσῃς in Frg. 2b, par. 34.2. Cf.
Freudenthal, 209.

11. This fragment, tracing the major leaders of Israel
from Moses to Solomon, and concentrating on the accomplishments of the latter, is preceded by quotations from Polyhistor witnessing to Moses (Ezekiel the Tragedian, Demetrius, et al.), and followed by other quotations from Polyhistor describing the geography of Jerusalem.

12. The title is problematic. No such work is attested
elsewhere, and it is not related to the Apocalypse of
Elijah (cf. Denis, Introduction, 163-69). Elijah is nowhere mentioned in the following paragraphs, nor in any
of the other fragments. Accordingly, Freudenthal, 208,
rejected this as the title of Eupolemus' work, favoring
instead the one cited by Clement (cf. Frg. 1a). Jacoby
conjectures that Polyhistor referred to a numbered sub-
division of the larger work which preceded Eupolemus'
discussion of 'Ελεί (Eli), who is mentioned in Frg. 2b,
par. 8. Fallon and Attridge note that the title as given,
or perhaps some variation thereof, may not be entirely inappropriate, given the recurrent interest in prophecy
exhibited in the fragments: Moses and Joshua prophesy (Frg.
1b, par. 30.1); Nathan (Frg. 1b, par. 6); Jeremiah (Frg. 4).
Fallon and Attridge, 8, "Perhaps Eupolemus wrote in part
to clarify the place of prophecy in the Jewish state" (cf.
1 Macc 4:46). Cf. above note 2. Also Wacholder, Eupolemus,
21-26.

13. Cf. Deut 29:5; also Exod 7:7 and Deut 34:7.

14. Josh 24:29; 14:7; Num 14:30-34 (110-(40+40)=30).
Cf. Walter, JS, ad loc.; Wacholder, Eupolemus, 107-108.

15. Josh 18:1. LXX: Σηλω   MT: שׁילה   Cf. Frg. 1b, par.
14: Σηλωμ.

16. Because the abrupt transition from Joshua to Samuel
completely omits the period of the judges, Freudenthal,
121, proposes a lacuna after par. 1. Cf. app. crit.

17. 1 Sam 8:4-22; 9:27-10:27.

18. How Eupolemus derived a 21-year reign for Saul is unclear. The most pertinent OT reference is 1 Sam 13:1 (MT:
"Saul was one year old when he became king, and he reigned
two years"), but the textual traditions, especially the LXX,
are unclear. Josephus provides conflicting testimony as
to the length of Saul's reign: 20 years (Ant. 10.143) and
40 years, i.e., 18 years prior to Samuel's death, after that
22 years (Ant. 6.378). For the various solutions offered
in the textual tradition, cf. notes in LCL, ad loc. A 40-
year reign is given in Acts 13:21. Cf. Beginnings 4.151;
Wacholder, Eupolemus, 108.

19. Doubtless, Polyhistor's error, though an understandable one for a pagan unfamiliar with the biblical text. He
may, however, have conflated the story of Ishbosheth, Saul's
son who reigned for 2 years, with the account of David's
accession (2 Sam. 2:8-11). Cf. Fallon and Attridge, 9-10.
The solution proposed by B, that David was Saul's son-in-
law (γαμβρόν) has biblical support (1 Sam 18:27), but is
clearly secondary since υἱόν is the more difficult reading.

20. Eupolemus' account of David's exploits and the extent
of his reign considerably exceeds the biblical account. The
OT records his victories over the Syrians (2 Sam 8:3-8; 10:
6-19; cf. 1 Chr 18:3-8; 19:10-19), Idumeans, i.e., Edomites
(2 Sam 8:13-14; cf. 1 Chr 18:12-13; also 1 Kgs 11:15-17),
Ammonites (2 Sam 10:1-19; 11:1-27; 12:26-31; cf. 1 Chr 19:
1-15; 20:1-3), and Moabites (2 Sam 8:2; cf. 1 Chr 18:2).
David's exploits over Assyrians, Phoenicians, Itureans
(cf. 1 Chr 5:18-19), Nabateans, and Nabdeans are not mentioned in the biblical accounts. Oddly, Eupolemus omits
entirely David's wars with the Philistines (2 Sam 5:17-25;
8:1; 21:15-22; 23:8-39; cf. 1 Chr 14:1-17; 18:1; 20:4-8).
The political and geographical situation envisioned here is
Maccabean, not Davidic. Commagene, a region in northern
Syria, is not mentioned in the LXX, though frequent in
Josephus (cf. Ant. 18.53, 140; 19.276, 338, 355; J.W. 5.461;
7.219, 224-25). "Assyrians in Gilead" is puzzling. Γαλα-
δηνη, the Hellenized form of Γαλααδ (גלעד) occurs frequently in Josephus, who commonly identifies biblical place
names with names in use in his own time (cf. Ant. 1.324;
2.32; 4.96, 173 passim). Cf. Gifford 4.317; Wacholder,
Eupolemus, 133. "Assyrians" (cf. Gen 10:11) here may refer
to the Ammonites (cf. 2 Sam 10-12 and 1 Chr 19), or more
likely to the Syrians. Eupolemus may be drawing on Ps 82
(83):2-8 (cf. Freudenthal, 115), which may also account
for his inclusion of Phoenicians. His references to Nabateans and Nabdeans are clearly anachronistic. The Nabateans
entered Edom and Moab sometime prior to the 4th century
B.C.E., but there is no evidence of their existence in
Davidic times. They had become well established and power-
ful by the Maccabean period (cf. 1 Macc 5:25; 9:35; cf.
2 Macc 5:8; Gen 25:13 ?; also Ovid, Metam. 1.61; Juvenal,
Sat. 11.26). "Nabdeans" may be a corrupt doublet, or a
scribal error for Ζαβαδαιους (cf. 1 Macc 12:31; Walter,
JS, ad loc.). Gifford, 4.312, suggests that it is perhaps
a variation of Ναβαιωϑ, first-born son of Ishmael (Gen 35:
13). Also, cf. 1QapGen 21:8-19. Cf. Wacholder, Eupolemus,
131-39.

21. Obviously Hiram, though the spelling is unusual. MT:
חירם, חורם, חירום. LXX: Χειραμ, Χιραμ. Josephus: Ειρωμος,
'Ιερωμος, Ειραμος, Χειραμος. Cf. Herodotus, 7.98: Σιρωμος.
Cf. Freudenthal, 108, 209; Wacholder, Eupolemus, 135-37.

22. In the biblical account, David's only contact with
Hiram is recorded in 2 Sam 5:11-12 (cf. 1 Chr 14:1), where
they are on friendly terms (cf. 1 Kgs 5:1,7 = MT/LXX 5:15,
21). Ps 82:8 (LXX), however, includes the inhabitants of
Tyre among the adversaries of the psalmist, whom Eupolemus
doubtless would have taken to be David (Walter, JS, ad loc.).
Tribute payments are mentioned in 2 Sam 8:11-12.

23. The treaty with Vaphres is apocryphal. In the biblical account, David has no dealings with an Egyptian king.
Where Eupolemus derives the name Vaphres is not known
(cf. Wacholder, Eupolemus, 135-36). Jer 44:30 (LXX: 51:30)
mentions a Pharaoh Hophra (LXX: Ουαφρη; MT: יחפרע), probably the Ουαφρης mentioned in the Egyptian king lists as
the seventh (or eighth) king in the 26th dynasty (cf. Frg.
68 of Manetho in Waddell, LCL, 170), who ruled as successor
of Psammetichus ca. 588-69 B.C.E. He is referred to by
Herodotus as 'Απρίης   (2.161; 4.159; also Diodorus Siculus
1.68.1). He may have been introduced here in connection
with Hiram because he was a near contemporary with Hiram
III, king of Tyre (552-32 B.C.E.). Cf. Attridge and Fallon,
11.

24. 2 Sam 7:1-29; cf. 1 Chr 17:1-27.

25. ἰδρύω, perf. mid./pass. inf. = "to be situated," "lie,"
though also used in an active sense (LSJ, s.v.). Cf.
Herodotus, 2.42; also, cf. Gifford, 4.318; Wacholder,
Eupolemus, 140.

26. Cf. 2 Sam 24:15-25; cf. 1 Chr 21:14-22:1; also
2 Chr 3:1.

27. ἰδρύω, pres. mid./pass. inf. (so Mras) = "set up,"
"found," "dedicate," esp. temples (LSJ, s.v.). Cf. Plato,
Prt. 322 A. Also, cf. app. crit.

28. 1 Kgs 5:3; 1 Chr 22:8; 28:3; cf. 2 Sam 7:1-17.

29. The OT nowhere refers to an angel named Dianathan.
The two separate traditions concerning David and the temple
site may have become conflated here, the one mentioning an
angel (2 Sam 24; 1 Chr 21), the other the prophet Nathan
(2 Sam 7; 1 Chr 17). Freudenthal, 119-21, conjectures that
the text originally read: ἄγγελον δ' αὐτῷ ἔπεμψε διὰ Νάθαν
(cf. app. crit.), with ἄγγελον, or perhaps ἀγγελίαν, understood as "message." Consequently, διὰ Νάθαν was misunder-
stood as the proper name of the sender: ΔΙΑΝΑΘΑΝ. Attridge
and Fallon, 12, suggest another possibility: εἶναι δ' αὐτῷ
ῥῆμα διὰ Νάθαν (cf. 2 Sam 7:4 and 1 Chr 17:3) might have
been misconstrued so that ῥῆμα was understood as ὄνομα
and ΔΙΑΝΑΘΑΝ as the proper name itself. Whether either of
these is plausible, some such misunderstanding must have
occurred, probably by Polyhistor, for the present form of
the text to have resulted. Cf. Wacholder, Eupolemus,
142-43.

30. David's preparations for the construction of the temple
are recorded only in Chr. Cf. 1 Chr 14 and 22, esp. verses
2-5, 14-15, and 1 Chr 28 and 29, esp. 29:1-5. Also, cf.
Exod 25:3-7. On the conspicuous absence of iron in
Eupolemus' list, cf. Wacholder, Eupolemus, 146-47.

31. David's commissioning ships to be built represents
another embellishment of the OT account. It doubtless
derives from 1 Kgs 9:26-28 and 2 Chr 8:17-18, which mention
Solomon's shipbuilding activity at Eziongeber near Eloth
(LXX: Αιλαϑ) "on the shores of the Red Sea, in the land
of Edom." Cf. Wacholder, Eupolemus, 148. "Elana" is
another geographical anachronism. Cf. Strabo 16.4.4;
16.2.30; also Freudenthal, 209-10; Wacholder, Eupolemus,
146-47.

32. Eupolemus expands the OT account by attributing the
initiative for procuring the gold for the temple to
David. Cf. 1 Kgs 9:28; 10:11; 1 Chr 22:14; 29:4; 2 Chr 8:
18. On Ophir, cf. Wacholder, Eupolemus, 149-50.

33. So, 2 Sam 5:4; 1 Kgs 2:11; 1 Chr 29:27.

34. The transfer of power is peaceful, as in Chr (contrast
1 Kgs 1-2). Solomon's age at the time of his accession to
the throne is not stated in the MT (cf. 1 Kgs 2:12), although he is said to have been young (1 Kgs 3:7; 1 Chr 22:
5; 29:1; also Josephus, Ant. 8.1). Eupolemus here agrees
with, and possibly provides independent testimony to, the
LXX textual tradition on 1 Kgs 2:12, represented by Codex
A, among others, which gives his age as 12 years. Also,
S. 'Olam. Rab. 14; Sipre Deut. 357; Gen. Rab. C 1294-95.
Josephus, Ant. 8.211, implies that he was 14 years old when
he became king ("having reigned 80 of his 94 years").
This age given here agrees with the length of reign given
in Frg. 3. Cf. Wacholder, Eupolemus, 109-110.

35. This is another striking departure from the biblical
text. Eli, of course, was the priest of Shiloh in the
time of Samuel (cf. 1 Sam 1-4), not a "high priest" in the
time of Solomon. In 1 Kgs 1:32, Solomon's accession occurs
in the presence of Zadok the priest, Nathan the prophet,
and Benaniah, the son of Jehoiada. According to the
Chronicler (1 Chr 29:22), Zadok becomes the priest under
Solomon. How and why "Eli" occurs in Eupolemus' text is
unclear. He may have written "Abiathar, the last priest
of the family of Eli" (cf. 1 Kgs 2:27; 1 Chr 27:34), all
of which may have dropped out except the name of Eli (cf.
Walter, JS, ad loc.). Or, "Zadok" may have originally stood
in the text, only to have been changed because of the dis-
pute over the legitimacy of priestly families, especially
during the Maccabean period. Cf. Wacholder, Eupolemus,
131, 151-54. Or, again, the fault may be Polyhistor's.
Cf. Freudenthal, 121.

36. Cf. 1 Chr 28:1; 29:6, 24; 1 Kgs 4:7 ?. The reference
to the twelve tribes may have been inspired by Ezra 6:17
(=1 Esdras 7:8 LXX).

37. The letters exchanged between Solomon and Vaphres in
31.1 and 32.1 have no biblical basis, though in 1 Kgs 3:
1-2 Solomon is said to have entered a marriage alliance
with an Egyptian king (also, cf. 1 Kgs 11:40). Though at
one time thought to be genuine archival materials (Movers,
Kuhlmey), they are now regarded as Eupolemus' own fabri-
cations. Cf. Freudenthal, 109-12, and discussion in
Wacholder, Eupolemus, 155-58, also 167-78, where a similar
tradition is noted in late rabbinic texts. As Eupolemus'
own compositions, they illustrate the practice among
Hellenistic historians of composing letters and other
archival documents to include in their works. Cf., e.g.,
Ep. Arist. 28; 1 Macc 11:30; 12:6,19; 15:1; Josephus, Ant.
8.50-55; also, E. Norden, Die Antike Kunstprosa (2 vols.;
8th ed., Leipzig/Berlin: Teubner, 1915; repr. Darmstadt:
Wissenschaftliche Buchgesellschaft, 1981) 1.88; J. Sykutris,
"Epistolographie," PW Suppl. 5 (1931) 185-220, esp. 208-10.
These first two letters are built on and modeled after the
second set of letters between Solomon and Hiram, which do
have biblical basis. Cf. 1 Kgs 5:3-6, 8-9; 1 Chr 2:3-10,
11-16; also, cf. Josephus, Ant. 8.50-54. Useful in
assessing their conformity to Hellenistic epistolographic
conventions is F. J. X. Exler, The Form of the Ancient
Greek Letter. A Study in Greek Epistolography (Washington,
D.C.: Catholic University of America, 1923); also, C. B.
Welles, Royal Correspondence in the Hellenistic Period. A
Study in Greek Epigraphy (New Haven: Yale University Press,
1934), esp. xxxvii-xli on "The Use of Letters in Hellenistic
Diplomacy"; W. Schubart, "Bemerkungen zum Stile hellenistischer Königsbriefe," Archiv für Papyrusforschung 6 (1920)
324-47; recent bibliography in N. Dahl, "Letter," IDB
Suppl., 538-41. On their structural similarities to Ep.
Arist., cf. Freudenthal, 110; Wacholder, Eupolemus, 168-69;
on similarity of language with that of Hellenistic Egypt,
cf. Freudenthal, 210.

38. Cf. below, note 49.

39. Mras's conjectural deletion is based on the omission
of καί in the MS tradition at the comparable point in par.
33.1.

40. Cf. below, note 59.

41. Cf. below, note 61.

42. The Greek syntax is awkward here, but is improved
somewhat by Mras's conjectural addition: ὧν καὶ τὰ πλήθη
<καὶ> ἐξ ὧν εἰσι κ.τ.λ. The translation here follows
Mras's suggestion.

43. This spelling follows Kuhlmey's emendation of
Σεβριθίτου (cf. app. crit.), thus conforming it to known
Egyptian geographical divisions. Cf. Herodotus 2.164-67;
Strabo 17.1.2-54, esp. 1.18-20, 24, 27; Pliny, Nat. Hist.
5.9.49-50. All the nomes mentioned by Eupolemus are
located in the Nile Delta. Cf. Freudenthal, 210; Wacholder,
Eupolemus, 163-64.

44. Supplying this phrase follows the suggestion of
Müller. Cf. app. crit.

45. Cf. app. crit. for alternative renderings of this
nome in the textual tradition. Also, Freudenthal, 210.

46. Since "ὡς 'when' scarcely ever takes ἄν" (Smyth, par.
2399a), ὡς ἄν should perhaps be emended to ἕως ἄν. Cf.
Sophocles Aj. 1117; Ph. 1330. Cf. discussion in Giff., 4.
319. Also, Viger's emendation of γενομένης is supported by
Plutarch Alex. 683 C and Polybius 5.14.7. Cf. Giff., 4.319.

47. 1 Kgs 5:2-6 (MT/LXX: 3 Kgdms 5:17-20); 2 Chr 2:2-9;
Josephus, Ant. 8.51-52. The Hebrew, Greek, and Latin
versions of the letters may be compared in P. Vannutelli,
Libri Synoptici Veteris Testamenti (2 vols.; Rome: Pontifi-
cal Biblical Institute, 1931-34) 1.212-21, where the MT,
LXX (with app. crit.), and Vulgate are arranged in parallel
columns, accompanied by the texts from Josephus.

        The letters in Chr are generally longer, and more
elaborate than those in Kgs. The temple as the center of
cultic activity is more prominently emphasized (2 Chr 2:
4,6). The language of the letters is more liturgical, with
special emphasis on the preeminent position of God (2 Chr
2:5-6, 12). The request for a skilled architect to oversee
the work is unique (2 Chr 2:7, 13-14). The list of materials
needed for the work is more detailed (2 Chr 2:7-8, 14), as
is the list of provisions for the workers (2 Chr 2:10, 15).
The building project is more grandiose, including a royal
palace in addition to the temple (2 Chr 2:1,12). In contrast to Kgs and Chr, the letters in Eupolemus and Josephus
are cast in formal epistolary style, complete with salu-
tation. Josephus, Ant. 8.55, also reports that the
Solomon-Hiram correspondence was still present in the
Tyrian archives in his own day. Cf. AgAp 1.106-27. On
Eupolemus' dependence on 1 Esdras, cf. Wacholder, Eupolemus,
160-61.

48. With the addition of "Sidon and Phoenicia" to the
biblical description of Hiram as "king of Tyre" (also
Josephus), Eupolemus enlarges his sphere of influence,
thereby enhancing Solomon's status as a world ruler, since
the letters cast Hiram in the role of a subordinate vassal
king.

49. If φίλος πατρικός is used here in the technical sense
of "royal advisor," as it commonly is in Hellenistic royal
correspondence, it may reduce Hiram's status before Solomon even further. Cf. Welles, Royal Correspondence, Nos.
22.9 and 25.8, though the phrase occurs in the plural.
Cf., however, SEG 1. No. 364.2-3: [Pelops, son of Alex-
ander], φίλος ὢν τοῦ βασιλέως Πτολεμαίου. Also, SIG 1. No.
189.3. Examples of φίλοι in the technical sense of the
"king's advisors": Welles, Nos. 6.6; 14.9; 22.13; 25.25;
45.3; 49.2; 75.2; also, cf. SEG 7. Nos. 1.6; 3.2; 8.1;
62.3; 8. No. 357.1; OGIS 100.1; 219.45; 256.3. Also, cf.
1 Macc 10:65; 2 Macc 11:14. On φίλοι as a group of royal
advisors and later as a court title in the Hellenistic
period, cf. F. Geyer, "Lysimakos," PW 14 (1928) 23-24; G.
Corradi, Studi ellenistici (Torino: Societa editrice
internazionale, 1929) 231-55; 318-47; A. Momigliano,
"Honorati amici," Athenaeum 11 (1933) 136-41; M. Holleaux,
"Une inscription de Séleucie-de Piérie," Bulletin de
Correspondance Hellenique 57 (1933) 6-67, esp. 31-35;
Welles, Royal Correspondence (1934), p. 44; H. Kortenbeutel,
"Philos," PW 20 (1941) 95-103; Fraser, Ptolemaic Alexandria,
1.102-104, and extensive bibliography in 2.183, n. 62.

50. Eupolemus alone includes the formal greeting χαίρειν
which is typical of royal letters of the period. Cf.
Welles, Royal Correspondence 2.4; 4.1; 5.2; passim. Also,
cf. Acts 23:26. Cf. H. G. Meecham, Light from Ancient
Letters (New York: Macmillan, 1923) 96-127, esp. 116.

51. The title appropriately expresses the sentiments of
2 Chr 2:5. Cf. Add Esth 8:12q (LXX); 2 Macc 3:36; also
1:16.

52. Cf. 2 Chr 2:12; Gen 14:18-22.

53. God's command for Solomon to request the services
of Hiram is another unbiblical detail.

54. These regions are not specified in the biblical accounts. As before (cf. above, note 20), the list (including
Judaea and Arabia mentioned below) appears to reflect
the geographical realities of Eupolemus' own day, though
he may have derived the names themselves from the biblical
account. On "Galilee," cf. 1 Kgs 9:11; 2 Kgs 15:29; Isa
9:1; also 1 Macc 5:9-10, 14-23, 55; Josephus, J.W. 3.35-37.
On "Samaria," cf. 1 Kgs 13:32; 16:24; also Ezra 4:8-24;
Neh 4:2; Josephus, J.W. 3.48. In any case, the extent of
Solomon's influence is exaggerated. Ammon and Moab were
ruled by their own kings independently of Solomon. Cf.
Wacholder, Eupolemus, 164-65.

55. The numbers differ from the biblical accounts. In
1 Kgs 5:11 Solomon gave Hiram 20,000 cors of wheat and
20,000 cors of oil - annually. In 2 Chr 2:10, the amount
of provisions is larger: 20,000 cors of wheat, 20,000 cors
of barley, 20,000 baths of wine, and 10,000 baths of oil.
In Eupolemus, the amounts are smaller, but are distributed
monthly, thus making the total provisions far exceed both
Kgs and Chr (cf. Josephus, Ant. 8.57). The cor (כור) is
a Hebrew measure, the artaba Persian. As a dry measure,
a cor was approximately 3-6 bushels; as a liquid measure,
approximately 35-60 gallons. Cf. IDB 4.834. The use of
such measures, as Eupolemus illustrates, inevitably re-
required their translation into meaningful equivalents,
not always successfully. Cf. Josephus, Ant. 3.321; 15.314;
also 11.16; 12.140; also Herodotus 1.192. Cf. Wacholder,
Eupolemus, 165-67.

56. The provision of oil is mentioned in 1 Kgs 5:11 and
2 Chr 2:15, but Judaea as its supplier is unique to
Eupolemus.

57. ἱερεῖα, usually sacrificial animals, but also "cattle
slaughtered for food" (Hippocrates, Aff. 52; Xenophon,
Cyr. 1.4.17. LSJ, s.v.). Cf. Giff., 4.320. Eupolemus
alone mentions cattle from Arabia. Walter, JS ad loc.,
suggests that he might have been influenced by Ps 71:10
(LXX). Cf. Diodorus Siculus 2.50.2. Arabia here apparently refers to the provice between the Dead Sea and the Gulf
of Aqaba. Cf. Wacholder, Eupolemus, 165; also cf. Frg. 2b,
par. 30.7.

58. 1 Kgs 5:8-9 (MT/LXX: 3 Kgdms 5:21-23); 2 Chr 2:10-15;
Josephus, Ant. 8.53-54.

59. In the biblical account, Hiram praises Solomon
effusively (2 Chr 2:11-12), but his subordination to Solomon
is not explicit as it is here when he addresses him as
βασιλεὺς μέγας. In fact, they cut a treaty as equals (1 Kgs
5:12). The use of this title reflects Hellenistic practice:
Antiochus III: OGIS 230.5; 237.12; 239.1; 240.1; 245.18,
40; 249.2; 250.2; 746.1; Antiochus VII Sidetes: OGIS 255.1,
2; 256.2, 3. References cited in Hengel, Judaism and
Hellenism, 2.64, n. 284, who notes that the title is
rare with the Ptolemies, e.g. Ptolemy III Euergetes:
OGIS 54.1ff.

60. 2 Chr 2:12; also Gen 14:19. For a structural comparison with the berakoth of 1 Kgs 5:7 and 2 Chr 2:10-11,
cf. Wacholder, Eupolemus, 120.

61. The number of those sent by Hiram is unspecified in
the biblical account. Eupolemus' 80,000 workers supplied
by Vaphres and Hiram each are apparently derived by rounding off the number of workers conscripted by Solomon
(153,300 in 1 Kgs 5:13-16; 153,600 in 2 Chr 2:16-17; also

61. (cont.) 2:2), and dividing it by half. Or, the figure
80,000 may have been derived from 2 Chr 2:10, where the
total amount of provisions is 80,000 cors.

62. A skilled artisan is requested by Solomon in 2 Chr
2:7 and agreed to by Hiram in 2 Chr 2:13-14, where he is
named Huramabi (a detail omitted by Eupolemus), and identified as "the son of a woman of the duaghters of Dan,"
whose father was "a man of Tyre" (2 Chr 2:14; also 4:16).
In 1 Kgs 7:13-14, he is identified as "Hiram from Tyre"
(not to be confused with the king himself) "the son of a
widow of the tribe of Naphtali," whose father was a "man
of Tyre." All the MSS in Eupolemus, however, read "David,"
an error probably resulting from the similarity between
the abbreviation for David ($\overline{\Delta A \Delta}$) and Dan ($\Delta AN$). Accordingly, Freudenthal, 55, emends the text to read "Dan."
Cf. Frg. 2a, line 9, and note 9 above.

63. His credentials are equally impressive, indeed more
detailed, in the biblical account. Cf. 2 Chr 2:7, 14; 1 Kgs
7:14. In 1 Kgs 7:15-44, his smelting work is detailed.
Cf. 2 Chr 4:6.

64. Cf. 1 Chr 28:1; cf. above, note 49.

65. There is no record in the biblical account of a trip
by Solomon to Lebanon. Cf. 1 Kgs 5:2; 2 Chr 2:3.

66. Solomon's transporting the lumber by sea to Joppa and
by land to Jerusalem is unbiblical. Cf. 2 Chr 2:16;
Ezra 3:7.

67. This would have been a year after his accession (cf.
above, Frg. 2b, par. 30.8), whereas in the biblical account,
the temple is begun in the fourth year of his reign (1 Kgs
6:1; 2 Chr 3:2). Cf. above, note 34. Wacholder, Eupolemus,
155: "This is supposedly the first allusion to the bar
mitzvah tradition found anywhere."

68. Cf. above, note 61. In 1 Kgs 5:13-18 the labor force
consists of conscripted Israelites (cf. 1 Kgs 9:22; 12:4),
whereas in 2 Chr 2:17-18 they are said to have been aliens
living in Israel.

69. The method of distributing provisions mentioned by
Eupolemus is unbiblical.

70. These dimensions for the sanctuary (ναός, cf.
Wacholder, Eupolemus, 174, n. 4) agree with neither the
biblical accounts nor with Josephus, and may be compared
as follows:

		Length	Width	Height (in cubits)
1 Kgs 6:2	MT	60	20	30
	LXX	40	20	25
2 Chr 3:4	MT	60	20	120
	LXX	60	20	120
Josephus, Ant. 8.64 J.W. 5.215		60	20	60/120 ?
Eupolemus		60	60	unspecified (20?)

The 60-cubit width Eupolemus may have derived from Ezra
6:3, where the width of the Second Temple is given as 60
cubits. The reference to a 60-cubit width is omitted by
BON (cf. app. crit.). Kuhlmey suggested that it was
originally a reference to the height: ὕψος πηχῶν ξ´, or
that the κ´ was misconstrued as ξ´: πλάτος πηχῶν κ´.
Cf. Freudenthal, 211; Wacholder, Eupolemus, 176-77

71. Wacholder, Eupolemus, 175, renders οἰκοδομή as
"masonry," hence "the thickness of the masonry and its
foundations." Freudenthal, 211, takes it as a reference
to the vestibule, otherwise unmentioned by Eupolemus. In
any case, the width of the foundations is not specified
in the biblical accounts. Eupolemus also omits reference
to the dimensions of the Holy of Holies (cf. 1 Kgs 6:3;
2 Chr 3:4, 8-9). In fact, several significant features
of the biblical description of the temple are absent from
Eupolemus: the elaborate three-story side chambers sur-
rounding the central structure (1 Kgs 6:5-6), the Most
Holy Place (1 Kgs 6:5, 16, 19-20; 2 Chr 3:8-9; Ezek 41:3-4),
the cherubim within the Most Holy Place (1 Kgs 6:23-28; 2 Chr
3:10-14), the details of the palace and administrative
complex (1 Kgs 7:1-8), separate account of Hiram's work
(1 Kgs 7:15-47), the ten bronze lavers on wheeled stands
(1 Kgs 7:27-37; 2 Chr 4:6), the speech of dedication
(1 Kgs 8:12-53; 2 Chr 6:1-42). It has been plausibly
suggested that Eupolemus' account actually describes the
Second Temple. Cf. Wacholder, Eupolemus, 177.

72. The reference to Nathan is perhaps inferred from 1 Chr
28:11-12, where David is said to have transferred the
building plans to Solomon. Nathan, however, is not
mentioned by name. Cf. 2 Sam 7; 1 Chr 17.

73. Precisely what is envisioned in the mode of wall construction described here is unclear. No such details of how the outer walls of the temple were constructed are provided in Kgs and Chr, though Eupolemus may have been influenced here by 1 Kgs 6:36 and 7:12. Also, cf. Ezra 5:8; 6:4. Cf. Freudenthal, 211; Wacholder, Eupolemus, 178.

74. 1 Kgs 6:15-30; 2 Chr 3:5-7; cf. Ezek 41:16.

75. Here the translation follows the suggested emendation of Freudenthal, 211: χωνεύοντα rather than MSS χωννύντα, "stacking up." Cf. app. crit.

76. 1 Kgs 6:19-22; 2 Chr 3:4-9. The details about gold bricks and silver nails are added by Eupolemus. Cf. 2 Chr 3:9. Cf. Wacholder, Eupolemus, 179-80.

77. These details of the ceiling and the roof are unbiblical. Cf. however, 1 Kgs 6:9; 2 Chr 3:7; Ezek 40:13 (MT).

78. The finger-thick layer of gold covering the two pillars is added by Eupolemus to the biblical account (cf. 1 Kgs 7:15-22; 2 Chr 3:15-17; 4:12-13; also 2 Kgs 11:14; 23:3; 25:16-17; Ezek 40:49; 42:6; Jer 52:17,20). These dimensions differ slightly from the biblical account. In 1 Kgs 7:15 the circumference of each pillar is 12 cubits (LXX: 14 cubits; cf. Jer 52:21). Eupolemus wisely leaves the height of the pillars unspecified, a detail on which Kgs and Chr disagree: 18 cubits + 5-cubit capital according to 1 Kgs 7:15-16 (also Jer 52:21-22; though, cf. 2 Kgs 25:17), but 35 cubits + 5-cubit capital in 2 Chr 3:15 (LXX: Jer 52:21). Cf. also Herodotus 2.44; also Wacholder, Eupolemus, 181-83.

79. The translation here follows Seguier's emendation. Cf. app. crit.; also Freudenthal, 211.

80. Cf. 1 Kgs 7:49; 2 Chr 4:7, 20; also Exod 25:31-40; 37:17-24.

81. The seventy gold lamps are added by Eupolemus, rendering the description of the menorah more explicit. Cf. Wacholder, Eupolemus, 184-85.

82. Cf. 1 Kgs 6:33-36; 7:50; 2 Chr 4:22; also Ezek 41: 23-25. Cf. Wacholder, Eupolemus, 186-87.

83. The north portico supported by 48 bronze pillars is unbiblical, and it is not clear where Eupolemus derived this bit of information. He is perhaps dependent on 1 Kgs 7:31 (LXX), which refers to 48 pillars. Cf. Ezek 42:1-10; also Josephus, J.W. 5.185; Ant. 20.220-21. Cf. Freudenthal, 118; Wacholder, Eupolemus, 187-90, suggests that the LXX version of 1 Kgs 7:31 may have been dependent on Eupolemus.

84. In 1 Kgs 7:23-26 and 2 Chr 4:2-6 the bronze laver
(= Exod 30:18 passim), or "molten sea," is circular, not
square as in Eupolemus, with a diameter of 10 cubits, circumference of 30 cubits, and height of 5 cubits. Though
the dimensions are the same in Kgs and Chr, the laver in
Chr is said to have 1/3 more capacity. Cf. 1 Kgs 7:26
and 2 Chr 4:5. Cf. Wacholder, Eupolemus, 190-93.

85. The syntax describing what appears to be a rim sur-
rounding the base is difficult, and not altogether clear.
Cf. Exod 30:17-21; also Ezek 43:13.

86. In the biblical account, the laver rests on "twelve
bronze bulls" (Jer 52:20), whose height is not given. Cf.
1 Kgs 7:25-26; 2 Chr 4:4. Freudenthal, 211, emends the
text to conform to the biblical account. Cf. app. crit.
Eupolemus' description of how the pedestals were positioned
underneath the laver is unclear, as is its position within
the outer court. The syntax seems to suggest that the
laver was positioned "at the right of the altar" in the
outer court. His description of the pedestals may represent a conflation of the biblical account of the molten
sea and the ten lavers resting on wheeled stands.

87. The "speaker's podium" is mentioned only in 2 Chr 6:13,
and its dimensions are 5 x 5 x 3 cubits. From it Solomon
delivers the dedicatory speech (2 Chr 6:14-42; cf. 1 Kgs
8:12-57), which is omitted by Eupolemus. Cf. Wacholder,
Eupolemus, 193-94.

88. Cf. app. crit. Kuhlmey, apud Freudenthal, 211,
proposes κε' owing to dittography: κ' ἐπί. Cf. Wacholder,
Eupolemus, 195.

89. The presence of the altar is presupposed in 1 Kgs 8:22,
64; 9:25 (cf. 2 Kgs 16:14-15), but only described in 2 Chr
4:1, where its dimensions are given as 20 x 20 x 10 cubits.
Cf. Ezek 43:13-17. Also, cf. Josephus, AgAp 1.198;
Ant. 8.88. Also, Wacholder, Eupolemus, 194-96.

90. This elaborate device for protecting the temple from
defilement is not mentioned in the biblical account, but
appears to be derived by Eupolemus from the detailed description of the capitals of the two bronze pillars in
1 Kgs 7:15-22 and 2 Chr 3:15-17; cf. also 4:11-13. 2 Chr
4:13 mentions 400 pomegranates in connection with the
capital decoration. Cf. also Exod 39:25-26; 28:33; Sir
45:9; Josephus, J.W. 5.224; Mid. 4.6; cf. Lieberman, Hellenism, 173-6; Hengel, Judaism and Hellenism, 2.64, n. 285.

91. Cf. 1 Kgs 3:1; 9:15; Ezek 40:5; also Freudenthal,
211-12; Wacholder, Eupolemus, 196-201.

92. In the biblical account, the building project also
entails the palace and administrative complex (cf. 1 Kgs
3:1; 2 Chr 2:1; 8:2), with a fairly detailed architectural
description in 1 Kgs 7:1-12. In fact, this part of the
project is said to have taken 13 years to build (1 Kgs
7:1; cf. 9:18), whereas the building of the temple took
7 years (1 Kgs 6:38). Eupolemus does not mention the
duration of the building project.

93. Similar etymologies are given in Josephus, J.W. 6.348;
Ant. 7.67; AgAp 1.174; also Hecataeus of Abdera apud
Diodorus Siculus 40.3.3 = Stern, Greek and Latin Authors,
Frg. 11. Cf. Freudenthal, 212; Wacholder, Eupolemus,
204-208.

94. This detail is apparently derived from 1 Kgs 3:4 and
2 Chr 1:3, even though it is out of sequence here. The
reference to Shiloh is puzzling. Cf. 1 Sam 1:3; 4:3. Cf.
Freudenthal, 212; Wacholder, Eupolemus, 208-11.

95. 1 Kgs 8:4; 2 Chr 5:5.

96. 1 Kgs 7:48-51; 2 Chr 4:19-22; also 1 Macc 4:49.
Cf. Wacholder, Eupolemus, 212-13.

97. The size of the offering is considerably smaller than
the one described in 1 Kgs 8:62 and 2 Chr 7:4 (22,000 oxen
and 120,000 sheep) -- one of the few instances where
Eupolemus is more modest in his description. Cf. also
1 Kgs 8:5; 2 Chr 5:6.

98. These fantastic "grand totals" exceed even the
exaggerated figures of 1 Chr 22:14 (cf. 29:4,7) where
David is said to have provided 100,000 talents of gold,
1,000,000 talents of silver, and immeasurable amounts of
bronze and iron for the building of the temple. More
modest figures are given in 1 Kgs 9:14, 28. Cf. also
2 Chr 9:13; 1 Kgs 10:10, 14; Exod 38:24-31. For the
various efforts to emend the text, cf. app. crit. Cf.
Wacholder, Eupolemus, 213-15; Freudenthal, 212, suggests
that μυριάδων was added later to enhance the otherwise
unimpressive amount of 460 talents.

99. The workers' return home is recorded in 1 Kgs 8:66
and 2 Chr 7:10, but the 10-shekel bonus is added by
Eupolemus, effectively underscoring the generosity of
Solomon. The talent, however, did not equal one shekel,
as Eupolemus states; it was rather equivalent to approximately 3,000 shekels. Cf. IDB 4.832; Wacholder, Eupolemus,
215-16.

100. Cf. 1 Kgs 5:11.

101. In 1 Kgs 9:11, Solomon is said to have given Hiram
20 cities in Galilee as a gesture of gratitude, though
the biblical account oddly notes Hiram's displeasure. 2 Chr
8:2 smooths over this feature, noting that Solomon rebuilt
cities given to him by Hiram. (cf. Josephus, Ant. 8.141-43).
In any case, the biblical account makes no mention of the
golden pillar given by Solomon to Hiram as a token of
gratitude. This tradition, however, is mentioned elsewhere. Immediately after this fragment (P.E. 9.34.19),
Polyhistor cites Theophilus (2nd cent. B.C.E.; cf. R.
Laqueur, PW, ser. 2, 5(1934) 2137-38 = FGrH 733, Frg. 1),
who reported that Solomon returned to Hiram the unused
gold (cf. 1 Kgs 9:11-14), and that Hiram made a full-
length statue of his daughter, using the golden pillar to
cover it. Another tradition relates that this was the
daughter Hiram had given Solomon in marriage (cf. Laetus,
apud Tatian, Oratio ad Graecos 37 = Stern, Greek and
Latin Authors, No. 29, pp. 128-30). The golden pillar
tradition is also mentioned by Menander of Ephesus (2nd
cent. B.C.E. = FGrH 783, Frg. 1), apud Josephus, AgAp
1.118; cf. also Ant. 8.144-49; also Dio = FGrH 785, Frg.
1 = Josephus, AgAp 1.113. Herodotus 2.44 mentions a golden
pillar which stood in the temple of Heracles. Cf.
Wacholder, Eupolemus, 217-23.

102. Immediately after the long quote from Eupolemus
(taken from Polyhistor) describing Solomon's accomplishments (= Frg. 2b), Eusebius includes a brief text from
Theophilus (from Polyhistor) relating to Hiram. Then
follows this snippet (taken again from Polyhistor) which
completes his treatment of Solomon. It is followed by
descriptions of Jerusalem.

103. Literally, "each of which was of 500 gold (pieces)."
Cf. 1 Kgs 10:16-17 and 2 Chr 9:15-16 which mention 500
shields. Eupolemus is perhaps influenced here by Cant 4:4.

104. 1 Kgs 11:42 and 2 Chr 9:30 record a 40-year reign,
though his age at the time of his death is not given.
1 Kgs 11:4 implies an older age. Josephus, Ant. 8.211
says that he reigned 80 of his 94 years. Eupolemus'
figures here agree with Frg. 2b, par. 30.8.

105. Following various witnesses to the geography of
Jerusalem, Eusebius continues his treatment of major
events of Israel's history with this fragment (again
taken from Polyhistor), followed by other testimonies
to the captivity, and to the rise of Persia.

106. This is probably a reference to Jehoiakim, king of
Judah (609-598 B.C.E.), during whose reign Jeremiah prophesied (Jer 1:3; 26:1; cf. 2 Kgs 23:31-24:6; 2 Chr 36:
4-8), and against whom he railed (Jer 22:18-19). It may,
however, refer to his son and successor Jehoiachin, also
called Jeconiah (1 Chr 3:16) and Coniah (Jer 22:24), who
ruled 598-597 B.C.E. (cf. 2 Kgs 24:6-17; 2 Chr 36:8-10).
The two would be easily confused because the LXX transliteration of their Hebrew names (יהויקים and יהויכין) is
often identical: 'Ιωακειμ/'Ιωακιμ (cf. 2 Kgs 24:6 and
2 Chr 36:5). Jehoiachin is rendered Ιεχονιας/Ειεχονιας
in 2 Chr 36:8,9. Not all the events mentioned in this
fragment occurred in the reign of Jehoiakim, however.
The king of Judah exiled to Babylon (par. 5) was Jehoiachin (2 Kgs 24:12; 2 Chr 36:10), though 2 Chr 36:6 implies
that Jehoiakim was also exiled. The seizure of the
temple booty mentioned at the end of the fragment occurred
under Zedekiah (cf. 2 Kgs 25:1-17; Jer 52:1-23; 2 Chr 36:
11-21). Eupolemus has telescoped events from the reigns
of Jehoiakim, Jehoiachin, and Zedekiah and placed them
under the reign of "Jonacheim." Cf. Wacholder, Eupolemus,
227-28.

107. Polemics against idol worship are frequent in Jeremiah (1:16; 2:8; 7:9; 11:11-14; 17:2-4; passim), though
the reference to the "golden idol" is unusual here, and
may recall Exod 21:1-20.

108. Cf. Jer 2-6.

109. The details of this paragraph, though unbiblical,
appear to be based on Jer 26 and 36. The threat of being
burned alive may reflect Maccabean times. Cf. 2 Macc 7:3-6;
4 Macc 9:19-21; also Heb 11:34. Cf. Wacholder, Eupolemus,
229-30.

110. Astibares is not mentioned in the biblical account,
nor are the Medes said to have collaborated with the Babylonians in destroying Jerusalem. Ctesias of Cnidos (late
5th cent. B.C.E.) mentions a Median king Astibares, along
with Aspandas, in his fanciful history of Persia (cf.
Diodorus Siculus 2.34.6; Herodotus 1.74, 103, 106-107),
as the last two kings of Persia. In Herodotus they are
Cyxares and Astyges, and "Astibares" may be a variation
of the latter. Ctesias appears to have been a source for
Eupolemus for this tradition. Cf. Freudenthal, 118;
Wacholder, Eupolemus, 231-34.

111. Neither 2 Kgs 24 nor 2 Chr 36 mentions the number
of troops accompanying Nebuchadrezzar. Eupolemus may
be dependent here on Herodotus 7.113 and 9.32 for these
figures (so Wacholder, Eupolemus, 234). Cf. Jdt 2:5.

112.   On Eupolemus' use of anachronistic geography, cf.
above, note 20. Scythopolis is the Hellenistic name of
Beth-shan. Cf. Josephus, Ant. 5.84; 1 Macc 5:9-10, 14-15,
52, 55-62; 2 Macc 12:29.

113.   Cf. 2 Kgs 24:10-15; 2 Chr 36:9-10.

114.   The biblical account provides a detailed inventory
of the temple booty taken by Nebuchadrezzar (cf. 2 Kgs
25:13-17; 2 Chr 36:18; Jer 52:17-23). Even though the
ark and the decalogue are not mentioned in these lists,
Jeremiah's rescue of them is an unbiblical detail, and he
appears to have been in no position to retrieve them
(cf. Jer 39:14; 40:1-42:7). Understandably, the fate of
the sacred temple objects became the topic of various
later traditions. Cf. 2 Macc 2:1-8; 2 Bar 6; Paraleipomena
Jeremiou 3:8-11; Josephus, Ant. 18.85-87; 2 Esdr 10:22.
For rabbinic sources, cf. Wacholder, Eupolemus, 242, n. 74.

115.   In Book 1, chapter 21, Clement seeks to establish
the high antiquity of Jewish laws and institutions, and
naturally devotes much space to chronology. This fragment
from Eupolemus, which appears to be a summary rather than
a direct quotation, occurs in the section which treats the
exile and the post-exilic period. It follows immediately
a quotation or chronological summary from Demetrius (= Frg.
6), and precedes a discussion of the origin of the various
human dialects.

116.   That is, similar to Demetrius' work On the Kings in
Judaea which precedes this. Cf. Frg. 1a, and notes 2 and
12 above.

117.   Doubtless referring to Demetrius I Soter (162-150
B.C.E.), and thus bringing the chronology to the year
158/157 B.C.E. Cf. Freudenthal, 124, 212-13; Gutschmid,
"Zeit und Zeitrechnung," 2.191; Wacholder, Eupolemus,
6, 40-44.

118.   Most likely, Ptolemy VIII Euergetes II Physcon
(170-163 and 145-116 B.C.E.). The identity of "Demetrius"
and "Ptolemy" has been much debated, primarily because it
is difficult to synchronize the 5th year of the reign of
any of the Seleucids named Demetrius with the 12th year
of the reign of any of the Ptolemies. Müller, FHG 3.208,
identifies "Demetrius" as Demetrius II Nicator (145-139
and 129-125), and emends τὸ δωδέκατον to read τὸ ἕκτον,
thus identifying the "Ptolemy" as Ptolemy VIII Euergetes
II Physcon, who ruled jointly with Ptolemy VI Philometor
from 170-164, alone from 164-163, was then king in Cyrene
from 163-145, and finally ruled again in Egypt from 145-116.
Freudenthal, 123, 212-13, convincingly argued against
Müller's idenfitifcation of Demetrius, insisting rather
that Demetrius I Soter (162-150 B.C.E.) was meant. He did
agree to Müller's identification of Ptolemy. Since 158

118. (cont.) B.C.E., "the fifth year of Demetrius I Soter's
reign," was the year when the latter established a formal
peace with Jonathan, this would have been a suitable terminus ad quem for his work. Gutschmid, "Zeit und Zeitrechnung," 2.191, while agreeing with Freudenthal about
Demetrius I, argued against Ptolemy VIII Euergetes II
Physcon, since the latter was not "ruling over Egypt"
(as Eupolemus states), but was rather in Cyrene in 158/
157 B.C.E. Moreoever, a strict calculation puts 158/157
B.C.E. in the 13th year of his reign, not the 12th. This
accounts for Gutschmid's conjectural deletion (cf. app.
crit.), and his suggestion that Πτολεμαίου τὸ δωδέκατον
βασιλεύοντος Αἰγύπτου belongs later in par. 5 with the
mention of the consulship of Gnaeus Domitius and C.
Asinius (also Walter, JS, ad loc.). He further suggests
that both phrases are attributable to Clement of Alexandria
who borrowed them from Julius Cassianus, a 2nd century
Christian chronographer. Cf. below, note 121. Also, Freudenthal, 124, 212-15; Denis, Introduction, 253-54; Wacholder,
Eupolemus, 6, 40-42.

119. Thus placing the creation ca. 5307 B.C.E.

120. Or, 1,580 years, if one accepts Clinton's conjectural
deletion {διο}χίλια, as Stählin does, thus dating the
exodus (using Eupolemus' figures) 3560 anno mundi or 1738
B.C.E. The higher figure (2580) would place the exodus
2569 years after creation, or 2738 B.C.E., approximately
a thousand years too early. The unemended text conforms
more closely to the date of the exodus in MT chronology
(2668 anno mundi), while the emendation brings Eupolemus
into closer harmony with the date of the exodus in LXX
chronology (3819 anno mundi). Cf. IDB 1.580-83. The
higher figure is defended by Wacholder, Eupolemus, 112,
250-54, who stresses Eupolemus' reliance on MT and pre-MT
traditions. Cf. Freudenthal, 212-13; Gutschmid, "Zeit und
Zeitrechnung," 2.192-95; Schlatter, "Eupolemus als Chronolog," 633-35; Wacholder, Eupolemus, 111-17; Walter, JS,
ad loc., 1.95, n. 7.

121. If this last sentence represents Eupolemus' own
calculation, he obviously would have flourished in the
mid-1st century B.C.E. More likely, it is a later addition
which has become fused with Eupolemus' time scheme, and is
perhaps attributable to Polyhistor (assuming this is
Clement's source; cf. Introduction), or even Clement.
Wacholder, Eupolemus, 42-44, attributes it to Ptolemy of
Mendes, an Egyptian priest who flourished in the mid-1st
century B.C.E. The textual tradition is corrupt. The
reading of L: γαίου δομετιανοῦ κασιανοῦ, i.e., "until the
consulship in Rome of Gaius Domitius (and) Cas(s)ian,"
is clearly impossible. Kuhlmey's emendation, adopted by
Stählin (and attributed to Freudenthal), is based on
Josephus, Ant. 14.389, and further refined by Gutschmid

121. (cont.)(cf. app. crit.): "And from that time until
the time of the consulships in Rome of Gnaeus Domitius
and Asinius is calculated by Cas(s)ian as 120 years."
This suggestion is based on Clement's earlier reference
to a Cassian in the same chapter (Strom. 1.21.101.2 =
Eusebius, P.E. 10.12.1), whom Gutschmid identifies as a
2nd-century gnostic and chronographer (cf. Eusebius, Hist.
eccl. 6.13.7). Though, cf. N. Walter, "Der angebliche
Chronograph Julius Cassianus," in Studien zum Neuen
Testament und zur Patristik. Erich Klostermann zum 90.
Geburtstag dargebracht (Berlin: Akademie-Verlag, 1961)
177-92. In any case, the emended text as translated here
brings the terminus to ca. 40 B.C.E., the date of the
Roman consuls Gnaeus Domitius Calvinus and Gaius Asinius
Pollio. Cf. Freudenthal, 214-15; Wacholder, Eupolemus,
6-7, 42-44.

PSEUDO-EUPOLEMUS (ANONYMOUS)

The two fragments commonly designated Pseudo-Eupolemus[1] or Anonymous are now widely thought to have been written by an unknown Samaritan author who flourished in a Syrian-Palestinian[2] setting in the mid-second century B.C.E.[3] Both fragments are preserved by Eusebius in P.E., Book 9, in the section which treats Abraham. Eusebius extracts both fragments from Alexander Polyhistor who directly attributes the first to Eupolemus, but traces the second to "some anonymous writings."

Contents. The central figure in both fragments is Abraham, though minor attention is given to other patriarchal figures, most notably Enoch. Fragment 1, consisting of some 56 lines, treats biblical incidents recorded in Gen 6-14, including mention of the period of the settlement following the flood, the tower of Babel, Abraham's origins in Ur, his sojourn in Egypt (in this order), his migration to "Phoenicia," i.e., Canaan, his battle with the four foreign kings, and the Melchizedek episode. Frg. 2, consisting of only 10 lines, is a summary rehearsal of Abraham's origins among the giants, the building of the tower of Babel by Belus, Abraham's journey from Babylon to Egypt via Phoenicia, and his role as inventor and teacher of astrology.

Sources. The Bible is a primary source for Pseudo-Eupolemus. His use of the LXX is certain,[4] the MT probable.[5] The biblical story is freely interwoven with haggadic traditions[6] and mythological traditions drawn from both Greek and Babylonian sources:[7] colonization of the world by giants in the postdiluvian period, the building of the tower of Babel by the Babylonian hero Belus, Abraham as cultural benefactor who discovered astrology while in Babylon and transmitted this "Chaldean science" to the

157

Phoenicians, and later to the Egyptians, Abraham's association with the temple at Mount Gerizim, the miraculous
protection of Sarah's chastity in her marriage to Pharaoh
during Abraham's sojourn in Egypt, Abraham's civilizing
activities in Heliopolis, and Enoch as the original
discoverer of astrology.

Authorship. Because Polyhistor explicitly attributed
the first fragment to Eupolemus, earlier scholarship quite
naturally grouped it with the other five fragments attributed to him.[8] Doubts about the identity of its author
persisted, however, because of its contents. Though all
the Eupolemus fragments handled the biblical story freely,
often departing from the biblical text and contradicting
it,[9] this fragment seemed too syncretistic.[10] It freely
incorporated into the genealogy of Gen 10 names drawn
from pagan mythology, including Belus, Kronos, and Asbolus;
it facilely identified Enoch with Atlas; astrology it
viewed in a thoroughly positive light, in sharp contrast
to its negative assessment in other Jewish traditions.
The other Eupolemus fragments, by contrast, exhibited fewer
traces of pervasive pagan influence.[11] Most decisive was
their apparently mutually exclusive cultic loyalty. This
fragment identified Abraham with the temple at Mount
Gerizim and heralded the latter as the "mount of the Most
High God," whereas the other Eupolemus fragments gave
primacy to the Jerusalem temple whose location had been
signified by an angel of God, and which had been lavishly
built and furnished by David and Solomon, both depicted
in heroic terms.[12]

Taken together, it was difficult to imagine that all
the Eupolemus fragments stemmed from either a Jewish or
a Samaritan author,[13] yet the themes were too biblical to
have come from a pagan.[14] For Freudenthal, these considerations were decisive enough to call for their separation:
this fragment, especially because of the central prominence
it gave to Mount Gerizim, could best be explained as having
originated within Samaritan circles, while the other five

Eupolemus fragments could stand together as the work of
a Jewish author named Eupolemus.[15]

Coupled with this was the fact that the second fragment which occurs in the same section of Book 9 was acknowledged by Polyhistor as being from an anonymous source.
Yet, it had clear affinities with the first fragment. In
both, the building of the tower of Babel is traced to the
postdiluvian giants. The Babylonian figure Belus played
a prominent role in both. Abraham was also central in
each fragment, and was similarly depicted as having
descended from the giants, and as being the one who discovered astrology while in Babylon and taught it to the
Phoenicians and Egyptians. Also, in both fragments
"Phoenicia" is used to designate Canaan. In general, both
fragments reflect similar levels and types of pagan
influence. These lines of continuity, as well as similarity
of terminology,[16] suggested that the two fragments stood
or fell together, and attributing them both to an anonymous
Samaritan author Freudenthal saw as the best solution.[17]
This has emerged as the scholarly consensus.[18]

Title. Alexander Polyhistor credits the first fragment to Eupolemus' work Concerning the Jews of Assyria,
but this title is seriously disputed. The phrase "of
Assyria" may very well belong to the phrase following it,
and "concerning the Jews" may be a generic description
of the content of the work rather than a title in a technical sense.[19] Most likely, its correct title has not
survived.

Date. The terminus a quo is provided by Berossus'
Babyloniaca, a source used by Pseudo-Eupolemus written
after 293-292 B.C.E.[20] Since both fragments were first
preserved by Polyhistor, who flourished in the mid-first
century B.C.E., this provides their terminus ante quem.
The reference to the temple at Mount Gerizim appears to
presuppose its existence; if so, the fragments would
antedate its destruction by the Hasmoneans in 132 B.C.E.[21]
Their pro-Phoenician[22] and anti-Egyptian[23] bias, if any

indication of the political realities in which they were
produced, would point to the first half of the second
century B.C.E.[24]

Importance. If genuinely Samaritan, as they are
widely held to be, these two fragments are important
primary sources for reconstructing the history of the
Samaritans[25] and for understanding their traditions in the
Hellenistic period.[26] In this respect, they should be
considered alongside other ancient Samaritan fragments,
including Theodotus, Thallus, and possibly Cleodemus
Malchus.[27] Unlike many later sources which frequently
present polemical descriptions of the Samaritans,[28] these
fragments would represent the Samaritans' own midrashic
traditions from a very early period.[29] Because they
reflect an outlook which both knows and values pagan mythological traditions,[30] it may be necessary to modify the
common view of Samaritans as a sect immune to outside
influences.[31] The type of midrashic tradition which freely
fuses haggadic with pagan traditions provides a useful
counterpoint to similar traditions both inside and outside
Palestine.[32] As "one of the first Palestinians to present
the biblical history in the form of Hellenistic history
writing,"[33] Pseudo-Eupolemus is an important testimony to
Israelite historiography in the Hellenistic period. These
two fragments also provide evidence of early appropriation
of Enochic legends within Samaritan circles, although
explicit apocalyptic motifs are not in evidence. Equally
significant is Pseudo-Eupolemus' use of the LXX[34] and
the implications of this for determining the relationship
between the Samaritan and Greek versions of the Pentateuch.[35]

NOTES

1. For testimonia, cf. Introduction to Eupolemus, note 1.

2. Since Samaritan communities are known to have existed outside Palestine (cf. Schürer, 3.51-52), it is conceivable that Pseudo-Eupolemus reflects a non-Palestinian provenance. Egypt would be a likely candidate were it not for the strong anti-Egyptian bias reflected in the fragments: Egyptian culture is consistently said to have derived from Babylonian culture. It should be noted, however, that a similar tendency is also seen in Artapanus who is generally thought to have flourished in Egypt. For this reason, an Egyptian provenance is not an impossibility (cf. Walter, JS (1,2) 139-40). In any event, a Syrian-Palestinian setting is generally favored. Cf. Freudenthal, 99. Hengel, Judaism and Hellenism, 2.59, n. 240, favors a direct derivation from Samaria because the fragments are acquainted with Palestinian Haggada and the Enoch traditions. Also, cf. Wacholder, "Pseudo-Eupolemus," 112.

3. Cf. below for discussion of date.

4. Especially decisive is the orthography of proper names: Ἀβρααμ, Ἐνωχ, Μαθουσαλα, Μελχισεδεκ, Μεστραειμ, Χανααν, Χους, Χαμ. Cf. Freudenthal, 98; Wacholder, "Pseudo-Eupolemus," 87-88, n. 30.

5. So, Freudenthal, 83; Wacholder, 87-88, though doubted by Walter, "Pseudo-Eupolemus," 284-86 and JS (1,2) 139, n. 9.

6. E.g., his use of Enochic traditions which may reflect acquaintance with 1 Enoch, Jubilees, and Genesis Apocryphon. Cf. Wacholder, "Pseudo-Eupolemus," 88, 98, 109. Similar haggadic traditions are discussed in Ginzberg, Legends, 1.143-308 and notes in vol. 5, and Gaster, Asatir, 9-61.

7. In Frg. 1, par. 9 Pseudo-Eupolemus indicates his use of Babylonian and Greek traditions. Freudenthal, 96, notes how striking is the degree to which Hebrew, Babylonian, and Greek traditions are reflected in Pseudo-Eupolemus, as well as the way in which they are interwoven. Specifically, Berossus (cf. Freudenthal, 94), Hesiod (cf. Wacholder, "Pseudo-Eupolemus," 92-93), and possibly Ctesias (cf. Gutschmid, Kleine Schriften (1890) 2.575-76). Cf. Freudenthal, 94; Schnabel, Berossos, 67-70; Gutman, Beginnings, 1.100-101; Wacholder, "Pseudo-Eupolemus," 58, 90-91, Hengel, Judaism and Hellenism, 2.59, n. 241.

8. For a review of the earlier history of interpretation, cf. Freudenthal, 82-83.

9.   On the divergence of the Eupolemus fragments from the
biblical text, cf. Introduction to Eupolemus, and notes
2, 17-19. As to Pseudo-Eupolemus, the following may be
noted: Abraham is dated in the thirteenth generation
after Noah (assuming no textual corruption; Frg. 1, par.
3); Armenians as the enemies of Abraham and the "Phoenicians" (Frg. 1, par. 4); Abraham's capture of the women
and children in his battle with the kings of the east
(Frg. 1, par.4); the miraculous protection of Sarah's
chastity (Frg. 1, par. 7).

10.   The term is used advisedly. As Hengel, _Judaism and
Hellenism_, 1.91, notes, Pseudo-Eupolemus does not adopt
a polytheistic outlook despite his use of pagan traditions.
(Cf. however "the gods" in Frg. 2). Freudenthal, 96,
notes the evidence of Assyrian-Babylonian, Median-Persian,
Syrian-Phoenician, Greek, and Israelite traditions within
the fragments.

11.   Freudenthal, 88, also pointed to contradictory claims
within the fragments. Most important, Abraham was depicted
as the cultural benefactor "who surpassed all in nobility
and wisdom," while Moses was cast in the same role in the
other Eupolemus fragments. This difference can be easily
exaggerated, however, since their respective roles do not
specifically overlap: Abraham as the inventor of astrology,
but Moses as the inventor of laws and letters. Also, it
should be noted that even within the Pseudo-Eupolemus
fragment, a contradiction occurs. Both Abraham and Enoch
are said to have been the "original discoverer" of astrology. Cf. Frg. 1, par. 4 and par. 8. Cf. Wacholder,
"Pseudo-Eupolemus," 84; also, Hengel, _Judaism and Hellenism_,
1. 90, where Abraham becomes the "(re)discoverer of
astrology."

12.   Cf. Eupolemus, Frg. 2.

13.   Cf. Freudenthal, 85-86, who notes that, assuming the
strained relations between Jews and Samaritans in the
Hellenistic period, it would have been inconceivable for a
Jewish author to have spoken so favorably of Mt. Gerizim.
Equally inconceivable would have been an author with
Samaritan loyalties acknowledging Saul, David, and Solomon
as legitimate Israelite kings, Eli as high priest, or
Samuel, Elijah, and Jeremiah as prophets of God. Nor would
he have conceded Samaritan dependence on Solomon.

14.   Besides the fact that he knew and used the LXX, the
various features of their content which would have been
inconceivable for a pagan are enumerated by Freudenthal,
83-84, e.g. the report "in good biblical language" that
Abraham had gone to Phoenicia at the command of God, or
that an angel had instructed Methuselah in all knowledge,
and that this revelation was the source of all knowledge.
The point of view presupposed is also telling, since he

14. (cont.) cites other traditions, e.g. "the Babylonians
say," or "the Greeks say," as if he were not a pagan
himself.

15.   This represents a refinement of a position advocated
earlier by Dähne, and defended by Movers and Ewald, which
had detected Samaritan interpolations within an otherwise
pagan author. Cf. Freudenthal, 89 and 91, where he notes
that it was through the carelessness of Polyhistor that
the fragment was wrongly attributed to Eupolemus, an arch-
enemy of the Samaritans. Walter, JS (1,2), 137, also notes
the inappropriateness of the title "On the Kings of Judaea"
for the contents of the two Pseudo-Eupolemus fragments.

16.   κατοικεῖν (Frg. 1, par. 4, line 3; par. 6, line 20;
and Frg. 2, line 5); παραγενέσθαι (Frg. 1, par. 5, line 11
and Frg. 2, line 10). Ἀβρααμ is more problematic than
Freudenthal allows. Throughout Frg. 1 and at the beginning
of Frg. 2, Ἀβρααμ is used, but Ἀβραμον occurs in line 7
of Frg. 2 with no significant variations within the textual
tradition. Cf. Freudenthal, 91.

17.   Frg. 2 had also been attributed to Artapanus (cf.
Müller, FHG 3.212 = No. 4, and followed by Riessler, 186 =
Artapanus, Frg. 1, par. 4-6). Freudenthal, 14, 90, notes
that unlike this fragment, Artapanus never cites his
sources.

18.   Accepted by Graetz, Schürer, Susemihl, Stearns, as
noted in Wacholder, "Pseudo-Eupolemus," 84, n. 11; also
Walter, "Pseudo-Eupolemus," 282. So designated in collections of the fragments by Jacoby, Denis, and Walter.
Bousset-Gressmann, RJ 21, n. 2, still assigns the first
fragment to Eupolemus; also, Schlatter, Geschichte, 189-90.

19.   On the title, cf. Annotations, No. 2; also Wacholder,
"Pseudo-Eupolemus," 84-85.

20.   So, Wacholder, "Pseudo-Eupolemus," 85.

21.   Cf. Josephus, Ant. 13.256-57; 275-83; J.W. 1.64-66.

22.   Cf. Annotations, No. 13.

23.   In the cultural more than the political sense, since
Egyptian culture is finally said to be derivative from
Babylonian culture. Freudenthal, 97, notes other
ancient writers who treat the Egyptians in similar fashion.

24.   Especially significant is the fact that the Samaritans
sided with the Seleucids against the Maccabeans (1 Macc
3:10; cf. 2 Macc 6:2; Josephus, Ant. 12.252-64; also 11.34).
In this connection, Freudenthal suggests that Eupolemus
and Pseudo-Eupolemus in their respective loyalties to
Jerusalem and Gerizim cultic centers, and Philo Epicus and

24. (cont.) Theodotus in their respective portraits of
Jerusalem and Shechem, may stem from an environment produced by the hostility of the Maccabean period when
Samaritan and Jewish relations were especially strained.
Freudenthal, 102-103, also suggests that out of this
conflict may have arisen a collection of pro- and anti-
Samaritan documents which would have been used in the dis-
pute before Ptolemy VI Philometor in Alexandria (cf.
Josephus, Ant.   13.74-79) concerning the legitimacy of
each cultic center. This would account for their presence
in Egypt where Polyhistor was likely to have been introduced to them. If the fragments pre-date this conflict,
this would provide an even earlier terminus ante quem.
According to Wacholder, "Pseudo-Eupolemus," 86, use of
Pseudo-Eupolemus is reflected in Sibylline Oracles 3.97,
reliably dated ca. 140 B.C.E. Cf. J. Geffcken, ed.
Oracula Sibyllina (Leipzig, 1906) 53 (on 3.97) and 59 (on
3.218). Accordingly, Wacholder allows for a date as early
as 200 B.C.E.   Cf., however, Walter, "Pseudo-Eupolemus,"
283-84, who sees the possibility for such a level of syncretism in a pre-Maccabean setting. Hengel, Judaism and
Hellenism, 1.88: "between the Seleucid conquest and the
Maccabean revolt."

25. Hengel, Judaism and Hellenism, 1.91, for example,
notes that "despite the competing sanctuaries and the
border disputes reported by Josephus, contacts between
Jewish upper classes and Samaritans did not break off
completely in the third century B.C.E."

26. Pseudo-Eupolemus is utilized by Montgomery, 284;
Gaster, Asatir, 9-61; Kippenberg, 80-85; Hengel, Judaism
and Hellenism, 1.88-92, 94-95. He is not cited, however,
in the indices of Thomson, Bowman, Problem and Documents,
MacDonald, Theology, Lowy, and other recent works.

27. Other Samaritan sources are noted by Freudenthal,
101, including Sib. Or. 11.238-42, Thallus (= FGrH 256,
Frg. 2; cf. Hengel, Judaism and Hellenism, 2.61, n. 249)
in Josephus, Ant. 18.167, Marinos in Photius 345b, 20
(Bekker). Also, Eusebius, P.E. 10.10.8; Justin, Coh. 102;
Theophilus, Ad Autolycum 3.29.

28. Cf. Josephus, Ant. 12.156; 13.74-79; Sirach 50:25-26.

29. For example, the central prominence of Abraham is
confirmed, and Pseudo-Eupolemus illustrates the types
of traditions about him generated within the Samaritan
community. Freudenthal, 91, refers to Pseudo-Eupolemus,
and the other fragments, e.g. Theodotus, as "the sole
remains of the older Samaritan-Hellenistic literature."

30. Hengel, Judaism and Hellenism, 1.90, remarks Pseudo-
Eupolemus' "explicit interest in the history of culture;"
also, 1.91, the fragments' "rational and universalist
trait." He also contrasts (1.95) their universalist and
international outlook with the more narrow nationalism
of Eupolemus. Hengel, 1.89, also speaks of the "demytholo-
gizing euhemerism" of Pseudo-Eupolemus, noting that he
freely incorporates pagan mythological traditions, yet
the figures from the OT story remain mortal men. Cf.
also Wacholder, "Pseudo-Eupolemus," 96, 99, 113; Walter,
JS (1,2) 139, n. 15.

31. Especially the view of earlier scholarship.

32. Useful comparisons may be made with Jubilees,
Sibylline Oracles, and the haggadic legends collected
in Ginzberg, Legends.

33. So, Hengel, Judaism and Hellenism, 1.91.

34. Cf. above, note. 4.

35. Especially useful are comparisons with the Samaritan
Greek translations of portions of the Pentateuch, the
Σαμαρειτικόν, from which fragments were quoted in early
Christian writers. Cf. P. Glaue and A. Rahlfs, Fragmente
einer griechischer Übersetzung des samaritanischen Pentateuchs (cf. bibliography). Walter, JS (1,2) 139, n. 8,
notes the similarities between the Samaritan Pentateuch
and the LXX over against the MT, and suggests that this
may result from their common use of an older Hebrew
text type.

Bibliography

Bousset-Gressmann, RJ, 20-22, 74, 494-95; cf. 9-10, 72, 435.

Bowman, J. The Samaritan Problem: Studies in the Relation-
    ships of Samaritanism, Judaism, and Early Christianity
    (Pittsburgh Theological Monograph Series, 4; Pitts-
    burgh: Pickwick Press, 1975).

_____. Samaritan Documents Relating to Their History,
    Religion and Life (Pittsburgh Original Texts and Trans-
    lation Series, 2; Pittsburgh: Pickwick Press, 1977).

Burstein, S. M. The Babyloniaca of Berossus (Sources and
    Monographs on the Ancient Near East, vol. 1, fascicle
    5; Malibu, CA: Undena Publications, 1978) 39 pp.

Charlesworth, PAMRS, 77-78, 273.

Cohen, J. M. A Samaritan Chronicle. A Source-Critical
    Analysis of the Life and Times of the Great Samaritan
    Reformer, Baba Rabbah (Studia Post-Biblica, 30;
    Leiden: Brill, 1981).

Collins, Athens and Jerusalem, 38-39.

Conzelmann, HJC, 145-48.

Denis, A.-M. "L'Historien anonyme d'Eusèbe (Praep. Ev. 9,
    17-18) et la crise des Macchabées," JSJ 8 (1977) 42-49.

_____, Introduction, 261-62.

Doran, R. "Pseudo-Eupolemus," in Charlesworth, OTP.

Ewald, History, 8.63.

Feldman, L. H. "Abraham the Greek Philosopher in Josephus,"
    in Transactions and Proceedings of the American
    Philological Association 99 (1968) 143-56.

Fraser, Ptolemaic Alexandria, 2.962:101(ii).

Freudenthal, Alexander Polyhistor, 82-103; also 105-30.

Gall, A. F. von (ed.). Der Hebräische Pentateuch der
    Samaritaner (Giessen: A. Töpelmann, 1918).

Gaster, M. The Asatir. The Samaritan Book of the "Secrets
    of Moses."   (London/Leipzig: The Oriental Translation
    Fund, New Series 26, 1927) 9-42.

_____. The Samaritan Oral Law and Ancient Traditions.
    Vol. I: Samaritan Eschatology (London: Search
    Publishing Co., 1932).

_____. The Samaritans. Their History, Doctrines, and
    Literature (The Schweich Lectures, 1923; London:
    The British Academy, 1925).

Graetz, Geschichte, 3.51, 625.

Gutman, Beginnings, 2.95-108.

Gutschmid, Kleine Schriften (1890) 2.180-95.

Hengel, Judaism and Hellenism, 1.88-92, 94-95.

Karpeles, Geschichte, 1.180.

Kippenberg, H. G. Garizim und Synagoge: Traditionsgeschicht-
   liche Untersuchungen zur samaritanischen Religion der
   aramäischen Periode (Religionsgeschichtliche
   Versuche und Vorarbeiten, 30; Berlin: Walter de
   Gruyter, 1971) 80-85.

Kuhlmey, C. Eupolemi Fragmenta prolegomenis et commentario
   instructa (Berlin, 1840).

Lowy, S. The Principles of Samaritan Bible Exegesis
   (Studia Post-Biblica, 28; Leiden: Brill, 1977).

MacDonald, J. (ed. and trans.). Memar Marqah: The Teaching
   of Marqah (2 vols.; vol. I (text) and vol. II (translation); BZAW, 84; Berlin: Töpelmann, 1963).

_____. The Samaritan Chronicle No. II (BZAW, 107; Berlin:
   Walter de Gruyter, 1969).

_____. The Theology of the Samaritans (London: SCM
   Press, 1964).

Montgomery, J. A. The Samaritans. The Earliest Jewish
   Sect: Their History, Theology and Literature
   (Philadelphia: J. C. Winston, 1907).

Poehlmann, W. and J. Miller. "Pseudo-Eupolemus." Unpublished
   seminar paper. Harvard New Testament Seminar.
   April 26, 1970. 20 pp.

Schlatter, Geschichte, 187-91.

Schmid-Stählin, Geschichte, 2,1.591.

Schnabel, P. Berossos und die babylonisch-hellenistische
   Literatur (Leipzig/Berlin, 1923) 67-93, 246.

Schürer, Geschichte, 3.482.

Susemihl, Geschichte, 2.652.

Thomson, J. E. H. The Samaritans: Their Testimony to the
   Religion of Israel (Edinburgh/London: Oliver and
   Boyd, 1919).

Wacholder, B. Z. "Biblical Chronology," esp. 458-62.

_____, Eupolemus, 104-106, 135, 162-63, 205-206, 287-93,
   313-14.

_____, "How Long."

_____, "Pseudo-Eupolemos' Two Greek Fragments on the Life
   of Abraham," HUCA 34 (1963) 83-113.

Walter, N. "Pseudo-Eupolemos (Samaritanischer Anonymus),"
   JSHRZ, 1,2. 137-43.

_____, "Zu Pseudo-Eupolemos," Klio: Beiträge zur alten
   Geschichte 43-45 (1965) 282-90.

_____, Untersuchungen, 112-27, 236-57.

Index to Editions and Translations

Fragment One

    Source: Eusebius, P.E. 9.17.1-9.

    Reference Number in P.E.: Steph., 244-45;
        Vig. 418c - 419d.

    Greek Text Used: Mras, GCS (43,1) 8.1, p. 502,
        line 12 - p. 504, line 9.

    Editions: Steph., 244-45; Vig., 418c - 419d;
        Hein., 2.19-21; Gais., 2.370-73; Müll., FHG
        3.211 (= No. 3); Migne, PG (21) col. 705 D -
        709 A (notes, cols. 1565-67); Dind., 1.484-86;
        Freu., 223-24 (= Frg. 1); Giff., 1.528-29
        (notes, 4.298-301); Stearns, 68-70 (= Frg. 2);
        Mras, GCS (43,1) 8.1, 502-503; Jac., FGrH 3.678-79
        (= No. 724, Frg. 1); Denis, 197-98 (= Frg. 1).

    Translations:

        English: Giff., 3.450-51; Wacholder, Eupolemus,
               313-14.

        French:

        German: Riessler, 11-12 (notes, 1266); Walter,
               JS (1.2), 141-43.

Fragment Two

    Source: Eusebius, P.E. 9.18.2.

    Reference Number in P.E.: Steph., 245-46; Vig. 420 b-c.

    Greek Text Used: Mras, GCS (43.1) 8.1, p. 504,
        line 18 - p. 505, line 3.

    Editions: Steph., 245-46; Vig., 420 b-c; Hein., 2.21;
        Gais., 2.374; Müll., FHG 3.212 (= No. 4,
        "Artapanus"); Migne, PG (21) col. 709 B-C; Dind.,
        1.486-87; Freu., 225 (= Frg. 2); Giff., 1.530
        (notes, 4.302); Stearns, 67-68 (= Frg. 1);
        Mras, GCS (43,1) 8.1, 504-505; Jac., FGrH 3.679
        (= No. 724, Frg. 2); Denis, 198 (= Frg. 2).

    Translations:

        English: Giff., 3.452; Wacholder, Eupolemus, 314.
        French:

        German: Riessler, 186 (= Artapanus, Frg. 1,
               par. 4-6); Walter, JS (1.2), 143.

FRAGMENT ONE   (Eusebius, P.E. 9.17.1-9)

(1) Συνᾴδει δὲ τούτοις καὶ ὁ Πολυΐστωρ   (1)
Ἀλέξανδρος, πολύνους ὢν καὶ πολυμαθὴς ἀνὴρ τοῖς   418c
τε μὴ πάρεργον τὸν ἀπὸ παιδείας καρπὸν πεποιη-
μένοις Ἕλλησι γνωριμώτατος, ὃς ἐν τῇ Περὶ
5   Ἰουδαίων συντάξει τὰ κατὰ τὸν Ἀβραὰμ τοῦτον
ἱστορεῖ κατὰ λέξιν τὸν τρόπον·

ΕΥΠΟΛΕΜΟΥ ΠΕΡΙ ΑΒΡΑΑΜ· ΑΠΟ ΤΗΣ ΑΛΕΞΑΝΔΡΟΥ

ΤΟΥ ΠΟΛΥΙΣΤΟΡΟΣ ΠΕΡΙ ΙΟΥΔΑΙΩΝ ΓΡΑΦΗΣ

(2) "Εὐπόλεμος δὲ ἐν τῷ περὶ Ἰουδαίων   (2)
10   τῆς Ἀσσυρίας φησὶ πόλιν Βαβυλῶνα πρῶτον μὲν
κτισθῆναι ὑπὸ τῶν διασωθέντων ἐκ τοῦ κατακλυσμοῦ·
εἶναι δὲ αὐτοὺς γίγαντας, οἰκοδομεῖν δὲ τὸν
ἱστορούμενον πύργον. (3) πεσόντος δὲ τούτου   (3)
ὑπὸ τῆς τοῦ θεοῦ ἐνεργείας τοὺς γίγαντας διασπα-
15   ρῆναι καθ᾿ ὅλην τὴν γῆν. δεκάτῃ δὲ γενεᾷ, φησίν,   418d
ἐν πόλει τῆς Βαβυλωνίας Καμαρίνῃ, ἥν τινας
λέγειν πόλιν Οὐρίην (εἶναι δὲ μεθερμηνευομένην
Χαλδαίων πόλιν), <ἢ> ἐν τρισκαιδεκάτῃ γενέσθαι
Ἀβραὰμ γενεᾷ, εὐγενείᾳ καὶ σοφίᾳ πάντας ὑπερ-
20   βεβηκότα, ὃν δὴ καὶ τὴν ἀστρολογίαν καὶ Χαλδαϊκὴν

BION

2-6 ἀνὴρ -- τρόπον: καὶ γνώριμος τοῖς Ἑλλήνων σοφοῖς,
τάδε φάσκων B | 7-8 ΕΥΠ. -- ΓΡΑΦ. BION |
10 φησὶ I: φησιν post δὲ (lin. 9) transp. BON |
16 Καμαρίνη ἥν B | 18-19 <ἢ> ἐν τρισκαιδεκάτῃ γενέσ.
Ἀβ. γενεᾷ Mras: ἐν τοίνυν δεκάτῃ γενέσ. Ἀβ. γενεᾷ
Freu. (not.; cf. 93-94): {ἐν τρισκαιδεκάτῃ} γενέσ. Ἀβ.
{γενεᾷ} Jac. | 20 καὶ² MSS: τὴν Dähne (Jüd. Alex.
Relig., 2.221, apud Freu., p. 224) |

FRAGMENT ONE[1]

(1)   (1) And on these matters Alexander Polyhistor is also in agreement. He is a man with a great intellect and much learning and is well known to those Greeks who have reaped the benefits of education by effort not by accident. In his collection <u>Concerning the Jews</u> he records the story of this man Abraham, word for word, in the following manner:

> <u>Eupolemus' Remarks Concerning Abraham --</u>
> <u>From the Same Work Concerning the Jews By</u>
> <u>Alexander Polyhistor</u>

(2)   (2) "Eupolemus[2] in his work <u>Concerning the Jews</u> <u>of Assyria</u>[3] says that the city of Babylon was first founded by those who were saved from the flood.[4] He also says that they were giants and built the well-

(3) known tower.[5] (3) When it fell as the result of the action of God,[6] the giants were scattered throughout the whole earth. In the tenth generation,[7] he reports, in Camarine,[8] a city of Babylon, which some call the city Ur (and is interpreted 'a city of the Chaldeans'),[9] in the thirteenth generation[10] Abraham was born. He excelled all men in nobility of birth and wisdom.[11] In fact, he discovered both astrology and Chaldean

εὑρεῖν ἐπί τε τὴν εὐσέβειαν ὁρμήσαντα εὐαρεστῆσαι τῷ θεῷ. (4) τοῦτον δὲ διὰ τὰ προστάγματα   (4)
τοῦ θεοῦ εἰς Φοινίκην ἐλθόντα κατοικῆσαι, καὶ
τροπὰς ἡλίου καὶ σελήνης καὶ τὰ ἄλλα πάντα
5   διδάξαντα τοὺς Φοίνικας εὐαρεστῆσαι τῷ βασιλεῖ
αὐτῶν. ὕστερον δὲ Ἀρμενίους ἐπιστρατεῦσαι
τοῖς Φοίνιξι· νικησάντων δὲ καὶ αἰχμαλωτισαμένων
τὸν ἀδελφιδοῦν αὐτοῦ τὸν Ἀβραὰμ | μετὰ οἰκετῶν   419a
βοηθήσαντα ἐγκρατῆ γενέσθαι τῶν αἰχμαλωτισαμένων
10 καὶ τῶν πολεμίων αἰχμαλωτίσαι τέκνα καὶ γυναῖκας.
(5) πρέσβεων δὲ παραγενομένων πρὸς αὐτὸν ὅπως   (5)
χρήματα λαβὼν ἀπολυτρώσῃ ταῦτα, μὴ προελέσθαι
τοῖς δυστυχοῦσιν ἐπεμβαίνειν, ἀλλὰ τὰς τροφὰς
λαβόντα τῶν νεανίσκων ἀποδοῦναι τὰ αἰχμάλωτα
15 ξενισθῆναί τε αὐτὸν ὑπὸ πόλεως ἱερὸν Ἀργαριζίν,
ὃ εἶναι μεθερμηνευόμενον ὄρος ὑψίστου· (6) παρὰ   (6)
δὲ τοῦ Μελχισεδὲκ ἱερέως ὄντος τοῦ θεοῦ καὶ   419b
βασιλεύοντος λαβεῖν δῶρα. λιμοῦ δὲ γενομένου
τὸν Ἀβραὰμ ἀπαλλαγῆναι εἰς Αἴγυπτον πανοικίᾳ
20 κἀκεῖ κατοικεῖν τήν τε γυναῖκα αὐτοῦ τὸν βασιλέα
τῶν Αἰγυπτίων γῆμαι, φάντος αὐτοῦ ἀδελφὴν εἶναι.
(7) περισσότερον δ' ἱστόρησεν ὅτι οὐκ ἠδύνατο   (7)
αὐτῇ συγγενέσθαι καὶ ὅτι συνέβη φθείρεσθαι
αὐτοῦ τὸν λαὸν καὶ τὸν οἶκον, μάντεις δὲ αὐτοῦ
25 καλέσαντος τούτους φάναι μὴ εἶναι χήραν τὴν

BION
2 τῷ om. B | 3 ἐλθόντα <ἐκεῖ> ? Jac. | 4 τἆλλα B |
8 ἀδελφιδοῦν B: -δὸν ION | 9 αἰχμαλωτισθέντων Jac. |
10-14 καὶ¹ -- αἰχμ. om. B | 15 ἱερὸν: <εἰς> ἱερὸν ?
Giff.: ΄Ιερὸν ? Jac. | Ἀργαρίζειν B | 16 μεθερμηνευ-
όμενον I: -νευθὲν BON | 16-18 παρὰ -- δῶρα om. B |
20 sqq. περὶ τῆς γυναικὸς τοῦ Ἀβραὰμ καὶ τοῦ βασιλέως
τῶν Αἰγυπτίων οἷα ἱστορεῖ Iᵐᵍ | 21 τῶν Αἰγυπτίων:
Αἰγύπτου B | 22 περισσ. -- ὅτι om. B | ἠδύνατο BI:
ἐδύνατο ON | 23 αὐτῇ: δ' αὐτῇ B | 23-25 καὶ ὅτι --
φάναι: φθειρομένου τοῦ λαοῦ αὐτοῦ καὶ τοῦ οἴκοῦ, μάντεις
δ' αὐτοῦ κεκληκότος εἶπον B | 25 τούτους ON: τοῦτο I
Jac. | 25 χήραν (!) εἶναι B |

science.[12]   Because he was eager in his pursuit of

(4)   piety, he was well-pleasing to God.   (4)   In response
to the commandments given by God he came into
Phoenicia[13]   and dwelt there.[14]   By teaching the
Phoenicians the movements of the sun and moon,[15]
and everything else as well, he found favor with
their king.   Later, the Armenians[16]   waged war against
the Phoenicians.   After the Armenians won a victory
and had taken Abraham's nephew[17] as prisoner, Abraham,
accompanied by his household servants, came to the
assistance of the Phoenicians, gained mastery of
the captors,[18]   and captured the enemies' children

(5)   and women.   (5)   When the ambassadors approached him,[19]
requesting that he might release the prisoners in
exchange for money, he did not choose to take advantage
of those who had been unfortunate enough to lose.
Instead, after he had obtained food for his young men,
he returned the booty.   He was also received as a
guest by the city at the temple Argarizin,[20]   which
is interpreted 'mountain of the Most High.'[21]

(6)   (6)   He also received gifts[22]   from Melchizedek who
was a priest of God and a king as well.   When a
famine occurred,[23]   Abraham removed into Egypt with
all his house and dwelt there.   The king of the
Egyptians took his wife in marriage because Abraham

(7)   had said that she was his sister.   (7)   He also
reported rather remarkably that the king was unable
to have intercourse with her,[24] also that it happened
that his people and his household were perishing.
When he had his diviners summoned, they told him
that the woman was not a widow.   Consequently, the

γυναῖκα· τὸν δὲ βασιλέα τῶν Αἰγυπτίων οὕτως   419c
ἐπιγνῶναι ὅτι γυνὴ ἦν τοῦ Ἀβραὰμ καὶ ἀποδοῦναι
αὐτὴν τῷ ἀνδρί. (8) συζήσαντα δὲ τὸν Ἀβραὰμ   (8)
ἐν Ἡλιουπόλει τοῖς Αἰγυπτίων ἱερεῦσι πολλὰ
5 μεταδιδάξαι αὐτοὺς καὶ τὴν ἀστρολογίαν καὶ τὰ
λοιπὰ τοῦτον αὐτοῖς εἰσηγήσασθαι, φάμενον Βαβυλωνίους ταῦτα καὶ αὐτὸν εὑρηκέναι, τὴν δὲ εὕρεσιν
αὐτῶν εἰς Ἐνὼχ ἀναπέμπειν, καὶ τοῦτον εὑρηκέναι
πρῶτον τὴν ἀστρολογίαν, οὐκ Αἰγυπτίους. (9) Βαβυ-   (9)
10 λωνίους γὰρ λέγειν πρῶτον γενέσθαι Βῆλον, ὃν
εἶναι Κρόνον· ἐκ τούτου δὲ γενέσθαι Βῆλον καὶ
Χαναάν, τοῦτον δὲ τὸν Χαναὰν γεννῆσαι τὸν πατέρα
τῶν Φοινίκων, τούτου δὲ Χοὺμ υἱὸν γενέσθαι, ὃν   419d
ὑπὸ τῶν Ἑλλήνων λέγεσθαι Ἄσβολον, πατέρα δὲ
15 Αἰθιόπων, ἀδελφὸν δὲ τοῦ Μεστραείμ, πατρὸς
Αἰγυπτίων· Ἕλληνας δὲ λέγειν τὸν Ἄτλαντα
εὑρηκέναι ἀστρολογίαν, εἶναι δὲ τὸν Ἄτλαντα τὸν
αὐτὸν καὶ Ἐνώχ· τοῦ δὲ Ἐνὼχ γενέσθαι υἱὸν
Μαθουσάλαν, ὃν πάντα δι' ἀγγέλων θεοῦ γνῶναι καὶ
20 ἡμᾶς οὕτως ἐπιγνῶναι."

BION

1-3 τῶν -- ἀνδρί: γνόντα γαμετὴν αὐτὴν Ἀβραὰμ ἀποδοῦναι
τούτῳ B | 3-9 συζήσ. -- Αἰγυπτίους om. B |
3 sqq. ὅτι τὴν ἀστρολογίαν εἰς Ἐνὼχ ὡς εὑρετὴν ἀνα-
πέμπει Iᵐᵍ | 7 αὐτὸν Steph.: αὐτὸν ION |
10-11 ὃν -- Βῆλον om. B | 11 Βῆλον I: Βῆλον εἰς
Αἴγυπτον ON: εἰς Αἴγ. B | 12 Χαναάν¹ MSS:
Χάμ Bochart apud Freu. (p. 208): τὸν <Χάμ> Χαναάν Gutschmid
apud Freu. (p. 224) | 13 τούτου: τοῦτον B |
Χοὺμ I: Χοῦν BON: καὶ Χοῦν Bochart apud Freu. (p. 208):
Χοὺς Gutschmid apud Freu. (p. 224) | 15 τοῦ: τούτου
Gutschmid apud Freu. (p. 208) | πατρὸς G Mras:
πατέρα BION | 19 Μαθουσάλαν I: -σάλα BON |

king of the Egyptians learned that she was Abraham's

(8)   wife, and he returned her to her husband. (8) While
Abraham was living in Heliopolis[25] with the Egyptian
priests, he taught them many new things.[26]   He
introduced them to astrology and other such things,
saying that he and the Babylonians had discovered
these things. But the original discovery he traced
back to Enoch,[27] saying that this man Enoch, not the

(9)   Egyptians,[28] had discovered astrology first. (9) For
the Babylonians say[29] that first there was Belus[30]
(who was Kronos[31]), and that from him was born Belus[32]
and Canaan.[33] This Belus fathered Canaan, the father
of the Phoenicians.[34] To him was born a son, Cush,[35]
whom the Greeks called Asbolus,[36] the father of the
Ethiopians, the brother of Mizraim,[37] the father of
the Egyptians. The Greeks say that Atlas[38] discovered
astrology. (Atlas and Enoch[39] are the same.) To Enoch
was born a son, Methuselah,[40] who learned all things
through the help of the angels of God,[41] and thus we
gained our knowledge."

FRAGMENT TWO (Eusebius, P.E. 9.18.2)

(2) "ἐν δὲ ἀδεσπότοις εὕρομεν τὸν ᾿Αβραὰμ ἀνα-   (2)
φέροντα εἰς τοὺς γίγαντας, τούτους δὲ οἰκοῦντας
ἐν τῇ Βαβυλωνίᾳ διὰ τὴν ἀσέβειαν ὑπὸ τῶν θεῶν
ἀναιρεθῆναι, ὧν ἕνα Βῆλον ἐκφεύγοντα τὸν θάνατον
5 ἐν Βαβυλῶνι κατοικῆσαι πύργον τε κατασκευάσαντα   420c
ἐν αὐτῷ διαιτᾶσθαι, ὃν δὴ ἀπὸ τοῦ κατασκευάσαντος
Βήλου Βῆλον ὀνομασθῆναι. τὸν δὲ ῎Αβραμον τὴν
ἀστρολογικὴν ἐπιστήμην παιδευθέντα πρῶτον μὲν
ἐλθεῖν εἰς Φοινίκην καὶ τοὺς Φοίνικας ἀστρολογίαν
10 διδάξαι, ὕστερον δὲ εἰς Αἴγυπτον παραγενέσθαι."

BION

1-4 ἐν -- θάνατον om. B | 5 ἐν Βαβ. κατ. πύργ. τε ION:
τισ Βῆλος ὀνόματι κατ. ἐν Βαβ. πυργ. τε B |
7 ῎Αβραμον B | 9-10 ἀστρολογίαν διδάξαι I: ἀστρολογεῖν
διδ. ON: οὓς καὶ διδ. ταύτην B | 10 παραγενέσθαι:
ἀπιέναι B |

FRAGMENT TWO[42]

(2)   (2)   "In some anonymous writings we found that
        Abraham traced his family to the giants.[43]   While
        these giants were living in Babylonia, they   were
        destroyed by the gods[44] because of their wickedness.[45]
        One of them, Belus,[46]   escaped death and came to
        dwell in Babylon.   There he built a tower and lived
        in it.[47]   It was named Belus, after Belus who built
        it.   After Abraham had been instructed in the
        science of astrology, he first came into Phoenicia
        and there taught the Phoenicians astrology.   Then
        he went to Egypt."

ANNOTATIONS

1. In Book 9, chs. 16-20, Eusebius cites various pagan
witnesses to Abraham (e.g. Berossus, Hecataeus, Nicolaus
of Damascus, and Apollonius Molon), gleaned from Josephus
and Alexander Polyhistor. Among them is this fragment
taken from Polyhistor who attributes it to Eupolemus. It
is preceded by an excerpt from Josephus (Ant. 1.158-68),
and followed by an excerpt from Artapanus (= Frg. 1), also
taken from Polyhistor.

2. I.e., Pseudo-Eupolemus, an anonymous Samaritan author.
Cf. Introduction.

3. The title is problematic in two respects. "Of Assyria"
seems inappropriate for an account of the Jewish patriarchs.
"Of Syria" may have been read originally, since the two
names were easily and frequently confused (cf. Kuhlmey,
46). Rather than being part of the title, "of Assyria"
more likely modifies πόλιν Βαβυλῶνα (so Freudenthal, 207;
Gifford, 4.299; Susemihl, 2.652, n. 87; Wacholder, "Pseudo-
Eupolemus," 85). Thus, "Eupolemus says ... that the
Assyrian city of Babylon was first founded ..." As to the
first part, Περὶ ᾽Ιουδαίων, it is difficult to imagine a
Samaritan author using a descriptive title so despised
within Samaritan circles where other self-designations were
preferred, e.g. Israel, Hebrews, the 'Sidonians in
Shechem' (Josephus, Ant. 12.262; cf. also Ant. 11.344;
also, Freudenthal, 89; Hengel, Judaism and Hellenism, 2.
195, n. 233; Coggins, 8-12). Apart from this instance,
᾽Ιουδαῖοι occurs nowhere else in the fragments. The
original title may have been Περὶ ᾽Εβραίων (so, Freudenthal,
207), or περὶ ᾽Ιουδαίων may have been a generic description
adopted by Polyhistor rather than an actual title. Cf.
Wacholder, "Pseudo-Eupolemus," 85.

4. Cf. Gen 10:1-32, esp. 10-12.

5. The midrashic tradition that the settlers were giants
stems from the statement in Gen 10:8 that Nimrod, the son
of Cush, who settled in the "land of Shinar" was a "mighty
man" (גבר), which the LXX renders as "giant" (γίγας).
Similarly, Gen 6:1-8, on which cf. Ginzberg, Legends, 1.
158-59; also Josephus, Ant 1.113-15 and Frg. 2 below.
Linking the giants with the building of the tower of
Babel would easily be prompted by Gen 10:10, which asserts
that the beginning of Nimrod's kingdom was "Babel" (בבל;
LXX Βαβυλων). In other traditions, Nimrod, the builder
of cities, is the anti-hero responsible for building the
tower of Babel (cf. Josephus, Ant. 1.113-15; Ginzberg,
Legends, 1.179; 5.198, n. 77; 200, n. 83. For the tower
in other traditions, hence "well-known tower," cf.
Enuma Elish 6.60-62 (= ANET, 69); also Homer, Od. 7.59, 206;
10.120; Hesiod, Th. 185. Cf. Freudenthal, 93, for references to other traditions.

6.   In the biblical account (Gen 11:1-9), the tower is
deserted, not destroyed.   Cf. Jub 10:26; Josephus, Ant.
1.118; also Ginzberg, Legends, 1.180.

7.   So, Gen 11:10-32.   Also, cf. below, note 10.   Compare
Berossus, apud Josephus, Ant. 1.158 (= FGrH   680, Frg. 6;
Burstein, 21): "In the tenth generation after the flood
there lived among the Chaldeans a just man and great, and
versed in the celestial lore."   Whether Pseudo-Eupolemus
is directly dependent on Berossus for this tradition (so,
Freudenthal, 94; Wacholder, "Pseudo-Eupolemus," 92, 102),
or derives the tradition independently (so, Schnabel,
Berossos, 246; Feldman, "Abraham," 155, n. 44) is disputed.
In any case, the biblical springboard is provided by
Gen 15:5.

8.   How Camarine came to be identified with Ur is not
clear.   There was a Camarine on the southern coast of
Sicily (cf. Sib. Or. 3.736), but no such city is known in
ancient Babylon.   Since C. Alexandre, ed., Orac. Sibyll.
(Paris, 1841), 3.218, it has been suggested that the name
is related to the Arabic word qamar, "moon," since Ur in
the third millennium B.C.E. was a center of lunar worship.
"Camarine" is used to fill a lacuna in Sib. Or. 3.218,
based on the supposition that Sib. Or. 3.218-35, which
asserts that the righteous people of Ur eschewed astrologi-
cal speculation, is a polemic against Pseudo-Eupolemus.
Cf. Ewald, History, 1.283; Charles, APOT 2.382; Wacholder,
"Pseudo-Eupolemus," 100-101; Walter, JS (1,2), 141, n. 3b.
Its similarity to Shamerine, the self-designation of the
Samaritans, should also be noted (cf. Gaster, Samaritan
Eschatology, 14).

9.   The "interpretation" of the name Ur, which makes
explicit that Ur is the name of a city, may be prompted
by the fact that the LXX, rather than transliterating אור,
regularly renders אור כשדים as ἡ χώρα τῶν Χαλδαίων (cf. Gen
11:28, 31; 15:7; Neh. 9:7 = LXX 2 Esdr 19:7).   Freudenthal,
87-88, suggests that Χαλδαίων πόλιν may have resulted from
אור being read as עיר.   If Pseudo-Eupolemus is dependent
on the MT for the etymology, he appears to have misconstrued
it (so, Freudenthal, 87-88, and Wacholder, "Pseudo-Eupolemus," 88; cf. Freudenthal, 93).   If he is dependent on the
LXX solely, he must have known of Ur from extra-biblical
traditions about Abraham (so Walter, "Pseudo-Eupolemus,"
286).   Cf. Josephus, Ant. 1.151; Ewald, History, 1.283,
n. 1.   The occurrence of the "interpretation" here may
point to an early recognition of the well-known crux in
Gen 11:31. Cf. Speiser, Genesis, 79.

10.   Gen 11:10-32 places Abraham in the tenth generation
from Noah.   Accordingly, the phrase "in the thirteenth
generation" is either a gloss (Niebuhr and Kuhlmey, apud
Freudenthal, 93, and thus bracketed by Jacoby and followed
by Walter, JS; also Hengel, Judaism and Hellenism, 2.61,
n. 252), an additional tradition of the dating of Abraham's

10. (cont.) birth supplied by Pseudo-Eupolemus (N.B.
φησίν), with the qualifying phrase (e.g. ἢ ὡς ἔνιοι λέγου-
σιν) having dropped out, or omitted by Polyhistor (so,
Freudenthal, 93-94, and reflected in Mras's conjecture
<ἢ>), or an interpolation based on Molon (P.E. 9.19.2)
who says that Abraham was born in the third generation
after the flood (μετὰ τρεῖς γενέας; cf. Freudenthal, 94;
Gifford, 4.300). Wacholder, "Pseudo-Eupolemus," 100,
suggests that it may reflect a different method of compu-
tation which used Enoch as the starting point. According
to Freudenthal, 94-95, since Pseudo-Eupolemus connects
Abraham with Nimrod (i.e. Belus), and the latter lived in
the 13th generation after Adam according to Gen 10, of
necessity Abraham too would have to be placed in the 13th
generation. (Similar looseness in calculating the generations in which the patriarchs lived is reflected in Sib.
Or. 1.284; 3.108.)

11. Cf. 1 Cor 1:26.

12. "Chaldean science," with τέχνην implied (so Mras);
otherwise, the text should be emended (as, e.g. Dähne
τὴν ἀστρολογίαν τὴν Χαλδαϊκὴν), thus resulting in a single
discovery. Cf. Philo, Abr. 71 τὴν Χαλδαϊκὴν ἐπιστήμην;
also 77 and 82. Hengel, 2.61, n. 253, observes that
Χαλδαική (τέχνη ?) may refer to manticism and visions of
the future. He also notes Asatir 2.6 (Gaster, 198), where
Enoch is said to have received the "book of signs" from
Adam.

     Hellenistic-Jewish portraits of Jewish heroes typical-
ly include motifs asserting preeminence in nobility, wisdom,
and piety, but with variations. Pseudo-Eupolemus' claim
that Abraham was the "discoverer" (or re-discoverer, so
Hengel, Judaism and Hellenism, 1.90, since Enoch in Frg. 1,
par. 8, shares the same distinction) of Chaldean science
and astrology is distinctive, though elsewhere he is said
to have transmitted the knowledge of astrology to the
Egyptians (Pseudo-Eupolemus, Frg. 1, par. 8; also, cf. par.
9; Artapanus, Frg. 1; Josephus, Ant. 1.166-67; perhaps
1QapGen 19:25-26). The discovery of the "science of the
heavenly bodies" is also attributed to Seth's progeny
(Josephus, Ant. 1.69-71) and Enoch (Jub 4:17; cf. 1 Enoch
2; 17-18; 41:3-9; 43-44; 72-82; 2 Enoch, esp. 11-17).
Jub 11:23-24 possibly depicts him as the inventor of the
plough, but certainly as an innovator in agricultural
technology. The role of "cultural discoverer" is also
attributed to Joseph and Moses by Artapanus (cf. Frg. 2,
par. 3; Frg. 3, par. 4; cf. Annotations to Eupolemus, Nos.
5-7). Philo, Abr., similarly stresses Abraham's wisdom
(68, 255, 275) and piety (60, 114), but Pseudo-Eupolemus'
positive valuation of Chaldean science, with Abraham as its
inventor, contrasts sharply with Philo's negative assessment in Abr. 68-72. In Philo, Abraham's departure from
"the land of Chaldea" symbolizes his conversion; he
abandons his preoccupation with the created order, i.e.,

12. (cont.) celestial bodies, and gives sole allegiance
to the Creator. Similarly, Mut. 16, 70-76. His study
of celestial bodies is also viewed negatively in Jub 12:
16-18, as well as in certain rabbinic traditions (cf.
Wacholder, "Pseudo-Eupolemus," 103, n. 130; also Ginzberg,
Legends, 1.186-89). Astrology is also viewed negatively
in 1 Enoch 8 and Sib. Or. 3.218-30. Abraham's adversarial
relationship with Chaldea is also reflected in other
traditions (cf. Josephus, Ant. 1.157; Jdt 5:7-8; Pseudo-
Philo, Bib. Ant. 6.3-18). According to Feldman, "Abraham,"
a more sophisticated form of the cultural benefactor topos
as applied to Abraham occurs in Josephus, Ant. 1.161-68,
where he is portrayed as a philosophic innovator in a much
more nuanced, and original, fashion. Cf. also B. E. Schein,
Our Father Abraham (Unpublished Yale Ph.D. dissertation,
1972) esp. 24-40 on Abraham as philosopher and sage;
S. Sandmel, Philo's Place in Judaism: A Study of Abraham
in Jewish Literature (New York: KTAV, 1971). It is also
worth noting that Jews were viewed by pagans as those
interested in astrological speculation. Cf. Theophrastus
= Stern, Authors , No. 4. Also, cf. extensive note on
role of astrology in Jewish and Samaritan traditions in
Hengel, Judaism and Hellenism, 2.62, n. 264.

13. Pseudo-Eupolemus' consistent use of Phoenicia for
Canaan is unusual, though technically correct (so, Wacholder, "Pseudo-Eupolemus," 103). It doubtless derives
from Gen 10:19 where Canaanite territory is said to
extend from Sidon to the southern tip of the Dead Sea,
the probable location of Sodom and Gomorrah, Admah, and
Zeboiim. In the LXX, כנען is generally rendered Χανααν
(e.g. Gen 12:5), but occasionally Φοινίκη (Exod 16:35;
cf. 6:15; Josh 5:1, 12; Job 40:25; Prov 31:24 [v.l.]; but
= אדני in Deut 3:9; Isa 23:2). In any case, this change,
along with his claim that Canaan was the father of the
Phoenicians (Frg. 1, par. 9) reflects a pro-Phoenician
bias, and provides further evidence of the author's
Samaritan provenance (so, Freudenthal, 96-97; also
Wacholder, "Pseudo-Eupolemus," 103-104; on the Sidonian-
Samaritan connection, cf. Josephus, Ant. 11.344; 12.257-
64). Cf. Hengel, Judaism and Hellenism, 1.90-91.

14. The translation follows Jacoby's emendation. Cf.
app. crit.

15. Cf. Frg. 2; also Eupolemus, Frg. 1, where Moses is
said to transmit knowledge of the alphabet to the Phoenicians. Elsewhere, Abraham teaches astrology to the
Egyptians. Cf. par. 8; also Artapanus, Frg. 1; Josephus,
Ant. 1.167-68.

16. Armenians are not mentioned in Gen 14:1-12 among the
kings who waged war against the five Canaanite kings. In
later Jewish traditions (cf. Josephus, Ant. 1.171-78;
1QapGen 21.23; Jub 13:22-29) the latter are identified as
Assyrian or Babylonian kings. Poehlmann and Miller, 7,
note that the Armenians may be cast here as enemies of
the Phoenicians owing to the strained relations between
Armenians and the Seleucids which resulted when Artaxias
and Zariadres, the two Armenian underlords of the Seleucids,
deserted Antiochus the Great after his defeat at Magnesia
in 189 B.C.E. and subsequently sided with the Romans who
established them as kings (cf. Strabo 11.14.15). Cf. also
Hengel, Judaism and Hellenism, 2.61, n. 254.

Armenians are the antagonists of Israel in other
Samaritan traditions, e.g. the Samaritan Chronicle (on
Joshua), chs. 26-37, where Joshua fights king Shobhach and
his allies, who include "Greater and Lesser Armina" (cf.
MacDonald, Samaritan Chronicle No. II, 194-204). Ginzberg,
Legends, 4.13-17, records another version where Joshua
fights forty-five kings of Persia and Media, led by
Shobach, king of Armenia. "Armenia" may have derived from
"Aramaean," since Shobach is an Aramaean general in 2 Sam
10:16,18; also 1 Chr 19:16, 18 (so, Ginzberg, Legends,
6.179, n. 45).

17. I.e. Lot. Cf. Gen 14:12, 16. ἀδελφιδοῦν (or,
ἀδελφιδόν, cf. app. crit.; also Cant 2:3 et al.) is more
precise than the LXX (Gen 14:16 ἀδελφόν [ἀδελφιδοῦν *v. l.*])
and Josephus, Ant. 1.176 συγγενής. Cf. Freudenthal,
207-208.

18. Or, if one adopts Jacoby's emendation (cf. app. crit.),
"(re)gained possession of those who had been taken captive."
Gen. 14:16 does not state that Abraham captured the
enemies' women and children, although this is not an
unjustified inference.

19. In Gen 14:17-24, Abraham negotiates exclusively with
the king of Sodom. The transfer of the negotiations from
the Valley of Shaveh (Gen 14:17) to Shechem, i.e. "the
city at the temple Argarizin," is the most significant
change. Otherwise, Pseudo-Eupolemus generally conveys
the gist of the biblical narrative, though Abraham as
generous victor is more sharply profiled. Cf. Wacholder,
"Pseudo-Eupolemus," 105.

20. Perhaps, "was admitted as a guest into a temple
of the city called Argarizin," assuming that εἰς may have
fallen out after πόλεως (so, Giff., 4. 300).

21. 'Αργαριζίν = גרזים הר, commonly written as one word
in the Samaritan Pentateuch (cf. Deut 11:29; 27:4 app.
crit. in A. F. von Gall (ed.), Der Hebräische Pentateuch
der Samaritaner [Giessen: A. Töpelmann, 1918]); also,
regularly הרגריזים in the Samaritan liturgy (cf. A. E.
Cowley (ed.), The Samaritan Liturgy (Oxford: Oxford University Press, 1909) 2. p. LIV). In the LXX, however, it is
consistently rendered ὄρος Γαριζιν (Deut 11:29; 27:12;
Josh 9:2d; Jud 9:7; cf. 2 Macc 5:23; 6:2). In the Greek
translation of the Samaritan Pentateuch (Deut 27:4 and 12):
αργαριζιμ (Cf. P. Glaue & A. Rahlfs, Fragmente einer
griechischer Übersetzung des samaritanischen Pentateuchs
[Nachrichten der K. Gesellschaft der Wissenschaften zu
Göttingen. Philologische-historische Klasse (1911) 167-
200, 263-66; repr. 68 pp.), 37, and 47-48 (note), 49.
Similarly, Josephus, J.W. 1.63 ('Αργαριζίν); Pliny, Nat.
Hist. 5.14.68 (Argaris); Damascius (6th cent. C.E.) =
Photius, Bibl. cod. 242, ed. Bekker, p. 345b (πρὸς ὄρει...
τῷ 'Αργαρίζῳ καλουμένῳ). References given in Glaue-Rahlfs,
who note that an "interpretation" would be required for
Aramaic speaking Samaritans who only knew הרגריזים as the
name of their holy city, not as the original description
of the mountain. If a tradition of etymological interpretation already existed in Samaritan circles, this may
explain its inclusion in Pseudo-Eupolemus. ὄρος ὑψίστου,
however, is unusual, since ὕψιστος normally rendered
עליון. Doubtless, the etymology has been influenced by the
occurrence (4x) of ὕψιστος in Gen 14, and may have arisen
through the association of Salem, or Melchizedek, with
Gerizim in Samaritan traditions (cf. Walter, "Pseudo-
Eupolemos," 286). It should be noted that in Gen 33:18
שלם is translated Σαλημ in the LXX, thus "Jacob came to
Salem, a city of Shechem." Epiphanius, Panarion 55.2.1
(GCS, Holl) 2.326, also associates Melchizedek with Shechem.
Cf. Hengel, Judaism and Hellenism, 2.89. It is possible
that the etymology resulted from a confusion of the Greek
(cf. Freudenthal, 87). On the temple at Gerizim, cf.
Kippenberg, Garizim und Synagoge.

22. Conceivably, δῶρα could refer to the bread and wine
proffered by Melchizedek (Gen 14:18). According to
Josephus, Ant. 1.181, Melchizedek lavishly entertained
Abraham's army. More likely, Pseudo-Eupolemus has diverged
from the biblical text, where Abraham is said to have
offered a "tenth of everything" to Melchizedek (Gen 14:2).
Both the MT and LXX are admittedly ambiguous as to who
actually gave the tithe, but the context seems to require
that Abraham is the giver (so 1QapGen 22.17; Josephus,
Ant. 1.181; cf. Jub 13:24-26). In any case, Pseudo-
Eupolemus' version enhances further the status of
Abraham.

23. The following episode is out of sequence. Cf. Gen
12:10-20.

24. Similar accounts of the miraculous protection of
Sarah's chastity are found in 1QapGen 20.1-32; Josephus,
Ant. 1.162-65; Philo, Abr. 96-98; cf. Jub 13:13-15.
Also, Gen. Rabbah 41.2. Also, on the role of diviners,
cf. Asatir 6.16-19.

25. In Gen 12:10-20 no Egyptian nome is mentioned as
Abraham's place of residence. 1QapGen 19.25 locates him
in Tanis (cf. Jub 13:11). In other traditions, Jews are
associated with Heliopolis, largely owing to Joseph's
marriage to Asenath, daughter of Potiphera, priest of On,
the Hebrew rendering of the Egyptian name iwnw (Gen 41:45,
50; 46:20). Later Hellenistic texts specifically mention
Heliopolis (Artapanus, Frg. 2, par. 3-4; Jub 40:10; 44:24;
T.Jos. 18.3), and Jacob is said to have settled there
(Josephus, Ant. 2.91). Traditions about Moses also locate
him there (Artapanus, Frg. 3, par. 2 and 8; Josephus, AgAp
1.238, 250, 261, 265, 279 (Manetho); 2.10 (Apion)). The
only biblical references are Isa 19:18, and Jer 43:13
(50:13 LXX), where its status as a major cultic center
is implied, though no mention is made of the worship of
the sun-god, Atum-Re, for which it was well known. Given
its later assocation with the patriarchs, and its reputation
for sun worship, Pseudo-Eupolemus' placement of Abraham
there, associating with Egyptian priests, and instructing
them in astrology is quite understandable. Hengel, Judaism
and Hellenism, 1.90, also notes the tradition of the
wisdom of the priests of Heliopolis and of the Egyptians
in general; he also refers to Herodotus 2.3.1; 77.1; 160.2
and 54-60.

26. Visits by Greek philosophers to Egypt for the purpose
of philosophical inquiry and instruction became a frequent
occurrence, and thus a Hellenistic topos (cf. Feldman,
"Abraham," who refers to Aristoxenes, frg. 12 (Wehrli);
Isocrates, Busiris 28; 12.33; Diogenes Laertius 8.3;
Iamblichus, Vita Pyth. 11). Cf. Josephus, Ant. 1.161,
where Abraham goes to Egypt initially to "learn," but
eventually emerged as a philosophical colleague of "the
most learned of the Egyptians" (Ant. 1.165; also 1.154).
1QapGen 19.26-27, though corrupt, may point to a similar
tradition. In Artapanus, Frg. 1, Abraham actually instructs
the Pharaoh himself, representing yet another variation
of the tradition where the philosopher becomes the teacher
of the king.

27. Cf. 1 Enoch 41-44, esp. 72-82, where Enoch is introduced to the mysteries of the heavens. Also, cf. above,
note 12.

28. In the genealogy in the following paragraph, the
Egyptians are placed in the 3rd or 4th generation after
the flood, that is, after Belus and Canaan (or, perhaps
Ham). The antediluvian Enoch, by contrast, acquired
astrological knowledge much earlier. Cf. Freudenthal,
95-96, who noted that here, too, Pseudo-Eupolemus is
probably dependent on Babylonian tradition drawn from
Berossus, who locates Edor-ankos and A-memp-sinos
in the 7th or 8th generation. Cf. Burstein, 19.

29. It should be noted that the Babylonians and Greeks
are quoted here as independent testimony for the claim
made in par. 8: they reaffirm the priority of Abraham,
and that of the Babylonians, especially over the Egyptians.

30. Βῆλος ("Belus," "Belos," "Bel," from Hebrew בֵּל,
shortened form of בַּעַל) is the title designating the pre-
eminent status of Marduk (also Merodach) in the Babylonian
pantheon (cf. Bel 1-22; Arrian, Anabasis 3.16.4; also
M. Jastrow, The Civilization of Babylonia and Assyria
(Philadelphia: Lippincott, 1915) 213; Aspects of Religious
Belief and Practice in Babylonia and Assyria (New York:
Blom, 1911; repr. 1971) 63-142, esp. 19, 38, 100; H. W. F.
Saggs, The Greatness That Was Babylon (New York: Hawthorn,
1962) 342). In Babylonian mythology, Belus assumes the
role of Creator god (cf. Berossus, FGrH 680, Frg. 1(8),
p. 373 = Burstein, 15 (Frg. 2, par. 3a & 3b, 4); also
Enuma Elish 6.134 = ANET, 69. In some traditions, he is
the founder of Babylon, having emigrated from Egypt
(Diodorus Siculus 1.28.1; also Abydenus, FGrH 685, Frg. 1
& 6). In other traditions, his son Ninus, and Ninus' wife
Semiramis, founded Babylon (cf. Ctesias, FGrH 688, Frg. 1a;
cf. Herodotus 1.7; also Wacholder, "Pseudo-Eupolemus,"
90-91). The Belus of Greek mythology is the son of Poseidon by Libya; his twin brother Agenor is said to have
settled Phoenicia, and his twin sons Aegyptus and Danaus
are said to have settled in Egypt, at least initially
(Apollodorus 2.1.4). His competitive status, alongside
Yahweh, is reflected in Isa 46:1; Jer 50:2; 51:44 (= 27:2
LXX), and, of course, Bel and the Dragon. Also, cf. Ep
Jer 41; Ahikar 6.16. As Creator of the heavenly bodies,
his association with astrological knowledge was natural
(cf. Berossus (Burstein, 15); Enuma Elish 5.1-45 (ANET,
501), though his status as an authority on astrology and
astronomy is debated. Cf. Burstein, 15, n. 19; also
Jastrow, Aspects, 207-54.

31. The identification of Belus as Kronos, the father
of Zeus in Greek mythology (cf. OCD², 573-74; W. K. C.
Guthrie, The Greeks and Their Gods [Boston: Beacon, 1950],
39-53), is unusual, though fusion of Greek theogonical
and cosmogonical stories with Babylonian and Egyptian
elements is already well established by the Hellenistic
period (cf. G. S. Kirk and J. E. Raven, The Presocratic
Philosophers [Cambridge: Cambridge University Press, 1969],
9, 36.) On Kronos, cf. Philo of Byblos, Frg. 2C, par. 15-30

31. (cont.)   = P.E. 1.10.15-30 in H. W. Attridge and
R. A. Oden, Philo of Byblos: The Phoenician History (CBQ
Monograph Series, 9; Washington, D.C.: Catholic Biblical
Association, 1981) 47-55.   In Philo of Byblos, Frg. 2C,
par. 26, one of the three children of Kronos is Zeus
Belus.   On the myth of the revolt of the Titans, and its
relation to Pseudo-Eupolemus and later Jewish and Christian
traditions, esp. Sibylline Oracles, cf. Wacholder,
"Pseudo-Eupolemus," 90-91; also Hengel, Judaism and Helle-
nism, 1.89 and 2.60, n.246.

32.   Jacoby suspects dittography in this repetition of
Βῆλος; if so, Βῆλον καὶ should be deleted.   In some
genealogical lists of Babylonian deities, however, there
is a double occurrence of Bel.   Cf. T. G. Pinches, The
Religion of Babylonia and Assyria (London: Constable, 1906)
46-49.   The variant readings of ON and B represent
secondary attempts to resolve the textual difficulty
(cf. app. crit.).   Freudenthal, 95, accounts for the
second Belus as an attempt to bring the second fragment
into conformity with the first.

33.   Bochard's emendation of Χάμ for Χανααν is adopted
by Jacoby (cf. app. crit.), and followed by Walter, thus
bringing what is clearly a corrupt text into somewhat
closer conformity with Gen 10:6-9: "... from this one
(Belus) was born Ham; this one (Ham) fathered Canaan, the
father of the Phoenicians.   To him (i.e. Canaan) was born
a son, Cush ... "   Cf. Freudenthal, 208; Hengel, Judaism
and Hellenism, 1.89.

34.   Cf. Gen 10:15, where Canaan is the father of Sidon.
Nevertheless, another indication of pro-Phoenician bias.

35.   In the biblical genealogy (Gen 10:6), Cush is the
brother of Canaan, not his son, as in Pseudo-Eupolemus.
Χουμ is most likely a corruption of Χους (cf. Gen 10:6, 8
LXX).   On the debate concerning the orthography (cf. app.
crit.), cf. Freudenthal, 208; Giff. 4.301; Wacholder,
"Pseudo-Eupolemus," 94-95; Walter, "Pseudo-Eupolemos,"
285.   Also, cf. Ezekiel the Tragedian, Frg. 1, par. 28.4.

36.   Asbolus, an augur, is mentioned in Hesiod, Sc. 185.
According to Wacholder, "Pseudo-Eupolemus," 95, he is here
connected with the Ethiopians because of the literal
meaning of ἀσβολος, i.e. "soot," "darkened."

37.   Cf. Gen 10:6, where Μεσραιμ (= Egypt) is the brother
of Χους.

38.   On Atlas as the discoverer of astrology, cf.
Herodorus of Heracleia, FGrH 31, Frg. 13, p. 218; Xenagorus
of Heracleia, FGrH 240, Frg. 32, p. 1010; Dionysius
Scytobrachion, FGrH 32, Frg. 7, p. 237 in Diodorus
Siculus 3.60.2; also cf. Diodorus Siculus 4.27.5; also
cf. Hesiod, Th. 517; Homer, Od. 1.53.   References cited
in Wacholder, "Pseudo-Eupolemus," 96, notes 82 and 83.
Cf. also Cleanthes, SVF 1.125, No. 549, apud Hengel,
Judaism and Hellenism, 2.60, n. 243.

39.   Traditions concerning Enoch's access to the heavens
(cf. above, notes 12 and 27) doubtless prompted this
identification with Atlas, otherwise unattested in
Hellenistic Jewish writings.   Accordingly, Enoch supplants
the Greek mythological hero.

40.   On Methuselah as the recipient of Enoch's heavenly
knowledge, and the transmitter of tradition, cf. Jub 7:
38-39; 1 Enoch 76:14; 81:5; 82:1; 83:1, 9; 85:2; 91:1-2;
107:3; 2 Enoch 1:10; also 1 QapGen 2.19-26.

41.   Cf. 1QapGen 2.19-21; 1 Enoch 106.13; Jub 4:21; also
Hengel, Judaism and Hellenism, 2.60, n. 243 and 2.164,
notes 859-62.

42.   This fragment also occurs in Eusebius' section on
Abraham (cf. note 1 above).   It is excerpted from Poly-
histor, and occurs immediately after a fragment from
Artapanus (= Frg. 1), and precedes an excerpt from
Apollonius Molon, also taken from Polyhistor.

43.   Cf. Gen 6:4.

44.   Perhaps this represents his adoption of a pagan
mythological outlook.

45.   Though no mention is made of the flood (cf. Gen 6:5-
8:24), it is the event presupposed here.

46.   Belus here is doubtless to be identified with Noah
(contra Wacholder, "Pseudo-Eupolemus," 94).   Other traditions record survivors from the flood and these may have
influenced Pseudo-Eupolemus (cf. Apollonius Molon in P.E.
9.19; Nicolaus of Damascus in Josephus, Ant. 1.94-95;
Berossus in Burstein, 20-21).   Cf. Hengel, Judaism and
Hellenism, 1.89 and 2.60, n. 294.

47.   In other traditions, it is Nimrod (cf. Gen 10:9-11)
who is reponsible for building the tower of Babel.
According to Wacholder, "Pseudo-Eupolemus," 90, Belus
has supplanted Nimrod in Pseudo-Eupolemus through fanciful
etymological interpretation of "Babel," as "Bel came"
(בל בא).   On the identification of Belus as Nimrod, cf.
Freudenthal, 94, with numerous references.

Three fragments from the work of Artapanus[1] are
extant.[2] First preserved by Alexander Polyhistor, from
whom Eusebius quoted them,[3] they treat respectively
Abraham, Joseph, and Moses, primarily as they relate
to Egypt.

Title. Two titles of the work are given: Judaica
(Frg. 1) and Concerning the Jews (Frg. 2, par. 1; Frg. 3,
par. 1). The latter is to be preferred since it is also
supported, independently, by Clement.[4] Neither title
provides any clear indication of the nature and extent
of the work.

Author. Nothing certain is known of the author himself. The name Artapanus is of Persian origin, and this
may point to a mixed descent.[5] He has always been regarded as something of an enigma. The essential dilemma has
always been that the fragments appeared far too syncretistic
to have been produced by a Jew, however liberal;[6] yet,
they are so thoroughly committed to the glorification of
Jewish heroes and Jewish history that a pagan origin is
impossible.[7] Accordingly, scholarly debate has been
especially preoccupied with establishing his ethnic identity
and ultimate loyalties, i.e. whether he was Jewish or
pagan. Although at one time regarded as a pagan,[8] there
is broad scholarly consensus now that whatever his motives,
Artapanus was Jewish.[8a]His social setting has been confidently established through analysis of the contents of
the fragments. He is now seen to reflect a less sophisticated, popular outlook, perhaps even from a center other
than Alexandria.[9]

Date and Provenance. It is only known for certain
that he predated Alexander Polyhistor (fl. ca. 50 B.C.E.)
from whom Eusebius quoted him. The terminus post quem

is more difficult to establish. Since he appears to be
responding to pagan polemics against the Jews, especially
reminiscent of Manetho (3rd cent. B.C.E.),[10] he is normally dated from the mid-third to the mid-second century
B.C.E.[11] Efforts have been made to establish his dependence
on Hecataeus (ca. 300 B.C.E.),[12] Pseudo-Hecataeus, and
Eupolemus (ca. 167 B.C.E.), but these have not produced
any consensus. Since the existence of the Jewish temple
at Leontopolis appears to be presupposed in the fragments,
the period of Ptolemy VI Philometor (180-145 B.C.E.) is
perhaps the most plausible period in which to locate him.[13]

Given the pervasively Egyptian cast of the fragments,[14]
Artapanus' citation of Egyptian local traditions, and his
dependence on Egyptian traditions as mediated through
Herodotus, and probably Hecataeus, an Egyptian provenance
is virtually certain.[15] No other setting has been proposed
which adequately accounts for both the mood and content
of the work. Broad scholarly agreement exists on this
point.

Genre. Generally classified among Hellenistic Jewish
historical writings, in no sense do the Artapanus fragments
belong to the category of serious history in the way
Herodotus and Thucydides do; but, neither are they mere
biblical paraphrases. Because they provide a glorified
treatment of Israel's heroes, they are now widely regarded
as belonging to the genre of popular romance literature.[16]
Their patriotic, even nationalistic flavor, is to be explained in this way, and it is at this level that they
should be read as popular religious propaganda. Since
this type of literature often arises among peoples with
mutual interest in each other's history and culture, be
it Egyptian, Greek, Babylonian, or Jewish, this helps to
account for the inclusion of traditions from other
cultural traditions, and thus explains its universalistic
flavor. Similarly, the apologetic dimension of the fragments is to be understood.[17] Such popular romance writing
often arose to combat ignorance about one's own cultural

tradition. Because they originally were part of popular
Jewish historical romance writing, they were not thereby
to be taken any less seriously, for they embodied the
sacred traditions through which their religious, ethnic,
and national identity was preserved.

Content. Frg. 1, consisting of only a few lines,
gives an etymology of the name Jews ("Hermiouth"), and
depicts Abraham as an emigrant to Egypt who taught
Pharaoh astrology and returned to Syria after twenty years.
Frg. 2, consisting of some thirty lines, condenses the
Joseph story from Gen 37, 39-47, focusing on his rise to
Egyptian fame, his eventual elevation to "lord of Egypt,"
and his role as cultural benefactor of Egypt. Frg. 3,
by far the longest of the three fragments, treats Moses
from his birth to his death, following in the main the
storyline of Exodus, but with many non-biblical additions.[18]
The account is thoroughly Egyptianized, however, as otherwise nameless biblical characters, such as Pharaoh and
his daughter, as well as place names, are given Egyptian,
or Egyptian-sounding names. As was Abraham and Joseph,
so Moses in this fragment is presented as cultural
benefactor, though on a greater scale. He is also portrayed as a military strategist who protects Egypt by
fending off the Ethiopians. Perhaps most striking is the
emphasis on Moses as the founder of Egyptian cults who
organized religious life and came to be revered by the
Egyptians as himself divine. This fragment is remarkable
for its inclusion of Moses' battle with the Ethiopians
(par. 7-10), the plot by the king to assassinate Moses
(par. 13-18), and his eventual encounter with Pharaoh
in which the king died for blaspheming the name of God,
but was restored to life by Moses (par. 23-25). Also
included is an abbreviated and rearranged account of the
plagues, though conspicuously omitting the Passover (par.
27-33). A summary account of the exodus is also given.
Also noteworthy is the inclusion of local traditions
providing rationalistic accounts of the crossing of the

Red Sea (par. 35). Throughout this fragment, Moses
emerges not as the lawgiver of the Jews, as he does,
for example, in Eupolemus, Aristobulus, Philo, or
Josephus, but as hero and thaumaturge who accomplishes
marvelous, if not magical feats, and never meets defeat.

 Sources. Clearly, the LXX is a primary source,[19]
and there is little weighty evidence that Artapanus knew,
or used, the Hebrew Bible.[20] A variety of traditions are
included, however, which are also found in Herodotus,
Hecataeus, Pseudo-Hecataeus, Diodorus Siculus, and
Plutarch, but he is likely to have known these traditions
through popular, oral sources rather than through any
use or familiarity with literary traditions.

 History of Transmission. Artapanus is mentioned
nowhere in ancient pagan[21] or Jewish sources[22] other
than in connection with these three fragments. Josephus
almost certainly knew, and used, his work, but does not
mention him by name;[23] nor does Philo. The first Christian
writer to mention him is Clement of Alexandria who cites
two paragraphs from Frg. 3.[24] Freudenthal has reconstructed
the history of the transmission of the Artapanus tradition
as follows:[25]

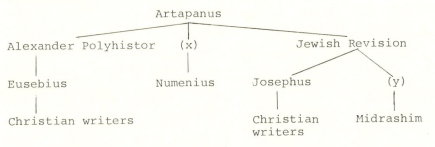

 Importance. Artapanus has figured centrally in
scholarly discussion of theios aner traditions, particularly as they became formulated in Hellenistic Jewish circles.[26]
His portrait of Moses as a thaumaturge, as well as his
general encomium on Moses, has created interest in romance
literature as a form of religious propaganda.[27] Historical
value has been attached to several references in the

fragments as they bear on the Hyksos invasion of Egypt.[28]
The fragments are perhaps most useful in assessing mode
and degree of cultural assimilation and accommodation of
Diaspora Jews to a pagan setting.[29] Worth noting especially is Artapanus' adoption of a distinctly euhemeristic
outlook in his depiction of Moses.[30] Artapanus has been
seen to reflect a much more liberal outlook, typical of
a large segment of Diaspora Jews who did not find pagan
traditions threatening or compromising to fidelity to
their religious tradition.

NOTES

1. No early testimonia exist other than the references
to Artapanus in the fragments themselves. For the
medieval period: Chronicon Paschale (7th cent.), ed. L.
Dindorf (1832) [Corpus Scriptorum Historiae Byzantinae,
16] 1.117 = PG (92), par. 64, col. 201A. Also, Chron.
anonym. in Cramer, Anecdota, Paris, 2.176, apud Schürer,
Literature, 207.

2. Among older treatments, the fragment now recognized
as belonging to Pseudo-Eupolemus (Frg. 2) was attributed
to Artapanus. Cf. Müller, FHG, 3.212; Riessler, 186.

3. Frg. 1 = P.E. 9.18.1; Frg. 2 = P.E. 9.23.1-4; Frg. 3 =
P.E. 9.27.1-37 (par. 23-25 are also quoted in Clement of
Alexandria, Stromata 1.23.154.2-3). Cf. Index to Editions
and Translations.

4. Cf. Frg. 3, par. 23 = Strom. 1.23.154.2. So, Freudenthal, 216.

5. On the name, cf. Freudenthal, 216. On the presence
of Persians and Jews in Egypt, and the occurrence of the
name Artapanus in Egyptian papyri and epigraphy, cf.
Fraser, Ptolemaic Alexandria, 2.985, n. 199, who also
mentions the suggestion of Meyer, Papyrusfunde der Eleph.,
28, that Artapanus might have been a descendent of the
Elephantine garrison.

6. Among the most striking statements are Artapanus'
claim that Joseph founded sanctuaries at Athos and Heliopolis (Frg. 2, par. 4), that Moses venerated the worship of
Isis (Frg. 3, par. 13), and that Moses consecrated Egyptian
deities, especially the worship of animals, and played a
leading role in establishing Egyptian polytheistic worship
(Frg. 3, par. 4, 9, & 12). This positive attitude towards
Egyptian worship is commonly contrasted with the negative
attitude reflected in other Jewish sources, e.g., Sib. Or.
3.29-31; Frg. 3.22-32; Wis 11:15-16; 12:24-25; 15:18-19;
Ep. Aris. 138-39; Philo, De Decal. 76-80; Josephus, Ag.Ap.
1.224-25. So, Walter, JS (1,2) 123, n. 9. Hengel,
Judaism and Hellenism, 1.91, speaks for most modern scholars: "In him (i.e. Pseudo-Eupolemus) we find no traits
tending towards polytheism, and one could with much greater
justification apply the term syncretistic to the fictional
biography of Moses by the Egyptian Jew Artapanus."

7. Besides the generally embellished portraits of the
Jewish heroes Abraham, Joseph, and Moses, there are
specific motifs: Moses is exonerated in the slaying of
the Egyptian, since it is an act of self-defense (Frg. 3,
par. 18); he raises the Egyptian king back to life (Frg.
3, par. 25); Chenephres is struck with disease as

7. (cont.) punishment for forcing Jews to wear conspicuous garments (Frg. 3, par. 20).

8. E.g., by Dähne, Geschichtliche, 2.201; Ewald, History, 2.89; Seguier, PG (21) col. 1567, note on 709 B7; cf. Freudenthal, 148, 216.

8a Valckenaer, De Diatribe Aristobulo (1806), 26, had already regarded him as Jewish, as did Herzfeld (1847-57) and Graetz (1878³) (against Holladay, THEIOS ANER, 201-202), but the case was first convincingly argued by Freudenthal, 143-53, who explained the pagan overlay as the result of a Jewish author writing under a pseudonym, affecting a pagan outlook (esp. based on Ep. Arist. 6). He characterized the work as a Trugschrift, and also proposed that the same author wrote the Epistle of Aristeas to Philocrates, Pseudo-Hecataeus, and other pseudonymous works, including the Solomon-Vaphres correspondence in Eupolemus, and the pseudonymous citations in Aristobulus. Although Freudenthal's pseudonym hypothesis never gained acceptance, the Jewishness of Artapanus has never been seriously questioned since. With various qualifications, he has been regarded as Jewish by Schwartz (1895), Willrich (1900), Friedländer (1903), Schürer (1901-1909³⁻⁴), Braun (1938), Dalbert (1954), Merentites (1957-61), Hengel (1969), and Fraser (1972). The generous inclusion of pagan traditions, and their thorough assimilation within Artapanus' work, was variously explained: as not unexceptional among ancient Jewish writers, even the rabbis (Heinemann); as apologetically motivated, and therefore as necessary accommodations (Schürer, Schlatter, Friedländer); as naive (Heinemann, Dalbert), and therefore indefensible (Ginzberg); as the result of pagan redaction, e.g. by Alexander Polyhistor (discussed, but not defended by Freudenthal, 145, 147). For a more detailed review of the debate, cf. Collins-Poehlmann, 1-7; Holladay, THEIOS ANER, 201-204.

9. Fraser, 1.704, "...his work ... points to a humbler milieu than that portrayed in the Letter (of Aristeas);" 1.706, "He is familiar with the native life of Egypt and the pure priestly traditions, and it is most natural to see in him not a member of the influential Jewish circles around Philometor or a later Ptolemy, but (as his Persian name suggests) as a Jew of mixed descent, possibly resident in another centre such as Memphis, where the residence of Jews from an early date exacerbated a problem which was still only nascent in the capital."

10. That he was responding to Manetho's account of Moses, or a similar tradition, has long been recognized. Cf. Freudenthal, 161-62; Braun, 26-31; Fraser, 1.706; Collins-Poehlmann, 7; Holladay, THEIOS ANER, 212-14.

11.   Cerfaux, "Influence," dates him as early as the reign
of Ptolemy IV Philopator (221-205 B.C.E.) because of the
importance of Isis worship within the fragments, and other
allusions to mystery religions; followed by Denis, Introduction, 257. He is dated in the second century B.C.E.
by Schwartz, 1306; Dalbert, 44; Ginzberg, 145; Wacholder,
"Biblical Chronology," 460, n. 34 (prior to the Maccabean
revolt; also based on the reference to elephantiasis).
He is dated ca. 100 B.C.E. by Hopfner, 52; Reitzenstein,
Poimandres, 182; Walter, JS (1,2) 125.

12.   Cf. Dalbert, 44; Willrich, Judaica, 111-12;
Geffcken, Apologeten, xiii.

13.   Cf. Frg. 2, par. 4, and note 28; also Conzelmann,
HJC, 149. So, Fraser, Ptolemaic Alexandria, 1.704.

14.   Cf. esp. Freudenthal, 157-60, who notes Artapanus'
use of and familiarity with Egyptian traditions.

15.   Fraser, Ptolemaic Alexandria, 1.704, following
Freudenthal, notes that Artapanus makes limited use of
the current language of administration, but that the
native Egyptian element is very marked; also, cf. 1.706.

16.   As to former classifcations, Schürer, Literature,
206-208, is typical in treating him under "historical
literature." The shift in genre classification is indicated in Charlesworth, OTP, which treats Artapanus in the
separate category of "Romance." Interpreting Artapanus
as representative of popular romance literature had already
begun with Schwartz, "Artapanus," (1895) 1306, and was
continued by Weinreich, "Gebet und Wunder" (1929) and
Heinemann, "Moses," (1935). It was treated more fully
by Braun, History and Romance, who explored the national
character of hero romance literature as it developed among
subject peoples. Braun distinguished between two levels
of such literature. An aristocratic, more literary
level, as carried on by priests or upper-class, educated
figures, would be addressed to audiences of comparable
social status within the dominant culture. Examples would
include Berossus, Manetho, and (later) Josephus. At a
more popular, non-literary level, the literature would
tend to be anonymous, and in it history, myth, and legend
would be less clearly distinguished, indeed if at all.
As the romance literature developed, it became "the spiri-
tual bread without which a proud people can stand the
pressure of alien domination, and it is individual heroic
figures in whom the feeling and longing of the masses
come to a concentrated expression" (pp. 3-4). Such hero-
romances developed around a variety of figures: Ninus and
Semiramis (Assyria); Sesostris (Egypt); Manes and Metiochus
(Phrygia); Cyrus (Persia); Alexander and Achilles (Macedonia). Accordingly, Artapanus' work reflects the development of a Moses romance within Judaism intended to project

16. (cont.) Moses into the arena of national heroes, but
also to respond to anti-Jewish Egyptian polemics, although
not directly traceable to Manetho, at least as old as the
2nd century B.C.E. Thus, "In the fragments of Artapanus
which provide us with the oldest available version of this
romance, Moses combines in a single life political, military, religious, philosophical, technical and civilizing
achievements, which in the Egyptian-Hellenistic view
were shared by the deities Isis, Osiris, Thot-Hermes and
the national hero Sesostris. Not only does he surpass
each one individually, but also all of them combined"
(p. 26). Hengel, Judaism and Hellenism, 2.62, n. 262:
"(Artapanus')... whole work, which is probably a romantic
aretalogy, expresses a strong nationalistic feeling."
Cf. also Walter, JS (1,2) 122: "eine Art historischer
Roman." Cf. Conzelmann, HJC, 149.

17. Cf. Freudenthal, 161-62, who notes that in response
to the charge that Jews were native Egyptians, later
expelled, Artapanus emphasized their origin from "Syrian
lands" (Frg. 1; Frg. 2, par. 3; Frg. 3, par. 21). He also
stressed that Moses was not an Egyptian priest, as Manetho
charged, but the child of Jewish parents, not adopted by
Merris, but "cared for" by her (Frg. 3, par. 3). In a
similar vein, Moses did not form a nation from a collection
of Egyptian rejects, but was in fact the cultural benefactor of Egypt (Frg. 3, par. 4-7). The Jews, rather
than being those who hate other nations' gods and customs,
recognize the value of popular religion, as seen through
the work and example of Moses himself (Frg. 3, passim).
In response to the charge that Jews never produced any
great men, Artapanus presents Abraham, Joseph, and Moses
as great cultural benefactors who contribute especially to
the welfare of Egyptian life. In response to the charge
that circumsion is not a divine covenantal sign because
Egyptians taught it to other people, Artapanus shows that
Moses actually introduced it to the Ethiopians and the
Egyptian priests (Frg. 3, par. 10). The apologetic aim
of Artapanus is similarly recognized by Vermes, "La
figure," 73; Walter, JS (1,2) 125; Tiede, Charismatic
Figure, 148-49; Holladay, THEIOS ANER, 212-229.

18. Schürer, Literature, 206, "... methodically embellished
... remodelled by fantastic and tasteless additions."

19. Cf. esp. Freudenthal, 152, 215-16, who notes the
following: Frg. 3, par. 27 σημεῖον ποιῆσαι (Exod 4:8);
ῥάβδον ἐκβάλοντα ὄφιν ποιῆσαι (Exod 4:2,3); ἐπιλαβόμενον
τῆς οὐρᾶς (Exod 4:4); Νεῖλον τῇ ῥάβδῳ πατάξαι (Exod 7:20);
par. 30 διὰ ... ἐπαοιδῶν δράκοντα ποιῆσαι (Exod 7:12,22);
par. 32, in regard to the terminology for the plagues
βάτραχον (Exod 8:2); ἀκρίδας (Exod 10:4); σκνίπας
Exod 8:16 (11); χάλαζαν (Exod 9:24). Also, on Frg. 3, par.
31, Freudenthal notes that ζῷόν τι πτηνόν could only be
derived from the LXX (Exod 8:21 [17]) κυνόμυια (cf. Ps
77 (78):14), not Exod 8:17 MT עָרֹב, "swarm."

20.   Cf., however, Freudenthal, 216; also Annotations, Note 5.

21.   Freudenthal, 173, suggests that the Pythagorean Numenius drew upon the Artapanus tradition. Noting the similarity of spelling of Μουσαῖος in both Artapanus and Numemius, Freudenthal also suggests that the Jannes-Jambres story as recorded in Numemius reflects the earlier version of Moses' conflict with the Egyptian magicians/priests found in Artapanus, Frg. 3, par. 29-31. The story is preserved in other pagan traditions, including Pliny, Nat. Hist. 30.2.11; Apuleius, Apology 90. Cf. Gager, Moses, 137-40; Walter, JS (1,2) 122-23, n. 7.

22.   S. Applebaum, "The Jewish Community of Hellenistic and Roman Teucheira in Cyrenaica," Scripta Hierosolymitana 7 (1961) 27-51, esp. 49, apud Walter, JS (1,2) 124, n. 13, reports two instances where Αρταφαν, apparently as applied to a Jew, occurs in an inscription from Teucheira.

23.   Cf. Freudenthal, 169-73, for a detailed comparison of Artapanus and Josephus; also, Bloch, Quellen, 60-62; Walter, JS (1,2) 121, and references in n. 3 to S. Rappaport, Agada und Exegese bei Flavius Josephus, 25-32, 113-20; Walter, Untersuchungen, 70-76. According to Walter, JS (1,2) 121, Josephus worked either from the original or from a reworked version of Artapanus.

24.   Parts of Artapanus' work are used, or alluded to in later Christian works. Cf. testimonia for the medieval period in note 1, above. Also, traditions from Artapanus appear to have been preserved, independent of Josephus and Eusebius, in a medieval Syrian work, traceable to Isho'dad of Merw. Cf. Annotations, Note 56.

25.   Freudenthal, 174.

26.   Cf. especially, Weinreich, "Gebet und Wunder" (continued in the work of his student Merentites in his commentary); Bieler, THEIOS ANER, 2.30-33; Georgi, Gegner, 147-51, 201; Tiede, Charismatic Figure, 146-77; Holladay, THEIOS ANER, 199-232.

27.   E.g., Hadas, Hellenistic Culture, 90, 96, 125, 172.

28.   Especially emphasized by Freudenthal, 156-57; though, cf. Walter, Untersuchungen, 68-69; also JS (1,2) 125, n. 19.

29.   Especially, Hengel, Judaism and Hellenism, passim; Walter, JS (1,2) 123.

30.   Cf. Freudenthal, 146; Heinemann, "Moses," 368; Walter, JS (1,2) 123-24.

Bibliography

"Artapan," DB 1/2 (1926) 1038.

Bieler, L. ΘΕΙΟΣ ANHP, Das Bild des "Göttlichen Menschen"
    in Spätantike und Frühchristentum (2 vols; Wien:
    Höfels, 1935 (Bd. I); 1936 (Bd. II); repr. 2 vols
    in 1, Darmstadt: Wissenschaftliche Buchgesellschaft,
    1967) 2.26, 30-33.

Bloch, H. Die Quellen des Flavius Josephus in seiner
    Archäologie (Leipzig: Teubner, 1879) 60-62.

Bousset-Gressmann, RJ, 20-21, 486, 494-95.

Braun, History and Romance, 26-31, 99-102.

Cassuto, U. "Artapanus," EncJud 3 (1930) 405-406.

Cerfaux, L. "Influence des Mystères sur le Judaïsme
    Alexandrin avant Philon," in Recueil L. Cerfaux
    (BETL, 6-7; Gembloux: J. Duculot, 1954) 1.105.

Charlesworth, PAMRS, 82-83, 275.

Collins, J. J. and W. Poehlmann. "Artapanus." Unpublished
    Seminar Paper. Harvard New Testament Seminar.
    April 6, 1970. 50 pp.

_____, "Artapanus," in Charlesworth, OTP.

_____, Athens and Jerusalem, 32-38.

Colpe, C. "Artapanos," KP 1 (1964) 615.

Conzelmann, HJC, 149-52.

Dähne, Geschichtliche, 2.200-203.

Dalbert, Missionsliteratur, 42-52.

Denis, Introduction, 255-57.

Eisler, R. Orphisch-dionysische Mysterien-Gedanken in
    der christlichen Antike (Vorträge der Bibliothek
    Warburg, 2; Vorträge, 2. Teil, Ed. F. Saxl.;
    Leipzig/Berlin: Teubner, 1925; repr. Hildesheim:
    Georg Olms, 1966) 6-7, 10.

Ewald, History, 1.50; 2.89-90.

Fraser, Ptolemaic Alexandria, 1.704-706, 714; 2.983, n.
    177, 986, n. 201.

Freudenthal, Alexander Polyhistor, 143-74; 215-18.

Friedländer, Geschichte, 112-14.

Geffcken, Apologeten, xiii-xiv.

Georgi, Gegner, 147-51, 201.

Ginzberg, L. "Artapanus," JE 2 (1904) 145.

Goodenough, E. By Light, Light. The Mystic Gospel of
    Hellenistic Judaism (New Haven: Yale University
    Press, 1935; repr. Amsterdam: Philo Press, 1969)
    291.

Graetz, Geschichte, 3.624-25.

Gutman, Beginnings, 2.109-35.

Gutschmid, Kleine Schriften, 2.184-85.

Hadas, Hellenistic Culture, 90, 96, 125, 172.

Halevy, M. A. Moïse dans l'histoire et dans la légende
     (Judaisme VI; Paris, 1927) 54-55, 61.

Hanhart, R. "Artapanus," BHH 1 (1962) 131-32.

Heinemann, I. "Moses," PW 16.1 (1935) 365-69.

Hengel, "Anonymität," 239-41.

_____, Judaism and Hellenism, 1.90-94, passim.

Holladay, THEIOS ANER, 199-232.

Hopfner, T. Orient und Griechische Philosophie (Beihefte
     zum Alten Orient, ed. W. Schubart, Heft 4; Leipzig:
     J. C. Hinrichs, 1925) 52.

Karpeles, Geschichte, 1.177-78.

Lagrange, M. J. Le Judaïsme avant Jesus-Christ   (Paris:
     J. Gabalda, 1931) 499-500.

Merentites, K. J. "Ο ΙΟΥΔΑΙΟΣ ΛΟΓΙΟΣ ΑΡΤΑΠΑΝΟΣ ΚΑΙ ΤΟ
     ΕΡΓΟΝ ΑΥΤΟΥ (Γλωσσικόν, φιλολογικὸν καὶ θρησκειολογικὸν
     ὑπόμνημα εἰς κείμενα τῆς ἐλληνιστικῆς γραμματείας),"
     Ἐπετηρὶς τῆς Ἑταιρείας Βυζαντινῶν Σπουδαιῶν
     (= Annuaire de l'Association d'Etudes Byzantines)
     27 (1957) 292-339; 29 (1959) 273-321; 30 (1960-61)
     281-350. Reprinted as single volume, Athens, 1961.

_____, "Τὸ πρόβλημα τῆς γνησιότητος τῆς συγγραφῆς τοῦ
     Ἰουδαίου λογίου Ἀρταπάνου," Ἐπιστημονικὴ Ἐπετηρὶς
     τῆς φιλοσοφικῆς Σχολῆς τοῦ ταπεπιστημίου Ἀθηνῶν
     11 (1960-1961) 467-98.

_____, "Artapanus," ThEE 3 (1962) 257-58 [in Greek].

Meyer, E. Der Papyrusfund von Elephantine (Leipzig:
     J. C. Hinrichs, 1912) 28.

Rappaport, S. Agada und Exegese bei Flavius Josephus
     (Wien: Alexander Kohut Memorial Foundation, 1930)
     25-32, 113-26.

Reitzenstein, R. Poimandres. Studien zur griechisch-
     ägyptischen und frühchristlichen Literatur (Leipzig:
     Teubner, 1904) 182.

Schalit, A. "Artapanus," EncJud 3 (1971) 645-46.

_____. קדמוניות היהדים (Jerusalem, 1955[2]) xlvii-xlix.

Schlatter, Geschichte, 193-96.

Schmid-Stählin, Geschichte, 2,1.590.

Schürer, Geschichte, 3.477-80.

Schwartz, "Artapanos," PW 2/1 (1895) 1306.

Susemihl, Geschichte, 2.646-47.

Tiede, Charismatic Figure, 146-77.

Tonneau, R. M. "Moïse dans la tradition syrienne," in
    Moïse: l'homme de l'alliance (Paris: Desclee &
    Cie., 1955) 245-65.

Vaillant, Historicis, 74-83.

Vermes, G. "La figure de Moïse au tourant de deux testa-
    ments," in Moïse, l'homme de l'alliance (Paris:
    Desclee & Cie., 1955) 63-92.

Wacholder, "Biblical Chronology," 459-60.

Walter, N. "Artapanus," JSHRZ (1,2) 121-36.

_____, Untersuchungen, 57-85, 176-215.

Weinreich, O. "Gebet und Wunder. Zwei Abhandlungen zur
    Religions- und Literaturgeschichte." (1. Abhandlung:
    "Primitiver Gebetsegoismus," 169-99; 2. Abhandlung:
    "Türöffnung im Wunder-, Prodigien- und Zauberglauben
    der Antike, des Judentums und Christentums," 200-452)
    in Festschrift Genethliakon Wilhelm Schmid (edd.
    F. Focke, et al.; Tübinger Beiträge zur Altertums-
    wissenschaft, 5; Stuttgart: W. Kohlhammer, 1929;
    repr. in O. Weinreich, Religionsgeschichtliche
    Studien (Darmstadt: Wissenschaftliche Buchgesell-
    schaft, 1968) 1-298) 298-309, esp. 299, 307.

Willrich, Judaica, 111-17.

_____. Juden und Griechen vor der makkabäischen
    Erhebung (Göttingen, 1895) 160.

Index to Editions and Translations

Fragment One

Source: Eusebius, P.E. 9.18.1.

Reference Number in P.E.:   Steph., 245; Vig., 420 a-b.

Greek Text Used: Mras, GCS (43,1) 8.1, p. 504,
     lines 10-18.

Editions: Steph., 245; Vig., 420 a-b; Hein., 2.21;
     Gais., 2.373-74; Müll., FHG 3.212-13 (= No. 4);
     Migne, PG (21), col. 709 B (notes, col. 1567);
     Dind., 1.486; Freu., 231 (= Frg. 1); Giff.,
     1.529-30 (notes, 4.301-302); Stearns, 42-43
     (= Frg. 1); Mras, GCS (43,1) 8.1, 504; Jac.,FGrH
     3.680-81 (= No.726,Frg. 1); Denis, 186 (= Frg. 1).

Translations:

     English: Giff., 3.451.

     French:

     German: Riessler, 186 (= Frg. 1); Walter
                (JS, 1.2), 127 (= Frg. 1).

Fragment Two

Source: Eusebius, P.E. 9.23.1-4.

Reference Number in P.E.:   Steph., 251; Vig., 429b -
     430b.

Greek Text Used: Mras, GCS (43,1) 8.1, p. 516,
     line 11 - p. 517, line 14.

Editions: Steph., 251; Vig., 429b-430b; Hein.,
     2.31-32; Gais., 2.390-92; Müll., FHG 3.219
     (= No. 10); Migne, PG (21), col. 725 A-D
     (notes, col. 1573); Dind., 1.496-97; Freu.,
     231-32 (= Frg. 2); Giff., 1.539-40 (notes,
     4.309-10); Stearns, 44-46 (= Frg. 2); Mras,
     GCS (43,1) 8.1,   516-17; Jac., FGrH 3.681
     (= No. 726, Frg. 2); Denis, 186-87 (= Frg. 2).

Translations:

     English: Giff., 3.460.

     French:

     German: Riessler, 186-87 (= Frg. 2);
                Walter (JS, 1.2), 127-28 (= Frg. 2).

Fragment Three

Source: Eusebius, P.E. 9.27.1-37.

Reference Number in P.E.: Steph., 252-55; Vig. 431d - 436d.

Greek Text Used: Mras, GCS (43,1) 8.1, p. 519, line 8 - p. 524, line 12.

Editions: Steph., 252-55; Vig., 431d-436d; Hein., 2.33-38; Gais., 2.394-404; Müll., FHG 3.220-24 (= No. 14); Migne, PG (21), col. 728 C - 736 B (notes, col. 1573-74); Dind., 1.498-505; Freu., 232-36 (= Frg. 3); Giff., 1.542-47 (notes, 4.312-15); Stearns, 46-56 (= Frg. 3); Mras, GCS (43,1) 8.1, 519-24; Jac., FGrH 3.682-86 (= No. 726, Frg. 3); Denis, 187-95 (= Frg. 3).

Translations:

   English: Giff., 3.462-67; Tiede, Charismatic Figure, 317-24.

   French:

   German: Riessler, 187-91 (= Frg. 3); Walter (JS, 1.2), 128-36 (= Frg. 3).

Fragment 3b = Frg. 3, par. 23-25.

Source: Clement of Alexandria, Stromata 1.23.154.2-3.

Greek Text Used: Stählin-Früchtel, GCS (52), p. 96, lines 9-18.

Editions: Dind., 2.124 (notes, 4.228); Migne, PG (8), col. 900 B - 901 A; Caster, SC (30), 1.155; Jac., FGrH 3.684-85 (= No. 726, Frg. 3. 23-25b); Stählin-Früchtel, GCS (52) p. 96; Denis, 192 (= Frg. 3.23-25 parallel).

Translations:

   English: Wilson (ANF), 2.335.
   French: Caster (SC, 30), 1.155.
   German: Stählin (BK, 17), 3.128-29.

FRAGMENT ONE (Eusebius, P.E. 9.18.1)

ΑΡΤΑΠΑΝΟΥ ΠΕΡΙ ΤΟΥ ΑΥΤΟΥ· ΑΠΟ ΤΗΣ ΑΥΤΗΣ   420a
ΤΟΥ ΠΟΛΥΙΣΤΟΡΟΣ ΓΡΑΦΗΣ

(1) |"Ἀρτάπανος δέ φησιν ἐν τοῖς Ἰουδαϊκοῖς   (1)
τοὺς μὲν Ἰουδαίους ὀνομάζεσθαι Ἑρμιούθ, ὃ εἶναι
5 μεθερμηνευθὲν κατὰ τὴν Ἑλληνίδα φωνὴν Ἰουδαῖοι·
καλεῖσθαι δὲ αὐτοὺς Ἑβραίους ἀπὸ Ἀβραάμου.
τοῦτον δέ φησι πανοικίᾳ ἐλθεῖν εἰς Αἴγυπτον πρὸς
τὸν τῶν Αἰγυπτίων βασιλέα Φαρεθώθην καὶ   τὴν   420b
ἀστρολογίαν αὐτὸν διδάξαι· μείναντα δὲ ἔτη ἐκεῖ
10 εἴκοσι πάλιν εἰς τοὺς κατὰ Συρίαν ἀπαλλαγῆναι
τόπους· τῶν δὲ τούτῳ συνελθόντων πόλλους ἐν
Αἰγύπτῳ καταμεῖναι διὰ τὴν εὐδαιμονίαν τῆς
χώρας."

FRAGMENT TWO (Eusebius, P.E. 9.23.1-4)

Τούτοις καὶ τὰ ἑξῆς περὶ τοῦ Ἰωσὴφ ἐκ τῆς
15 αὐτῆς τοῦ Πολυΐστορος γραφῆς ἐπισυνήφθω·
ΑΡΤΑΠΑΝΟΥ ΠΕΡΙ ΤΟΥ ΙΩΣΗΦ· ΑΠΟ ΤΗΣ ΑΥΤΗΣ
ΤΟΥ ΠΟΛΥΙΣΤΟΡΟΣ ΓΡΑΦΗΣ

(1) "Ἀρτάπανος δέ φησιν ἐν τῷ Περὶ Ἰουδαίων   (1)
τῷ Ἀβραὰμ Ἰωσὴφ ἀπόγονον γενέσθαι, υἱὸν δὲ   429c
20 Ἰακώβου· συνέσει δὲ καὶ φρονήσει παρὰ τοὺς

BION

1-2 ΑΡΤ. -- ΓΡΑΦ. ON: om. I: Ἀρτ. -- Αὐτοῦ Β |
8 τῶν Αἰγυπτίων om. Β | Φαρεθώνην Steph. |
9-10 εἴκοσι ἐκεῖ Β | 11 τούτῳ: τούτων Ι | 14 ἑξῆς Ι:
om. ΒΟΝ | 14-15 τῆς αὐτῆς om. Β | 15 γραφῆς om. Β |
ἐπισυνῆφθαι Ι | 16-17 ΑΡΤ. -- ΓΡΑΦ. Ο: Ἀρτ. περὶ
τοῦ Ἰωσ.· Ἀπὸ τοῦ αὐτοῦ τοῦ Πολ. γραφῆς Ν: Ἀρτ. περὶ
Ἰωσ. Β: om. Ι | 18 Ἀρταπάνος ΟΝ | 19 Ἀβραὰμ Β |

FRAGMENT ONE[1]

Artapanus' Remarks Concerning the Same Man;[2]
From the Same Work by Polyhistor

(1)   (1) "Artapanus, in his work Judaica,[3] says that
the Jews were named Hermiouth,[4] which means "Jews"[4a]
when translated into the Greek language; and he says
that they were called Hebrews[5] from the time of
Abraham. He also says that Abraham came with his
entire household into Egypt to Pharethothes,[6] the
king of the Egyptians, and taught him astrology.[7]
After he had remained there twenty years,[8] he
returned to the regions of Syria,[9] but many of those
who had accompanied him remained behind in Egypt,
attracted by the prosperity of the country."[10]

FRAGMENT TWO[11]

In addition to these things, let me also relate
from this same work of Polyhistor what is said next
concerning Joseph:

Artapanus' Remarks Concerning Joseph;
From the Same Work of Polyhistor

(1)   (23.1) "Artapanus says in his book Concerning
the Jews[12] that Joseph, the son of Jacob, was
descended from Abraham. Because he excelled all the

ἄλλους διενεγκόντα ὑπὸ τῶν ἀδελφῶν ἐπιβουλευθῆναι·
προϊδόμενον δὲ <u>τὴν ἐπισύστασιν</u> δεηθῆναι τῶν
ἀστυγειτόνων Ἀράβων εἰς τὴν Αἴγυπτον αὐτὸν
διακομίσαι· τοὺς δὲ τὸ ἐντυγχανόμενον ποιῆσαι·
5 εἶναι γὰρ τοὺς τῶν Ἀράβων βασιλεῖς ἀπογόνους
Ἰσραήλ, υἱοὺς τοῦ Ἀβραάμ, Ἰσαὰκ δὲ ἀδελφούς.
(2) ἐλθόντα δὲ αὐτὸν εἰς τὴν Αἴγυπτον καὶ συσ-   (2)
ταθέντα τῷ βασιλεῖ διοικητὴν τῆς ὅλης γενέσθαι
χώρας. καὶ πρότερον ἀτάκτως τῶν Αἰγυπτίων γεω-   429d
10 μορούντων, διὰ τὸ τὴν χώραν ἀδιαίρετον εἶναι καὶ
τῶν ἐλασσόνων ὑπὸ τῶν κρεισσόνων ἀδικουμένων,
τοῦτον πρῶτον τήν τε γῆν διελεῖν καὶ ὅροις
διασημήνασθαι καὶ πολλὴν χερσευομένην γεωργήσιμον
ἀποτελέσαι καί τινας τῶν ἀρουρῶν τοῖς ἱερεῦσιν
15 ἀποκληρῶσαι. (3) τοῦτον δὲ καὶ μέτρα εὑρεῖν   (3)
καὶ μεγάλως αὐτὸν ὑπὸ τῶν Αἰγυπτίων διὰ ταῦτα
ἀγαπηθῆναι. γῆμαι δ᾽ αὐτὸν Ἡλιουπολίτου ἱερέως
Ἀσενὲθ θυγατέρα, ἐξ ἧς γεννῆσαι παῖδας. μετὰ
δὲ ταῦτα παραγενέσθαι | πρὸς αὐτὸν τόν τε πατέρα   430a
20 καὶ τοὺς ἀδελφοὺς κομίζοντας πολλὴν ὕπαρξιν καὶ
κατοικισθῆναι ἐν τῇ Ἡλίου πόλει καὶ Σάει καὶ
τοὺς Σύρους πλεονάσαι ἐν τῇ Αἰγύπτῳ. (4) τούτους   (4)
δέ φησι καὶ τὸ ἐν Ἀθὼς καὶ τὸ ἐν Ἡλιουπόλει
ἱερὸν κατασκευάσαι τοὺς Ἑρμιοὺθ ὀνομαζομένους.
25 μετὰ δὲ ταῦτα τελευτῆσαι τόν τε Ἰωσὴφ καὶ τὸν

BION

2 προϊδόμενον Dind.: προειδόμενον B (ει ras. partim)
ION | δεηθῆναι BO²: δεθῆναι I: δειχθῆναι O¹N |
4 δὲ τὸ ἐντυγχ.: δ᾽ οὕτω B | 6 Ἰσμαήλ, υἱοῦ Gais. |
Ἀβραάμ ON: Ἀβραάμ BI | 9-15 καὶ -- εὑρεῖν om. B |
17 Ἡλιουπολίτου om. B |18 Ἀσενὲθ Steph. (cf. Demetrius,
Frg. 2, par. 12): Ἀσσενέθ ION: Ἀσενεθὲμ Bᵃᶜ: Ἀσεκε-
θὲμ B¹ |18-19 ἐξ -- ταῦτα om. B | 19 παραγ. δὲ B |
21 κατοικῆσαι B | Ἡλίου πόλει BON: πόλει I Steph. |
καὶ Σάει Giff.: καὶ Σαεὶ ON: καὶ Σαὶν I: om. B:
Καισὰν Steph.: καὶ Σὰν (= Tanis) Freu. (p. 217): ἐν
πόλει καλουμένῃ Σάν (vel Κεσσὰν) ? Jac. (cf. Frg. 3, par.2)|
22 τοῦτον B | 23 τὸ ἐν Ἀθὼς: τὸ ἐν Πειθῶ Seguier (PG
(21), col. 1573) | ἐν Ἀθὼς καὶ τὸ om. B | 24-p.208, 1
τοὺς -- Αἰγυπτίων om. B | 25 τε ON: om. I | Ἰωσήφ:
Ἀβραάμ vel Ἰακὼβ ? Jac. (cf. Frg. 3, par. 1) |

other sons of Jacob in wisdom and understanding,[13]
his brothers plotted against him. Anticipating the
conspiracy, however, he besought the neighboring
Arabs[14] to transport him to Egypt,[15] and they did as
he requested, for the kings of the Arabs, being the
sons of Abraham and brothers of Isaac, are descendants

(2) of Israel.[16]   (2)   After he came into Egypt and became
acquainted with the king, he became minister of
finance for the entire country.[17] Prior to that time
the Egyptians had farmed the land haphazardly because
the countryside was not divided into allotments, and
consequently the weak were treated unfairly by the
strong. Joseph was the very first to subdivide the
land, to indicate this with boundaries, to render
much of the waste land tillable, to assign some of

(3) the arable land to the priests.[18]   (3) In addition,
it was he who discovered measures, and he was greatly
loved by the Egyptians because of these accomplishments.[19] He married Asenath,[20] the daughter of a
priest of Heliopolis,[21] by whom he fathered children.[22]
Later, both his father and his brothers came to him,
bringing with them many possessions.[23] They settled
in Heliopolis and Sais,[24] and the Syrians[25] multiplied

(4) in Egypt.   (4)   He says that these people named
Hermiouth[26] built both the temple in Athos[27] and the
one in Heliopolis.[28] Eventually Joseph and the king

βασιλέα τῶν Αἰγυπτίων. τὸν οὖν Ἰωσὴφ κρατοῦντα
τῆς Αἰγύπτου τὸν τῶν ἑπτὰ ἐτῶν σῖτον, γενόμενον
κατὰ τὴν φορὰν ἄπλετον, παραθέσθαι καὶ τῆς
Αἰγύπτου δεσπότην γενέσθαι."

FRAGMENT THREE   (Eusebius, P.E. 9.27.1-37)

5   ΑΡΤΑΠΑΝΟΥ ΠΕΡΙ ΜΩΣΕΩΣ ΟΜΟΙΩΣ   431d

          (1) "Ἀρτάπανος δέ φησιν ἐν τῇ Περὶ Ἰουδαίων,   (1)
    Ἀβραὰμ τελευτήσαντος καὶ τοῦ υἱοῦ αὐτοῦ Μεμψασ-
    θενώθ, ὁμοίως δὲ καὶ τοῦ βασιλέως τῶν Αἰγυπτίων,
    τὴν δυναστείαν παραλαβεῖν τὸν υἱὸν αὐτοῦ Παλ-
10 μανώθην. (2) τοῦτον δὲ τοῖς Ἰουδαίοις φαύλως   (2)
    προσφέρεσθαι· καὶ πρῶτον μὲν τήν τε Σάιν οἰκο-
    δομῆσαι τό τε ἐπ' αὐτῇ ἱερὸν καθιδρύσασθαι, εἶτα
    τὸν ἐν Ἡλιουπόλει | ναὸν κατασκευάσαι.   432a
    (3) τοῦτον δὲ γεννῆσαι θυγατέρα Μέρριν, ἣν   (3)
15 Χενεφρῇ τινι κατεγγυῆσαι, τῶν ὑπὲρ Μέμφιν τόπων
    βασιλεύοντι· πολλοὺς γὰρ τότε τῆς Αἰγύπτου
    βασιλεύειν· ταύτην δὲ στεῖραν ὑπάρχουσαν ὑπο-
    βαλέσθαι τινὸς τῶν Ἰουδαίων παιδίον, τοῦτο δὲ
    Μώϋσον ὀνομάσαι· ὑπὸ δὲ τῶν Ἑλλήνων αὐτὸν
20 ἀνδρωθέντα Μουσαῖον προσαγορευθῆναι. (4) γενέσθαι   (4)
    δὲ τὸν Μώϋσον τοῦτον Ὀρφέως διδάσκαλον. ἀνδρω-
    θέντα δ' αὐτὸν πολλὰ τοῖς ἀνθρώποις εὔχρηστα
    παραδοῦναι· καὶ γὰρ πλοῖα καὶ μηχανὰς πρὸς τὰς
    λιθοθεσίας καὶ τὰ Αἰγύπτια ὅπλα καὶ τὰ ὄργανα τὰ   432b
25 ὑδρευτικὰ καὶ πολεμικὰ καὶ τὴν φιλοσοφίαν ἐξευρεῖν·

BION

1 Αἰγυπτίων <   > Freu. (p. 145) | 1-3 τὸν² -- παραθέσ-
θαι om. B | 2 ἐτῶν om. I | 3 ἄπλετον I: ἄπλητα ON |
5 ΑΡΤ. -- ΟΜ.   ΟΝ: om. ΒΙ | 6-p.224,19 Ἀρτάπανος --
ἐννέα om. B | 7-8 Μεμψασθενώθ, ante τοῦ βασιλέως transp.
Freu. (p. 217) | 11 τε Σάιν Mras (cf. Frg. 2, par. 3):
Τέσσαν ΙΟΝ: † Τέσσαν Jac.: Κεσσὰν Steph. | 20 {ἀνδρω-
θέντα} Freu. (p. 217) | 20sqq. Ὀρφέως διδάσκαλος ὁ Μωϋσῆς.
καὶ ὅρα οἷα περὶ τούτου διέξεισιν I^mg |

of the Egyptians died. As long as Joseph held power
over the financial affairs of Egypt, he stored up
the grain surplus which had accumulated during the
seven years as a result of the immense production,
and consequently he became the lord of Egypt."[29]

FRAGMENT THREE[30]

Artapanus' Remarks Concerning Moses -- In Similar Fashion

(1)   (27.1) "Artapanus says in his book Concerning
the Jews that after Abraham[31] and his son Mempsasthenoth[32] died, the king of the Egyptians died as well,

(2) and his son Palmanothes[33] received the crown. (2) Now
Palmanothes dealt meanly with the Jews.[34] First he
built Sais,[35] then he set up the temple there. Later

(3) he built the sanctuary in Heliopolis.[36] (3) He
fathered a daughter Merris[37] whom he betrothed to a
certain Chenephres,[38] a ruler of the regions above
Memphis. At that time there were many rulers in
Egypt.[39] But since she was barren,[40] she took as her
own a child of one of the Jews[41] and named him Moses.[42]
When he became a man,[43] he was called Mousaios[44] by

(4) the Greeks. (4) This Moses became the teacher of
Orpheus.[45] When he reached manhood, he bestowed on
humanity many useful contributions[46], for he invented
ships, machines for lifting stones, Egyptian weapons,
devices for drawing water and fighting, and philosophy.[47]

ἔτι δὲ τὴν πόλιν εἰς λς' νομοὺς διελεῖν καὶ
ἑκάστῳ τῶν νομῶν ἀποτάξαι τὸν θεὸν σεφθήσεσθαι
τά τε ἱερὰ γράμματα τοῖς ἱερεῦσιν, εἶναι δὲ καὶ
αἰλούρους καὶ κύνας καὶ ἴβεις· ἀπονεῖμαι δὲ καὶ
5   τοῖς ἱερεῦσιν ἐξαίρετον χώραν. (5) ταῦτα δὲ πάντα   (5)
ποιῆσαι χάριν τοῦ τὴν μοναρχίαν βεβαίαν τῷ
Χενεφρῇ διαφυλάξαι. πρότερον γὰρ ἀδιατάκτους
ὄντας τοὺς ὄχλους ποτὲ μὲν ἐκβάλλειν, ποτὲ δὲ
καθιστάνειν βασιλεῖς, καὶ πολλάκις μὲν τοὺς   432c
10 αὐτούς, ἐνιάκις δὲ ἄλλους. (6) διὰ ταῦτα οὖν   (6)
τὸν Μώϋσον ὑπὸ τῶν ὄχλων ἀγαπηθῆναι καὶ ὑπὸ τῶν
ἱερέων ἰσοθέου τιμῆς καταξιωθέντα προσαγορευθῆναι
Ἑρμῆν, διὰ τὴν τῶν ἱερῶν γραμμάτων ἑρμηνείαν.
(7) τὸν δὲ Χενεφρῆν ὁρῶντα τὴν ἀρετὴν τοῦ   (7)
15 Μωϋσου φθονῆσαι αὐτῷ καὶ ζητεῖν αὐτὸν ἐπ' εὐλόγῳ
αἰτίᾳ τινὶ ἀνελεῖν. καὶ δή ποτε τῶν Αἰθιόπων
ἐπιστρατευσαμένων τῇ Αἰγύπτῳ τὸν Χενεφρῆν ὑπολαβόντα εὑρηκέναι καιρὸν εὔθετον πέμψαι τὸν
Μώϋσον ἐπ' αὐτοὺς στρατηγὸν μετὰ δυνάμεως· τὸ δὲ
20 τῶν γεωργῶν αὐτῷ συστῆσαι πλῆθος, ὑπολαβόντα   432d
ῥᾳδίως αὐτὸν διὰ τὴν τῶν στρατιωτῶν ἀσθένειαν
ὑπὸ τῶν πολεμίων ἀναιρεθήσεσθαι. (8) τὸν δὲ   (8)
Μώϋσον ἐλθόντα ἐπὶ τὸν Ἑρμοπολίτην ὀνομαζόμενον
νομόν, ἔχοντα περὶ δέκα μυριάδας γεωργῶν, αὐτοῦ
25 καταστρατοπεδεῦσαι· πέμψαι δὲ στρατηγοὺς τοὺς
προκαθεδουμένους τῆς χώρας, οὓς δὴ πλεονεκτεῖν
ἐπιφανῶς κατὰ τὰς μάχας· λέγειν δέ φησιν Ἡλιουπολίτας γενέσθαι τὸν πόλεμον τοῦτον ἔτη δέκα.
(9) τοὺς οὖν περὶ τὸν Μώϋσον διὰ τὸ μέγεθος τῆς   (9)
30 στρατιᾶς πόλιν ἐν τούτῳ κτίσαι τῷ τόπῳ καὶ τὴν

ION

1 νομοὺς Mras: νόμους MSS | 2 νομῶν Mras: νόμων MSS |
3 καὶ I: om. ON | 4 ἴβεις I: ἴβις ON | 7 γὰρ ON: om. I |
12 καταξιωθέντα I: ἀξιωθέντα ON | 16 αἰτίᾳ τινὶ I:
τινὶ αἰτίᾳ ON | 20 γεωργῶν ON: γονέων I |
24 νομόν Mras: νόμον MSS | 25 καταστρατεῦσαι I |
30 στρατιᾶς Steph.: στρατίας (!) I: στρατείας ON |

He also divided the state[48] into thirty-six nomes,
and to each of the nomes he assigned the god to be
worshipped;[49] in addition, he assigned the sacred
writings[50] to the priests. The gods he assigned were
cats, dogs, and ibises.[51] He set aside as well land

(5) exclusively for the use of the priests.[52] (5) He
did all these things for the sake of keeping the
monarchy stable for Chenephres,[53] for prior to this
time the masses were disorganized and they would
sometimes depose, sometimes install rulers, often

(6) the same persons, but sometimes others. (6) Thus,
for these reasons Moses was loved by the masses,
and being deemed worthy of divine honor[54] by the
priests, he was called Hermes because of his ability

(7) to interpret the sacred writings.[55] (7) When
Chenephres saw the fame of Moses, he became jealous
and sought to kill him on some reasonable pretext.
Thus when the Ethiopians[56] marched against Egypt,
Chenephres, supposing that he had found the right
moment, sent Moses against them as the commander of
a force of troops. He conscripted a band of farmers
for Moses, rashly supposing that Moses would be killed

(8) by the enemy because his troops were weak. (8) Moses
came to the nome called Hermopolis[57] with approximately
100,000 farmers, and he camped there. He commissioned
as generals those who would eventually preside as
rulers[58] over the region, and they won every battle
with distinction. He[59] says that the Heliopolitans

(9) report that the war lasted ten years.[60] (9) Thus,
Moses and those with him, because of the size of
army, founded a city in this place, and they

ἶβιν ἐν αὐτῇ καθιερῶσαι, διὰ τὸ ταύτην τὰ
βλάπτοντα ζῷα τοὺς ἀνθρώπους ἀναιρεῖν· | προσ-   433a
αγορεῦσαι δὲ αὐτὴν Ἑρμοῦ πόλιν. (10) οὕτω δὴ   (10)
τοὺς Αἰθίοπας, καίπερ ὄντας πολεμίους, στέρξαι
5   τὸν Μώϋσον ὥστε καὶ τὴν περιτομὴν τῶν αἰδοίων
παρ' ἐκείνου μαθεῖν· οὐ μόνον δὲ τούτους, ἀλλὰ
καὶ τοὺς ἱερεῖς ἅπαντας. (11) τὸν δὲ Χενεφρῆν   (11)
λυθέντος τοῦ πολέμου λόγῳ μὲν αὐτὸν ἀποδέξασθαι,
ἔργῳ δὲ ἐπιβουλεύειν. παρελόμενον γοῦν αὐτοῦ
10   τοὺς ὄχλους τοὺς μὲν ἐπὶ τὰ ὅρια τῆς Αἰθιοπίας
πέμψαι προφυλακῆς χάριν, τοῖς δὲ προστάξαι τὸν
ἐν Διὸς πόλει ναὸν ἐξ ὀπτῆς πλίνθου κατεσκευασ-
μένον καθαιρεῖν, ἕτερον δὲ λίθινον κατασκευάσαι   433b
τὸ πλησίον ὅρος λατομήσαντας· τάξαι δὲ ἐπὶ τῆς
15   οἰκοδομίας ἐπιστάτην Ναχέρωτα. (12) τὸν δὲ   (12)
ἐλθόντα μετὰ Μωύσου εἰς Μέμφιν πυθέσθαι παρ'
αὐτοῦ εἴ τι ἄλλο ἐστὶν εὔχρηστον τοῖς ἀνθρώποις·
τὸν δὲ φάναι γένος τῶν βοῶν, διὰ τὸ τὴν γῆν ἀπὸ
τούτων ἀροῦσθαι· τὸν δὲ Χενεφρῆν, προσαγορεύσαντα
20   ταῦρον Ἄπιν, κελεῦσαι ἱερὸν αὐτοῦ τοὺς ὄχλους
καθιδρύσασθαι καὶ τὰ ζῷα τὰ καθιερωθέντα ὑπὸ τοῦ
Μωύσου κελεύειν ἐκεῖ φέροντας θάπτειν, κατακρύ-
πτειν θέλοντα τὰ τοῦ Μωύσου ἐπινοήματα.
(13) ἀποξενωσάντων δὲ αὐτὸν τῶν Αἰγυπτίων   (13)
25   ὁρκωμοτῆσαι τοὺς φίλους μὴ ἐξαγγεῖλαι τῷ Μωύσῳ   433c

ION

1 αὐτῇ I: αὐτῷ ON | 7 ἱερεῖς: πέριξ Diels apud
P. Wendland (Berliner philologische Wochenschrift 22
(1902) 1322) apud Mras | 11 προφυλακῆς Steph.:
πρὸς φυλακῆς MSS | 12 Διὸς πόλει: Διὸς πολει I:
Διοσπόλει ON | 13 post λίθινον verbum ὅρος addunt ON |
16 Μωυσοῦ ON | 23 θέλοντα Vig. (in not.): -τας MSS |
Μωυσοῦ ON | 24 ἀποξενωσάντων Steph.: ἀποξενώσαντας
MSS | 25 ὁρκομωτῆσαι ON | Μωύσῳ Steph.: Μωυσῆ
MSS |

consecrated the ibis[61] in the city because of its
reputation for killing those animals that were harmful
(10) to men.   They named it "The City of Hermes."[62]   (10) So
then, although the Ethiopians had been enemies, they
came to love Moses, and as a result learned from him
the practice of circumcising the genitalia -- not only
(11) they but all the priests as well.[63]   (11)   When the
war was over, Chenephres welcomed him back in word
but plotted against him in deed.   In fact, after
taking away Moses' troops, Chenephres sent some of
them to the borders of Ethiopia as a defense garrison
and ordered others to destroy the temple in Diospolis.[64]
This temple was constructed with baked bricks, but he
ordered them to build another one of stone quarried
from the mountain nearby.   He appointed Nacheros to
(12) be in charge of the construction.   (12)   When he[65]
came with Moses to Memphis, Chenephres inquired of
him[66] whether there was anything else useful to man-
kind, and he suggested a breed of oxen because of their
usefulness in tilling the land.   Chenephres named   a
bull Apis[67] and commanded the people to dedicate a
temple to it.   He also ordered that the animals which
had been consecrated by Moses be brought there and
buried,[68] wishing thereby to conceal the ideas of
(13) Moses.   (13)   But when the Egyptians began to reject
Chenephres,[69]   he swore his advisors to an oath not

τὴν ἐπισυνισταμένην αὐτῷ ἐπιβουλὴν καὶ προβαλέσ-
θαι τοὺς ἀναιρήσοντας αὐτόν. (14) μηδενὸς δ'   (14)
ὑπακούσαντος ὀνειδίσαι τὸν Χενεφρῆν Χανεθώθην,
τὸν μάλιστα προσαγορευόμενον ὑπ' αὐτοῦ· τὸν δὲ
5 ὀνειδισθέντα ὑποσχέσθαι τὴν ἐπίθεσιν, λαβόντα
καιρόν. (15) ὑπὸ δὲ τοῦτον τὸν καιρὸν τῆς   (15)
Μέρριδος τελευτησάσης ὑποσχέσθαι τὸν Χενεφρῆν τῷ
τε Μωύσῳ καὶ τῷ Χανεθώθῃ τὸ σῶμα διακομίσαντας   433d
εἰς τοὺς ὑπὲρ Αἴγυπτον τόπους θάψαι, ὑπολαβόντα
10 τὸν Μώυσον ὑπὸ τοῦ Χανεθώθου ἀναιρεθήσεσθαι.
(16) πορευομένων δὲ αὐτῶν τὴν ἐπιβουλὴν τῷ Μωύσῳ   (16)
τῶν συνειδότων ἐξαγγεῖλαί τινα· τὸν δὲ φυλάσσοντα
αὐτὸν τὴν μὲν Μέρριν θάψαι, τὸν δὲ ποταμὸν καὶ
τὴν ἐν ἐκείνῳ πόλιν Μερόην προσαγορεῦσαι· τιμᾶσ-
15 θαι δὲ τὴν Μέρριν ταύτην ὑπὸ τῶν ἐγχωρίων οὐκ
ἐλαχίστως ἢ τὴν Ἴσιν. (17) Ἀάρωνα δὲ τὸν τοῦ   (17)
Μωύσου ἀδελφὸν τὰ περὶ τὴν ἐπιβουλὴν ἐπιγνόντα
συμβουλεῦσαι τῷ ἀδελφῷ φυγεῖν εἰς τὴν Ἀραβίαν·
τὸν δὲ πεισθέντα, ἀπὸ Μέμφεως τὸν Νεῖλον δια-
20 πλεύσαντα ἀπαλλάσσεσθαι εἰς τὴν Ἀραβίαν. | 434a
(18) τὸν δὲ Χανεθώθην πυθόμενον τοῦ Μωύσου τὴν   (18)
φυγὴν ἐνεδρεύειν ὡς ἀναιρήσοντα· ἰδόντα δὲ
ἐρχόμενον σπάσασθαι τὴν μάχαιραν ἐπ' αὐτόν, τὸν
δὲ Μώυσον προκατατασχήσαντα τήν τε χεῖρα κατασχεῖν
25 αὐτοῦ καὶ σπασάμενον τὸ ξίφος φονεῦσαι τὸν
Χανεθώθην· (19) διεκδρᾶναι δὲ εἰς τὴν Ἀραβίαν   (19)
καὶ Ῥαγουήλῳ τῷ τῶν τόπων ἄρχοντι συμβιοῦν,
λαβόντα τὴν ἐκείνου θυγατέρα· τὸν δὲ Ῥαγουῆλον
βούλεσθαι στρατεύειν ἐπὶ τοὺς Αἰγυπτίους, κατά-
30 γειν βουλόμενον τὸν Μώυσον καὶ τὴν δυναστείαν τῇ

ION

1-2 προβάλλεσθαι I | 4 προσαγορευόμενον I: προσ-
αγόμενον ON | 7 Μερίδος I | 8 Μωύσῳ I^ac: Μωύση I¹ |
10 Χανεθώθου I: Χανεθώθη ON | 11 Μωύσῳ edd.:
Μωσεῖ MSS | 13 αὐτὸν Mras: αὐτόν MSS | 16 ἐλαχίστως
ION: ἔλαττον Steph. | 24 προκατατασχήσαντα I: προκατα-
τα^ρχήσαντα O: προκαταχχήσαντα N: προκαταχ. D |
27 τῷ om. ON |

to inform Moses of the plot which was being formed
(14) against him and he appointed his assassins. (14) But
no one obeyed, and Chenephres reprimanded Chanethothes
whom he had especially designated for the task.
Duly censured, Chanethothes promised to make the
assault as soon as he found an appropriate
(15) time. (15) About this time Merris died, and
Chenephres entrusted[70] her body to both Moses and
Chanethothes for them to transport it to the region
above Egypt[71] for burial, supposing that Moses would
(16) be killed by Chanethothes. (16) But while they were
en route, one of those who knew about the plot reported it to Moses.[72] He guardedly buried Merris, then
named the river and the city in that place Meroe.[73]
This Merris was honored by the inhabitants no less
(17) highly than Isis.[74] (17) Aaron, the brother of
Moses, upon learning of the plot, advised his brother
to flee into Arabia. He was persuaded and sailed
across the Nile from Memphis, escaping into
(18) Arabia. (18) Now when Chanethothes learned that
Moses had fled, he lay in wait in order to kill him.
When he saw Moses approaching, he drew his dagger
on him, but Moses reacted too quickly for him,
restrained his hand, and then drew his own sword and
(19) killed Chanethothes.[75] (19) He then fled into
Arabia where he took up residence with Raguel,[76]
the chieftain of the region, and he married Raguel's
daughter. Raguel wanted to wage war against the
Egyptians because he wished to return Moses from

τε θυγατρὶ καὶ τῷ γαμβρῷ κατασκευάσαι· τὸν δὲ
Μώϋσον ἀποκωλῦσαι, στοχαζόμενον τῶν ὁμοφύλων·   434b
τὸν δὲ ʽΡαγουῆλον διακωλύοντα στρατεύειν τοῖς
ʺΑραψι προστάξαι λῃστεύειν τὴν Αἴγυπτον. (20) ὑπὸ   (20)
5   δὲ τὸν αὐτὸν χρόνον καὶ τὸν Χενεφρῆν πρῶτον
ἁπάντων ἀνθρώπων ἐλεφαντιάσαντα   μεταλλάξαι·
τούτῳ δὲ τῷ πάθει περιπεσεῖν διὰ τὸ τοὺς ʼΙουδαίους προστάξαι σινδόνας ἀμφιέννυσθαι, ἐρεᾶν
δὲ ἐσθῆτα μὴ ἀμπέχεσθαι, ὅπως ὄντες ἐπίσημοι
10   κολάζωνται ὑπ᾽ αὐτοῦ. (21) τὸν δὲ Μώϋσον εὔχεσθαι   (21)
τῷ θεῷ, ἤδη ποτὲ τοὺς λαοὺς παῦσαι τῶν κακο-
παθειῶν. ἱλασκομένου δ᾽ αὐτοῦ αἰφνιδίως φησὶν   434c
ἐκ τῆς γῆς πῦρ ἀναφθῆναι καὶ τοῦτο κάεσθαι, μήτε
ὕλης μήτε ἄλλης τινὸς ξυλείας οὔσης ἐν τῷ   τόπῳ.
15   τὸν δὲ Μώϋσον δείσαντα τὸ γεγονὸς φεύγειν· φωνὴν
δ᾽ αὐτῷ θείαν εἰπεῖν στρατεύειν ἐπ᾽ Αἴγυπτον καὶ
καὶ τοὺς ʼΙουδαίους διασώσαντα εἰς τὴν ἀρχαίαν
ἀγαγεῖν πατρίδα.   (22) τὸν δὲ θαρρήσαντα δύναμιν   (22)
πολεμίαν ἐπάγειν διαγνῶναι τοῖς Αἰγυπτίοις·
20   πρῶτον δὲ πρὸς ʼΑάρωνα τὸν ἀδελφὸν ἐλθεῖν. τὸν
δὲ βασιλέα τῶν Αἰγυπτίων πυθόμενον τὴν τοῦ
Μώϋσου παρουσίαν καλέσαι πρὸς αὐτὸν καὶ πυν-   434d
θάνεσθαι ἐφ᾽ ὅ τι ἥκοι· τὸν δὲ φάναι, διότι
προστάσσειν αὐτῷ τὸν τῆς οἰκουμένης δεσπότην
25   ἀπολῦσαι τοὺς ʼΙουδαίους. →

ION

2 τὸ στοχαζ. Ι | 3 ʽΡαγούηλον ΟΝ | διακωλυθέντα Jac.|
8 ἐρεᾶν Steph.: ἐρέαν MSS | 12 φασὶν ? Jac. |
13 κάεσθαι Ι: καίεσθαι ΟΝ | 15 γεγονὸς ΟΝ: γένος Ι |
21 ἐκ τοῦ Ι | 22 αὐτὸν Steph.: αὑτὸν MSS |
23 ἐφ᾽ ὅ τι: ἐφ᾽ ὅτῳ Steph. | 23-24 διότι προστάσσειν:
προστάξαι Steph. |

exile and thereby establish the throne for his
daughter and son-in-law. But Moses would not hear
of it because he had regard for his own people.
With his proposal for an attack blocked, Raguel
(20) ordered the Arabs to plunder Egypt.[77] (20) About
this time Chenephres also died, the first man ever
to contract elephantiasis.[78] This suffering befell
him because he had ordered the Jews to be clothed
with linen and not to wear woolen clothing. He
did this so that once they were so marked, they could
(21) be harrassed by him.[79] (21) Moses prayed to God
that the people might soon have respite from their
sufferings. While he was making his appeal to God,
suddenly, he[80] says, fire appeared out of the earth,
and it blazed even though there was neither wood nor
any other kindling in the vicinity. Frightened at
what happened, Moses fled but a divine voice spoke
to him and told him to wage war against Egypt, and
as soon as he had rescued the Jews, to return them
(22) to their ancient fatherland.[81] (22) Taking courage
from this, he resolved to lead a fighting force
against the Egyptians, but first he went to Aaron
his brother.[82] The king of the Egyptians,[83] upon
learning of the arrival of Moses, summoned him and
inquired of him why he had come.[83a] Moses replied
that he had come because the Lord of the universe[84]
had commanded him to liberate the Jews.

FRAGMENT 3b

Clement of Alexandria,
Stromata 1.23.154.2-3

(23)   τὸν   δὲ   πυθόμενον   (23)
εἰς φυλακὴν αὐτὸν καθεῖρ-
ξαι· νυκτὸς δὲ ἐπιγενομέ-
νης   τάς τε θύρας πάσας
5 αὐτομάτως ἀνοιχθῆναι τοῦ
δεσμωτηρίου   καὶ   τῶν
φυλάκων οὓς μὲν τελευτῆ-
σαι,   τινὰς δὲ ὑπὸ τοῦ
ὕπνου παρεθῆναι τά τε
10 ὅπλα   κατεαγῆναι.
(24) ἐξελθόντα δὲ τὸν   (24)
Μώϋσον ἐπὶ τὰ βασίλεια
ἐλθεῖν· εὑρόντα δὲ ἀνε-
ῳγμένας τὰς θύρας εἰσ-
15 ελθεῖν καὶ ἐνθάδε τῶν
φυλάκων παρειμένων τὸν
βασιλέα ἐξεγεῖραι. τὸν
δὲ   ἐκπλαγέντα ἐπὶ τῷ
γεγονότι   κελεῦσαι   τῷ
20 Μώϋσῳ τὸ τοῦ πέμψαντος
αὐτὸν θεοῦ | εἰπεῖν
ὄνομα,   διαχλευάσαντα
αὐτόν·   (25)   τὸν δὲ   (25)
προσκύψαντα   πρὸς   τὸ
25 οὖς εἰπεῖν,   ἀκούσαντα
δὲ τὸν βασιλέα πεσεῖν
ἄφωνον, διακρατηθέντα δὲ
ὑπὸ τοῦ Μώϋσου πάλιν
ἀναβιῶσαι·

(2)   'Αρτάπανος γοῦν ἐν τῷ
περὶ 'Ιουδαίων συγγράμματι
ἱστορεῖ κατακλεισθέντα εἰς
φυλακὴν Μωυσέα ὑπὸ Χενεφρέους τοῦ Αἰγυπτίων βασιλέως
ἐπὶ τῷ παραιτεῖσθαι τὸν λαὸν ἐξ Αἰγύπτου ἀπολυθῆναι,
νύκτωρ ἀνοιχθέντος τοῦ δεσμωτηρίου κατὰ βούλησιν τοῦ
θεοῦ ἐξελθόντα καὶ εἰς τὰ
βασίλεια παρελθόντα ἐπιστῆ-
ναι κοιμωμένῳ τῷ βασιλεῖ
καὶ   ἐξεγεῖραι   αὐτόν,
(3) τὸν δὲ καταπλαγέντα
τῷ γεγονότι κελεῦσαι τῷ
Μωυσεῖ τὸ τοῦ πέμψαντος
εἰπεῖν ὄνομα θεοῦ καὶ τὸν
μὲν προσκύψαντα πρὸς τὸ οὖς
εἰπεῖν, ἀκούσαντα δὲ τὸν
βασιλέα ἄφωνον πεσεῖν, δια-
435a κρατηθέντα δὲ ὑπὸ τοῦ Μωυσέως πάλιν ἀναβιῶναι.

ION
16-17 καὶ τὸν βασιλέα ON |

L
4 Χενεφρέους Potter (Clem.,
Opera (Oxford, 1715)p. 413)
emend ex Eus. P.E. 9.27.3-
20 passim: Νεχχεφρέους L¹|

(23) Upon learning this,
the king imprisoned him. [86]
When night came, all the
doors of the prison open-
ed of their own accord, [87]
and some of the guards
died while others were
overcome with sleep; also,
their weapons broke into
pieces. [88] (24) Moses left
the prison and went to
the palace. Finding the
doors open, he entered
the palace and aroused
the king while the guards
were sleeping on duty.
Startled at what happened,
the king ordered Moses
to declare the name of
the god who had sent him.
He did this scoffingly. [89]
(25) Moses bent over and
spoke into the king's ear,
but when the king heard
it, he fell over speech-
less. [90] But Moses
picked him up and he came
back to life again. [91]

(2) And so Artapanus reports
in his work Concerning the
Jews that Moses was shut up
in prison by Chenephres,
the king of the Egyptians,
because of his request that
the people be released from
Egypt. At night when the
prison was opened by the
will of God, Moses departed,
came to the palace, stood
over the king who was sleeping, and aroused him.
(3) Frightened at what
happened, the king ordered
Moses to declare the name
of the god who had sent him.
Moses bent over and spoke
into the king's ear, but
when the king heard it, he
fell over speechless. But
Moses picked him up and he
came back to life again.

(26)   γράψαντα δὲ τοὔνομα εἰς δέλτον κατασφραγί-   (26)
σασθαι τῶν τε ἱερέων τὸν φαυλίσαντα ἐν   τῇ
πινακίδι   τὰ   γεγραμμένα   μετὰ   σπασμοῦ τὸν βίον
ἐκλιμπάνειν·   (27) εἰπεῖν τε τὸν βασιλέα σημεῖόν   (27)
5   τι αὐτῷ ποιῆσαι·   τὸν δὲ Μώϋσον ἣν εἶχε   ῥάβδον
ἐκβαλόντα   ὄφιν   ποιῆσαι·   πτοηθέντων δὲ πάντων
ἐπιλαβόμενον τῆς οὐρᾶς ἀνελέσθαι καὶ πάλιν ῥάβδον   435b
ποιῆσαι·   (28)   προελθόντα δὲ μικρὸν τὸν Νεῖλον   (28)
τῇ   ῥάβδῳ   πατάξαι,   τὸν   δὲ   ποταμὸν   πολύχουν
10   γενόμενον   κατακλύζειν   ὅλην τὴν Αἴγυπτον·   ἀπὸ
τότε   δὲ καὶ τὴν κατάβασιν αὐτοῦ γίνεσθαι·   συν-
αγαγὸν   δὲ   τὸ   ὕδωρ   ἐποζέσαι   καὶ τὰ ποτάμια
διαφθεῖραι   ζῷα   τούς   τε   λαοὺς διὰ τὴν   δίψαν
φθείρεσθαι.   (29) τὸν δὲ βασιλέα τούτων γενομένων   (29)
15   τῶν τεράτων φάναι μετὰ μῆνα τοὺς λαοὺς ἀπολύσειν,
ἐὰν ἀποκαταστήσῃ τὸν ποταμόν·   τὸν δὲ Μώϋσον
πάλιν   τῇ   ῥάβδῳ πατάξαντα τὸ ὕδωρ συστεῖλαι   τὸ   435c
ῥεῦμα.   (30) τούτου δὲ γενομένου τὸν βασιλέα τοὺς   (30)
ἱερεῖς τοὺς ὑπὲρ Μέμφιν καλέσαι καὶ φάναι αὐτοὺς
20   ἀναιρήσειν   καὶ   τὰ ἱερὰ κατασκάψειν, ἐὰν μὴ καὶ
αὐτοὶ τερατουργήσωσί τι.   τοὺς δὲ τότε διά τινων
μαγγάνων καὶ   ἐπαοιδῶν δράκοντα ποιῆσαι καὶ τὸν
ποταμὸν μεταχρῶσαι.   (31)   τὸν δὲ βασιλέα φρονη-   (31)
ματισθέντα ἐπὶ   τῷ   γεγονότι, πάσῃ τιμωρίᾳ   καὶ
25   κολάσει καταικίζειν τοὺς Ἰουδαίους.   τὸν   δὲ

ION

2 τε: δὲ Steph. | φαυλίσαντα: ἐκφαυλίσαντα Steph. |
3 τὰ   ante   ἐν   (lin. 2) transp. Steph. |
{τὰ γεγραμμένα}   ? Jac. | 8 προελθόντα   I: προσ-
ελθόντα ON | 9 πολύχουν N: πολυχ^ρουν N² |
11-12 συναγαγὸν Steph.:   συναγαγῶν   MSS |
12 ἐποζέσαι: ἀποζέσαι Steph. | 17 τῇ ῥάβδῳ   I: om. ON |

(26) (26) He[92] wrote the name on a tablet and sealed
      it securely, but one of the priests who showed
      contempt for what was written on the tablet died
(27) in a convulsion.   (27) The king then told Moses
      to perform some sign for him. So Moses threw out
      the rod[93] which he held and made it a snake. Since
      everyone was terrified, he seized it by the tail,
(28) picked it up, and made it a rod again.[94]   (28) He
      then stepped forward a few steps, struck the Nile
      with his rod, and the river flooded, inundating all
      of Egypt.[95] It was from that time that the flood-
      ing of the Nile began.[96] When the stagnant water
      began to smell,[97] the animals in the river perished
      and the people as well began to die of thirst.[98]
(29) (29) Once these mighty wonders were accomplished,
      the king said that he would release the people
      after a month if Moses would restore the river to
      its banks.[99] So Moses again struck the water with
(30) his rod and the waters subsided.   (30) When this
      had been done, the king summoned the priests[100] who
      were over Memphis and threatened to kill them and
      destroy their temples unless they too performed some
      marvelous act. Then, using charms and incantations,[101]
      they made a serpent and changed the color of the
(31) river.[102]   (31) The king became arrogant as a
      result of such performances as this and consequently
      mistreated the Jews with every kind of vindictive

Μώϋσον ταῦτα ὁρῶντα ἄλλα τε σημεῖα ποιῆσαι καὶ
πατάξαντα τὴν γῆν τῇ ῥάβδῳ ζῷόν τι πτηνὸν
ἀνεῖναι λυμαίνεσθαι τοὺς Αἰγυπτίους, πάντας τε
ἐξελκωθῆναι τὰ σώματα. τῶν δὲ ἰατρῶν μὴ δυνα-   435d
5   μένων ἰᾶσθαι τοὺς κάμνοντας, οὕτως πάλιν ἀνέσεως
τυχεῖν τοὺς Ἰουδαίους. (32) πάλιν τε τὸν   (32)
Μώϋσον βάτραχον διὰ τῆς ῥάβδου ἀνεῖναι, πρὸς
δὲ τούτοις ἀκρίδας καὶ σκνίφας. διὰ τοῦτο δὲ
καὶ τοὺς Αἰγυπτίους τὴν ῥάβδον ἀνατιθέναι εἰς
10 πᾶν ἱερόν, ὁμοίως δὲ καὶ τῇ Ἴσιδι, διὰ τὸ τὴν
γῆν εἶναι Ἶσιν, παιομένην δὲ τῇ ῥάβδῳ τὰ τέρατα
ἀνεῖναι. (33) τοῦ δὲ βασιλέως ἔτι ἀφρονουμένου   (33)
τὸν Μώϋσον χάλαζάν τε καὶ σεισμοὺς διὰ νυκτὸς
ἀποτελέσαι, ὥστε τοὺς τὸν σεισμὸν φεύγοντας ἀπὸ
15 τῆς χαλάζης ἀναιρεῖσθαι τούς τε τὴν χάλαζαν
ἐκκλίνοντας ὑπὸ τῶν σεισμῶν διαφθείρεσθαι. | συμ-   436a
πεσεῖν δὲ τότε τὰς μὲν οἰκίας πάσας τῶν τε ναῶν
τοὺς πλείστους. (34) τελευταῖον   τοιαύταις   (34)
συμφοραῖς περιπεσόντα τὸν βασιλέα τοὺς Ἰουδαίους
20 ἀπολῦσαι· τοὺς δὲ χρησαμένους παρὰ τῶν Αἰγυπτίων
πολλὰ μὲν ἐκπώματα, οὐκ ὀλίγον δὲ ἱματισμὸν
ἄλλην τε παμπληθῆ γάζαν, διαβάντας τοὺς κατὰ τὴν
Ἀραβίαν ποταμοὺς καὶ διαβάντας ἱκανὸν τόπον ἐπὶ
τὴν Ἐρυθρὰν τριταίους ἐλθεῖν θάλασσαν.
25 (35) Μεμφίτας μὲν οὖν λέγειν ἔμπειρον ὄντα τὸν   (35)
Μώϋσον τῆς χώρας τὴν ἄμπωτιν τηρήσαντα διὰ ξηρᾶς   436b
τῆς θαλάσσης τὸ πλῆθος περαιῶσαι. Ἡλιουπολίτας

ION
3 λυμαίνεσθαι: ὃ λυμήνασθαι Steph. | πάντας ON:
πάντα I | 6 τὸν I: om. ON | 8 σκνίφας: σκνίπας
Steph.: σκνῖπας Giff. | 14 ἀπὸ I: ὑπὸ ON |
18 πλείστους <   > Freu. (p. 216) | 21 ἐκπτώματα I |
22 παμπληθεῖ I | διαβῆναι τοὺς vel 23 καὶ {διαβάντας}
? Jac. | 25 οὖν om. I |

chastisement.[103] When Moses saw this, he performed
more signs and struck the ground with his rod and
raised up a certain species of winged creatures to
scourge the Egyptians.[104] As a result of his actions,
they all broke out in body sores.[105] Even the
physicians were unable to cure those who were suffering with the sores.[106] Thus once again relief came
(32) to the Jews.[107] (32) Once again, Moses used his
rod to raise up frogs as well as locusts and flees.[108]
It was for this reason that the Egyptians set up a
rod in every temple. They do the same with Isis[109]
because the earth is Isis and it produced these
(33) wonders when it was struck with the rod. (33) Since
the king persisted in playing the fool, Moses produced
hail and earthquakes throughout the night so that
those who fled the earthquakes perished in the hail
and those who tried to avoid the hail were destroyed
by the earthquakes.[110] Also at that time all the
(34) houses and most of the temples collapsed.[111] (34)
Finally, after enduring such calamities, the king
released the Jews.[112] After they had procured from
the Egyptians many drinking vessels as well as not
a little clothing and numerous other treasures,[113]
they crossed the river towards Arabia. They covered
a considerable distance and then came to the Red
(35) Sea in three days.[114] (35) Now the Memphians claim
that Moses, being familiar with the countryside,
watched for the ebb tide, then led the multitudes
through the dry part of the sea. The Heliopolitans,

δὲ λέγειν ἐπικαταδραμεῖν τὸν βασιλέα μετὰ πολλῆς
δυνάμεως, <ἅμα> καὶ τοῖς καθιερωμένοις ζῴοις,
διὰ τὸ τὴν ὕπαρξιν τοὺς Ἰουδαίους τῶν Αἰγυπτίων
χρησαμένους διακομίζειν. (36) τῷ δὲ Μωῦσῳ φωνὴν   (36)
5 θείαν γενέσθαι πατάξαι τὴν θάλασσαν τῇ ῥάβδῳ καὶ
διαστῆσαι. τὸν δὲ Μώϋσον ἀκούσαντα ἐπιθιγεῖν τῇ
ῥάβδῳ τοῦ ὕδατος, καὶ οὕτως τὸ μὲν νᾶμα διαστῆναι, τὴν δὲ δύναμιν διὰ ξηρᾶς ὁδοῦ πορεύεσθαι.
(37) συνεμβάντων δὲ τῶν Αἰγυπτίων καὶ διωκόντων   (37)
10 φησὶ πῦρ αὐτοῖς ἐκ τῶν ἔμπροσθεν ἐκλάμψαι, τὴν   436c
δὲ θάλασσαν πάλιν τὴν ὁδὸν ἐπικλύσαι· τοὺς δὲ
Αἰγυπτίους ὑπό τε τοῦ πυρὸς καὶ τῆς πλημμυρίδος
πάντας διαφθαρῆναι· τοὺς δὲ Ἰουδαίους δια-
φυγόντας τὸν κίνδυνον τεσσαράκοντα ἔτη ἐν τῇ
15 ἐρήμῳ διατρίψαι, βρέχοντος αὐτοῖς τοῦ θεοῦ
κρίμνον ὅμοιον ἐλύμῳ, χιόνι παραπλήσιον τὴν
χρόαν. γεγονέναι δέ φησι τὸν Μώϋσον μακρόν,
πυρρακῆ, πολιόν, κομήτην, ἀξιωματικόν. ταῦτα δὲ
πρᾶξαι περὶ ἔτη ὄντα ὀγδοήκοντα ἐννέα."

ION
2 <ἅμα> Steph. | ζωῆς ON | 4 sqq. τὸ θαῦμα τῆς
ἐρυθρᾶς I^mg | 4 Μωσῆ ON | 5-6 καὶ διαστῆσαι Mras:
καὶ διαστῆναι MSS: {καὶ διαστῆναι} Steph.: καὶ
διαστήσειν ? Jac. | 6 ἐπιθιγεῖν Dind.: -θίγειν I:
-θήγειν ON | 14 τεσσαράκοντα: μ̄ ON: τριάκοντα I |
17 φασι ON | 19 ὄντα I: om. ON |

on the other hand, claim that the king rushed down
on them with full force, carrying with them all the
sacred animals[115] because the Jews were crossing the
sea, having taken the possessions of the Egyptians.[116]

(36) (36)   The divine voice came to Moses instructing him
to strike the sea with his rod and divide it.[117]
When Moses heard this, he touched the water lightly
with his rod and the stream divided, and the multi-
(37) tude passed through the dry channel.[118] (37) When
the Egyptians went in together in hot pursuit, he[119]
says that a fire blazed in front of them, and the
sea again flooded their path. All the Egyptians were
consumed by the fire and the flood.[119] After the
Jews had escaped the danger, they spent forty years
in the desert.[120] Meanwhile, God showered upon them
meal similar in texture to rolled millet resembling
the color of snow.[121] He[122] reports that Moses was
tall, ruddy complexioned, with long flowing gray
hair, and dignified.[123] He accomplished these things
when he was about eighty-nine years old."[124]

ANNOTATIONS

1.   This fragment occurs in the section of P.E., Book 9,
that treats Abraham (chs. 16-20). It belongs to a catena
of excerpts which Eusebius takes directly from Alexander
Polyhistor. It is preceded by a quotation from "Eupolemus" (= Pseudo-Eupolemus, Frg. 1), and is immediately
followed by an anonymous quotation (= Pseudo-Eupolemus,
Frg. 2), then quotations from Apollonius Molon and Philo
Epicus.

2.   I.e., Abraham.

3.   This is most likely a reference to the work mentioned
in Frg. 2, par. 23.1. Cf. below, note 12.

4.   Various explanations have been offered for this
puzzling designation. Viger, PG (21) col. 709 B, n. 29
(cf. Seguier's note, col. 1567), suggests that it is
possibly a corruption of 'Ερμιούδ, a compound form derived
from יהוד + ארם = Ερμ + ιουθ, i.e., Syrian Jews. He also
refers to Herodotus 1.11 and 2 Kgs 23:29. Freudenthal,
153 (note), attributes it to the creative imagination of
Artapanus, based on its connection with 'Ερμῆς, the name
given to Moses by the Egyptian priests (Frg. 3, par. 6;
also cf. par. 9); accordingly, it would have been selected
by Artapanus for its Egyptian ring and because it would
have designated the Egyptian Jews as "Moses-ites," i.e.,
'Ερμ(ῆς) + 'Ιουδ(αῖοι) = "Moses Jews," just as the name
"Hebrews" related Jews to Abraham "the Hebrew" (Gen 14:13).
Freudenthal also notes that 'Αραμαῖοι could easily become
'Ερεμβοί (Strabo 1.41-42; 16.784). Cf. Walter, JS (1,2),
127, n. 1a; also Collins-Poehlmann, 8-9.

4a On the derivation of "Jews," cf. Conzelmann, HJC,
149-50.

5.   If Artapanus' claim here is based on Gen 14:13, this
would suggest his dependence on the Hebrew text
(אברם העברי) rather than the LXX (Αβραμ τῷ περάτῃ). Elsewhere in the Bible, however, the Israelites are called
Hebrews, although this is frequently a designation used
of them by outsiders (Gen 39:14; Exod 1:16) or by the
Israelites to identify themselves to foreigners (Gen 40:15;
43:32; Exod 1:19). Cf. Speiser, Genesis, 103; Georgi,
Gegner, 51-60; Kuhn, TDNT, 3.367-68; Conzelmann, HJC, 149.
Whether this statement relates to Artapanus' Jewishness,
cf. Seguier, PG (21) col. 1567, note on 709 B7.

6.   The Egyptian king is unnamed in the biblical account
(Gen 12:10-13:1), where Pharaoh is used as a title rather
than a name. By contrast, the title becomes a name in
Artapanus, as commonly happens (cf. Herodotus 2.111; also
Josephus). Φαρεθώθης is an orthographical variation of

6. (cont.) Φαραω, the Hellenized form typically used by
the LXX to render פַּרְעֹה. Normally, Φαραωϑης in Josephus
(cf. Ant. 1.163, et al.), though v.l. Φαραωνης (cf. Ant.
8.151) and Φαραων. Consistently, Φαραω in Philo. Seguier,
PG (21) col. 1567, n. on 709 B9, notes the absence of the
name in Manetho's king lists, and sees it as a corruption.
Mras, P.E. (GCS, 43.1) 8,1.504, proposes an Egyptian
derivation: Φα + ʿΡα (= Re) + Θωϑ (=Thoth), and is followed
by Merentites, EHBS 27 (1957) 306; also Walter, JS (1,2),
127, n. 1c. Cf. note in Stearns, 43, n. 6.

7. Cf. Pseudo-Eupolemus, Frg. 1, par. 3 & 8; Frg. 2;
also Annotations, Nos. 12, 26-27, & 38. Cf. Pseudo-
Hecataeus II, Frg. 1, par. 167 (apud Walter).

8. The length of his stay in Egypt is not given in the
biblical account, nor in Pseudo-Eupolemus, Frg. 1, par.
6-8, nor Josephus and Philo. Cf., however, Jub 13:11
(5 years); S. ʿOlam Rab. 1 (3 months); 1 QapGen 20.18
(2 years at least). Cf. Ginzberg, Legends 1.224 and 5.272,
n. 78. Also, Freudenthal, 216-17.

9. I.e., the land of Canaan (Gen 13:12) which is frequently designated "Syria," or more correctly "Coele-Syria" in
the Hellenistic period. Cf. OCD², 1030-31; A. H. M.
Jones, The Cities of the Eastern Provinces (Oxford:
Clarendon, 1971) 226-94. Cf. Sib. Or. 4.125. Literally,
the text reads "again ... departed," which Freudenthal,
161, sees as apologetic, showing their non-Egyptian
origin, in response to pagan charges that the Jews were
originally expelled Egyptians (Josephus, Ag.Ap. 1.228-92;
2.28-32; Diodorus Siculus 1.28.2). Cf. also Frg. 2.

10. This is another unbiblical detail. According to
Gen 12:20-13:1, Abraham, his wife and Lot, were dis-
patched from Egypt "with all that he had." Freudenthal,
156-57, sees here traces of an old tradition about the
Hyksos invasion which is independent of Manetho (cf.
Josephus, Ag.Ap. 1.73-92; 227-50) and which related the
entry of some ancient Semitic peoples into Egypt. On the
Hyksos, cf. now J. van Seters, The Hyksos: A New Investigation (New Haven: Yale University Press, 1966); also,
cf. Fraser, Ptolemaic Alexandria, 1.506-507, and notes.
Also, cf. Frg. 2, par. 1, and below notes 39 and 77.

11. After treating Jacob in chapters 21-22 of P.E., Book 9,
Eusebius cites this fragment from Artapanus, and one from
Philo Epicus, as witnesses to Joseph. Both are quoted
directly from Alexander Polyhistor.

12. This was likely the original title of the work,
since it is independently attested by Clement (cf.
Frg. 3, par. 23 and parallel); so, Freudenthal, 216.
Cf. the title in Frg. 1, above.

13. Cf. Gen 41:33, 39; Josephus, Ant. 2.17, 63, 65, 80, 87.

14. Arabs, an anachronistic description, frequently used in the Hellenistic period. Cf. esp. Strabo 1.2.34; Herodotus 2.11; Ps 71:10 (LXX); Ep. Arist. 114; 1 Macc 5:39; 11:17, 39; 12:31; 2 Macc 5:8; 12:10; Acts 2:11; Josephus, passim; cf. parallel account in Ant. 2.32: Ἄραβας τοῦ Ἰσμαηλιτῶν γένους.

15. This modified version of Gen 37:18-36 which not only serves to exonerate the brothers but underscore Joseph's prescience is perhaps apologetically motivated. Cf. Demetrius, Frg. 2, par. 11.

16. "Israel" here can be understood (mistakenly by Artapanus, or perhaps by Alexander Polyhistor) as Abraham's actual father (so, Mras, GCS (43,1) 8.1, 516, note to lin. 20), as the ordinary name of the nation (Giff. 4.309), or as a corrupt form of "Ishmael," hence Ἰσμαήλ, υἱοῦ, which would then require a singular form of ἀδελφούς (Gais. 2.391; also Seguier, PG (21), col. 1573, note on 725 B9; also read by Freudenthal, 232; Merentites, EHBS 27 (1957) 313). Cf. Walter, JS (1,2) 127, n. 1b on Frg. 2. Also, cf. Apollonius Molon in P.E. 9.19.1-3 = FGrH 728, Frg. 1, par. 2 = Stern, GLAJJ, 150-51.

17. Cf. Gen 39-41. On διοικητής as an apparently genuine Egyptian title, cf. Freudenthal, 216; Fraser, Ptolemaic Alexandria, 2.983, n. 178.

18. Artapanus' description of Joseph's land reforms are more humane than the agrarian program described in Gen 47:13-26, where the landowners are reduced to royal tenant farmers. On the privileged status of the priests, cf. Gen 47:22, 26; also Diodorus Siculus 1.21.7. Similar pioneering land reforms and agricultural "firsts" are attributed to Sesostris (Diodorus Siculus 1.54.3,6; Herodotus 2.107), Isis (Diodorus Siculus 1.14.1; 27.3-4), and Osiris (Diodorus Siculus 1.15.6,8; 17.3; 18.4). On the priority topos (πρῶτος), cf. Thraede, Erfinder. Cf. also similar claims made of Abraham (Pseudo-Eupolemus, Frg. 1, par. 3 & 8, and Annotations, No. 12) and Moses (Artapanus, Frg. 3, par. 4; Eupolemus, Frg. 1, and Annotations, Nos. 5-7).

19. On good will and popularity resulting from discoveries and benefactions, cf. Diodorus Siculus 1.54.2; 55.12; 56.1-2; 57.2; Herodotus 2.109.

20. Cf. Gen 41:45, 50; also Demetrius Frg. 2, par. 12; Josephus, Ant. 2.91; T.Jos. 18.3; 20.3(a); Jub 34:20; 44:24; and, of course, Joseph and Asenath. Note the orthographical variants in app. crit.

21. On Heliopolis, cf. Pseudo-Eupolemus, Frg. 1, par. 8,
Annotations, No. 25, and below, note 24.

22. I.e., Ephraim and Manasseh; cf. Gen 41:50-52.

23. Cf. Gen 42-47:12. According to Gen 45:10; 46:28-29;
47:1-4, 27, Jacob and his family settle in Goshen.

24. Sais: much disputed in the textual tradition (cf.
app. crit.). Heliopolis was widely recognized, and used,
as the Greek name for the biblical On (Gen 41:45, 50; cf.
esp. Exod 1:11 LXX; also Jer 43:13 = 50:13 LXX; also
Jub 40:10; 44:24; T.Jos. 18.3; Josephus, Ant. 2.188). On
Heliopolis, cf. Pseudo-Eupolemus, Frg. 1, par. 8, esp.
Annotations, No. 25. Sais (Σάϊς), the chief city of the
Saite nome located in the western Delta (cf. Plato, Ti.
21e; Herodotus 2.59, 62, 163, 165; Diodorus Siculus 5.57.5;
Plutarch, Is. et Osir. 354C; references in Giff. 4.310;
also, cf. Jones, Cities, 99) is not mentioned in the Bible
(though, cf. Ezek 30:15: Σάϊς (-ιν) = סוֹן, i.e., Pelusium,
on the eastern frontier; so, BDB, 695), nor are the
patriarchs elsewhere located there. It is not clear why
MS I omitted ῾Ηλίου, thus reading ἐν τῇ πόλει καὶ Σαίν,
though conceivably it was influenced by Ezek 30:15. Even
so, the syntax remains problematic. This variant, however, apparently prompted Stephanus' emendation, dropping
῾Ηλίου and reading ἐν τῇ πόλει Καισάν, which is slightly,
though remotely, reminiscent of Γεσεμ, i.e., Goshen (גֹּשֶׁן;
cf. Gen 45:10; 47:1-4, 27), where the biblical account
locates the family of Joseph. Seguier, PG (21), col. 1573,
note on 725 BC9, regards it as a corruption of Γεσεμ.
Stephanus is further refined by Freudenthal, 159, 217, who
retains ῾Ηλίου because of its MS support, but reads ἐν τῇ
῾Ηλίου πόλει καὶ Σάν. He suggests that Sais was misread
for San (Σαν), i.e., Tanis/Tanais, also Avaris, Per-
Ramses, and in Hebrew Zoan (צֹעַן). Precedent is provided
by similar confusion in Herodotus 2.17 and Strabo 17.1.20,
noted by F. Kees, art. "Tanis," PW 4 (1931) col. 2178.
Freudenthal's suggestion also has merit because it is
elsewhere associated with Heliopolis (Exod 1:11) and
because Jews are elsewhere associated with and located
in Tanis (cf. Num 13:22; Ps 77:12, 43 LXX; Isa 19:11, 13;
30:4; Jub 13:12; Jdt 1:10). Jacoby's suggestion, which
presumably (though this is not clear from his apparatus)
reads ἐν τῇ ῾Ηλίου πόλει ἐν πόλει καλουμένῃ Σάν (or
Κεσσάν), attempts to bring this reading into closer
conformity with Frg. 3, par. 2, where the MSS read
Τέσσαν, though Mras reads Σάιν.

25. Cf. above, note 9.

26. Cf. above, note 4.

27.   Athos, otherwise unattested as a city in Egypt.
Thus, since Seguier, PG (21), col. 1573, note on 725 C10,
seen as a corruption of Pithom (Πιθωμ, cf. Exod 1:11). Cf.
app. crit.   Conceivably, the initial Π has elided (cf.
Πατουμον, Herodotus 2.158).   So, Freudenthal, 158.
Also, cf. Giff. 4.310.   Collins-Poehlmann, 17, also see
a connection with the Egyptian form of Pithom, Pr Jtm
= House/Temple of Athum.

28.   Conceivably, an allusion to the Jewish temple at
Leontopolis established by Onias IV ca. 167-164 B.C.E.
(cf. Josephus, Ant. 12.387-88; 13.62-73; 20.236-37; also
14.21; J.W. 7.423-32).   Since Leontopolis was located in
the Heliopolite nome (cf. Josephus, Ant. 13.70), this
association would be natural.   The temple at Leontopolis
appears to lie behind Isa 19:1-25 and Sib. Or. 5.484-530.
The letters to Egyptian Jewry in 2 Macc 1:1-9 and 1:10-
29 are plausibly seen as attempts to realign the loyalty
of Egyptian Jews away from Leontopolis toward the Jerusalem
temple (so, E. Bammel, Cambridge lectures, February, 1971).
Cf. Smallwood, Jews, 221-22, 367-68, and bibliography
cited therein.   Could "the temple at Athos" be an allusion
to the sanctuary at Elephantine?   The connection, however,
is not obvious.

29.   This last sentence, according to Walter, JS (1,2),
128, n. 4c, does not belong to Artapanus, but probably
with Demetrius, Frg. 2, after par. 12.   Cf. JS (3,2) 287,
n. 12c.

30.   This fragment occurs at the beginning of the section
of P.E., Book 9, which treats Moses (chs. 26-29).   It is
preceded by a brief excerpt from Eupolemus (ch. 26 = Frg.
1) and followed by excerpts from Ezekiel the Tragedian
and Demetrius variously intercalated.   All of the quotations
in this section of Book 9 Eusebius takes directly from
Alexander Polyhistor.

31.   Doubtless, Jacob is meant here, especially since the
preceding sections (P.E. 9.21-24) dealt with Jacob and
Joseph.   Cf. Merentites, EHBS 27 (1957) 317.   On the
death of Jacob, cf. Gen 47:28-31.

32.   The translation here adheres to Mras's punctuation.
A name of similar length is given to Joseph by Pharaoh
in Gen 41:45LXX: Ψονθομφανηχ.   According to Freudenthal,
217, Mempsasthenoth is Artapanus' fabricated name of the
deceased Pharaoh.   Accordingly, he transposes it to the
following phrase (cf. app. crit.).

33.   No such name appears in the Egyptian king lists in
the 18th or 19th dynasties.   According to Freudenthal,
158, it is a corruption of known Egyptian names: Pamenothes
or Pamonthes.

34.   Cf. Exod 1:9-14.

35.   The MSS (ION) read Τέσσαν (cf. app. crit.), most
likely a corruption of τε Σάν, hence Mras's emendation
τε Σάιν, which conforms to Frg. 2, par. 3. Cf. above,
note 24. According to Stephanus (followed by Freudenthal,
158, 217), the text should read Κέσσαν, i.e., Goshen
(Γεσεμ, cf. e.g., Gen 47:27). Cf. Seguier, PG (21) col.
1573, note on 725 C9.

36.   Heliopolis is one of the three cities built by
the Jews at Pharaoh's direction mentioned in Exod 1:11 LXX.
On Heliopolis, cf. above, notes 21, 24, 28.

37.   Pharaoh's daughter remains unnamed in Scripture
(cf. Exod 2:1-10; also Sib. Or. 3.253; Philo, V. Mos.
1.5-17; Ps.-Philo, Bib. Ant. 9.15). Elsewhere, she is
called Thermuthis (Josephus, Ant. 2.224-43), Tharmuth
(Jub 47:5), Pharia (alias, Isis; cf. Syncellus, 1.227,
apud Charles, APOT, 2.78; also, cf. below, par. 16),
Bithiah (Talmud, after 1 Chr 4:17). References in
Thackeray, Josephus (LCL) 4.261. Cf. Ginzberg, Legends,
1.266 and 5.398, n. 48; 5.401, n. 60; Freudenthal, 217.

38.   Chenephres: properly, Χεφρήν (Seguier, PG (21) col.
1573-74, note on 729 A2), brother and successor of
Cheops. Cf. Herodotus 2.127; Diodorus Siculus 1.64.1. Cf.
Scholiast on Clement of Alexandria, Protrepticus, 44,
apud Seguier, op. cit.; also Giff., 4.312. Also, identified
with Chenceres (18th dynasty) and Menophres (19th dynasty).
Cf. Freudenthal, 158.

39.   According to Freudenthal, 157, such a political situation with many rulers could only refer to the time of the
Hyksos.

40.   Her barrenness is an unbiblical detail. Cf., however,
Philo, V. Mos. 1.13; Josephus, Ant. 2.232.

41.   In contrast to the biblical account, Philo, and
Josephus, some pagan authors (Pseudo-Manetho, Chaeremon,
Apion, and possibly Tacitus) regarded Moses as a native
Egyptian. Cf. Gager, Moses, 19; Freudenthal, 161.

42.   On the naming of Moses, cf. Exod 2:10 (from משה, "to
draw out." Cf. Philo, V. Mos. 1.17 (Μωυσῆν, from μῶυ, "the
Egyptian word for water"); Josephus, Ant. 2.228 (from μῶυ,
"the Egyptian word for water" + ἐσῆς, "those who are
saved").

43.   Freudenthal, 217, suspects dittography here (cf.
lines 21-22), hence his conjectural deletion of ἀνδρωθέντα
(cf. app. crit.).

44.   Μουσαῖος: a pre-Homeric, mythical Greek poet and seer
of Attica to whom were ascribed various oracular sayings,
songs, and poems, including cosmogonies. In P.E. 9.8.1-2

44. (cont.) Moses is also designated Mousaios by Numenius,
a 2nd cent. C.E. Pythagorean philosopher. Cf. Kirk &
Raven, Pre-Socratic Philosophers, 21-24; Rzach, "Musaios,"
PW 16 (1935) cols. 757-67.

45.   In Greek literature, Musaios is ordinarily associated
with Orpheus (cf., e.g., Aristophanes, Ra. 1032-34; Plato,
Rep. 2.364e; Diodorus Siculus 1.96.2), either as his son
(Diodorus Siculus 4.25.1; Justin, Cohort. ad Graec. 15)
or his disciple (Tatian, Or. ad Graec. 41 = Eusebius, P.E.
10.11.27-28, 30; Clement, Strom. 1.21.131.1), but not as
his teacher, as in Artapanus. Cf. M. P. Nilsson, "Early
Orphism and Kindred Religious Movements," HTR 28 (1935)
181-230, esp. 192 on the relationship between Orpheus and
Musaeus. Also, Holladay, THEIOS ANER, 224. Walter, JS
(1,2), 129, n. 4a, notes the tradition in Hecataeus of
Abdera (FGrH 264, Frg. 25 = Diodorus Siculus 1.96.2),
according to which Orpheus transmits to the Greeks the
sacred wisdom gained in his Egyptian travels (cf. also
Diodorus Siculus 1.23; 92; Freudenthal, 160). It is
altered by Artapanus so that Moses, not the Egyptian
priests, becomes the ultimate source of Greek wisdom.

46.   The following portrait of Moses as cultural benefactor,
with its special emphasis on his role as inventor, draws
on diverse strands from a well-established tradition of
national romance literature and patriotically motivated
propaganda. On the tradition as a whole, and its several
genres and sub-genres, cf. Thraede, "Erfinder II," and
"Das Lob." Individual accomplishments and inventions are
elsewhere attributed to various heroic figures, such as
Ninus, Semiramis, Sesostris, Isis and Osiris. Cf. Braun,
History and Romance, 3-35. For similar claims elsewhere
in the fragments, cf. Artapanus, Frg. 2, par. 3 (of Joseph);
Eupolemus, Frg. 1 A & B (of Moses), and Annotations, Nos.
5-7; Pseudo-Eupolemus (of Abraham), Frg. 1, par. 3, and
Annotations, No. 12. Numerous pagan parallels exist for
individual items in the portrait. Similar claims are made
for Hermes Thoth: the inventor of writing (Plato, Phdr.
274-75; Diodorus Siculus 1.16.1; Philo of Byblos, FGrH
790, Frg. 1 = P.E. 1.9.24, on which cf. Attridge-Oden,
Philo of Byblos, 72, n. 8; Cicero, de nat. deor. 3.22);
the inventor of culture and scholarship (Diodorus Siculus
1.16.43; Plutarch, Is. et Osir. 352B); founder of
Egyptian worship and author of priestly liturgical books
(Diodorus Siculus 1.20.6; Clement of Alexandria, Stromata
6.3,35.1-37.3; on the designation of ibis as the sacred
animal, cf. Herodotus 2.67; Apion in Aelian, NA 10.29).
Cf. Freudenthal, 155; R. Hanhart, "Fragen um die Entstehung
der LXX," VT 12 (1962) 139-63, esp. 143, n. 1; Conzelmann,
HJC, 151. As to the individual motifs in Artapanus'
portrait of Moses: many useful contributions (Osiris:
Diodorus Siculus 1.13.5; 17.1-2; 18.5; 19.5; 20.5; 27.5;
Isis: Diodorus Siculus 1.22.1; 27.1; 27.3-4); the invention
of ships (Sesostris: Diodorus Siculus 1.55.2; Herodotus
2.102; also cf. Pliny, Nat. Hist. 7.206; Herodotus 1.171;

46. (cont.) Thucydides 1.4); machines for lifting stones
(crowbars? cf. Herodotus 2.125; Pliny, Nat. Hist. 7.195;
Manetho, Frgs. 11 & 12); weapons and devices for fighting
(Pliny, Nat. Hist. 7.200; Pindar, Frg. 281 B; Schol. Ven.
Homer, Il. 10.439; Strabo 10.3.19; Hellanicus, Frg. 71b,
189); devices for drawing water (Archimedean screw ?,
though κοχλίας; cf. Strabo 17.1.30, 52; Diodorus Siculus
1.34.2; 5.37.3; P. Lond. 3.1177.73); philosophy (cf.
Plato, Phdr. 274 c-e; Plutarch, Quaest. conv. 9.3.2.;
Isocrates, Or. 11.11-14, 17-20, 28, 30; Diodorus Siculus
1.96); division of state into 36 nomes (Sesostris: Diodorus
Siculus 1.54.3); assignment of local deities and the
building of sanctuaries and temples (Osiris: Diodorus
Siculus 1.15.3; Isis: Diodorus Siculus 1.21.56; Hermes:
Diodorus Siculus 1.61.1; Sesostris: Diodorus Siculus
1.56.2; 57; Herodotus 2.108); the assignment of hieroglyphics (Sesostris: Diodorus Siculus 1.55.7); assignment
of land for priests (Isis: Diodorus Siculus 1.21.7;
cf. 1.54.6; Sesostris: Herodotus 2.107) the founding of
cities (Osiris: Diodorus Siculus 1.15.1; 18.6; 19.7;
Isis: Diodorus Siculus 1.27.4; Semiramis: Diodorus Siculus
2.14.4, Ps.-Callisthenes 3.18; Cambyses: Diodorus 1.33.1);
military sagacity (Sesostris: Diodorus Siculus 1.54-56;
94.4; Herodotus 2.102-106); gaining popular approval
(Sesostris: Diodorus Siculus 1.54.2; 55.12; 56.1-2; 57.2;
Herodotus 2.109). Many of these references are given
in Tiede, Charismatic Figure, 146-77.

Clearly, Artapanus' portrait is indebted to numerous
pagan strands. Its thoroughly Egyptian cast represents
his own contribution. The portrait has apologetic value
as a response to the pagan charges that Jews had produced
no figures who had made genuine contributions to humanity.
Cf. Josephus, Ag.Ap. 2.135-36.

47. On Moses as the first philospher, cf. Eupolemus, Frg.
1 and n. 5. The motif is developed on a grand scale in
Philo, V. Mos. Also, cf. Numenius, apud P.E. 9.6.9: τί γάρ
ἐστι Πλάτων ἢ Μωσῆς ἀττικίζων; on which, cf. Gager, Moses,
63-69.

48. πόλις, ordinarily "city," but occasionally "country."
Cf. Homer, Od. 1.170; 6.177; Hesiod, Sc. 380. LSJ, s.v.

49. The translation here follows Freudenthal, 147, who
also notes par. 12: τὰ ζῷα τὰ καθιερωθέντα ὑπὸ τοῦ Μωύσου,
and similar language in Diodorus Siculus 1.89.5: καθ'
ἕκαστον δ' αὐτῶν καταδεῖξαι τοῖς ἐγχωρίοις σέβεσθαί τι ζῷον.
Also, Walter, JS (1,2), 129, n. 4a; Tiede, Charismatic
Figure, 161; Collins-Poehlmann, 23. Contra Schürer,
Geschichte 3.478, who regards σεφθήσεσθαι as deponent:
"Moses directs each province to honour God," presumably
Yahweh. Freudenthal, 160-61, noting the close similarity
of Artapanus with Diodorus Siculus, sees a comparable
euhemeristic outlook reflected. On the practice of making
provisions for native patron deities, cf. Plato, Leg. 8.
848 c-e.

50. ἱερὰ γράμματα: "sacred writings" (OGIS 56.36 [3rd
cent. B.C.E.], Philo, V. Mos. 2.290, 292; 2 Tim 3:16;
Josephus, Ag.Ap. 1.54), or "hieroglyphics" (OGIS 90.54
[Rosetta stone, 2nd cent. B.C.E.]; Philo, V. Mos. 1.23;
cf. Herodotus 2.36). If the latter here, perhaps "he gave
(taught?) the priests hieroglyphics." Contrast Philo,
V. Mos. 1.23. Cf. Walter, JS (1,2), 130; Giff., 4.313.

51. The syntax is unclear. This final phrase is
presumably governed by ἀποτάξαι. Cf. Walter, JS (1,2),
130, n. 5e; Tiede, Charismatic Figure, 161, n. 103. On
the Egyptian worship of animals, cf. Herodotus 2.65-76;
Diodorus Siculus 1.83.1-90.4 (abbreviated in P.E. 2.1.33-
50); Strabo 17.1.40. Critiques developed in pagan (Strabo
16.2.35; Plutarch, Is. et Osir. 71; Cicero, de nat. deor.
1.36.101; Juvenal 15.1-13; Athenaeus, Epit. 7.299-300;
Lucian, Deor. Conc. 10.11; Im. 11; JConf. 42), Jewish
(Philo, DVC 8-9; Decal. 76-80; Leg. ad Gaium 139, 163-66;
Josephus, Ag.Ap. 1.224-25, 254; 2.66, 81, 86, 139; Sib.
Or. Frg. 3.22, 27; Bk. 3.30; 5.77, 279; Wis 12:24; 15:18)
and Christian (Aristides, Apol. 12; Justin, Apol. 1.24;
Tatian, Or. ad Graecos 9) traditions.

52. Cf. Frg. 2, par. 2. On the special privileges of
priests, cf. Herodotus 2.37; Diodorus Siculus 1.21.7.

53. Land and religious reforms produce similar stabilizing
effects in Diodorus 1.89.5; Plutarch, Is. et Osir. 379F-380C.

54. ἰσόθεος, frequently used to ascribe divine status to
heroes. LSJ, s.v.: Homer, Il. 2.565; Od. 1.374; Aeschylus,
Pers. 80, 857; Sophocles, Ant. 837; Euripides, IA 626;
Plato, Phdr. 255; Isocrates 2.5; Hippocrates, Decent.;
Antiphanes 1.47.2.

55. Or, "because of his interpretation of the hieroglyphs."
In Greek mythology, Hermes is the herald of the gods, and
(later) the patron god of literature and the arts, and the
god of rhetoric. In Iamblichus, De mysteriis Aegypt. 1,
Hermes is θεὸς ὁ τῶν λόγων ἡγεμών (apud, Haenchen, Acts,
426, n. 3). Cf. Acts 14:12. Hermes became appropriated
in Egyptian traditions as the inventor of language,
especially the alphabet, and the god of the art of interpretation (ἑρμηνεία), and thus was identified with his
Egyptian counterpart Thoth (cf. Diodorus Siculus 1.16.1-2;
also Fraser, Ptolemaic Alexandria, 1.208, esp. 2.353, n.
150, and the references to Rusch, "Thoth," PW 6 (1937) cols.
379-88, and Festugière, Hermes Tris. i², 67-88;   Also,
on Thoth, cf. ANET, 5, 8-9. According to Mras, GCS (8,1)
43,1., 520, note on line 9, this mention of Hermes is
clearly an allusion to the alleged name of the Jews
"Hermiouth" in Frg. 1 and Frg. 2, par. 4. Cf. above, note
4. The identification of Moses with Hermes-Thoth is made
easier because of the similarity with Tut-Mosis. Cf.
Freudenthal, 154, who also notes Hermes-Thoth's role as

55 (cont.) teacher of righteousness and lawgiver (cf.
Diodorus Siculus 1.94.1; Plutarch, Is. et Osir. 375 F;
Cicero, de nat. deor. 3.22). Cf., also Hengel, Judaism
and Hellenism, 1.92-93; 2.62, n. 262.

56.   Moses' battle with the Ethiopians (par. 7-9) is
another haggadic addition to the biblical account, most
likely deriving from the reference in Num 12:1 to Moses'
marriage to a Cushite woman (cf. also Hab 3:7; also,
Ginzberg, Legends, 3.256 and 6.90, n. 488). The account
in Josephus, Ant. 2.238-53, is more detailed and perhaps
dependent on Artapanus.   An abbreviated medieval Syrian
version, which occurs in Isho'dad of Merw (9th cent.),
is reported by R. M. Tonneau, "Moïse dans la tradition
syrienne," in Moïse: l'homme de l'alliance   (Paris:
Desclee & Cie, 1955) 245-65, esp. 257-59. Cf. Walter,
JS (1,2), 130, n. 7b.   Because of the legendary invinci-
bility of the Ethiopians (cf. Strabo 16.4.4; Herodotus
3. 17-26), in the Hellenistic romance literature military
victories over them became a frequent motif used to
enhance the status of heroic figures, e.g., Osiris
(Diodorus Siculus 1.17.1; 18.3-4), Cambyses (Herodotus
3.17-26), Sesostris (Diodorus Siculus 1.55.1; cf. 94.4;
Herodotus 2.110; Strabo 16.4.4), and Semiramis (Diodorus
Siculus 2.14.4).   Cf. Collins and Poehlmann, 26; Tiede,
Charismatic Figure, 158-59. Yet another variation of the
Moses-Ethiopian story, in which Moses becomes their ally
and king, occurs in rabbinic sources. Cf. Ginzberg,
Legends, 2.283 and 5.407-10, note 80. On Ethiopians in
antiquity, cf. F. Snowden, Blacks in Antiquity (Cambridge,
Mass.: Harvard University Press, 1970). Also, cf. Vermes,
"La figure," 69-70; I.Levi, "Moïse en Ethiope," REJ 53
(1907) 201-11; I. Heinemann, "Moses (1)," PW 16.1 (1933)
cols. 359-75, esp. 367; Freudenthal, 155-56; Collins-
Poehlmann, 25-27.

57.   Hermopolis was the southernmost nome mentioned in
the Ptolemaic lists (cf. Jones, Cities, 298), located on
the boundary line between Upper and Middle Egypt. It
was an important center of Egyptian religion and the
location of the main shrine of Thoth and the birthplace
of the sun-god Re. Cf. Collins-Poehlmann, 27.

58.   Cf. Polybius 2.24.8, apud Giff. 4.313.

59.   I.e., Artapanus.

60.   Sesostris' battle with the Ethiopians lasted nine
years. Cf. Diodorus Siculus 1.55.9.

61.   On the ibis, cf. Herodotus 2.75-76; Josephus, Ant.
2.245-47; Aelian, NA 2.38; Strabo 17.2.4. Cf. Fraser,
Ptolemaic Alexandria, 1.269 and 2.425, n. 661.

62. I.e., in honor of Moses, so designated in par. 6.

63. Artapanus, in one sense, here agrees with the widespread tradition that the practice of circumcision originated in Egypt (cf. Herodotus 2.36, 104; Agatharchides,
De Mari Erythraeo 61, in C. Müller (ed.), Geographi
Graeci minores (Hildesheim: Georg Olms, 1965; repr. of
1855 ed.) 1.154; Diodorus Siculus 1.28.3; 55.5; 3.32.4;
Strabo 16.4.17; 17.2.5; cf. 16.2.37; Celsus (dependent on
Herodotus) in Origen, Contra Celsum 1.22; also cf. 5.41,
47). The actual origins of the practice are obscure, but
the Egyptian practice is at least as old as the 3rd
millennium B.C.E. (cf. relief from the Sixth Dynasty tomb
at Saqqarah, in IDB 1.629), and is confirmed by numerous
papyri in the Hellenistic-Roman period (e.g. P.Lond. 1.
24.12-13 [164-163 B.C.E.]; P.Tebt. 2.292 [189-190 C.E.];
2.293 [ca. 187 C.E.]; also 2.291; P.Tebt. 2.314 [2nd cent.
C.E.]). The assocation of the practice with Egypt is also
attested in Christian writings (cf. Barn. 9.6; Origen,
Contra Celsum 5.41; Hom. in Jerem. 5.14 = GCS 6 (1901)
43; Jerome, Comm. in Jerem. 9.25-26 = PL (24), par. 910,
cols. 774C - 775A; Justin, Dial. Tryph. 28.4 [on Jer.
9:25-26]).
     By depicting Moses as the one who taught circumcision
to the Ethiopians and (if Walter's conjecture is sound
[JS (1,2), 131, n. 10b]), to all the Egyptian priests as
well, Artapanus continues the inventor-motif introduced
in par. 4, and posits the ultimate Hebrew origin of the
practice. This, in itself, is unusual for Hellenistic-
Jewish authors, though a similar claim is made by Origen,
(Contra Celsum 1.22), also presupposing the higher
antiquity of the Pentateuch (cf. Gen 17:9-27; 34:14-24;
Exod 4:24-26; Lev 12:3; Deut 10:16; 30:6; cf. Josh 5:2-7).
Absent in Artapanus is the defensive tone which later
surfaces in Hellenistic-Jewish writers who respond to
pagan ridicule of the practice (e.g. Josephus, Ag.Ap.
2.137; cf. 1 Macc 1:11-15; Herodotus 2.37; also Sallustius
9, on which cf. A. D. Nock, Sallustius (Cambridge: Cambridge
University Press, 1926) lxxii, n. 152; Petronius 68.4-8
[= Stern, GLAJJ, No. 193]; Martial [= Stern, GLAJJ, 238-46).
A typical response is to defend the practice by noting
its widespread usage among other nations, hence as
nothing peculiarly Jewish (cf. Philo, Spec. Leg. 1.2-11;
Ques. Gen. 3.47-52, esp. 47-48; Josephus, Ag.Ap. 1.168-71
[= Herodotus 2.104]; 2.140-42; cf. Ant. 8.262). It may
in fact have only been practiced by the Egyptian priests,
not by the general populace, as Herodotus suggests. Cf.
Freudenthal, 159. Also, cf. R. Reitzenstein, Zwei
religionsgeschichtliche Frage (Strassburg: K. J. Trübner,
1901) 1-46; I. H. Gray, G. Foucart, D. S. Margoliouth,
and G. A. Barton, "Circumcision," HERE 3 (1910) 659-80;
F. Stummer, "Beschneidung," RAC 2 (1954) cols. 159-69;
J. P. Hyatt, "Circumcision," IDB 1 (1962) 629-31; R. Meyer,
περιτέμνω, TDNT 6 (1968) 72-84; M. Stern, GLAJJ, 1.2-4.

64.   There were three Egyptian cities named Diospolis.
This one is Diospolis Magna, or Thebes, located in Upper
Egypt.   In the Bible, it is the city of No, or No-Ammon
(cf. Jer 46:25).   In Egyptian, it was niwt 'Imn, the
"city of Amon."   Formerly the capital of Egypt, it was
the cultic center for the worship of Amon, whom the Greeks
identified as Zeus, hence "the city of Zeus." Cf. Ezek
30:14, 16 LXX. Cf. Collins-Poehlmann, 28; Sethe, "Diospolis," PW 5 (1905) cols. 1144-45; Walter, JS (1,2) 131,
n. 11a; IDB, 4.615-17.

65.   I.e., Nacheros.

66.   I.e., Moses.

67.   On the veneration of the bull owing to its usefulness
in Egyptian agriculture, cf. Diodorus Siculus 1.21.10
(= P.E. 2.1.19). Generally, on the Egyptian worship of
Apis, cf. Herodotus 2.153; 3.28-29; Diodorus Siculus 1.84.
4, 8 (=P.E. 2.1.48); 1.85.1-5; 88.4 (= P.E. 2.1.41; also
cf. P.E. 3.13.2); Plutarch, Is. et Osir. 353A, 355C, 359B,
362 C-D, 363 C-D, 364 C-E, 368 C-F, 380 E; Aelian, NA
10.28; 11.10-11. Cf. Pietschmann, "Apis (5)," PW 1 (1894)
cols. 2807-09.

68.   On the famous necropolis at Memphis, cf. Fraser,
Ptolemaic Alexandria, 1.269.

69.   The translation here follows the conjecture of
Stephanus (adopted by Mras). The reading of the MSS
(ἀποξενώσαντας) is clearly impossible. Literally, "having
treated him as an alien." Cf. Giff. 4.313; Walter, JS
(1,2), 132, n. 13a.

70.   The translation here attempts to render ὑποσχέσθαι,
which is read by all MSS and retained by Mras. Ordinarily,
it is rendered "promise" (LSJ, s.v.), and "entrust" here
may be stretching it too far. Walter, JS (1,2), 132, n.
15a, plausibly emends the text to read ὑποθέσθαι, suspect-
ing dittography (cf. line 5). Thus, "Chenephres instructed
both Moses and Chanethothes to transport the corpse ..."

71.   I.e., Upper Egypt, most likely Ethiopia. So, Walter,
JS (1,2), 132, n. 15b.

72.   MSS: Μωσεῖ. (cf. app. crit.). Following earlier
editors, Mras brings the spelling here into conformity
with the rest of the text.

73.   Literally, "But he, while protecting himself (reading
with Mras the contracted reflexive αὐτὸν instead of the
more obscure reading of the MSS αὑτὸν), buried the
aforementioned Merris."   Meroe was the capital city of
Ethiopia (cf. Herodotus 2.29; Strabo 17.2.2), some 1100
miles (10,000 stadia; cf. Strabo 17.3.1) south of

73. (cont.) Alexandria. It was located on an island with the same name in the Nile (Diodorus Siculus 1.33.1; Strabo 17.1.2), and is said to have been founded by Cambyses and named by him for Meroe, variously designated as his mother (Diodorus Siculus 1.33.1-4) and sister (Strabo 17.1.5; Josephus, Ant. 2.249). No river by the same name is known among the ancient sources. Cf. Walter, JS (1,2) 132, n. 16b; Collins-Poehlmann, 30.

74. Strabo 17.2.3 lists Isis among the deities revered at Meroe. According to Diodorus Siculus 1.22.2, one tradition held that Isis and Osiris had been buried on an island in the Nile near the border of Ethiopia. Against the editorial tradition which prefers the comparative ἔλαττον, Mras follows the MS tradition in retaining ἐλαχίστως. On the use of the superlative for the comparative, cf. Mras, Rheinisches Museum N.F. 92 (1944) 231, apud P.E. (GCS, 8,1) 43,1.521.

75. Moses' murder of Chanethothes in self-defense represents a variation of the biblical account of his murder of the Egyptian (Exod 2:11-15). The episode is variously treated elsewhere. The biblical account is followed by Jub 47:10-12; also by Philo (V. Mos. 1.43-44, though freely allegorized in Leg. All. 3.37-39; Fuga 147-48). The episode is omitted entirely by Josephus (cf. Ant. 2. 254-57). Cf. Ginzberg, Legends, 2.278-82.

76. Ῥαγουήλ: so, Exod 2:18 LXX (though Ιοθορ in A, after Exod 3:1; 4:18; 18:1 passim.) Cf. Demetrius, Frg. 3, par. 1, and note 69.

77. The syntax is difficult, and perhaps results from abbreviation by Polyhistor. The translation here follows the suggestion of Jacoby to render διακωλύοντα in the passive: διακωλυθέντα. Giff., 3,1.464: "And Raguel forbidding him to march against the Arabs, ordered him to plunder Egypt." Mras, P.E., ad loc.: "At Moses' bidding, Raguel prevented his Arabs from launching a military campaign against the Egyptians, but led them in guerilla warfare instead." Also, Walter, JS (1,2) 133. Freudenthal, 157, by altering the punctuation, suggests: "And Moses, having prevented Raguel from launching an attack, ordered the Arabs to plunder Egypt." On the relation of this to the Hyksos, cf. Freudenthal, 217.

78. According to Plutarch, Quaest. conv. 8.9 (= Moralia 731A; also cf. 732A), elephantiasis was first noted in the time of Asclepiades of Prusa who flourished in Rome ca. 100 B.C.E. A work On Elephantiasis is attributed to Democritus by some ancient writers, but by Diels-Kranz (Frg. der Vorsok.8 68B 306.10, ii.216.8ff.) to Bolus of Mende (3rd cent. B.C.E.). Cf. note in Plutarch (LCL) 9.187; also Wacholder, "Biblical Chronology," 460, n. 34. Also, cf. Ptolemy, Tetr. 151. Elephantiasis was similar to

78. (cont.) leprosy and the name under which leprosy
was sometimes mentioned. The disease envisioned here
was most likely to have been a skin condition, so called
because it resembled the skin of an elephant. Accordingly,
it was sometimes used for leprosy. Later, the term also
came to be used for the enlarged leg condition, but this
condition was apparently unknown to the Greeks. Cf. H. A.
Skinner, The Origin of Medical Terms (Baltimore: Willimans
and Wilkins, 1949) 130. Frequent in Hellenistic-Jewish
literature is the theme of the villainous ruler/official
who in life seeks to obstruct the ways of God, but dies
an extraordinarily violent death. Cf. 2 Macc 9:5-11;
3 Macc 2:21-24; Philo, Flacc. 180-91; Acts 12:23. The
reference to the death of the king is perhaps based on
Exod 4:19. On elephantiasis, cf. further Deut 28:27 Symm;
also Ginzberg, Legends, 2.296-300.

79. Linen, or muslin, clothing would have been a remarkably honorable mark of distinction, given its fine quality
and association with honorable status, especially the
priesthood. Cf. Herodotus 2.37; Plutarch, Is. et Osir.
352 C-D; Diodorus Siculus 5.46.2; P.Tebt. 703.87-117;
Philostratus, VA 8.7.5; cf. also 3 Macc 2:29 where Jews
are branded with the Dionysiac ivy leaf. Cf. Heinichen
2.36, n. 10.

80. I.e., Artapanus.

81. Artapanus' portrait of Moses as the leader of a
military expedition against the Egyptians is distinctive.
Cf., however, Josephus' treatment of Moses as "general"
in Holladay, THEIOS ANER, 69-71. Also, cf. Freudenthal,
155, and 157, who takes this as evidence of Artapanus'
use of traditions about the Hyksos. Cf. Aristobulus,
Frg. 4, par. 3; Philo, V. Mos. 1.65-84; Josephus, Ant.
2.266-76; Ginzberg, Legends, 2.303-36.

82. On the consultation with Aaron, cf. Exod 4:27-31. As
Walter, JS (1,2) 133, n. 22a, notes, there is a sharp
break at this point, suggesting that Polyhistor has
omitted a section.

83. I.e., Chenephres' successor, although in the parallel
account in Clement (cf. following paragraph), Moses'
antagonist in Egypt is called Chenephres. Cf. app. crit.
on Clement parallel to par. 23 below. Also, cf. Josephus,
Ant. 2.277; Exod 4:19.

83a. Literally (following Stephanus' emendation, accepted
by Mras, against the MSS), "... he called (Moses) to
himself ..." Pharaoh's summons is an unbiblical detail.
Cf. Exod 5:1.

84. In Greek literature, δεσπότης is frequently used as
a divine appellation, especially when emphasizing the
power of the gods (cf. esp. Xenophon, An. 3.2.13). The
expression in Artapanus conforms to the typical LXX
pattern where δεσπότης is qualified with a more concrete
expression (cf. Wis 6:7; 8:3; Sir 36:1; 3 Macc 2:2; Jdt
9:12). It is frequently used of God in Philo (cf. esp.
Her. 22-29) and Josephus (cf. J.W. 7.323, 418-19; Ant.
8.111; 18.23). Cf. also Ezekiel the Tragedian, Frg. 2,
par. 11. The usage continues in Christian writings
(cf. Luke 2:29; Acts 4:24; 2 Pet 2:1; Jude 4; Rev 6:10).
Cf. BAG, s.v.; K. H. Rengstorf, TDNT 2 (1964) 44-49.

85. This fragment occurs in the final section of Book I
of the Stromata which is devoted to Moses and the Mosaic
law (chs. 23-29). Its immediate context (ch. 23) is a
panegyric on the life of Moses, specifically his education
in the wisdom of Egypt. It is preceded by a quotation
from Eupolemus (= Frg. 1a) and is followed by an excerpt
from Ezekiel the Tragedian (= Frg. 1, par. 2).

86. The imprisonment of Moses by Pharaoh is an unbiblical
detail.

87. The miraculous escape of the hero from prison is a
common motif in ancient literature. Cf. Euripides, Ba.
431-641 (Dionysus); Philostratus, VA 7.38; 8.30 (Apollonius
of Tyana). Cf. extensive discussion by O. Weinreich,
"Gebet und Wunder;" also Holladay, THEIOS ANER, 205-209.
Cf. Acts 5:17-26; 12:6-17; 16:23-30, on which see
Haenchen, Acts, 383-85; J. Jeremias, TDNT 3 (1965) 175-76;
also Matt 28:2-4; Origen, Contra Celsum 2.34.

88. Cf. Acts 12:7.

89. As Walter, JS (1,2) 134, n. 24a, notes, if the kings
jeers at the name of God, one would expect αὐτό, not
αὐτόν. Merentites, EHBS 30 (1960) 298, takes Moses as
the subject of διαχλευάσαντα, and Pharaoh as the antecedent
of αὐτόν, but this strains the already difficult syntax
too much. Literally, the phrase should be rendered "having
scoffed at him," i.e., either God, the "Lord of the
universe" (cf. par. 22), or Moses, his emissary.

90. The magical power of divine names is well established
in Egyptian magical texts. Cf. Nock, Essays, 1.37, 188-90.
Gager, Moses, 135, has noted the frequency of Jewish divine
names, including Adonai, Iao, Sabaoth, in magical texts.
Tiede, Charismatic Figure, 169, n. 118, notes PGM 2.126-28;
3.158-59; 5.108-18; 12.92-94. Similarly, Goodenough,
Symbols, 2.162, Cf. Josephus, Ant. 2.275-76; Acts 5:1-11;
16:18; also L. Cerfaux, "Influence;" Ginzberg, Legends,
2.331-41; Collins-Poehlmann, 33-34.

91. Cf. 1 Kgs 17:17-24; Acts 20:10; Philostratus, VA 4.45.

92.   Presumably, the king. Cf. Walter, JS (1,2) 134, n. 26a.

93.   Cf. Exod 4:2-3, 20; 7:8-13; also, Ezekiel the Tragedian, Frg. 2, par. 12; Bib. Ant. 19.11. On Moses' magical rod, cf. Collins-Poehlmann, 35; Tiede, Charismatic Figure, 171-73; Ginzberg, Legends, 2.320-21.

94.   Cf. Exod 7:8-13. The scene change required by par. 27 suggests that the text has been abbreviated here, probably by Polyhistor.

95.   On par. 28-30, cf. Exod 7:14-25.

96.   By attributing another cultural achievement to Moses, Artapanus reinforces his portrait of Moses as the bene-factor of Egypt (cf. above, par. 4-6). Cf. Freudenthal, 159. Providing such explanations of remarkable natural phenomena, especially the overflowing of the Nile, had become a well established tradition by the time of Artapanus. Cf. Herodotus 2.19-27; Diodorus Siculus 1.36.7-37.5. Alco, cf. Freudenthal, 217.

97. The reading of the MSS συναγαγών presupposes Moses as the subject, but was corrected by Stephanus to συναγαγόν, understood intransitively (contra Freudenthal, 217; so, Merentites, EHBS 30 (1960) 313, who adduces Theocritus 22.82; Polybius 11:184; Plutarch, Polit. 9.3).Cf. Exod 7:19 συνεστηκὸς ὕδωρ. References in Collins-Poehlmann, 36. It should also be noted that ἐποζέσαι, "to stink," supported by the MSS, is preferable to Stephanus' ἀποζέσαι, "to boil." So, Freudenthal, 217. Cf. Exod 7:18, 21.

98. Cf. Exod 7:21.

99.   Pharaoh makes so such promise in the biblical account. Cf., however, Josephus, Ant. 2.295, who either follows Artapanus, or reflects a common tradition. Cf. Collins-Poehlmann, 36.

100. Freudenthal, 173, sees here the core tradition which appears in modified form in Numenius, where Moses' competi-tors in magic are named Jannes and Jambres (P.E. 9.8.1-3; also Contra Celsum 4.51). The story is preserved in modified form in Pliny, Nat. Hist. 30.2.11; Apuleius, Apol. 90; 2 Tim 3:8. Cf. Gager, Moses, 137-40; IDB 2. 800-801; Ewald, History, 1.89, n. 1.

101. This may be a response to charges, such as those levelled by Molon and Lysimachus, that Moses was a charlatan and magician. Cf. Josephus, Ag.Ap. 2.145. So, Collins-Poehlmann, 36-37.

102. I.e., presupposing that the river had been changed
into blood. Cf. Exod 7:18.

103. An expansion of Exod 7:27, which mentions that
the king's heart was hardened.

104. Probably a reference to the flies, the fourth
biblical plague (Exod 8:20-24); if not, a midrashic
addition.

105. The sixth plague in the biblical account. Cf. Exod
9:8-12.

106. Another midrashic addition, but a common motif in
Hellenistic miracle stories. Parallels are given in
O. Weinreich, Antike Heilungswunder (Religionsgeschicht-
liche Versuche und Vorarbeiten, Bd. 8, Hft. 1; Giessen:
Töpelmann, 1909) 195, apud Collins-Poehlmann, 37.

107. Giff. 4.466: "And as the physicians were unable to
heal the sufferers, the Jews thus again gained relief."

108. Here, Artapanus combines three biblical plagues:
the second (frogs, Exod 7:25-8:15), eighth (locusts,
Exod 10:1-20), and the third (lice, Exod 8:16-19). On
σκνίπας, cf. Exod 8:16(22); Ps 104:31; Wis 19:10. Cf.
Freudenthal, 218.

109. The meaning is unclear. Walter, JS (1,2) 135, n. 32a,
suggests "... especially in the temple in which Isis is
worshipped." The point is vague, but appears to be that
the Egyptians, mistakenly perhaps, venerate a sacred object
which actually symbolizes Moses' power over the earth.
Cf. Diodorus Siculus 1.12.13; Plutarch, Is. et Osir.
363 D-E, 374 C. Cf. Freudenthal, 160.

110. In the biblical account, the seventh plague is hail
(Exod 9:13-35), but no nocturnal earthquakes are mentioned.
This may be an allusion to the ninth plague, darkness
(cf. Exod 10:21-29), which is otherwise omitted by
Artapanus. Cf. Ps 77:17-19; also Acts 16:18, 21.

111. The biblical account does not mention that the
Egyptian temples were destroyed, though cf. Num 33:4 LXX.

112. The death of the first-born (Exod 11:1-12:32) is
conspicuously omitted in Artapanus' account, and may be
Polyhistor's omission. So, Freudenthal, 216.

113. According to Exod 12:36, the Israelites "despoiled
the Egyptians" (σκυλεύω/לצנ). Artapanus' language here
(χρησαμένους) tones down the biblical account, though not
as much as Josephus, Ant. 2.314. Cf. Holladay, THEIOS
ANER, 213, n. 89.

114. Cf. Exod 12:37-39; 13:17-14:22. Also, Josephus, Ant. 2.315-16.

115. On the use of sacred animals in insuring victory in warfare, cf. Diodorus Siculus 1.86.1-5; 88.6-7; Plutarch, Is. et Osir. 379F - 380B. Cf. Freudenthal, 160. On ἄμα, cf. app. crit. and Freudenthal, 218.

116. As Walter notes, JS (1,2), 135, n.35a, the practice of supplying alternative explanations for remarkable events was a common literary device. Cf. Herodotus 2.3-4; also Philo, V. Mos. 1.163-80; Josephus, Ant. 2.347-48; Arrian, An. 1.26.

117. In contrast to the MS tradition, Mras correctly prefers the transitive to the intransitive form, and emends the text accordingly (cf. app. crit.). Likely, dittography has occurred, since διαστῆναι occurs in the next line. Cf. Freudenthal, 218, who regards καὶ διαστῆναι as a gloss.

118. Cf. Exod 14:10-25.

119. I.e., Artapanus. The reference to fire likely derives from Exod 14:24; also, cf. Josephus, Ant. 2.344, which, again, may reflect dependence on Artapanus. Cf. Exod 14:28; also Ps 78:53.

120. Cf. Deut 2:7. τριάκοντα is read by MS I to conform with the figure 89 in the final line, thus agreeing with the biblical account that Moses died at 120 years of age (cf Deut 34:7; also Josephus, Ant. 4.327). Obviously, Mras has preferred the more difficult reading. Cf. Freudenthal, 218, who prefers τριάκοντα.

121. Cf. Exod 16:4-36.

122. I.e., Artapanus.

123. This glowing description expands Deut 34:7. Cf. Josephus, Ant. 4.323-331; Philo, V. Mos. 2.288-92; As. Mos. 11-12. According to Freudenthal, 218, similar descriptions occur in Egyptian texts, including warrants and contracts. Cf. Diodorus Siculus 1.44.4.

124. Cf. Exod 7:7; also Josephus, Ant. 2.319 (eighty years). .

CLEODEMUS MALCHUS

Only one fragment from the work of Cleodemus Malchus[1] is extant, but it exists in two versions. The version of the fragment found in Eusebius (P.E. 9.20.2-4) is taken directly from Josephus (Ant. 1.239-41), who in turn attributes it to Alexander Polyhistor. Most likely, it derives ultimately not from Polyhistor's work Concerning the Jews, as do most of the other Hellenistic Jewish historians, but from another work of his Concerning Libya.[2] The two versions of the fragment (Frg 1 A and B) display some minor syntactic differences but differ primarily in the orthography of proper names, and the textual tradition for each displays immense variety in this regard (cf. app. crit.).

Title. Josephus merely states that Cleodemus Malchus "reported concerning the Jews" (ἱστορῶν τὰ περὶ ᾿Ιουδαίων). This is even less clearly a reference to the title of his work in a technical sense than are similar phrases in the other fragments.[3]

Content. The fragment, which consists of some dozen lines, deals chiefly with Abraham. More specifically, it represents an expansion of Gen 25:1-6, the genealogical description of Abraham's descendants through his second wife Keturah. The details of the biblical genealogy are rearranged: three children of Abraham by Keturah are mentioned: Iapheras/Apher, Sures/Assouri, and Iaphras/Aphran, after whom Africa, Assyria, and the otherwise unknown city of Aphra are said to be named. The most striking features of the fragment are (1) the tracing of Abraham's descendants to Libya; (2) the mention of the pagan tradition of Heracles' defeat of the Libyan giant Antaeus, and his subsequent conquest of Libya; and (3) the incorporation of Heracles into the genealogy of Abraham.

Author. Alexander Polyhistor attributes the fragment to Cleodemus, who is also designated "the prophet," and given the surname Malchus. He is variously seen as a Jew,[4] Samaritan,[5] and pagan,[6] either Syrian[7] or

245

Phoenician.[8] The continuing controversy over his identity
has centered on (1) the significance of his surname
Malchus,[9] and its ethnic origin; (2) his designation as
"prophet" and its significance;[10] and (3) the high level
of syncretism reflected in the fragments as seen by
his interweaving pagan mythological traditions with
biblical traditions. Certainly, none of these is an
a priori impossibility for either a Jewish author,[11] as
Freudenthal thought,[12] or for a Samaritan author.[13] It
is less likely that he was a pagan, although this too is
conceivable.[14]

Provenance. The brevity of the fragment makes it
difficult to establish the author's provenance. Most
frequently, it has been located in Syro-Palestine,
especially in Samaria.[15] Walter's suggestion, based on
the prominence of African, i.e., Libyan traditions, that
he was a member of the Jewish Diaspora in Carthage has
merit.[16]

Date. It is only known for certain that he preceded
Alexander Polyhistor (fl. mid-first century B.C.E.). His
mention of Heracles' progeny (Diodorus and Sophon), which
also occurs in the account of Libya by the historian-king
Juba II of Mauretania (ca. 50 B.C.E. - 23 C.E.) provides
no clear indication of date, since both could easily have
been drawing on widespread popular traditions. He is
generally dated between 200 B.C.E. and 50 B.C.E.[17]

Sources. It is inherently probable that he used the
Greek Bible, but the orthography of proper names shows
considerable divergence even here. There is no hint that
he knew, or used, the Hebrew text.[18]

Importance. To be sure, Cleodemus Malchus is an
obscure figure, but his willingness to combine pagan traditions with the biblical account places him somewhere
along the spectrum of Hellenization near Artapanus and
Pseudo-Eupolemus.[19] Positing Abraham as the universal
ancestor of all other cultures, in this case Africa and
Assyria, and even as prior to the heroic figure Heracles,

places Cleodemus Malchus in the same tradition as other
Hellenistic Jewish authors who sought to enhance their
own cultural and national tradition by establishing kinship
with other renowned peoples and by tracing all other
cultures to Jewish origins.[20]

NOTES

1. Testimonia: Cleodemus is otherwise unattested,
except in the references in the fragments (Josephus, Ant.
1.240; Eusebius, P.E. 9.20.3). Cf. Giff., 4.303, note on
422 bl. Also, cf. Index to Editions and Translations.

2. Suggested by Gutschmid, Kleine Schriften, 2.182; also,
cf. Susemihl, Geschichte, 2.652, 362, n. 78; Denis, 260.
Against Freudenthal, 14-15, cf. Walter, JS (1,2) 115, n. 3.
On Λιβυκά, cf. FGrH 273, Frg 32-47.

3. Freudenthal, 215, regarded περὶ ᾿Ιουδαίων as a title,
but because he saw the author as a Samaritan for whom
this would have been unacceptable, he posited the original
title as περὶ ᾿Εβραίων.

4. Walter, JS (1,2) 116; Hengel, Judaism and Hellenism,
1.74; 2.51, n. 135. The possibility is allowed by Schürer,
Geschichte, 3.481; Literature, 209; followed by Jacoby,
"Kleodemus," PW 11 (1921) 675.

5. Argued most strenuously by Freudenthal, 131-36, on
several grounds: (1) the reference to the books of Moses;
(2) that Malchus is a Semitic, but not demonstrably Jewish
name, occurring mostly in Syrian and Phoenician sources;
(3) the reference to Heracles, understood to be the Tyrian
god worshipped by the Samaritans in Mt. Gerizim; and
(4) the overall syncretistic complexion of the fragments,
which ruled out a Jew, especially one designated as "prophet." Followed by Dalbert, Missionsliteratur, 11; Fraser,
Ptolemaic Alexandria, 2.963, n. 101 [iii]; Denis, 261, 276.
Also, cf. Siegfried, 476-7.

6. Most recently defended by Wacholder, "Pseudo-Eupolemus,"
87, n. 27; "Cleodemus Malchus," 603; and Eupolemus, 54,
n. 114; 55, n. 119, for the following reasons: (1) Moses
is referred to as their lawgiver; (2) the designation
"prophet" is unlikely for a Jew of this period, but more
likely refers to a temple official, perhaps of Phoenician
or Nabataean origin; (3) Josephus quotes him as if he were
a pagan author.

7. Herzfeld, Geschichte, 3.498, 575; Schlatter, Geschichte,
409, n. 100: "Ein Jude war er sicher nicht, vermutliche
ein in die Nähe Palästinas gehörender Syrer."

8. Ewald, History, 8.62.

9. Cf. Annotations, No. 10.

10. Cf. Annotations, No. 9.

11. As seen, e.g., in Artapanus.

12. Freudenthal, 131-36.

13. As seen, e.g., in Pseudo-Eupolemus.

14. If he is dated late, e.g., in the first century B.C.E., it is no less likely that a pagan would have known the Abraham traditions than that Alexander Polyhistor knew and used Jewish traditions.

15. E.g., by Freudenthal, 130-36; Denis, 260-61; Fraser, Ptolemaic Alexandria, 2.963, n. 101 [iii].

16. Walter, JS (1,2) 116; also Conzelmann, HJC, 143. On the Jewish Diaspora in North Africa, cf. E. Schürer, "Diaspora," HDB 5 (1904) 91-109; also M. Stern, "The Jewish Diaspora," in Safrai and Stern, Jewish People, 1.117-83, esp. 133-37.

17. Schürer, 3,481: 200-100 B.C.E.; Charlesworth, PAMR, 93: "sometime in the second century B.C.E."; Walter, JS (1,2) 116-17: prior to Alexander Polyhistor; also, Jacoby, FGrH 3,686. As to the connection with Juba, Denis, 260, n. 54, suggests that the legends concerning Heracles' progeny were perhaps borrowed by Juba by his Jewish wife who had taken them from Cleodemus Malchus.

18. So, Walter, JS (1,2) 117.

19. Schürer, Literature, 209:"(Cleodemus Malchus) ... a classic example of that intermixture of native (Oriental) and Greek traditions, which was popular throughout the region of Hellenism."

20. Cf. Walter, JS (1,2) 117, who notes 1 Macc 12:5-23; 2 Macc 5:9, and B. Cardauns, "Juden und Spartaner. Zur hellenistisch-jüdischen Literatur," Hermes 95 (1967) 317-24, esp. 322-23. On the Jews and Spartans, also cf. APOT 1.112, n. 21.

Bibliography

Bickerman, E. "Un document relatif à la persécution
    d'Antiochus IV Épiphane," Revue de l'Histoire des
    Religions 115 (1937) 188-221.

Broydé, I. "Malchus (Cleodemus, Prophet)," JE 8 (1904) 277.

Charlesworth, PAMRS, 92-93, 276.

Collins, Athens and Jerusalem, 40.

Conzelmann, HJC, 143.

Dalbert, Missionsliteratur, 11.

Denis, Introduction, 259-61.

Doran, "Cleodemus Malchus," in Charlesworth, OTP.

Ewald, History, 8.62.

Fraser, Ptolemaic Alexandria, 2.963.101 [iii].

Freudenthal, Alexander Polyhistor, 13-15, 33-34, 130-36,
    215.

Graetz, Geschichte, 3.621.

Gutschmid, Kleine Schriften, 2.182.

Hengel, Judaism and Hellenism, 1.69, 74, 302; 2.50, 52.

Herzfeld, Geschichte, 3.498, 575.

Jacoby, F. "Kleodemus," PW 11.1 (1921) 675.

Karpeles, Geschichte, 3.180-81.

Müller-Bardorff, J. "Kleodemos," BHH 2.969.

Sanders, B. and D. Fraikin. "Cleodemos Malchos." Unpub-
    lished Seminar Paper. Harvard New Testament Seminar.
    April 13, 1970. 7 pp.

Schlatter, Geschichte, 408-409, n. 100.

Schmid-Stählin, Geschichte, 2,1.591.

Schürer, Geschichte, 3.481.

Siegfried, "Der jüdische Hellenismus," 476-77.

Susemihl, Geschichte, 2.652; also 362, n. 78.

Vaillant, Historicis, 72-74.

Wacholder, B. Z. "Cleodemus Malchus," EncJud 5 (1971) 603.

_____, Eupolemus, 7, 44, 46, 53-55, 95.

_____, "Pseudo-Eupolemus' Two Greek Fragments," 87,
    n. 27.

Walter, JSHRZ (1,2), 115-18.

_____, Untersuchungen, 97-107; 224-33.

Index to Editions and Translations

Fragment One

A.

Source: Josephus, Ant. 1.15.1, par. 239-41.

Greek Text Used: Niese, vol. 1, page 58, line 3 -
     page 59, line 2.

Editions: Müll., FHG 3.214 (= No. 7); Freu., 230;
     Naber, 1.48-49; Niese, 1.58-59; Stearns, 60-61;
     Thackeray, LCL 4.116-19; Jac., FGrH 3.686-87
     (= No. 727, Frg. 1); Denis, 196-97.

Translations:

English: Thackeray, LCL, 4.116-19.

French: Reinach, Antiquités Judaïque, 1.56-57;

German: Riessler, 667 (notes, 1311); Walter,
           (JS, 1.2) 115-19.

B.

Source: Eusebius, P.E. 9.20.2-4.

Reference Number in P.E.: Steph., 246-47; Vig., 422 a-c.

Greek Text Used: Mras, GCS (43,1) 8.1, p. 507,
     line 5 - p. 508, line 2.

Editions: Steph., 246-47; Vig., 422 a-c; Hein., 2.23;
     Gais., 2.377-78; Müll., FHG 3.214 (= No. 7);
     Migne, PG (21) col. 713 A-B (notes, col. 1569);
     Dind., 1.488-89; Freu., 230; Giff., 1.531-32
     (notes, 4.303-304); Stearns, 60-61; Mras, GCS
     (43,1) 8.1, 507-508; Jac., FGrH 3.686-87
     (= No. 727, Frg. 1); Denis, 196-97.

Translations:

English: Giff., 3.453-54.

French:

German: Riessler, 667 (notes, 1311); Walter,
           (JS, 1.2) 115-19.

FRAGMENT ONE

A. Josephus, Ant. 1.15.1, par. 239-41.

(239) ... λέγεται δέ, ὡς οὗτος ὁ Ἑώφρην στρα-   (239)
τεύσας ἐπὶ τὴν Λιβύην κατέσχεν αὐτὴν καὶ οἱ
υἱωνοὶ αὐτοῦ κατοικήσαντες ἐν αὐτῇ τὴν γῆν ἀπὸ
τοῦ ἐκείνου ὀνόματος Ἀφρικὰ προσηγόρευσαν.

5   (240) μαρτυρεῖ δέ μου τῷ λόγῳ Ἀλέξανδρος ὁ   (240)
πολυΐστωρ λέγων οὕτως· "Κλεόδημος δέ φησιν ὁ
προφήτης ὁ καὶ Μάλχος ἱστορῶν τὰ περὶ Ἰουδαίων,
καθὼς καὶ Μωυσῆς ἱστόρησεν ὁ νομοθέτης αὐτῶν,
ὅτι ἐκ τῆς Κατούρας Ἀβράμῳ ἐγένοντο παῖδες
10 ἱκανοί. (241) λέγει δὲ αὐτῶν καὶ τὰ ὀνόματα   (241)
ὀνομάζων τρεῖς Ἰαφέραν Σούρην Ἰαφράν. ἀπὸ
Σούρου μὲν τὴν Ἀσσυρίαν κεκλῆσθαι, ἀπὸ δὲ τῶν
δύο Ἰαφρᾶ τε καὶ Ἰαφέρου, πόλιν τε Ἐφρᾶν καὶ
τὴν χώραν Ἀφρικὰ ὀνομασθῆναι. τούτους γὰρ
15 Ἡρακλεῖ συστρατεῦσαι ἐπὶ Λιβύην καὶ Ἀνταῖον·
γήμαντά τε τὴν Ἀφράνου θυγατέρα Ἡρακλέα γεννῆσαι υἱὸν ἐξ αὐτῆς Δίδωρον· τούτου δὲ γενέσθαι
Σόφωνα, ἀφ' οὗ τοὺς βαρβάρους Σόφακας λέγεσθαι."

ROMSPLE Lat.   Zonaras, Chron.   Eustathius, Hex.
Hieron., Quaest. Gen.

1 Ἑώφρην: ἑώφρην O: ὤφρησ M: ὠφρὴν SP: ὠφρὸσ L:
ἀφρὴν E: opher Lat.: Σωφρὴν Eustath.: Apher Hieron. |
2 λιβύην, ι ex υ corr. R | 4 Ἀφρικὰ: RE(nomin. in E):
ἀφρικὴν OL Eustath.: ἄφρικα M: ἀφρίκαν SP: affricam
Lat.: Aphricam Hieron. | 9 Κατούρας: χατούρασ MSPE:
κατtούρασ L: cethura Lat. | 11 Ἰαφέραν: ἄφεραν ML:
ἀφέραν SP: ἀφεράν E: apheran Lat.: | Σούρην:
σούριν O: σουρείμ MLE: σουρίν SP: surim Lat. |
Ἰαφράν: ἴαφραν M: ἰαφράμ E | 12 Σούρου: σουρείμ MLE:
σουρεῖ S: σουρῆ P^pc: surim Lat.: Ἀσοὺρ Eustath. |
Ἀσσυρίαν: ἀσυρίαν S¹P¹ Eustath. | 13 Ἰαφρᾶ τε καὶ
Ἰαφέρου: iaphram et apheran Lat. | Ἰαφρᾶ τε:
φράτι M: φράτει S: φρατῆ P (ῆ i. ras.): φρᾶ τε L:
ἀφρά τε E | Ἰαφέρου: ἰαφράμου E | Ἐφρᾶν: ἀφρὰν
ME: ἄφραν SPL: abran Lat. | 14 Ἀφρικὰ: ἄφρικα M:
ἀφρίκαν SPE: ἀφρικὴν L: africam Lat. | 15 συνστρα-
τεῦσαι M | Ἀνταῖον: ἄνταιον SL: ἄντεον M: (cont.)

FRAGMENT ONE

A.[1]

(239)(239) ... It is reported[2] how this Heophre[3] waged
war against Libya[4] and conquered it[5] and how his
grandsons, after they had settled there, named the
(240) land Africa[6] after him.   (240) Alexander Polyhistor[7]
bears witness to my account when he says, "Cleodemus[8]
the prophet,[9] also called Malchus,[10] reported concerning the Jews, just as Moses their own lawgiver had
reported,[11] that numerous children were born to
(241) Abraham by Katoura.[12]   (241) He even gives their
names -- three of them are named -- Iapheras, Sures,
and Iaphras.[13] Assyria was named after Sures, while
the city of Ephra[14] and the country of Africa were
named after the other two, Iaphras and Iapheras
respectively. These, in fact, joined with Heracles
in fighting against Libya and Antaeus.[15] Heracles
married the daughter of Aphranes[16] and fathered a
son by her whose name was Didorus. Didorus fathered
Sophon, after whom the barbarian Sophakes are
named."[17]

---

haeteam Lat. | 16 γήμαντά: γήμασάν R | τε: om. Lat. |
'Αφράνου: ὄφραν M: ἄφρα SP: ἄφραν L: *iaphram* Lat.:
Οὐαφρῆ Eustath. | 17 Δίδωρον: δέδωρον M: δὲ δώρων L:
dodorim Lat.: Βόδωρον Eustath. | 18 Σόφωνα: σοφῶνα M:
σώφωνα SP[1]: *soron* Lat.: Σωφονά Eustath.: Σοφῶκα
Freu. | Σόφακας: σόφωνασ O: *osophaci* Lat.:
σοφιστὰς Eustath. |

FRAGMENT ONE

B.   Eusebius, P.E. 9.20.2-4.

(2)   Ταῦτα μὲν δὴ ἀπὸ τῆς προειρημένης τοῦ   (2)
Πολυΐστορος γραφῆς. καὶ ὁ Ἰώσηπος δὲ ἐν τῇ
πρώτῃ τῆς Ἀρχαιολογίας τοῦ αὐτοῦ μνημονεύει διὰ
τούτων·

5   "Λέγεται δὲ ὡς οὗτος ὁ Ἀφρὴν στρατεύσας
ἐπὶ τὴν Λιβύην κατέσχεν αὐτὴν καὶ οἱ υἱωνοὶ
αὐτοῦ κατοικήσαντες ἐν αὐτῇ τὴν γῆν ἀπὸ τοῦ
ἐκείνου ὀνόματος Ἀφρικὰ προσηγόρευσαν. (3) μαρ-   (3)
τυρεῖ δέ μου τῷ λόγῳ Ἀλέξανδρος ὁ Πολυΐστωρ   422b
10 λέγων οὕτως· Ἰκλεόδημος δέ φησιν ὁ προφήτης,
ὁ καὶ Μαλχᾶς, ἱστορῶν τὰ περὶ Ἰουδαίων, καθὼς
καὶ Μωσῆς ἱστόρηκεν ὁ νομοθέτης αὐτῶν, ὅτι ἐκ
τῆς Χεττούρας Ἀβραάμῳ ἐγένοντο παῖδες ἱκανοί·
λέγει δὲ αὐτῶν καὶ τὰ ὀνόματα, ὀνομάζων τρεῖς,
15 Ἀφέρ, Ἀσσουρί, Ἀφράν· (4) καὶ ἀπὸ Ἀσσουρὶ   (4)
μὲν τὴν Ἀσσυρίαν, ἀπὸ δὲ τῶν δύο, Ἀφρά τε καὶ
Ἀφέρ, πόλιν τε Ἀφρὰν καὶ τὴν χώραν Ἀφρικὰ
ὀνομασθῆναι. τούτους δὲ Ἡρακλεῖ συστρατεῦσαι
ἐπὶ Λιβύην καὶ Ἀνταῖον· γήμαντα δὲ τὴν Ἀφρὰ   422c
20 θυγατέρα Ἡρακλέα γεννῆσαι υἱὸν ἐξ αὐτῆς Διόδωρον.
τούτου δὲ γενέσθαι Σοφωνᾶν, ἀφ' οὗ τοὺς βαρβάρους
Σοφὰς λέγεσθαι.'"

Τὰ μὲν οὖν περὶ τοῦ Ἀβραάμ ὡς ἐν ὀλίγοις
τοσαῦτα παρακείσθω.

BION

1-2 ταῦτα -- ὁ: καὶ ταῦτα μὲν οὗτος. καὶ B | 3 τῆς
om. B | ἀρχαιολοΓʹ (signif. fort. -ίᾳ) B | 3-4 τοῦ --
τούτων: οὕτω φησίν B|5 sqq. ἀπὸ τῆς Ἰωσήπου ἀρχαιολογίας
BI ᵐᵍON | 5 Ἀφρὴν I: Σωφρὴν BON | 9 μου τῷ λόγῳ: μοι B |
10-11 Κλεόδ. -- Ἰουδαίων om. B | 11 καθὼς: ὅτι B |
12 αὐτῶν om. B | 13 τῆς BON: om. I | Χετούρας N |
Ἀβραάμῳ ION: Ἀβραὰμ B | 15 Ἀφέρ I: Ἄφερ BON |
Ἀσσουρί¹ B: Ἀσσουρί ON: Ἀσούρ I | Ἀφράν I:
Ἄφραν BON | Ἀσσουρὶ BON: Ἀσσουρὶ I |16-17 Ἀφρά τε
καὶ Ἀφέρ I: Ἄφρα τε καὶ Ἄφερ BON | 17 Ἀφράν I:
Ἄφραν BON | Ἀφρικα ON | 19 Ἄφρα BON | 20 Διόδωρον
BON: Διόδωρον I | 23 Ἀβραάμ B | 24 παρακείσθω om. B |

FRAGMENT ONE

B.[18]

(2)   (2)   These, then, are the things from the
aforementioned work of Polyhistor. And Josephus in
the first book of the <u>Antiquities</u> also mentions the
same author in the following remarks:

"It is reported how this Aphre waged war against
Libya and conquered it and how his grandsons, after
they had settled there, named the land Africa after

(3)   him.[19]   (3)   Alexander Polyhistor bears witness to
my account when he says, 'Cleodemus the prophet, also
called Malchus, reported concerning the Jews, just as
Moses their own lawgiver has reported, that numerous
children were born to Abraham by Kettourah. He even
gives their names -- three of them are named --

(4)   Apher, Assouri, and Aphran.   (4)   Assyria was named
after Assouri, while the city of Aphra and the
country of Africa were named after the other two,
Aphran and Apher respectively. These joined with
Heracles in fighting against Libya and Antaeus.
Heracles married the daughter of Aphran and fathered
a son by her whose name was Diodorus. Diodorus
fathered Sophon after whom the barbarian Sophakai
are named.'"

Let it suffice then that the story of Abraham
is briefly set forth in these quotations.

ANNOTATIONS

1. This fragment is quoted by Josephus in his treatment
of the story of Abraham as narrated in Genesis (<u>Ant</u>. 1.
150-256). In listing Abraham's descendants by his second
wife Keturah, expanding Gen 25:6 ("But to the sons of
his concubines Abraham gave gifts, and while he was still
living he sent them away from his son Isaac, eastward to
the east country."), he states that Abraham sent out his
children and grandchildren as colonizers of the regions
around the Red Sea ("Troglodytis and that part of Arabia
Felix which extends to the Red Sea," par. 239). The
one descendant whose accomplishments Josephus details was
Eophre, a grandson of Abraham, and he does this by quoting
Alexander Polyhistor's excerpt from Cleodemus Malchus.
Following this statement from Cleodemus, Josephus resumes
the Genesis account, recounting the story of Isaac and
Rebeccah.

2. I.e., in the following citation from Cleodemus
Malchus.

3. I.e., the grandson of Abraham. Josephus, <u>Ant</u>. 1.238-
39, summarizes Gen 25:1-4. Following Gen 25:2, Josephus
lists Abraham's six sons by Ketura, the third being Madan
who, according to Gen 25:4, had five sons, the second
being Epher/Eophre (עֵפֶר/Αφερ; 1 Chr 1:33 עֵפֶר/Οφερ). Cf.
app. crit. for the many orthographical variants. Also,
cf. Frg. 1 B, par. 2, and app. crit.

4. Cf. Ezekiel the Tragedian, Frg. 1, par. 4, where,
on the lips of Zipporah, Libya is said to be inhabited
by Ethiopians, and is apparently equated with Midian.
On the basis of this common occurrence, Denis, 260, 276,
following, Kuiper, <u>Ezechiele</u>, 278-79, raises the possibility that the work of Ezekiel the Tragedian was inspired
by Cleodemus Malchus, and that both were Samaritans.

5. Cf. par. 241, below.

6. On the geographical boundaries of Africa and Libya in
the Hellenistic-Roman period, cf. <u>OCD</u>[2], 22-23, 608.

7. According to Gutschmid, <u>Kleine Schriften</u>, 2.182,
Alexander Polyhistor's work <u>Concerning Libya</u> (Λιβυκά,
<u>FGrH</u> 273, Frg. 32-37) is the source of this quotation,
not his work <u>Concerning the Jews</u>. This suggestion is
supported by the fact that Eusebius (Frg. 1 B) breaks
his pattern of citing from Polyhistor's <u>Concerning the
Jews</u>, and quotes rather from Josephus. Since this is
Josephus' only reference to Alexander Polyhistor, it is
clear that the latter work was unknown to him. Cf. Denis,
260; Walter, <u>JS</u> (1,2) 115, n. 4, and esp. his "Zur Überlieferung einiger Reste früher jüdisch-hellenistischer
Literatur bei Josephus, Clemens, und Euseb," <u>Studia
Patristica VII</u> (TU, 92; Berlin, 1966) 314-20, esp. 316-19.

8. This Greek name is attested in Hellenistic Egypt. In
CPJ 1.227-230 (238-237 B.C.E.) = No. 126.20, Tlepolemos,
the son of Kleodemos (Τληπόλεμος Κλεοδήμου) is one of the
witnesses to a Greek will which also mentions a Jewish
slave. Cf. also Supp. Epigr. Gr. 18, No. 88.12, an
inscription from Delphi (137/136 B.C.E.): Κλεόδαμος.

9. According to Freudenthal, 133, this designation is
striking because of its infrequent use in Judaism in the
Hellenistic-Roman period owing to the demise of the prophetic movement (cf. 1 Macc 4:46; 9:27; 14:41; Ps 74:9;
Josephus, Ag.Ap. 1.41). This he saw as further proof of
Cleodemus' non-Jewish status -- such a title would have
been inappropriate and unlikely for a Jew so syncretistic.
(Followed by Denis, 260). This analysis is now seen to
be far too limited in scope. The development of the
Jewish prophetic movement in the Hellenistic period, and
the related phenomenon of apocalypticism, are now regarded
as far more complex and interrelated. As Freudenthal
himself recognized, the use of "prophet" and related terms
within pagan traditions was widespread (cf. TDNT, 6.781-
861). Consequently, the term itself, much less its
correlation with relative degrees of syncretism, is no
firm indicator of the author's ethnic status, nor even
of the nature of the work. Cf. Walter, JS (1,2) 119,
n. 240a.

10. Josephus: Μάλχος; Eusebius: Μαλχᾶς (cf. Frg 1 B,
par. 3). The latter is better attested. The name is
Semitic, and probably, though by no means certainly,
Jewish. Cf., e.g., John 18:10, as noted by Siegfried, 477.
Freudenthal, 131-32, notes the relative infrequency of it
and its cognate forms in the OT (מלוך/Μαλώχ, 1 Chr 6:29
(44); מלכם/Μελχάς, 1 Chr 8:9), apocryphal (though, cf.
1 Macc 11:39 v.l., and note in APOT 1.109, n. 39), and
other Jewish sources. This, along with the syncretistic
nature of the fragment, led Freudenthal to regard the
author as a Samaritan. Pagan use of the name may be
attested as early as the 6th century B.C.E., when used of
a Carthaginian general, although the actual form of the
name is uncertain, and may be a corruption of מלך (cf.
OCD[2], 642; also, on the use of מלך and its compounds as
proper names, cf. G. B. Gray, Studies in Hebrew Proper
Names (London: Black, 1896) 115-20). A first century B.C.E.
Nabataean king named Malchus is also known and mentioned
several times by Josephus who uses the name almost exclusively of Gentiles, especially of Nabataean Arabs (cf.
Index, LCL, 9.732). Moulton-Milligan, 387, note the occurrence of Ἰρμαῖος Μάλιχος, "the only Semite name in a ii/
A.D. military letter ...;" also, P. Magd. 15 verso[3] (221
B.C.E.). Certainly, at a later period its use by pagans
is documented, notably in the case of Porphyry who was
possibly originally called Malchus (Πορπύριος ὁ καὶ Μάλχος,
VP inscr.; also Plot. 17, apud BAG, 489-90, s.v.), though
his Tyrian origin should be noted. Other later uses

10.   (cont.)   include OGIS 640.3 (Palmyra, 3rd cent. C.E.);
P.Brem. 5,3 (117-119 B.C.E.); 6,3.   Cf. Walter, JS (1,2)
115, n. 1, and reference to Untersuchungen, 99, 226, for
instances of its presumed use of Jews in Egyptian sources.

11.   "Their own lawgiver" need not reflect the author's
pagan status (so, Wacholder, "Cleodemus Malchus," 613), so
much as Alexander Polyhistor's outlook and indirect citation of Cleodemus.   Nor is it significant that the Mosaic
authorship of Genesis is presupposed, since this was the
common assumption in antiquity.

12.   Cf. Gen 25:1-6.

13.   Schürer, 3.481, notes that in the biblical account
these are Arab tribes.   The genealogies in the biblical
account are conflated here, producing some confusion.
Iapheras (᾿Ιαφέραν) and Iaphras (᾿Ιαφράν) doubtless correspond to Ephah (עיפה/Γαιφα) and Epher (עפר/Αφερ), two
of the grandsons of Abraham and Keturah by their son
Midian (Gen 25:4).   Sures (Σούρην) appears to correspond
to Shuah (שוח/Σωυε, Gen 25:2), the sixth mentioned son of
Abraham and Keturah.   In the Eusebius manuscript tradition,
however, Assuri (᾿Ασσουρί) occurs instead of Sures, and
this appears to correspond to Asshurim (אשורם/Ασσουριιμ,
Gen 25:3), the grandson of Abraham and Keturah by their
son Dedan.   The orthographical differences in the Eusebius
MS tradition should be noted.   Cf. Frg 1 B, par. 3 (᾿Αφέρ,
᾿Ασσουρί, ᾿Αφράν), and app. crit.

14.   Presumably a, if not the chief, city of Africa, though
no such city is known in antiquity.   It is perhaps a
reference to Ephah in Isa 60:6. So, Denis, 260.

15.   On Heracles' defeat of Antaeus, the Libyan giant and
son of Poseidon and Ge, and his subsequent conquest and
civilizing of Libya, cf. Diodorus Siculus 4.17.4-5, which
is included as part of the longer account of Heracles'
Twelve Labors and other deeds (4.8-39; also 57-58). Cf.
also 1.21.4; 24.1-8.   Also, cf. Apollodorus, Bibliotheca
2.5.11., and the comprehensive list of references to
Hercules and Antaeus cited by J. G. Frazer in LCL 1.222-23,
n. 2.   In the Greek accounts, Heracles accomplishes these
feats singlehandedly.   On Antaeus, cf. Wernicke, "Antaios
(1)," PW 1 (1894) 2339-42.
        According to Freudenthal, 133, this is not the Heracles
of Greek mythology, the son of Poseidon and Ge, but the
Tyrian Heracles, identified in Phoenician circles with the
god Melkart who was worshipped by the Samaritans as Ζεὺς
Ξένιος on Mt. Gerizim.   Accordingly, because of the Samari-
tan-Phoenician connection (cf. 2 Macc 4:19; 6:2; Josephus,
Ant. 12.257-64), Freudenthal regarded this as further
evidence of a Samaritan origin for the fragment. He is
followed by Fraser, Ptolemaic Alexandria, 2.963, n. 101
[iii], in identifying Heracles with the Tyrian god and
in positing a Samaritan origin. Cf., however, Walter, JS

15. (cont.) (1,2) 116. Cf. also Giff. 4.304: "That the
Samaritans connected Heracles with the history of Abraham
is made probable by a statement of Epiphanius, Haer. 55.2.
1 Melchisedekiani εἶπον δέ τινες 'Ηρακλᾶν τινα καλεῖσθαι
τὸν αὐτοῦ (τοῦ Μελχισεδέκ) πατέρα, μητέρα δὲ 'Αστάρθ τὴν
δὴ καὶ 'Αστοριανήν. No Pagan, Jew, or Christian would have
spoken thus about Melchisedek, but the Hellenizing Samaritans in the time of Antiochus Epiphanes claimed to be
Phoenicians of Sidon (Josephus, Ant. 12.257-64), and as
such would be likely to claim descent from the union of
a grand-daughter of Abraham with the Phoenician Heracles,
Melcarth of Tyre, whose worship was still maintained
(2 Macc 4:18; 6:2)."

16. Though the spelling of Aphranes ('Αφράνου, line 16)
differs from that of Iaphras ('Ιαφράν, line 11) in Niese's
edition, the two should be equated, as they are in the
Eusebian text. Hence, according to Cleodemus Malchus,
Heracles marries the granddaugther of Abraham. Cf.
Frg 1 B, par. 4, and app. crit.

17. This represents a variation of the tradition related
in Plutarch, Sert. 9.3-5, where Heracles, after slaying
Antaeus, is said to have married his widow Tinga, who bore
him a son Sophax, who became king of Libya. To Sophax
was born a son, Diodorus. It is not clear why Cleodemus
reverses the order. Plutarch also states that this
genealogy is traceable to King Juba of Mauretania (ca.
50 B.C.E.-23 C.E.), the historian-king who traced his
ancestors to Sophax and Diodorus. The orthography in the
Eusebius version of the story (Frg 1 B, par. 4) agrees
with that of Plutarch: Διόδωρος. Cf. app. crit. On Juba,
cf. FGrH 275, T 10, and Kommentar in FGrH 3a (Leiden:
Brill, 1943) 323-24; also F. Jacoby, "Iuba(2)," PW 9 (1916)
2384-95.

18. This excerpt from Cleodemus Malchus occurs in the
section of Book 9 devoted to Abraham (chs. 16-20). It
occurs after a quotation from Philo Epicus (Frg. 1), and is
the final witness Eusebiues adduces for Abraham. After
this, he turns to Jacob (chs. 21-22), beginning with a
quotation from Demetrius (Frg. 2). It should be noted
that this fragment is taken directly from Josephus, who in
turn cites Alexander Polyhistor as his source. This is
the only time Eusebius cites Alexander Polyhistor indirectly. Cf. above, note 7.

19. I.e., Aphre.

One fragment from Aristeas'[1] work Concerning the Jews
is preserved by Eusebius, who quoted it directly from
Alexander Polyhistor.[2] Unless this is the work referred
to in Ep. Arist. 6,[3] it is otherwise unattested.

Contents. The fragment, consisting of some thirty
lines, summarizes the story of Job who is identified with
Jobab, the great-grandson of Esau (Gen 36:33), though here
he is said to be the son of Esau.[4] Job is thus included
among the patriarchs and portrayed as a descendant of the
Edomites. Apart from his identification with Jobab, the
Edomite connection, and the designation of Job's three
friends as kings (following Job 2:11 LXX), the fragment
presents no major divergencies from the biblical story.

Author. The author was a Jew, as seen from his close
adherence to the LXX.[5] He is variously designated as
"exegete" and "historian," primarily because he summarizes
the biblical text while showing some concern for historical
specificity and genealogy similar to that found in Demetrius; there is not, however, comparable chronographical
concern.[6]

Title. The title of his work Concerning the Jews may
be a general designation of the contents of the work rather
than a title in the strict sense. It is used elsewhere
of historical works, though it includes works ranging
from romance (Artapanus) to history in the stricter sense
(Eupolemus).

Sources. The fragment reflects an exclusive use of
the LXX, with no evidence of dependence on the Hebrew
text or rabbinic sources and traditions.[7] Nor is there
any influence of pagan traditions, as there is in Artapanus
and Pseudo-Eupolemus. In fact, it advances the interpretation of the Hebrew version of Job along the lines begun
by the Greek translators who had already established links

between Job and Gen 36, and translated the text accordingly.[8] It bears closest similarity with the epilogue of the
Greek version of Job (42:17b-e), and this constitutes one
of the chief critical problems: whether Aristeas used the
epilogue,[9] whether the author of the epilogue used
Aristeas,[10] or whether both used a common source or tradition.[11]

Date and Provenance. It is only known for certain
that Aristeas antedates Alexander Polyhistor (fl. mid-
first cent. B.C.E.) who first preserved it. The fragment
contains no historical or literary allusions which can
assist in pointing to a date any more precise. To be sure,
it presupposes a Greek translation of Genesis and Job,
thus suggesting a terminus post quem in the mid-3rd cent.
B.C.E., at the earliest. It is commonly dated in the
2nd cent. B.C.E.[12]

In light of its strict dependence on the LXX, and the
absence of any explicit Palestinian influence, an Egyptian
provenance is perhaps most likely, although the brevity of
the fragment makes any suggestion very tentative.[13]

Importance. It is valuable as an early testimony to
the Job tradition, and should be considered along with the
more complete documents which preserve this tradition,
e.g., the Testament of Job and 11QtgJob. It is an early
testimony to the Greek translation of Job, providing a
terminus ad quem for its date,[14] and also constitutes
valuable evidence for the critical assessment of the Greek
epilogue to Job (42:17b-e).[15] It also provides additional
testimony of early attempts to date Job in the patriarchal
period and to establish his connection with Edom.[16]

NOTES

1. Testimonia: Ep. Arist. 6 (?); Eusebius, P.E. 9.38.
2-3 (?).

2. P.E. 9.25.1-4. Cf. Index to Editions and Translations.

3. Ep. Arist. 6: "On a former occasion, too, I sent you
a record of the facts which I thought worth relating about
the Jewish race (περὶ τοῦ γένους τῶν Ἰουδαίων), -- the
record which I had obtained from the most learned high
priests of the most learned land of Egypt." This may be
an attempt of the author of Ep. Arist. to identify himself
with an already known and established work such as
Aristeas' Concerning the Jews. However, since the author
of Ep. Arist. presents himself as a pagan, this would
imply the pagan authorship of the work referred to, but
this is unlikely in light of its content (Freudenthal, 142,
notes the "slavish dependence" on the LXX). The reference
in Ep. Arist. may be to another work no longer extant nor
elsewhere attested. Cf. APOT, 2.95, n. 6. Since it cannot
be established that Ep. Arist. 6 is a reference to
Aristeas' Concerning the Jews, the two are best left unre-
lated. So, Schwartz, 879; Freudenthal, 141-43; Walter, JS
(3,2) 294; Denis, 259. Wendland, 92, suggests that the
author of Ep. Arist. probably borrowed his name from
Aristeas the historian-exegete.

4. This is a disputed point, however. Cf. par. 1.
Freudenthal, 23, emends the text by omitting the reference
to υἱόν; hence, τὸν Ἡσαῦ γήμαντα βασσάραν ἐν Εδὼμ γεννῆσαι Ἰώβ.

5. So, Ewald, History, 8.63; Freudenthal, 137-38; Dalbert,
Missionsliteratur, 68; Denis, Introduction, 259.

6. Cf. Dalbert, Missionsliteratur, 69.

7. In par. 1, Βασσάραν reflects Gen 36:33LXX ἐκ Βοσορρας
(MT מבצרה). Cf. below, Annotations, No. 3. Also, ἐν τῇ
Αὐσίτιδι (cf. Job 1:1 ἐν χώρᾳ τῇ Αυσίτιδι). The description of the animals in par. 2 conforms closely to Job 1:3.
In par. 3 Ἰωβάβ recalls Gen 36:33-34. Cf. below, Annotations, No. 3. In par. 4, the three friends are designated
as kings (βασιλεύς/τύραννος), following Job 2:11LXX (the
titles are absent in MT). Also, Ζωφὰρ τὸν Μινναίων (cf.
Job 2:11 Ζωφαρ ὁ Μιναίων; MT צופר הנעמתי). Cf. Freudenthal,
138-39; Swete, Introduction, 371.

8. So, Freudenthal, 137.

9. So, G. B. Gray, "The Additions in the Ancient Greek
Version of Job," The Expositor 19 (1920) 422-38, esp.
431-34, though tentatively; Wendland, 92; E. Dhorme, JoB
(London: Nelson, 1967) xvii-xviii, cxcvi, 653.

10. According to Freudenthal, 138-41, the epilogue is
based on direct use of Aristeas, nor the excerpted version
from Alexander Polyhistor. Also, Walter, JS (3,2) 293;
Denis, Introduction, 258, esp. n. 50. Wacholder, 438,
suggests that the epilogue is an attempt to correct
the earlier version of Aristeas.

11. E.g., M. Jastrow, Job (Philadelphia: Lippincott, 1920),
369, though he dates Aristeas much later in the second
century C.E.

12. So, Freudenthal, 143; Susemihl, 2.651; Dalbert,
Missionsliteratur, 68; Wendland, 92. Walter, JS (3,2)
294: ca. 100 B.C.E., or earlier. Wacholder, 438: second
or early first cent. B.C.E.

13. Freudenthal, 137-39; Dalbert, Missionsliteratur, 68,
Denis, Introduction, 259, allows Egypt as a possibility
but prefers a Palestinian setting.

14. As e.g., Dhorme, Job, cxcvi.

15. On the epilogue, cf. besides Gray, "Additions" (note
9 above), S. R. Driver and G. B. Gray, Job (ICC; Edinburgh: T. & T. Clark, 1921) lxv, lxxi; G. Fohrer, Das
Buch Hiob (KAT, 16; Gütersloh: G. Mohn, 1963) 542, 560;
Dhorme, Job (note 9 above), xviii-xix.

16. On the traditions of Job's homeland, cf. M. Pope,
Job (AB, 15; Garden City, New York: Doubleday, 1965) 3-5.

Bibliography

Charlesworth, PAMRS, 80-81, 274.

Collins, Athens and Jerusalem, 30-31.

Dalbert, Missionsliteratur, 67-70.

Denis, Introduction, 258-59.

Doran, "Aristeas the Exegete," in Charlesworth, OTP.

Ewald, History, 8.63.

Fraikin, D. "Alexander Polyhistor's Fragment from
    Aristeas." Unpublished Seminar Paper. Harvard New
    Testament Seminar. April 13, 1970. 11 pp.

Freudenthal, Alexander Polyhistor, 136-43, 231.

Ginzberg, Legends, 5.384.

Gutmann, J. "Aristeas," EncJud 3 (1930) 316.

Hengel, Judaism and Hellenism, 1.169.

Karpeles, Geschichte, 1.176.

Maugenot, E. "Aristée," DB 1/1 (1926) 963-64.

Schlatter, Geschichte, 75-76.

Schmid-Stählin, Geschichte, 2,1.590-91.

Schürer, Geschichte, 3.480.

Schwartz, E. "Aristeas (14)," PW 2/1 (1849) 879.

Siegfried, "Der jüdische Hellenismus," 477.

Susemihl, Geschichte, 2.651.

Swete, Introduction, 25, 256-57, 369-71.

Wacholder, B. Z. "Aristeas," EncJud 2 (1971) 438-39.

Walter, JSHRZ (3,2), 293-96.

_____, Untersuchungen, 86-92, 216-21.

Wendland, P. "Aristeas, the Historian," JE 2 (1904) 92.

Index to Editions and Translations

Fragment One

Source: Eusebius, P.E. 9.25.1-4.

Reference Number in P.E.: Steph., 251-52; Vig., 430d -
431b.

Greek Text Used: Mras, GCS (43,1) 8.1, p. 518, lines
5-22.

Editions: Steph., 251-52; Vig., 430d - 431b; Hein.,
2.32-33; Gais., 2.392-94; Müll., FHG 3.220
(= No. 12); Migne, PG (21) col. 728 A-B (notes,
col. 1573); Dind., 1.497-98; Freu., 231; Giff.,
1.540-41 (notes, 4.310-12); Stearns, 57-59;
Mras, GCS (43,1) 8.1, 518; Jac., FGrH 3.680
(= No. 725, Frg. 1); Denis, 195-96.

Translations:

English: Giff., 3.461.

French:

German: Riessler, 178 (notes, 1275); Walter,
(JS, 3.2) 293-96.

FRAGMENT ONE (Eusebius, P.E. 9.25.1-4)

    "Ακουε δὲ οἷα καὶ περὶ τοῦ Ἰὼβ ὁ αὐτὸς   430d
ἱστορεῖ·

ΑΡΙΣΤΕΟΥ ΠΕΡΙ ΤΟΥ ΙΩΒ ΟΜΟΙΩΣ

    (1) "Ἀριστέας δέ φησιν ἐν τῷ Περὶ Ἰουδαίων   (1)
5 τὸν Ἡσαῦ γήμαντα Βασσάραν υἱὸν ἐν Ἐδὼμ γεννῆσαι
Ἰώβ· κατοικεῖν δὲ τοῦτον ἐν τῇ Αὐσίτιδι χώρᾳ
ἐπὶ τοῖς ὅροις τῆς Ἰδουμαίας καὶ Ἀραβίας.
(2) γενέσθαι δ' αὐτὸν δίκαιον καὶ πολύκτηνον·   (2)
κτήσασθαι γὰρ αὐτὸν πρόβατα μὲν ἑπτακισχίλια,
10 καμήλους δὲ τρισχιλίας, ζεύγη βοῶν πεντακόσια,
ὄνους θηλείας νομάδας πεντακοσίας· εἶχε δὲ καὶ
γεωργίας ἱκανάς. (3) τοῦτον δὲ τὸν Ἰὼβ πρότερον   (3)
| Ἰωβὰβ ὀνομάζεσθαι. πειράζοντα δ' αὐτὸν τὸν   431a
θεὸν ἐμμεῖναι, μεγάλαις δὲ περιβαλεῖν αὐτὸν
15 ἀτυχίαις. πρῶτον μὲν γὰρ αὐτοῦ τούς τε ὄνους καὶ
τοὺς βοῦς ὑπὸ ληστῶν ἀπολέσθαι, εἶτα τὰ πρόβατα
ὑπὸ πυρὸς ἐκ τοῦ οὐρανοῦ πεσόντος κατακαῆναι σὺν
τοῖς ποιμέσι· μετ' οὐ πολὺ δὲ καὶ τὰς καμήλους
ὑπὸ ληστῶν ἀπελαθῆναι· εἶτα τὰ τέκνα αὐτοῦ
20 ἀποθανεῖν, πεσούσης τῆς οἰκίας· αὐθημερὸν δὲ

ΒΙΟΝ

1-2 οἷα -- ἱστορεῖ: καὶ τὰ περὶ Ἰὼβ μετὰ Ἰωσήφ Β |
3 ΑΡ. -- ΟΜ. Ι^mg ΟΝ: Ἀρισταίου -- Ομ. Β: Ἀρισταίου,
περὶ τοῦ Ἰὼβ ante 1-2 "Ακουε -- ἱστορεῖ transp. Vig. |
5 Ἡσαῦ Ι | Βασσάραν Β: Βασσάρας ΙΟΝ | 6 Ἰωβ ΒΟΝ:
υἱόν Ι (hic et post Βασσάρας) | 7 Ἰδουμαίας Ι:
Ἰουδαίας ΒΟΝ | 8 πολύκτημον Ο^ac Ν: πολύκτηνον ΒΙΟ^1? |
9 γὰρ: μὲν γὰρ Β | 10 δὲ om. Β | 13 Ἰωβὰβ ΒΟΝ:
Ἰωβὰμ Ι | 14 περιβ. αὐτ.: αὐτὸν περιβαλεῖν Β |
15 τε om. Β | 16 τούς: τάς ? Jac. | ἀπολέσθαι ΒΟΝ:
ἀπελαθῆναι Ι (cf. infra lin. 19) | 17 ὑπὸ -- πεσόντος:
ὑπουρανίου (!) πυρὸς Β | 19 sq. ὅτι τὸ σῶμα τοῦ
Ἰὼβ αὐθημερὸν οὗτος φησιν ἑλκῶσας τῆς γραφῆς τοῦτο μὴ
παρασημαινούσης Ι^mg |

FRAGMENT ONE[1]

Listen to what the same author[2] relates about
Job:

Aristeas' Remarks Concerning Job - Similarly:

(1)   (1) "Aristeas says in his book Concerning the
Jews[3] that after Esau took Bassara as his wife in
Edom, he fathered a son Job.[4] This Job dwelt in the
land of Ausitis[5] by the borders of Idumaea and
(2)   Arabia. (2) He was both righteous and rich in cattle,
for he owned 7,000 sheep, 3,000 camels, 500 yoke of
oxen, and 500 grazing she-asses. He also owned sub-
(3)   stantial farmland.[6] (3) This Job was formerly Jobab.[7]
As a way of testing his fidelity, God overwhelmed him
with great misfortunes.[8] First, his asses and cattle
were driven off by rustlers, then his sheep, along with
their shepherds, were consumed by a fire which fell
from heaven. Not long after this, his camels were also
stolen by rustlers. Then his children died when his
house collapsed. On the same day his body broke out

αὐτοῦ καὶ τὸ σῶμα ἑλκῶσαι.   (4) φαύλως δὲ αὐτοῦ   (4)
διακειμένου ἐλθεῖν εἰς ἐπίσκεψιν 'Ελίφαν τὸν   431b
Θαιμανιτῶν βασιλέα καὶ Βαλδὰδ τὸν Σαυχαίων
τύραννον καὶ Σωφὰρ τὸν Μινναίων βασιλέα, ἐλθεῖν
5   δὲ καὶ 'Ελιοῦν τὸν Βαραχιὴλ τὸν Ζωβίτην· παρα-
καλούμενον δὲ φάναι καὶ χωρὶς παρακλήσεως
ἐμμενεῖν αὐτὸν ἔν τε τῇ εὐσεβείᾳ καὶ τοῖς
δεινοῖς. τὸν δὲ θεὸν ἀγασθέντα τὴν εὐψυχίαν
αὐτοῦ τῆς τε νόσου αὐτὸν ἀπολῦσαι καὶ πολλῶν
10   κύριον ὑπάρξεων ποιῆσαι."

BION

1-5 φαύλως -- Ζωβίτην om. B | 3 Θεμανιτῶν ON |
Σαυχέων ON | 4 Σοφὰρ ON | 5 Ζωβίτην MSS:
Βωζίτην Freu. | 5-7 παρακαλούμ. -- ἐμμενεῖν: καὶ
ὑπὸ τῶν φίλων παρακαλούμενον ἐμμένειν B |
7 ἐμμένειν BON | αὐτὸν Steph.: αὐτὸν ION: om. B |

(4)   in sores.   (4)   While he was thus afflicted, Eliphaz,
      the king cf the Temanites, and Bildad, the ruler of
      the Shuhites, and Zophar, king of the Minnaites,
      visited him.[9]   Elihu, the son of Barachiel the Zobite,
      also came.[10]   Although he was exhorted by them, he
      said that even without their exhortation he himself
      would remain steadfast in his piety even with his
      affliction.[11]   In admiration of his fortitude God
      relieved him of his disease and made him master over
      many possessions." [12]

ANNOTATIONS

1. This fragment occurs in the section of P.E., Book 9,
where Eusebius adduces witnesses to early Jewish figures.
Having treated Abraham (16-20), Jacob (21-22), and Joseph
(23-24), Eusebius includes this fragment from Aristeas
as a witness to Job (25), after which he treats Moses
(26-29). It is quoted directly from Alexander Polyhistor.

2. I.e., Alexander Polyhistor.

3. Whether this is a title for the work in a technical
sense or a generic description of its contents cannot
be determined. Cf. Introduction.

4. Literally, the last phrase should be translated
"... Esau, having married Bassara, fathered a son in Edom
(named) Job." MS I omits υἱόν after Βασσάρας. In doing so,
MS I may be acknowledging the difficulty that the Bible
nowhere refers to Job as the son of Esau, but the substi-
tution of υἱόν for ᾿Ιώβ produces a senseless redundancy.
Hence, this reading is correctly rejected by Mras who
follows the majority reading of BON.
        Three features of Aristeas' statement are worth
noting: (1) that Job is said to be the son of Esau;
(2) the naming of Bassara as Esau's wife; and (3) Edom as
Job's birthplace. This doubtless represents an expansion
of Gen 36:33 (cf. 1 Chr 1:44). One of the kings mentioned
in the list of Edomite kings (Gen 36:31-39) is "Jobab
(יובב/Ιωβαβ) the son of Zera (זרח/Ζαρα) of Bozrah (מבצרה/
ἐκ Βοσορρας)." Aristeas identified Job with this Jobab,
and through a misreading or misunderstanding of the LXX,
took Bozrah as the name of his mother, thus understanding
ἐκ Βοσορρας not as a geographical location, but as his
genealogical descent. Or, through corruption בן זרח could
have become Βεν-σαρα → Βαρσαρα → Βασσαρα.
        A similar tradition occurs in the LXX addition to
Job (42:17b-e), which could easily serve as an explanation
of the more cryptic Aristeas statement, though the source-
critical relationship between the two remains unresolved
(See Introduction). There, we are told that "formerly his
(i.e. Job's) name was Jobab," that his father was Zerah
and his mother was Bozrah, and thus that he was a descendent of the children of Esau, fifth in descent from
Abraham. It is not at all unlikely that the tradition
preserved in Aristeas stemmed from the more elaborate
form which occurs in the epilogue to Job LXX, and that
the garbled form of the tradition is owing to Polyhistor's
carelessness. Cf. Walter, JS (3,2) 295, n. 1b.
        Given "the Edomite connections of the characters
and the setting of the story [of Job]" (IDB, 2.912), it
would have been natural to look for biblical links connect-
ing Job with Esau, even if it meant orthographical alteration.

4.   (cont.)
     Though remote, Gen 36:10 may also have influenced
this connection, with its mention of Eliphaz and Reuel
(elsewhere used as the name of Moses' father-in-law, also
called Hobab; cf. Num 11:29; Judg 4:11), the son of
Basemath (= Basarra ?).
     It would appear that Aristeas is working with a Greek
version of the Bible rather than with the MT. איוב is
not easily connected with יובב. Nor could מבצרה easily be
misconstrued as "from (his mother) Bozrah," as could
ἐκ Βοσορρας (e.g., by Polyhistor). Job is placed within
the patriarchal period in later Jewish traditions (e.g.,
Bib. Ant. 8.7; Targum of Job 2.9). On the identification
of Job with Jobab, cf. Testament of Job 1.2; 2.1-2; 3.1b,
and subscript. Also, cf. Fraikin, 3-4.

5.   The location of Job's homeland is unspecified in the
biblical book of Job.   There developed two traditions for
its location: the Hauran and Edom (Pope, Job, 3-5).   The
latter is reflected in the epilogue to Job (LXX 42:17b
ἐν μὲν γῇ κατοικῶν τῇ Αυσίτιδι ἐπὶ τοῖς ὁρίοις τῆς Ιδου-
μαίας καὶ ᾿Αραβίας), which Aristeas here doubtless
echoes.   The Hellenized form of Uz (i.e., the Hebrew form
עוץ transliterated Αυσ + adjectival ending -(ε)ῖτις; cf.
H. St. J. Thackeray, A Grammar of the Old Testament in
Greek (Cambridge: Cambridge University Press, 1909) 169-70.)
Aristeas could have easily derived from Job 1:1 LXX ἐν
χώρᾳ τῇ Αυσίτιδι, another indication of his dependence on
the LXX rather than the MT.   On Αυσιτις, cf. F. Delitzsch,
Job (Edinburgh: T. & T. Clark, 1881) 1.46; S. R. Driver &
G. B. Gray, Job (ICC; Edinburgh: T. & T. Clark, 1921)
xxviii.

6.   Cf. Job 1:3, although γεωργίας ἱκανάς   replaces
ὑπηρεσία πολλὴ σφόδρα.

7.   Cf. above, note 4.

8.   Cf. Job 1:13-2:10.

9.   On the three friends' status as kings, cf. Job 2:11
LXX, doubtless influenced by the description of Eliphaz
in Gen 36:10, 15, 31-43.   Similar dependence on the LXX
is seen in the description of Bildad as ὁ Μιναίων
(MT הנעמתי).

10.   Cf. Job 32:1-37:24, esp. 32:2, 6, where Elihu is
ὁ Βουζίτης. Freudenthal, 231, emends the text accordingly
(Βωζίτην), against the MS tradition. Cf. Giff. 4.311-12.

11.   Literally, "in his piety and afflictions." The original syntax must have intended an adversative sense, however
slight. So, Walter, JS (3,2) 296, n. 4f. Also, cf. Smyth,
Greek Grammar, par. 2974.

12.   Cf. Job 42. On εὐψυχία, cf. 4 Macc 6:11; 9:23.

Epilogue to Job 42:17b-e (LXX - Rahlfs)

17b Οὗτος ἑρμηνεύεται ἐκ τῆς Συριακῆς Βίβλου
     ἐν μὲν γῇ κατοικῶν τῇ Αὐσίτιδι ἐπὶ τοῖς ὁρίοις τῆς
        Ιδουμαίας καὶ ᾿Αραβίας,
     προϋπῆρχεν δὲ αὐτῷ ὄνομα Ιωβαβ·

17c λαβὼν δὲ γυναῖκα ᾿Αράβισσαν γεννᾷ υἱόν, ᾧ ὄνομα Εννων,
     ἦν δὲ αὐτὸς πατρὸς μὲν Ζαρε[θ], τῶν Ησαυ υἱῶν υἱός,
        μητρὸς δὲ Βοσορρας,
     ὥστε εἶναι αὐτὸν πέμπτον ἀπὸ Αβρααμ.

17d καὶ οὗτοι οἱ βασιλεῖς οἱ βασιλεύσαντες ἐν Εδωμ,
        ἧς καὶ αὐτὸς ἧρξεν χώρας·
     πρῶτος Βαλακ ὁ τοῦ Βεωρ, καὶ ὄνομα τῇ πόλει αὐτοῦ
        Δενναβα·
     μετὰ δὲ Βαλακ Ιωβαβ ὁ καλούμενος Ιωβ·
     μετὰ δὲ τοῦτον Ασομ ὁ ὑπάρχων ἡγεμὼν ἐκ τῆς Θαιμανίτι-
        δος χώρας·
     μετὰ δὲ τοῦτον Αδαδ υἱὸς Βαραδ ὁ ἐκκόψας Μαδιαμ ἐν τῷ
        πεδίῳ Μωαβ, καὶ ὄνομα τῇ πόλει αὐτοῦ Γεθθαιμ.

17e οἱ δὲ ἐλθόντες πρὸς αὐτὸν φίλοι·
     Ελιφας [υιος σωφαν/ρ] τῶν Ησαυ υἱῶν Θαιμανων
        βασιλεύς,
     Βαλδαδ [υιος αμ(μ)νων του χοβαρ] ὁ Σαυχαιων τύρρανος,
     Σωφαρ ὁ Μιναίων βασιλεύς.
     [θαιμαν υιος ελιφαζ εγεμων της ιδουμαιας·
     ουτος ερμηνευεται εκ της συριακης βιβλου εν μεν γη
        κατοικων τη αυσιτιδι επι των οριων του ευφρατου·
     προυπηρχεν δε το ονομα αυτου ιωβαβ, ην δε ο πατηρ
        αυτου ζαρεθ εξ ανατολων ηλιου]

Epilogue to Job 42:17b-e

17b This [man] is explained from the Syriac Book
     as living in the land of Ausis, on the borders of
        Edom and Arabia;
     formerly his name was Jobab.
17c He took an Arabian wife and sired a son whose name
        was Ennon.
     But he himself was the son of his father Zare[th],
        one of the sons of Esau, and of his mother Bosorra,
     so that he was the fifth from Abraham.
17d Now these were the kings that reigned in Edom, over
        which land he also ruled:
     first Balak, the son of Beor, and the name of his
        city was Dennaba;
     and after Balak, Jobab who is called Job;
     and after him, Asom, the governor from the country
        of Teman;
     and after him Adad, the son of Barad, who destroyed
        Midian in the plain of Moab, and the name of his
        city was Gethaim.
17e And the friends who came to him were
     Eliphaz, [a son of Sophan/r] of the sons of Esau,
        king of the Temanites;
     Bildad, son of Am(m)non [the son of Chobar], ruler
        of the Sauchaeans;
     Sophar, king of the Minaeans.
     [Teman, son of Eliphaz, ruler of Edom.
     This one is described in the Syriac Book as living
        in the land of Ausis, on the borders of the
        Euphrates;
     formerly his name was Jobab, but his father was
        Zareth from the rising of the sun.]

   (Translation from M. Pope, Job (AB, 15; Garden City,
   New York: Doubleday, 1965) 293.

PSEUDO-HECATAEUS

To Hecataeus of Abdera (or Teos) the Hellenistic ethnographer, philosopher, critic and grammarian[1] who flourished ca. 300 B.C.E., are attributed several fragments treating the Jews.[2] A former pupil of the Sceptic Pyrrhon of Elis,[3] he wrote a treatise on the poetry of Homer and Hesiod, a work about the Hyperboreans, and a more widely known work On The Egyptians based on his own travels in Egypt.[4] Only a few fragments from the works On the Hyperboreans and On the Egyptians are extant.[5] This last work, in keeping with the encomiastic tendency of Hellenistic ethnography, portrays Egypt as the source of civilization and stresses the antiquity, and therefore superiority, of Egyptian culture over Greek culture. It exercised influence on later authors who wrote about Egypt, including Manetho and Diodorus Siculus; in fact, major portions appear to be incorporated in Book I of Diodorus' History.[6]

In the course of his treatment of Egyptian history, Hecataeus (apud Diodorus Siculus 1.28.2) refers to the Jews, noting that they were emigrants from Egypt. He also gives a more detailed account of the Jews (apud Diodorus Siculus 40.3.1-8;[7] also cf. 40.2) which is remarkably informed and sympathetic in its treatment. These two passages, which qualify him as one of the earliest Greek authors to exhibit more than a superficial knowledge of the Jews,[8] are widely regarded as genuine and their authenticity is not disputed.[9]

Also attributed to this same Hecataeus, however, are several other passages whose genuineness is seriously contested and which are thought by many scholars to derive from Jewish pseudepigraphs. For this reason, they are treated here under "Pseudo-Hecataeus."[9a]

Besides the question of their authenticity, there is
considerable disagreement concerning the number of the
Pseudo-Hecataeus fragments, the extent of each fragment,
the nature and title of the work (or works) from which
they derive, their authorship (whether reflecting the work
of one or several authors, and the identity of such authors), and their historical setting. They have been
classified in various ways, depending on the interpretation
and use made of the testimonia that mention Hecataeus,
the fragments attributed to him, and other related evidence.[10]

The earliest testimony to a work of Hecataeus of
Abdera treating the Jews occurs in Ep. Arist. 31, where
Hecataeus is said to have reported that the Jews' concep-
tion of life is "so sacred and religious" that they were
ignored "by literary men and poets and the mass of historical writers."[11] The same statement, with slight modification, occurs in Josephus, Ant. 12.38, and later in
Eusebius, P.E. 8.3.3. The difficulty here is that none
of these versions of the statement mentions the name of
the work from which they are derived. It is conceivable
that Ep. Arist. 31 was prompted by Hecataeus' remarks about
the Jews in On the Egyptians, given the nature, content,
and tone of the extant fragments from this work preserved
by Diodorus Siculus.[12] On the other hand, this precise
form of argument, viz., that the Jews were ignored by
pagan writers because of the sacredness of their way of
life (cf. Ep. Arist. 313-36; also Josephus, Ag.Ap. 1.60-
68), is not explicitly articulated in the genuine Hecataeus
fragments. Thus, it is just as conceivable that Pseudo-
Hecataeus, i.e. a separate work treating the Jews and
attributed to Hecataeus of Abdera, is the source of this
argument and lies behind Ep. Arist. 31.[13]

Passages from a later period, beginning with Josephus,
do mention two specific works attributed to Hecataeus of
Abdera: On Abraham and On the Jews.

On Abraham. The earliest reference to a work with
this title is Josephus, Ant. 1.159: "Hecataeus (in contrast
to Berossus) has done more than mention him (Abraham); he
has left us a book which he composed about him" (= Eusebius,
P.E. 9.16.3).[14] A later reference to this work, apparently
independent of Josephus, occurs in Clement of Alexandria,
Strom. 5.14.113.1 (= Eusebius, P.E. 13.13.40), although
with an expanded title. Clement mentions the pagan author
Hecataeus and identifies him as the one who composed the
"histories ... the work about Abraham and the Egyptians."[15]
Because Clement names Hecataeus as the source of nine
lines of poetry attributed to Sophocles,[16] it appears that
the work On Abraham (and the Egyptians) contained quotations
from Greek authors, especially poets, perhaps those which
follow in Strom. 5.14.114.1-4 from Euripides and Aeschylus,
among others.[17] This work On Abraham, with its monotheistic
claims attributed to Sophocles, is widely regarded as a
forgery written by a Jewish apologist, and there is some
doubt whether the work even existed, especially as a
separate work.[18]

On the Jews. The earliest reference to this work is
Josephus, Ag.Ap. 1.183: "(Hecataeus of Abdera) ... makes
no mere passing allusion to us, but wrote a book entirely
about the Jews."[19] From this work Josephus quotes several
excerpts in Ag.Ap. 1.184-204. These excerpts mention the
emigration of the Jews to Egypt after the battle of Gaza
(312 B.C.E.), and single out one of the Jewish emigrants,
Ezekias, a high priest who heralded the benefits of emigration. They also mention the tenacious loyalty of the
Jews to their laws and ancestral faith, and include a
description of the Palestinian countryside, Jerusalem
itself, and especially the temple. A final incident,
involving a Jewish soldier Mosollamus who bests a pagan
seer, is reported as another triumph of Jewish faith and
wisdom over pagan superstition. An abbreviated version of
this section from Josephus is also quoted by Eusebius
(P.E. 9.4.1 = Ag.Ap. 1.183; P.E. 9.4.2-9 = Ag.Ap. 1.197-204)

who mentions Hecataeus' "special book on the history of
the Jews."[20] The existence of such a work is apparently
later attested by Origen, C. Cel. 1.15, who states that
"a book about the Jews is attributed to Hecataeus the
historian," but also mentions that Herennius Philo (2nd
cent. C.E.) had doubts about its authenticity.[21]

As to the content and scope of this work, Josephus'
remarks imply that On the Jews was a comprehensive treatment of Jewish history and customs,[22] presumably of the
same scope and genre as Hecataeus' On the Egyptians. If
so, it would have followed the traditional outline used
by ethnographers to treat (1) native cosmogony and theology;
(2) geography; (3) native rulers; and (4) customs.[23]

In addition to this fairly long fragment, or series
of excerpts, from Book I of Ag.Ap., another passage from
Book II (Ag.Ap. 2.42-43) is generally assigned to On the
Jews,[24] even though Josephus attributes the statement to
Hecataeus without naming the work from which it is taken.
In this brief fragment (which is sometimes extended to
include par. 47),[25] it is stated that the Jews were award-
ed Samaria by Alexander the Great because of "the consideration and loyalty shown to him by the Jews."

That there existed a work entitled On the Jews which
was attributed to Hecataeus of Abdera is not doubted. Yet,
concerning its authenticity there still exists no real,
nor even emerging, scholarly consensus.[26] Scholarly
opinion remains divided between those who regard the two
fragments from Josephus, Ag.Ap., Books I and II, as
deriving from an authentic work On the Jews written by
the pagan author Hecataeus of Abdera,[27] and those who
contest their genuineness and attribute them instead to a
Jewish apologist writing under the pseudonym of Hecataeus.[28]
Still others suspend judgment.[29]

Assigning these two fragments from Ag.Ap. to Hecataeus
of Abdera has been questioned for the following reasons:[30]
(1) Acknowledged precedent of attributing pseudonymous
works to Hecataeus. As noted earlier, the work On Abraham,

which Clement attributes to Hecataeus, is now regarded
with certainty as a forgery.[31] Since this work is admittedly
pseudonymous, it is equally likely that On the Jews was
pseudonymous as well. (2) Presence of anachronisms within
the work. The passages attributed to Hecataeus by Josephus
are thought by some scholars to reflect a later historical
setting. In particular, the understanding of the practice
of tithing (Frg. 1, par. 187) and the commendation of the
Jewish spirit of martyrdom (Frg. 1, par. 190-91) have been
taken to reflect a Maccabean, or post-Maccabean setting.
Also, the reference to Alexander's granting the Jews the
region of Samaria as a reward for their loyalty to him
(Frg. 2) is seen to reflect a much later period. (3) Explicit pro-Jewish tendency. The genuine Hecataeus fragments
preserved in Diodorus are more sober and objective in
their treatment of the Jews while those statements attributed to him by Josephus are more explicitly panegyrical.
Coupled with this is the anti-pagan tone of the remarks
in Frg. 1, par. 193, where Hecataeus reports approvingly
that the Jews destroyed pagan temples and altars that
were erected in Babylon; indeed, Hecataeus reportedly said
that they deserved admiration for this. (4) Ancient
doubts about their authenticity. As early as the second
century C.E., the authenticity of the work On the Jews
was questioned by Herennius Philo of Byblos (apud Origen,
C. Cel. 1.15).[32]

In response, those who favor the authenticity of the
fragments and attribute them to the pagan Hecataeus have
argued as follows: (1) The two works On Abraham and
On the Jews need not stand or fall together; the accepted
pseudonymity of the one does not necessarily prove the
pseudonymity of the other. (2) The anachronisms are by
no means unambiguous. These statements arguably reflect
the level of misunderstanding and confusion one might
expect from an intelligent and reasonably well-informed
pagan writing in the early Hellenistic period. (3) To be
sure, the tone of the remarks about the Jews in the

genuine fragments preserved by Diodorus is different from
that of the fragments preserved by Josephus. But given
the generally favorable tone of the former, the even more
positive portrait in the latter is not an unnatural extension.[33] Moreover, the literary context of the two sets
of fragments is different, the one having been taken from
a work On the Egyptians where one might expect a more
"objective" description of the Jews since they are treated
secondarily in the course of Hecataeus' description of
Egypt, the latter having been taken from a work On the Jews,
where one would expect explicit encomium, even as one
finds encomiastic description of Egypt in Hecataeus'
genuine work On the Egyptians. The statement that the
Jews destroyed pagan temples is indeed difficult to ascribe
to the pagan Hecataeus, and consequently has been taken
by some scholars as an editorial addition later made to
the version of Hecataeus used by Josephus. But, given the
sceptical outlook of Hecataeus, even this explanation may
not be required. The critique of popular worship by pagan
authors was well established by the time of Hecataeus,
and it is not inconceivable that an enlightened pagan would
have reported the destruction of Babylonian temples and
altars as an admirable act. (4) The testimony of Herennius
Philo should not be given too much weight; after all, the
statement only raises questions about the authenticity of
the work, it is not an outright denial. It actually concedes
the possibility of authenticity. Also, because Herennius
Philo flourished in the time of Hadrian, when the memory
of Jewish history for the past half-century was fresh, and
not altogether pleasant, it is easy to see why one would
have questioned the authenticity of a statement by a well-
known pagan author who spoke favorably of the Jews.

       To be sure, it is no longer possible, as it was in
an earlier period of scholarship, to deny a priori that an
educated Hellenistic author, such as Hecataeus of Abdera,
should exhibit this level of knowledge and sympathy with
things Jewish. The question of the authenticity of these

fragments remains open and awaits further investigation.
Even if they are inauthentic, it is probable that they
preserve some authentic portions of Hecataeus.[34] In any
case, the pseudonymity of the three fragments included
here under Pseudo-Hecataeus appears likely.

Nevertheless, assuming that the fragments from both
works are pseudonymous, other questions still persist.
Do they stem from the same work which has been assigned
different titles within the Hecataeus tradition? Or, do
they stem from two separate works? If separate works, are
they by the same author, or by different authors? If
different authors, are they from the same period and
provenance, or from different periods and provenances?

Author, Date, and Provenance. Because the various bits
of evidence pertaining to Pseudo-Hecataeus are complex
and interrelated, several proposals have been offered concerning authorship, date, and provenance. It will be
best to elaborate the various positions scholars have
taken in the history of scholarship on Pseudo-Hecataeus.

(a) Single work by a single author. The simplest
solution, offered by Schürer,[35] is to regard On Abraham
and On the Jews as variant titles of the same work:
"the work was indeed entitled περὶ Ἀβράμου, but dealt
in fact περὶ Ἰουδαίων."[36] Although the work is spurious
and is thus classified as "Jewish propaganda under a
heathen mask," it was probably based on genuine portions
of Hecataeus' work On the Egyptians. It was this pseudonymous work that was cited in Ep. Arist. 31 and consequently
is dated by Schürer prior to Ep. Arist. (200 B.C.E.)
in the third century B.C.E.

(b) Two works by the same author. Schaller,[37] while
allowing that the two works might have been composed by
two different authors, concludes that they were written
by the same author who, after having composed On the Jews,
then composed On Abraham. In this latter work, he
collected various (spurious) quotations from Greek poets
to demonstrate the antiquity and superiority of the Jewish

faith, the major theme of the first work.[38]   Schaller,
too, dates the two works prior to Ep. Arist., placing them
between 165 (145) and 100 B.C.E.[39]

   (c) Separate works by different authors.[40]

   (i) Jacoby. The four Pseudo-Hecataeus fragments
are treated by Jacoby, FGrH, No. 264, Frgs. 21-24, under
the two separate titles On the Jews (Frgs. 21-23) and
On Abraham (Frg. 24). In his Kommentar on the fragments
in FGrH 3a.61-75, this distinction is retained and elaborated. They are to be regarded as two separate works
primarily because Josephus, who mentions both titles
(Ag.Ap. 1.183, 214; Ant. 1.159) treats them as such. Their
content is also different. On the Jews, with its interest
in the Jewish people, their history, land, city and
temple, and its encomiastic tone, was clearly an ethnographical work, free of the clumsily composed forgeries,
such as the verses attributed to Sophocles, found in On
Abraham. As to the date and provenance, Jacoby thinks
On the Jews influenced, and thus antedated Ep. Arist.,
which Bickerman reliably dated ca. 145-127 B.C.E.[41]
Following Willrich, Juden und Griechen, 32, Jacoby sees
in the high priest Ezekias (Frg. 1, par. 187-88), a
veiled reference to Onias IV, the son of Simon the Just,
who fled to Egypt in the period immediately preceding
Antiochus IV Epiphanes' arrival in Palestine, thus
establishing a terminus post quem ca. 170-168 B.C.E.
Accordingly, he dates the work ca. 170 B.C.E., and further
suggests that the author, who was associated with Onias,
was a Palestinian Jewish priest who emigrated to Egypt
as a result of the turbulent events in Jerusalem ca.
170-168 B.C.E. On Abraham, by contrast, is to be regarded
as a separate work. Although Josephus mentions this work
only once (Ant. 1.159), he appears to have drawn extensively from it.[42] According to Jacoby, it was written by
a different Jewish author at a later period, though how
much later cannot be ascertained.[43]

(ii) _Walter_. Jacoby's position is made more explicit,
but modified somewhat by Walter,[44] who distinguishes between the two authors Pseudo-Hecataeus I, who wrote On the
Jews, and Pseudo-Hecataeus II, who wrote On Abraham.[45]
Unlike Jacoby, however, Walter sees no connection between
the reference to Hecataeus in Ep. Arist. 31 and these two
Jewish pseudepigraphs.[46] Rather, the most that can be
said is that Ep. Arist. reflects knowledge of Hecataeus'
treatment of the Jews in his work On the Egyptians. If
this is not the case, there is an outside chance that
Ep. Arist. 31 points to the existence of yet another
Jewish pseudonymous work attributed to Hecataeus, but
otherwise unattested. Consequently, Ep. Arist. 31 can
have no bearing whatever on the dating of Pseudo-Hecataeus
I and II.

As to date and provenance, Walter proposes that
Pseudo-Hecataeus I was an author of the Jewish Diaspora
who composed the work On the Jews sometime following the
Maccabean uprising. More specifically, because of its
reference to tithing, and the similarity of the arrange-
ments presupposed there with conditions obtaining during
the reign of John Hyrcanus (134-104 B.C.E.), he dates
the work in the last quarter of the second century B.C.E.,
probably ca. 100 B.C.E.[47] He proposes an Alexandrian
setting because of the attention given to the Ptolemies
in the fragment.

As to the date and provenance of On Abraham, because
of its heavy emphasis on Egypt in the fragments believed
to be derived from this work,[48] Walter attributes this
work to a Jewish Hellenist Pseudo-Hecataeus II who wrote
in Alexandria. As to its date, nothing certain can be
claimed except that it must have preceded Josephus.
Accordingly, its time of composition could have been any
time between the first century B.C.E. and the mid-first
century C.E.

(iii) <u>Wacholder</u>. This multiple work/multiple author
position is refined even further by Wacholder. In his
1971 article on Hecataeus of Abdera in <u>Encyclopaedia
Judaica</u>, he essentially reproduces Walter's proposal of
two works by the two authors Pseudo-Hecataeus I and II.
This position is expanded, however, in his 1974 book
<u>Eupolemus</u>.[49]

To begin with, he extends the number of pertinent
Pseudo-Hecataeus passages to seven, and treats together
both the testimonia and fragments attributed to Hecataeus.
Working with Walter's proposal of Pseudo-Hecataeus I and II,
Wacholder offers the novel suggestion that the two sets
of passages mentioned by Josephus in Books I and II of
<u>Ag.Ap.</u> do not stem from the same work, and should not be
treated together. The grounds for this separation are
that the two sets of passages reflect different authorial
perspectives, thematic interests, and attitudes towards
the Ptolemies. Accordingly, the excerpts in Book I of
<u>Ag.Ap.</u> are seen to have derived from a work composed in the
time of Ptolemy I Soter, perhaps as early as the last
decades of the fourth century B.C.E. The passage in
Book II of <u>Ag.Ap.</u>, by contrast, comes from a later period,
"during the second half of the second century B.C.E.,"
sometime after the composition of <u>Ep</u>. <u>Arist</u>.[50] This
reflects his conviction that the former work exercised
influence on <u>Ep</u>. <u>Arist</u>., and thus preceded it, while the
latter bears no demonstrable relationship with <u>Ep</u>. <u>Arist</u>.
Consequently, Wacholder proposes three separate authors
from three different periods: Pseudo-Hecataeus I (ca. 300
B.C.E.), Pseudo-Hecataeus II (after <u>Ep</u>. <u>Arist</u>. and before
Josephus), and Pseudo-Hecataeus III (before Aristobulus,
who incorporates excerpts of the Greek poets).[51]

Wacholder gives the most attention to the fragments
from the work of Pseudo-Hecataeus I which, on this showing,
are "the oldest remnants of a Greek treatise written by a
Jew."[52] The frequency of the first person in the fragments
suggests that they were written by an eyewitness who was

"expert in priestly law and well informed as to the conditions of the country during the Persian occupation,"[53]thus
a Palestinian author. The early date is defended on
archaeological grounds. Scholars at one time dated them
later in the second century because of such references
as those to Ezekias the high priest whose name does
not appear in the known lists of high priests and who
was thus thought to be unhistorical. However, the recent
discovery of a coin in the late Persian period bearing
the name of a high priest Hezekiah makes this early dating
much more probable. [54]

Thus, according to Wacholder, this work On the Jews
was written by a Jewish priest of Jerusalem, identifiable
only as Pseudo-Hecataeus I, in the last decades of the
fourth century B.C.E. Possibly writing ca. 312 B.C.E.,
shortly after the battle of Gaza, the author, "elated
by the prospects of the Macedonian occupation,"[55] wrote in
order to insure Ptolemy's kind treatment of the Jews,
and this accounts for the flattering remarks about Ptolemaic policies of open immigration. It accounts, as well,
for the panegyrical treatment of the Jews, since it represents an attempt to correct those few negative features
of Hecataeus' account of the Jews in his On the Egyptians.
The fact that it nowhere shows dependence on the Greek
Bible is explained because it was written much earlier.
Thus, the author of On the Jews actually knew the high
priest Ezekias, and wrote an eyewitness account of events
of this period. In fact, he "abandoned his priestly
garments to serve together with another Judaean named
Mosollamus (Meshulam) in a Jewish contingent of Alexander's
army marching towards the Red Sea."[56] In conclusion,
Wacholder states that "Pseudo-Hecataeus I may then be
regarded as the first Graeco-Palestinian writer, an
analogue of the Babylonian Berossus and the Egyptian
Manetho."[57]

Summary and Conclusions. As is clear from this review
of the various postions concerning the Pseudo-Hecataeus
fragments, the number of works attributed to Hecataeus of
Abdera, and the number of Jewish authors responsible for
writing them, tend to increase as the number of passages
attributed to or related to Pseudo-Hecataeus is expanded.
For the purpose of this collection of the Pseudo-Hecataeus
fragments, however, a minimalist position is adopted,
primarily on the grounds that the distinction between
testimonia and fragments should be adhered to more strictly.
This edition includes only those fragments explicitly
attributed to Hecataeus and does so under the titles
which occur in the sources themselves.

As indicated earlier, the fragments are here regarded
as pseudonymous. Moreover, the position that the fragments
stem from two separate works written by the same author
poses the fewest problems, and is thus adopted as the
organizing principle for arranging the fragments that
follow. They are most likely the work of a single Jewish
author writing with an apologetic purpose. Quite understandably, he writes under the pseudonym of Hecataeus of
Abdera who had previously written favorably of the Jews.[58]

Consequently, On the Jews is treated first, and
both passages from both books of Ag.Ap. (1.183-204 and
2.42-43) that are ordinarily regarded as excerpts from
this work are included. On Abraham is listed as a second
separate work because of the difference in title, and
because Josephus so regarded it. Although it is first
mentioned by Josephus in Ant. 1.159, this is, strictly
speaking, only a testimonium. Clement of Alexandria,
Strom. 5.14.113.1-2, by contrast, both mentions the title
and quotes the passage from Sophocles attributed to this
work. Because Clement only explicitly attributes the
Sophocles passage, and none of the others that follow,
to Hecataeus, this fragment (listed as Frg. 3) is
demarcated at that point. To enable the critical assessment of these fragments, however, the most relevant

passages have also been quoted after Frg. 3.

As to the date and provenance of the author, obviously,
the only certainty is that the terminus ante quem for On
the Jews is provided by Josephus.[59] Since the work is
cited neither by Alexander Polyhistor nor Philo Judaeus,
some scholars have understandably preferred to date the
work in the mid- to late first century C.E., immediately
prior to Josephus.[60] But, it is more likely that the
work existed as early as the mid-second century B.C.E.,
primarily because Ep. Arist. 31 appears to be dependent
on Pseudo-Hecataeus.[61] To be sure, this reference may
have been prompted by the authentic Hecataeus fragments
as preserved in Diodorus Siculus 40.3, but the tone of
the reference more nearly echoes that of the disputed
fragments in Ag.Ap. In addition, the dependence of Ep.
Arist. on Pseudo-Hecataeus at other points should be taken
more seriously than it usually is. Since Ep. Arist. has
been reliably dated in the first half of the second century
B.C.E., Pseudo-Hecataeus may be reliably placed as early
as the first quarter of the second century B.C.E., perhaps
during the reign of Philometor (ca. 180-164 B.C.E.).[62]
It is impossible to determine which of the two works was
composed first, but both On the Jews and On Abraham can be
confidently placed in the first half of the second century
B.C.E.

As to the provenance of the author, either a Palestinian or Egyptian setting is conceivable. Certainly,
nothing excludes a Palestinian setting, and the suggestion
that the author was a Palestinian who migrated to Egypt
has merit.[63] However, the favorable portrait of the
Ptolemies and the emphasis on the advisability of emigrat-
ing from Palestine to Egypt, combined with the less than
accurate description of Jerusalem and the location of the
temple, point to a setting outside Palestine.[64] An
Egyptian setting is also favored if Ep. Arist. is a
reference to Pseudo-Hecataeus, since Ep. Arist. is
generally given an Egyptian setting. Little else can

be affirmed about the author's identity or outlook.

Importance. If Pseudo-Hecataeus is dated as early
as the first quarter of the second century B.C.E., he
becomes an early witness to the Jewish apologetic tradition, especially of certain motifs which later became
standard apologetic features, such as the surpassing
wisdom of the Jews, their great numbers, their fidelity
to the law and readiness to suffer persecution, their
ridicule of pagan superstition, their political loyalty
to the ruling powers. If Pseudo-Hecataeus is written
in response to the genuine Hecataeus, and indeed preserves
portions of his work, it illustrates a Jewish author's
use and interpretation of a pagan's treatment of the Jews.
Because of the stylistic clues embedded within Josephus'
text, it may be possible to reconstruct to a considerable
degree the outline of the work; if so, it presents the
skeletal form of an early Jewish apologetic work. Pseudo-
Hecataeus is also very useful in further critical assess-
ments of Ep. Arist., since he may have been a major source
for this work. Although the work belongs to the genre of
ethnography, its value for historical reconstruction of
Jewish history in the early Hellenistic period is greater
than once believed. Further discussions of the Jews'
status under Alexander the Great, and certainly under
his successors, the tangled question of their Alexandrian
citizenship, the relationship between Jews and Samaritans
during the early Hellenistic period, the historicity of
the high priest Ezekias, the priesthood and the practice
of tithing during this period will inevitably take account
of Pseudo-Hecataeus' testimony. In tracing further the
history and development of Jewish apologetic in its
earliest stages, Pseudo-Hecataeus still remains valuable
testimony to the articulation of radical monotheism, and
the Jewish response to paganism during the Maccabean period.
The anecdote concerning Mosollamus also deserves further
attention as an example of the Jewish-pagan encounter in
the popular tradition, and the Jewish debt to the pagan
critique.

NOTES

1. The standard treatment of Hecataeus of Abdera, who is to be distinguished from Hecataeus of Miletus, the 6th century Ionian logographer, is F. Jacoby, "Hekataios (4)," PW 7 (1912) cols. 2750-69; also E. Schwartz, "Hekataeos von Teos," Rheinisches Museum 40 (1885) 223-62; also "Diodoros (38)," PW 5 (1905) col. 663-704, esp. 669-72; Susemihl, Geschichte, 1.310-14. More recently, Fraser, Ptolemaic Alexandria, 1.496-505; 2.718-27, notes 5-92; Gager, Moses, 26-37; Murray, "Hecataeus," 142-44; Stern, GLAJJ, 20-44, Nos. 11-13, and extensive bibliography, p. 25; also F. H. Diamond, Hecataeus of Abdera. A New Historical Approach. Ph.D. dissertation, University of California Los Angeles, 1974 (Summary in Dissertation Abstracts, 35 (1975) 5271A).

2. All the fragments from antiquity attributed to Hecataeus of Abdera are collected by Jacoby in FGrH 3A. 12-64 = No. 264, Frg. 1-25, with commentary in FGrH 3a. 29-87.

3. Cf. Diogenes Laertius 9.69.

4. Cf. Diodorus Siculus 1.46.8.

5. For references to this latter work, cf. Diodorus Siculus 1.46.8; Plutarch, De Is. et Osir. 354 C-D; also cf. Diogenes Laertius 1.9.

6. Cf. Murray, "Hecataeus," 144-45; cf., however, A. Burton, Diodorus Siculus. Book I. A Commentary (Leiden: Brill, 1972) 1-34, esp. 2-10.

7. This section is also preserved in Photius (9th cent.), Bibliotheca = Photii Bibliotheca 244, ed. I. Bekker (1824), col. 380 A (= PG [103] 1392-93). Photius attributes the passage to Hecataeus of Miletus (fl. ca. 500 B.C.E.), but this is widely regarded as incorrect, though an understandable identification. Cf. Aelian, NA 11.1. The mistake most likely entered the textual tradition of Diodorus Siculus 40.3.8 through Photius and not through Diodorus himself (cf. Diodorus Siculus 40 [LCL, 287, n. 1). Cf. Jacoby, Kommentar in FGrH 3a.46-7; however, cf. Dornseiff, Echtheitsfragen, 52-57, apud Walter, JS (1,2) 145, n. 9, who defends the attribution to Hecataeus of Miletus.

8. He is, in fact, the first pagan author known to refer to Moses. Cf. Gager, Moses, 26. Whether his is the "oldest account of Jewish origins in Greek literature" (so Stern, GLAJJ, 20), is disputed. Cf. Stern and Murray, "Hecataeus of Abdera." Also, cf. Jaeger, Diokles, 136-37.

9. For a fuller treatment of these authentic fragments, cf. Jacoby, Kommentar, FGrH 3a.29-87, esp. 46-52; Gager, Moses, 26-37; Stern, GLAJJ, 26-35.

9a. Testimonia: Ep. Arist. 31; Josephus, Ant. 1.159; 12.38; Ag.Ap. 1.183, 205, 213-14; 2.43; Clement of Alexandria, Strom. 5.14.113.1; Origen, C. Cel. 1.15; Eusebius, P.E. 8.3.3; 9.4.1,9; 13.13.40.

10. Reinach (1895), Textes, 227-36, includes five fragments under "Pseudo-Hecataeus":

    Frg. A   Josephus, Ag.Ap. 1.22, par. 183-205
    Frg. B   Josephus, Ag.Ap. 2.4, par. 42-43.
    Frg. C   Ep. Arist. 31 (= Josephus, Ant. 12.2.3 (?), par. 38)
    Frg. D   Josephus, Ant. 1.7.2, par. 159
    Frg. E   Clement of Alexandria, Strom. 5.14.113.1

Jacoby (1940), FGrH, No. 264, attributes to Pseudo-Hecataeus the following fragments:

From Περὶ 'Ιουδαίων:

    Frg. 21 Josephus, Ag.Ap. 1.186-205 (= Eusebius, P.E. 9.4.1-9)
    Frg. *22 Josephus, Ag.Ap. 2.42-47
    Frg. 23 Ep. Arist. 31 (= Josephus, Ant. 12.38; Eusebius, P.E. 8.3.3.)

From Κατ' "Αβραμον καὶ τοὺς Αἰγυπτίους:

    Frg. 24 Clement of Alexandria, Strom. 5.14.113.1
                (= Eusebius, P.E. 13.13.40)

Denis (1970), Fragmenta, 199-202, under the general rubric of Jewish historiographers, includes only two fragments under "Hecataeus Abderita":

    Frg. 1   Josephus, Ag.Ap. 1.22, par. 184-204
    Frg. 2   Josephus, Ag.Ap. 2.4, par. 42-43

In a footnote, Denis quotes these additional passages:

                Josephus, Ag.Ap. 1.23, par. 213-14
                Josephus, Ant. 1.7.2, par. 159
                Origen, C. Cel. 1.15

Walter (1976), JS (1,2), 144-60, assigns four fragments to "Pseudo-Hecataeus," but distinguishes between two separate authors:

Pseudo-Hecataeus I:

    Frg. 1   Josephus, Ag.Ap. 1.183b-205a, 213b-214a
    Frg. 2   Josephus, Ag.Ap. 2.43

Pseudo-Hecataeus II:
    Frg. 1   Josephus, Ant. 1.154-68
    Frg. 2   Clement of Alexandria, Strom. 5.14.113.1-2

10. (cont.) Wacholder (1974), Eupolemus, 262-73, further
refines Walter and distinguishes between three separate
authors from different periods:

Pseudo-Hecataeus I (ca. 300 B.C.E.):

    Frg. 1   Josephus, Ag.Ap. 1.183-205
    Frg. la   Ep. Arist. 83-120
    Frg. 2   Josephus, Ag.Ap. 1.213-14

Pseudo-Hecataeus II (after Ep. Arist. and before Josephus):

    Frg. 3   Josephus, Ag.Ap. 2.43-47
    Frg. 3a   Josephus, Ant. 12.3-8
    Frg. 3b   Ep. Arist. 12-27
    Frg. 4   Ep. Arist. 31

Pseudo-Hecataeus III (before Aristobulus):

    Frg. 5   Josephus, Ant. 1.159
    Frg. 6   Clement of Alexandria, Strom. 5.14.113.1-2
    Frg. 7   Herennius Philo in Origen, C. Cel. 1.15b

11. For the Greek text of Ep. Arist. 31, cf. Testimonia,
p. 320.

12. Cf. Spoerri, KP 2 (1967) 981; Hadas, Aristeas, 111.

13. How this question is resolved significantly affects
the dating of the Pseudo-Hecataeus fragments. It is widely
held that Pseudo-Hecataeus has influenced, and therefore,
antedates Ep.Arist. 31. So, Schürer, 3.604; Literature,
302-306; Jacoby, Kommentar in FGrH 3a.62, 65-6; Stein,
Eos, 474-75; Schaller, 30; Murray, "Aristeas," 342-43;
Fraser, Ptolemaic Alexandria, 2.968, n. 115. The problem
is especially illustrated by Jacoby who, in PW 7 (1912)
2767, denied that Ep. Arist. knew or used Pseudo-Hecataeus,
and consequently dated the latter immediately prior to
Josephus in the mid- to late first century C.E. Later,
in his commentary on the Hecataeus fragments in FGrH 3a
(1943) 62, he reversed himself, arguing that Ep. Arist.
had indeed used Pseudo-Hecataeus. Following Bickerman,
who dated Ep. Arist. ca. 145-127 B.C.E., Jacoby dated
Pseudo-Hecataeus ca. 170-168 B.C.E. Walter, JS (1,2) 146,
by contrast, denies any direct connection between Ep. Arist.
and Pseudo-Hecataeus, and thus disallows the use of Ep.
Arist. in establishing the date for Pseudo-Hecataeus.
Instead, he regards the reference in Ep. Arist. 31 as a
"free fiction of the author," and perhaps even a reference
to yet another, otherwise unattested, pseudonymous work
attributed to Hecataeus.

14. For the Greek text, cf. Testimonia, p. 320.

15. For the Greek text, cf. Frg. 3, p.320.

16. The lines attributed to Sophocles are also quoted
by Clement in Protr. 7.74.2, but without reference to
Hecataeus. For their occurrence in other Christian texts,
cf. Frg. 3, app. crit., p. 318.

17. These are attributed all too easily to Pseudo-Hecataeus by Wacholder, Eupolemus, 264. Cf. Schaller, 25.

18. Cf. Reinach, Contre Apion (Budé) 35, n. 3; Schaller, 16, n. 6; cf. Conzelmann, HJC, 165. Cf. below, pp. 283-87.

19. For the Greek text, cf. Frg. 1, par. 183.

20. P.E. 9.4.1: ʾΕκαταῖος δὲ ὁ ʾΑβδηρίτης, ἀνὴρ φιλόσοφος ἅμα καὶ περὶ τὰς πράξεις ἱκανώτατος, ἰδίαν βίβλον ἀναθεὶς τῇ περὶ ʾΙουδαίων ἱστορίᾳ, πλεῖστα περὶ αὐτῶν διέξεισιν...

21. For the Greek text, cf. Testimonia, p. 322.

22. Ag.Ap. 1.183: οὐ παρέργως, ἀλλὰ περὶ αὐτῶν ʾΙουδαίων συγγέγραφε βιβλίον. Also, Ag.Ap. 1.214: ἀλλ' ὅμως ʾΕκαταῖος μὲν καὶ βιβλίον ἔγραψε περὶ ἡμῶν.

23. Fraser, Ptolemaic Alexandria, 1.497, notes that these four main sections were "characteristic of philosophical and programmatic ethnographical writing."

24. With the notable exception of Wacholder, Eupolemus, 265-66, who assigns it to a separate work.

25. As e.g., Jacoby, FGrH, No. 264, Frg. *22; also Wacholder, 263, 266.

26. For a review of the earlier history of scholarship, beginning with Scaliger (d. 1609), cf. Müller, gegen Apion, 170-71; also LaFargue-Collins, 1-6. Also, Lewy, 117; Schaller, 16-17. Also, Müller, FHG 2.385.

27. Müller, gegen Apion (1877) 170-71; Elter, Gnomologiorum (1893-95) 9.247-54; Reinach, Oeuvres ... Josèphe (1900) 7,1.35, n.1; Wendland, "Aristeas," (1900), 2.1-2; Engers, Mnemosyne (1923) 232-33; Schlatter, Geschichte (1925³), 398, n. 50; Heinemann, PW (1931) 32; Lewy, ZNW (1932) 117-32; Dornseiff, Echtheitsfragen (1939) 52-65; Gutman, Beginnings (1958) 1.39-73, esp. 70-71; Tcherikover, Hellenistic Civilization (1966) 426-27; Gager, ZNW (1969) 130-39; Stern, GLAJJ (1974) 20-44; Jewish People (1976) 2.1105-1109.

28. Müller, FHG (1853) 2.385-86; Reinach, Textes (1895) 227 ?; cf. Contre Apion (Budé, 1930) xxxi-xxxii; Willrich, Juden und Griechen (1895) 48-51; Judaica (1900) 86-102; Schürer, Geschichte (1901-1909) 3.605-608; Geffcken, Apologeten (1907) x-xvi; Jacoby, PW (1912) 2766-67; FGrH 3a (1943) 46-52, 61-74; Schmid-Stählin, Geschichte (1920) 2,1.618-19; Bousset-Gressmann, RJ (1926) 26; Stein, Eos (1936) 463-78; Dalbert, Missionsliteratur (1954) 65-67; Hadas, Hellenistic Culture (1959) 88-89; Schaller, ZNW (1963) 15-31; Walter, Aristobulos (1964) 187-200; JS (1,2; 1976), 144-53; Murray, "Aristeas," JTS (1967); "Hecataeus," JEA (1970) 144; Denis, Introduction (1970) 262-67; Wacholder, "Hecataeus," EncJud (1971) 236-37; Eupolemus

28. (cont.) (1974), 272-73; Fraser, <u>Ptolemaic Alexandria</u>
(1972) 2.968, n. 115; Hengel, "Anonymität," (1972) 295-96,
301-303, 324-25; <u>Judaism and Hellenism</u> (1974) 1.69, 256.

29. Thackeray, Josephus, <u>Against Apion</u> (<u>LCL</u>, 1926) 1.236-
37; Olmstead, <u>JAOS</u> (1936) 243-44 (?); Jaeger, <u>Diokles</u>
(1938), 134-53, esp. 150. Others noted in Schaller,22,n.44.

30. These arguments are summarized in Stern, <u>GLAJJ</u>,
23-24; also, Conzelmann, <u>HJC</u>, 166-68.

31. Stern, <u>GLAJJ</u>, 22: "with almost absolute certainty."

32. Cf. the Greek text on p. 322. Cf. Chadwick, Origen,
<u>Contra Celsum</u>, 17, n. 4. Attridge-Oden, <u>Philo of Byblos</u>,
99; also J. Barr, "Philo of Byblos and His 'Phoenician
History,'" <u>BJRL</u> 57 (1974) 17-68, esp. 31-32.

33. Gager, "Pseudo-Hecataeus," 131-32, especially censures
scholars from an earlier period who treated any favorable
treatment of the Jews by pagan authors as later interpolations. He notes correctly that pagan attitudes towards
Jews varied according to time and place, and that in the
early Hellenistic period pagan attitudes towards the
Jews were decidedly more favorable than the harsher
attitudes displayed later by pagan authors such as Manetho
and Apion.

34. So, Reinach, <u>Textes</u>, 227; Schürer, <u>Literature</u>, 305;
Schmid-Stählin, 2,1.619.

35. Schürer, <u>Geschichte</u>, 3.605-608; <u>Literature</u>, 302-306.
A similar position is held by Freudenthal, 165-66; Susemihl,
Geschichte, 2.645; Willrich, <u>Judaica</u>, 108-109; Schmid-
Stählin, Geschichte, 2,1.618, n. 7; Stein, <u>Eos</u>, 467-68;
Dalbert, <u>Missionsliteratur</u>, 65; perhaps Reinach, <u>Textes</u>,
227.

36. Schürer, <u>Literature</u>, 305.

37. Schaller, "Hekataios," 15-31, esp. 26.

38. Schaller, 26.

39. Schaller, 31. Fraser, <u>Ptolemaic Alexandria</u>, 2.968,
n. 115, likewise regards the fragments as pseudonymous,
stemming from two separate works, but finds it difficult
to believe that they are from separate authors, much
less different periods.

40. This position is also held by Spoerri, <u>KP</u> 2 (1967)
981-82.

41. This, of course, in contrast to his earlier position
in <u>PW</u> (1912) when he argued for a later date. Cf. note 13.

42. Willrich, Judaica, 86-103, suggests that the following passages from Josephus are dependent on Pseudo-Hecataeus' On Abraham: Ant. 1.161, 164-66, and possibly Ant. 1.207-41, and all the citations in Ag.Ap. 1.166-83. Walter, JS (1,2), 158-59, also takes a maximalist approach, treating Ant. 1.154-68 under Pseudo-Hecataeus II, i.e., On Abraham. Cf. also Jacoby, FGrH 3a.75.

43. FGrH, 3a.75.

44. Walter, Aristobulos (1964), 187-200; JS (1,2; 1976), 144-53.

45. Murray, "Aristeas," 342, n. 4, also holds the "two works/two authors" view.

46. Cf. esp. JS (1,2), 146, esp. 148, n. 25; also, cf. above, n. 13.

47. JS (1,2), 148.

48. As noted earlier (cf. above, n. 42), Walter, JS (1,2), 144, thinks Josephus has used Pseudo-Hecataeus On Abraham throughout Ant. 1.154-68, thus is confident that more of this work is extant than is often supposed. Here, he continues the suggestion made earlier by Willrich and Jacoby.

49. Cf., esp. pp. 263-73.

50. Wacholder, Eupolemus, 266.

51. Wacholder, Eupolemus, 266. A fuller elaboration of his reconstruction is found in note 10 above.

52. Wacholder, Eupolemus, 266.

53. Wacholder, Eupolemus, 267.

54. Cf. Annotations, note 11.

55. Wacholder, Eupolemus, 272.

56. Wacholder, Eupolemus, 273.

57. Wacholder, Eupolemus, 272.

58. So, e.g., Conzelmann, HJC, 168.

59. As seen from the earlier review, suggested dates for Pseudo-Hecataeus (esp. On the Jews) range from the late fourth century B.C.E. to the mid- to late first century B.C.E. For a review of the range, cf. Schaller, 26, n. 60.

60. As e.g., Jacoby, in his earlier article in <u>PW</u> (1912);
Willrich, <u>Judaica</u>, suggests a date at the beginning of the
first century C.E.

61. So, Schürer, <u>Geschichte</u>, 3.604; Schaller, 30.
Similar dependence is reflected in <u>Ep</u>. <u>Arist</u>. 12-13, in
remarks reminiscent of Frg. 1, par. 186. Cf. <u>APOT</u> 2.95,
n. 12.

62. Cf. Jacoby, <u>FGrH</u> 3a.62; Fraser, <u>Ptolemaic Alexandria</u>,
2.968, n. 115.

63. Cf. Jacoby, <u>FGrH</u> 3a.61-63.

64. An Egyptian provenance is favored by Walter, <u>JS</u> (1,2),
148, 151; Dalbert, <u>Missionsliteratur</u>, 66; also Gager,
"Pseudo-Hecataeus," 135, although he regards them as
authentic. Denis, 266, favors a Palestinian setting.

Bibliography

Bernfield, I. "Hekatäus von Abdera," EncJud 7 (1930) 1135-
    36.

Bousset-Gressmann, RJ, 26-27.

Charlesworth, PAMRS, 119-22, 287.

Cohn, L. Review of Reinach, Textes in MGWJ 41 (1897) 285-88.

Collins, Athens and Jerusalem, 42-43.

Conzelmann, HJC, 164-70.

Dalbert, Missionsliteratur, 65-67.

Denis, Introduction, 223-28, 262-67.

Doran, R. "Pseudo-Hecataeus," in Charlesworth, OTP.

Dornseiff, F. Echtheitsfragen antik-griechischen Literatur.
    Rettungen des Theognis, Phokylides, Hekataios,
    Choirilos (Berlin: deGruyter, 1939) 52-65.

Droysen, J. G. Geschichte des Hellenismus (6 vols. in 3;
    Gotha: Perthes, 1877-78; repr. in 3 vols. Basel:
    Schwabe, 1953) 3.40-41.

Elter, A. De Gnomologiorum graecorum historia atque
    origine commentario (Bonn: C. Georgi, 1893-95)
    9. 247-54.

Engers, M. "De Hecataei Abderitae Fragmentis," Mnemosyne
    N.S. 51 (1923) 229-41.

Ewald, History, 1.202; 2.91-94; 5.246-48, 432.

Feist, S. "Ein Zeitgenosse Alexander des Grossen über
    die Juden," Menorah 19 (1931) 468-70.

Fraser, Ptolemaic Alexandria, 1.496-505, 695; 2.718-27,
    notes 5-92; 733, note 117; 968, n. 115.

Freudenthal, Alexander Polyhistor, 165-66, 178.

Gager, J. Moses, 26-37.

_____, "Pseudo-Hecataeus Again," ZNW 60 (1969) 130-39.

Geffcken, Apologeten, xii-xvi.

Graetz, Geschichte, 3.626-27.

Gutman, Beginnings, 1.39-73.

Hadas, M. Aristeas to Philocrates (Letter of Aristeas)
    (New York: Harper, 1951) 98-99, 110-11, 130, 222-23.

_____, Hellenistic Culture, 88-89.

Heinemann, I. "Antisemitismus," PW Suppl. 5 (1931) 32.

Hengel, "Anonymität," 295-96, 301-303, 324-25.

_____, Judaism and Hellenism, 1.69, 256; 2.76, 105.

Herrmann, L. "La lettre d'Aristée a Philocrate et
    l'empereur Titus," Latomus 25 (1966) 58-78, esp.
    76-78.

Jacoby, F. "Hekataios (4)," PW 7 (1912) 2750-69, esp.
    2766-67.

_____, Kommentar on FGrH, No. 264 ("Hekataios von
    Abdera"), Frg. 21-24 in FGrH 3a (Leiden: Brill, 1943)
    29-87, esp. 46-52 and 61-74.

Jaeger, W. Diokles von Karystos (Berlin: de Gruyter, 1938)
    134-53.

_____, "Greeks and Jews. The First Greek Records of
    Jewish Religion and Civilization," JR 18 (1938)
    127-43.

Karpeles, Geschichte, 1.188, 204.

La Fargue, M. and J. Collins. "The Allegedly Pseudo-
    Hecataeus." Unpublished Seminar Paper. Harvard New
    Testament Seminar. May 1, 1970. 24 pp.

Lewy, H. "Hekataios von Abdera περὶ Ἰουδαίων," ZNW
    31 (1932) 117-32.

Lohse, E. "Hekataeus aus Abdera," RGG³ 3 (1959) 206.

Müller, FHG, 2.385-86.

Müller, J. G. Des Fl. Josephus Schrift gegen den Apion
    (Basel: Bahnmaier Verlag, 1877) 170-78, 243.

Murray, O. "Aristeas and Ptolemaic Kingship," JTS N.S.
    18 (1967) 337-71, esp. 342-43.

_____, "Hecataeus of Abdera and Pharaonic Kingship,"
    JEA 56 (1970) 141-71.

Olmstead, A. T. "Intertestamental Studies," JAOS 56 (1936)
    242-57, esp. 243-44.

Pfeiffer, History, 201.

Posner, A. "Griechische Schriftsteller über Juden,"
    in Jüdische Lexikon 2 (1928) 1277.

Reinach, T. Flavius Josèphe Contre Apion (Budé; Paris:
    Société d'édition "Les belles lettres," 1930) xxxi-
    xxxii, 35-39, 65-66.

_____, Textes, 14-20, 227-36.

Safanov, A. "Greek Writers on Jews," Universal Jewish
    Encyclopedia 5 (1941) 94.

Schaller, B. "Hekataios von Abdera Über die Juden. Zur
    Frage der Echtheit und der Datierung," ZNW 54 (1963)
    15-31.

Schlatter, Geschichte, 10, 24, 31, 38, 68, 398-99.

Schmid, J. "Hekataios v. Abdera," LTK² 5 (1960) 206.

Schmid-Stählin, Geschichte, 2,1.618-19.

Schürer, Geschichte, 3.603-608.

_____, Literature, 302-306.

Sellers, O. The Citadel of Beth-Zur (Philadelphia:
    Westminster, 1933) 73-74.

Speyer, W. Die literarische Fälschung im heidnischen und
    christlichen Altertum (HAW 1,2; München: Beck, 1971)
    160-61.

Spoerri, W. "Hekataios (4)," KP 2 (1967) 980-82.

Stein, E. "Pierwsi apologeci hellenistyczno-zydowscy"
    ["Die ersten hellenistisch-jüdisch Apologeten"],
    Eos 37 (1936) 458-80, esp. 463-78; 38 (1937) 73-93;
    210-23; 470-91.

Stein, M. "The Pseudo-Hecataeus. The Date and Purpose of
    His Book on the Jews," Zion O.S. 6 (1934) 1ff.

Stern, GLAJJ, 1.20-44.

_____, Jewish People, 2.1105-1109.

_____ and O. Murray, "Hecataeus of Abdera and Theophras-
    tus on Jews and Egyptians," JEA 59 (1973) 159-68.

Susemihl, Geschichte, 2.644-45.

Tcherikover, Hellenistic Civilization, 426-27, note 49.

Wacholder, B. Z. Eupolemus, 60, 195, 235-36, 262-73, 289,
    292.

_____, "Hecataeus of Abdera," EncJud 8 (1971) 236-37.

Walter, N. Aristobulos, 86-88, 172-201.

_____, JSHRZ (1,2), 144-60.

Walton, F. R. "The Messenger of God in Hecataeus of
    Abdera," HTR 48 (1955) 255-57.

Wendland, P."Der Brief des Aristeas," in
    E. Kautzsch (ed.), Die Apokryphen und Pseudepigraphen
    des Alten Testaments (Tübingen: J. C. B. Mohr, 1900;
    repr. Hildesheim: G. Olms, 1962) 2.1-2.

_____, Review of Willrich, Judaica in Berliner Philolo-
    gische Wochenschrift 20 (1900) 1199-1202.

Willrich, Judaica, 86-130.

_____, Juden und Griechen, 20-33, 48-51.

Index to Editions and Translations

On the Jews

Fragment One

A.

Source: Josephus, Against Apion 1.22.7-16, par.
    183-204.

Greek Text Used: Thackeray, LCL, 1.236-46.

Editions: Müll., FHG 2.393-95 (= Frg. 14); Freu. (om.);
    J. G. Müller, Apion, 38-40 (commentary, 170-78);
    Naber, 6.217-21; Niese, 5.33-37; Stearns (om.);
    Reinach (Budé), 35-39; Jac., FGrH 3A1.19 (= No.
    264, Frg. 21; commentary, FGrH 3a.66-74); Denis,
    199-201 (= Frg. 1); Stern, GLAJJ, 35-44 (= No.
    12).

Translations:

    English: Thackeray, Josephus, Against Apion,
                 LCL, 1.236-46.

    French: Reinach, Textes, 227-34; Blum (Budé,
                 ed. Reinach), 35-39.

    German: Walter (JS, 1.2) 154-57.

B.   Parallel to Ag.Ap. 1.197-204.

Source: Eusebius, P.E. 9.4.2-9.

Reference Number in P.E.: Steph., 239-40; Vig., 408a-
    409b.

Greek Text Used: Mras, GCS (43,1) 8.1, p. 490,
    line 1 - p. 491, line 12.

Editions: Steph., 239-40; Vig., 408a-409b; Hein.,
    2.8-9; Gais., 2.351-53; Müll., FHG 2.393-95;
    Migne, PG (21) cols. 688D - 692A (notes, cols.
    1557-58); Dind., 1.473-74; Freu. (om.); Giff.,
    1.516-18 (notes, 4.289; cf. 4.255); Stearns (om.);
    Mras, GCS (43,1) 8.1, 490-91; Jac., FGrH 3A1.19
    (= No. 264, Frg. 21; commentary, FGrH 3a.66-74);
    Denis, 199-201 (= Frg. 1); Stern, GLAJJ, 35-44
    (= No. 12).

Translations:

    English: Giff., 3.439-40.

    French:

    German: Riessler (om.); Walter (JS, 1.2)
                 154-57.

Fragment Two

Source: Josephus, Against Apion 2.4, par. 42-43.

Greek Text Used: Thackeray, LCL, 1.308-309.

Editions: Müll., FHG 2.395 (= Frg. 15); J. G. Müller,
           Apion, 54-55 (commentary, 243); Naber, 6.247-48;
           Niese, 5.59; Reinach (Budé), 65-66; Jac., FGrH
           3A1.21 (= No. 264, Frg. *22; commentary, FGrH 3a.
           74); Denis, 201-202 (= Frg. 2); Stern, GLAJJ,
           44 (= No. 13).

Translations:

           English: Thackeray, Josephus, Against Apion,
                       LCL, 1.308-309.

           French: Reinach, Textes, 235; Blum (Budé,
                       ed. Reinach), 65-66.

           German: Walter (JS, 1.2) 157.

On Abraham (and the Egyptians)

Fragment Three

Source: Clement of Alexandria, Stromata 5.14.112.4-
           113.1-2.

Greek Text Used: Stählin-Früchtel, GCS (52) 15,
           p. 402, line 15 - p. 403, line 7.

Editions: Müll., FHG 2.396 (= No. 18); Migne, PG (9)
           col. 169 B - 172 A; Dind., 3.93-94; Freu. (om.);
           Reinach, Textes, 236 (= Frg. E); Stearns (om.);
           Jac., FGrH 3A1.22 (= No. 264, Frg. 24; commentary,
           FGrH 3a.75); Denis (om.); LeBoulluec, SC (228)
           1.210.

Translations:

           English: Wilson (ANF), 2.470-71.

           French: Voulet (SC, 278) 1.211, 213
                       (commentary by LeBoulluec, 2.336-37).

           German: Stählin, (BK, 19), 4.213-14; Walter
                       (JS, 1.2) 159-60 = Ps.-Hecataeus II,
                       Frg. 2); Riessler (om.).

Pseudo-Hecataeus, On the Jews

FRAGMENT ONE (Josephus, Ag. Ap. 1.22.7-16, ¶ 183-204;
       1.197-204 = Eusebius, P.E. 9.4.2-9)

(183) Κλέαρχος μὲν οὖν ἐν παρεκβάσει ταῦτ' εἴρη-   (183)
κεν, τὸ γὰρ προκείμενον ἦν αὐτῷ καθ' ἕτερον,
οὕτως ἡμῶν μνημονεῦσαι. Ἑκαταῖος δὲ ὁ Ἀβδηρίτης,
ἀνὴρ φιλόσοφος ἅμα καὶ περὶ τὰς πράξεις ἱκανώτα-
5   τος,   Ἀλεξάνδρῳ τῷ βασιλεῖ συνακμάσας καὶ
Πτολεμαίῳ τῷ Λάγου συγγενόμενος, οὐ παρέργως,
ἀλλὰ περὶ αὐτῶν Ἰουδαίων συγγέγραφε βιβλίον, ἐξ
οὗ βούλομαι κεφαλαιωδῶς ἐπιδραμεῖν ἔνια τῶν
εἰρημένων. (184) καὶ πρῶτον ἐπιδείξω τὸν χρόνον·   (184)
10 μνημονεύει γὰρ τῆς Πτολεμαίου περὶ Γάζαν πρὸς
Δημήτριον μάχης, αὕτη δὲ γέγονεν ἐνδεκάτῳ μὲν
ἔτει τῆς Ἀλεξάνδρου τελευτῆς, ἐπὶ δὲ ὀλυμπιάδος
ἑβδόμης καὶ δεκάτης καὶ ἑκατοστῆς, ὡς ἱστορεῖ
Κάστωρ. (185) προσθεὶς γὰρ ταύτην τὴν ὀλυμπιάδα (185)
15 φησίν· "ἐπὶ ταύτης Πτολεμαῖος ὁ Λάγου ἐνίκα
κατὰ Γάζαν μάχῃ Δημήτριον τὸν Ἀντιγόνου τὸν
ἐπικληθέντα Πολιορκητήν." Ἀλέξανδρον δὲ τεθνάναι
πάντες ὁμολογοῦσιν ἐπὶ τῆς ἑκατοστῆς τεσσαρεσκαι-
δεκάτης ὀλυμπιάδος. δῆλον οὖν ὅτι καὶ κατ'
20 ἐκεῖνον καὶ κατὰ Ἀλέξανδρον ἤκμαζεν ἡμῶν τὸ
ἔθνος. (186) λέγει τοίνυν ὁ Ἑκαταῖος πάλιν   (186)

L Lat.

1-3 Κλέαρχος -- μνημονεῦσαι: *clearchus siquidem facta
digressione, cum aliud propositum haberet, nostri generis
ita meminit* Lat. | 1-2 εἰρηκὼς cj. Nie. | 2 καθ' om.
Hud., apud Nie. | 2-3 καθ' ἕτερον οὕτως: ἕτερον καὶ οὐ
τὸ Gutschmid apud Nie. | 3 μνημονεύσας Hud. apud Nie.:
ἐμνημόνευσεν cj. Nie. | 6 Λάγου ed. pr.: λαγῶ L Lat. |
7 ἀλλὰ <ἴδιον> περὶ Reinach | 14 προθεὶς Colet apud
Reinach | 15 Λάγου ed. pr.: λαγὸ L Lat. | 16 κατὰ:
τῇ κατὰ cj. Nie. | 19-20 κατ' ἐκεῖνον: *secundum illud
tempus* Lat. |

FRAGMENT ONE[1]

(183) (183) This allusion of Aristotle to us is mentioned
parenthetically by Clearchus, who was dealing with
another subject. Of a different nature is the evidence of Hecataeus of Abdera,[2] at once a philosopher
and a highly competent man of affairs,[3] who rose to
fame under King Alexander, and was afterwards associated with Ptolemy, son of Lagus.[4] He makes no
mere passing allusion to us, but wrote a book entirely about the Jews,[5] from which I propose briefly to
(184) touch on some passages.[6] (184) I will begin with
fixing his date. He mentions the battle near Gaza
between Ptolemy and Demetrius, which, as Castor
narrates,[7] was fought eleven years after the death
(185) of Alexander, in the 117th Olympiad.[8] (185) For
under the head of this Olympiad he says:

> "In this period Ptolemy, son of Lagus,
> defeated in a battle at Gaza Demetrius,
> son of Antigonus, surnamed Poliorcetes."

And all agree that Alexander died in the 114th
Olympiad. It is evident, therefore, that our race
was flourishing both under Ptolemy and under
(186) Alexander.[9] (186) Hecataeus goes on to say that

τάδε, ὅτι μετὰ τὴν ἐν Γάζῃ μάχην ὁ Πτολεμαῖος
ἐγένετο τῶν περὶ Συρίαν τόπων ἐγκρατής, καὶ
πολλοὶ τῶν ἀνθρώπων πυνθανόμενοι τὴν ἠπιότητα
καὶ φιλανθρωπίαν τοῦ Πτολεμαίου συναπαίρειν εἰς
5 Αἴγυπτον αὐτῷ καὶ κοινωνεῖν τῶν πραγμάτων
ἠβουλήθησαν. (187) "ὧν εἷς ἦν," φησίν, "'Εζεκίας   (187)
ἀρχιερεὺς τῶν 'Ιουδαίων, ἄνθρωπος τὴν μὲν ἡλικίαν
ὡς ἐξήκοντα ἓξ ἐτῶν, τῷ δ' ἀξιώματι τῷ παρὰ τοῖς
ὁμοέθνοις μέγας καὶ τὴν ψυχὴν οὐκ ἀνόητος, ἔτι
10 δὲ καὶ λέγειν δυνατὸς καὶ τοῖς περὶ τῶν πραγμάτων, εἴπερ τις ἄλλος, ἔμπειρος.   (188) καίτοι,"   (188)
φησίν, "οἱ πάντες ἱερεῖς τῶν 'Ιουδαίων οἱ τὴν
δεκάτην τῶν γινομένων λαμβάνοντες καὶ τὰ κοινὰ
διοικοῦντες περὶ χιλίους μάλιστα καὶ πεντακοσίους
15 εἰσίν."   (189) πάλιν δὲ τοῦ προειρημένου μνημο-   (189)
νεύων ἀνδρός "οὗτος," φησίν, "ὁ ἄνθρωπος τετευχὼς
τῆς τιμῆς ταύτης καὶ συνήθης ἡμῖν γενόμενος,
παραλαβών τινας τῶν μεθ' ἑαυτοῦ τὴν {τε} διαφορὰν
ἀνέγνω πᾶσαν αὐτοῖς· εἶχεν γὰρ τὴν κατοίκησιν
20 αὐτῶν καὶ τὴν πολιτείαν γεγραμμένην." (190) εἶτα   (190)
'Εκαταῖος δηλοῖ πάλιν πῶς ἔχομεν πρὸς τοὺς
νόμους, ὅτι πάντα πάσχειν ὑπὲρ τοῦ μὴ παραβῆναι
τούτους προαιρούμεθα καὶ καλὸν εἶναι νομίζομεν.
(191) "τοιγαροῦν," φησί, "καὶ κακῶς ἀκούοντες   (191)
25 ὑπὸ τῶν ἀστυγειτόνων καὶ τῶν εἰσαφικνουμένων

L Lat.

6 ἐζεκίασ L | 7 ὁ ἀρχιερεὺς ed. pr. | 9 οὐκ Hud. apud
Nie.: οὗτ' L | 10 τοῖς περὶ damn. Hud., apud Nie.:
<τοῖς περὶ> ? Nie. | 10-11 τοῖς -- πραγμάτων: circa
causas Lat. | 12-13 τὴν δεκάτην: decatas Lat. |
18 †τὴν Reinach | τε Nie.: om. Lat. Hud., apud Nie. |
18-19 διαφορὰν ἀνέγνω πᾶσαν: differentiam cunctam exposuit
Lat., apud Reinach | 20 αὐτῶν: suam Lat. 21 πρὸς:
circa Lat.: περὶ cj. Nie. | 23 τούτους ed. pr.:
τοῦτο L: eas Lat. | καὶ om. ed. pr. | νομίζοντες
ed. pr. | 25 καὶ -- εἰσαφικνουμένων om. Lat. |

after the battle of Gaza Ptolemy became master of
Syria, and that many of the inhabitants, hearing of
his kindliness and humanity,[10] desired to accompany
him to Egypt and to associate themselves with his
realm.

(187)   (187) "Among these (he says) was Ezechias,[11]
a chief priest of the Jews,[12] a man of about
sixty-six years of age, highly esteemed by
his countrymen, intellectual, and moreover
an able speaker and unsurpassed as a man of

(188)   business. (188) Yet (he adds) the total
number of Jewish priests who receive a tithe[13]
of the revenue and administer public affairs
is about fifteen hundred."[14]

(189)   (189) Reverting to Ezechias, he says:

"This man, after obtaining this honour[15]
and having been closely in touch with us,[16]
assembled some of his friends and read to
them [a statement showing] all the advantages
[of emigration];[17] for he had in writing the
conditions attaching to their settlement
and political status."[18]

(190)   (190) In another passage Hecataeus mentions our
regard for our laws, and how we deliberately choose
and hold it a point of honour to endure anything
rather than transgress them.[19]

(191)   (191) "And so (he says), neither the
slander of their neighbours and of foreign

πάντες   καὶ   προπηλακιζόμενοι   πολλάκις   ὑπὸ   τῶν
Περσικῶν   βασιλέων   καὶ   σατραπῶν   οὐ   δύνανται
μεταπεισθῆναι   τῇ   διανοίᾳ,   ἀλλὰ   γεγυμνωμένως   περὶ
τούτων   καὶ   αἰκίαις   καὶ   θανάτοις   δεινοτάτοις
5   μάλιστα   πάντων   ἀπαντῶσι,   μὴ   ἀρνούμενοι   τὰ πατρῷα."
(192)   παρέχεται   δὲ   καὶ   τεκμήρια   τῆς   ἰσχυρογνω-   (192)
μοσύνης   τῆς   περὶ   τῶν   νόμων   οὐκ   ὀλίγα.   φησὶ   γάρ,
'Αλεξάνδρου   ποτὲ   ἐν   Βαβυλῶνι   γενομένου   καὶ
προελομένου   τὸ   τοῦ Βήλου   πεπτωκὸς   ἱερὸν   ἀνακα-
10   θᾶραι   καὶ   πᾶσιν   αὐτοῦ   τοῖς   στρατιώταις   ὁμοίως
φέρειν   τὸν   χοῦν   προστάξαντος,   μόνους   τοὺς
'Ιουδαίους   οὐ   προσσχεῖν,   ἀλλὰ   καὶ   πολλὰς   ὑπο-
μεῖναι   πληγὰς   καὶ   ζημίας   ἀποτῖσαι   μεγάλας,   ἕως
αὐτοῖς   συγγνόντα   τὸν   βασιλέα   δοῦναι   τὴν   ἄδειαν.
15   (193)   ἔτι   γε   μὴν   τῶν   εἰς   τὴν   χώραν,   φησί,   πρὸς   (193)
αὐτοὺς   ἀφικνουμένων   νεὼς   καὶ   βωμοὺς   κατασκευα-
σάντων   ἅπαντα   ταῦτα   κατέσκαπτον,   καὶ   τῶν   μὲν
ζημίαν   τοῖς   σατράπαις   ἐξέτινον,   περί   τινων   δὲ
καὶ   συγγνώμης   μετελάμβανον.   καὶ   προσεπιτίθησιν
20   ὅτι   δίκαιον   ἐπὶ   τούτοις   αὐτούς ἐστι   θαυμάζειν.
(194)   λέγει   δὲ   καὶ   περὶ   τοῦ   πολυανθρωπότατον   (194)
γεγονέναι   ἡμῶν   τὸ   ἔθνος·   πολλὰς   μὲν   γὰρ   ἡμῶν,
φησίν,   ἀνασπάστους   εἰς   Βαβυλῶνα   Πέρσαι   πρότερον
{αὐτῶν}   ἐποίησαν   μυριάδας,   οὐκ ὀλίγαι   δὲ   καὶ
25   μετὰ   τὸν   'Αλεξάνδρου   θάνατου   εἰς   Αἴγυπτον   καὶ

L Lat.

1 πάντων ed. pr. | ὑπὸ ed. pr.: ὑπὲρ L: *a* Lat. |
3 γεγυμνασμένως intellexit Lat. | 5 πάτρια cj. Nie.:
πατρῷα L | 12 προσχεῖν L: corr. Bekker, apud Nie. |
15 ἔτι cj. Nie.: ἐπεῖ L et ut vid. Lat.: τῶν ed. pr. |
16 νεὼς: καὶ νεὼς ed. pr. | 18 ἐξέτεινον L: corr.
Dind., apud Nie. | 19 προσεπιτίθησιν: *adicit* Lat.:
προστίθησιν cod. Eliensis recte, apud Nie. | 20 τούτοις
ed. pr.: τούτουσ L | 22 ἡμῶν[1] fort. spur.: αὐτῶν
Bekker, apud Nie. | 24 αὐτῶν Nie.: om. Lat. Bekker,
apud Nie. | ὀλίγοι ? Reinach |

visitors, to which as a nation they are
exposed, nor the frequent outrages of
Persian kings and satraps can shake their
determination;[20] for these laws, naked[21]
and defenceless, they face tortures and
death in its most terrible form, rather
than repudiate the faith of their fore-
fathers."[22]

(192) (192) Of this obstinacy in defence of their laws he
furnishes several instances.[23] He tells how on one
occasion Alexander, when he was at Babylon and had
undertaken to restore the ruined temple of Bel,[24]
gave orders to all his soldiers, without distinction,
to bring materials for the earthworks; and how the
Jews alone refused to obey, and even submitted to
severe chastisement and heavy fines, until the king
pardoned them and exempted them from this task.

(193) (193) Again, when temples and altars were erected in
the country by its invaders, the Jews razed them all
to the ground, paying in some cases a fine to the
satraps, and in others obtaining pardon. For such
(194) conduct, he adds, they deserve admiration.[25] (194) He
then goes on to speak of our vast population,[26]
stating that, though many myriads of our race had
already been deported to Babylon by the Persians,[27]
yet after Alexander's death myriads more migrated to

Φοινίκην μετέστησαν διὰ τὴν ἐν Συρίᾳ στάσιν.
(195) ὁ δὲ αὐτὸς οὗτος ἀνὴρ καὶ τὸ μέγεθος τῆς (195)
χώρας ἣν κατοικοῦμεν καὶ τὸ κάλλος ἱστόρηκεν·
"τριακοσίας γὰρ μυριάδας ἀρουρῶν σχεδὸν τῆς
5 ἀρίστης καὶ παμφορωτάτης χώρας νέμονται," φησίν·
"ἡ γὰρ Ἰουδαία τοσαύτη πλάτος ἐστίν." (196) ἀλλὰ (196)
μὴν ὅτι καὶ τὴν πόλιν αὐτὴν τὰ Ἱεροσόλυμα
καλλίστην τε καὶ μεγίστην ἐκ παλαιοτάτου κατοικοῦμεν καὶ περὶ πλήθους ἀνδρῶν καὶ περὶ τῆς τοῦ
10 νεὼ κατασκευῆς οὕτως αὐτὸς διηγεῖται· (197) "ἔστι (197)
γὰρ τῶν Ἰουδαίων τὰ μὲν πολλὰ ὀχυρώματα κατὰ
τὴν χώραν καὶ κῶμαι, μία δὲ πόλις ὀχυρὰ πεντή- 408b
κοντα μάλιστα σταδίων τὴν περίμετρον, ἣν οἰκοῦσι
μὲν ἀνθρώπων περὶ δώδεκα μυριάδες, καλοῦσι δ'
15 αὐτὴν Ἱεροσόλυμα. (198) ἐνταῦθα δ' ἐστὶ κατὰ (198)
μέσον μάλιστα τῆς πόλεως περίβολος λίθινος,
μῆκος ὡς πεντάπλεθρος, εὖρος δὲ πηχῶν ρ', ἔχων
διπλᾶς πύλας· ἐν ᾧ βωμός ἐστι τετράγωνος ἀτμήτων
συλλέκτων ἀργῶν λίθων οὕτω συγκείμενος, πλευρὰν
20 μὲν ἑκάστην εἴκοσι πηχῶν, ὕψος δὲ δεκάπηχυ.

Ag. Ap. - L Lat.

6 πλάτος Hud. apud Nie.: πλῆθός L Nie.: *amplitudinis*
Lat. | 8-9 κατοικοῦμεν ed. pr.: *inhabitamus* Lat.:
κατοικουμένην L | 9 καὶ -- ἀνδρῶν: *et virorum multi-*
tudine copiosam Lat. | 10 αὐτὸς: *idem ipse* Lat.:
αὖ vel ὁ αὐτός Bekker apud Nie. | ἔστι incip. Euseb.,
P.E. 9.4.2 | 14 μὲν om. L et ut vid. Lat. | δώδεκα
μυριάδες: *CL milia* Lat. | 17 μῆκος -- πεντάπλεθρος
om. Lat. | εὖρος -- ρ': *centum per circuitum cubitorum*
Lat. | δὲ om. L et ut vid. Lat. | 18-19 ἀτμήτων --
λίθων: *ex lapidibus non dolatis sed collectis atque*
iacentibus Lat. | 19 συλλεκτῶν L | οὕτως L Nie. |

P.E. - BION

10 ante ἔστι titulum ΕΚΑΤΑΙΟΥ ΠΕΡΙ ΙΟΥΔΑΙΩΝ habunt BON:
om. I | 11 μὲν BON: om. I | 12 πόλις BON: ἡ Ἱερουσαλὴμ
πόλις I | 15 δ' ἐστι: δέ ἐστι ION: δ' ἔστι B | 17
πήχεων BION | πήχεων ἑκατόν Mras | 19 οὕτως BION Mras |
20 μὲν: δὲ BION | πήχεων BION Mras | δὲ δεκάπηχυ:
δεκάπηχυ BON Mras: δωδεκάπηχυ I |

Egypt and Phoenicia in consequence of the disturbed
(195) conditions of Syria.[28]   (195) The same writer has
referred to the extent and beauty of the country[29]
which we inhabit in the following words:

> "They occupy almost three million arourae[30]
> of the most excellent and fertile soil,
> productive of every variety of fruits.
> Such is the extent of Judaea."[31]

(196) (196) Again, here is his description of Jerusalem
itself,[32] the city which we have inhabited from
remote ages,[33] of its great beauty and extent, its
numerous population, and the temple buildings:

(197)   (197)[34] "The Jews have many fortresses and
villages in different parts of the country,[35]
but only one fortified city, which has a
circumference of about fifty stades[36] and
some hundred and twenty thousand inhabitants;[37]
(198)   they call it Jerusalem. (198) Nearly in the
centre of the city stands a stone wall,[38]
enclosing an area about five plethra long
and a hundred cubits broad,[39] approached by
a pair of gates. Within this enclosure is
a square altar, built of heaped up stones,
unhewn and unwrought; each side is twenty
cubits long and the height ten cubits.[40]

καὶ παρ' αὐτὸν οἴκημα μέγα, οὗ βωμός ἐστι καὶ
λυχνίον, ἀμφότερα χρυσᾶ δύο τάλαντα τὴν ὁλκήν.   408c
(199) ἐπὶ τούτων φῶς ἐστιν ἀναπόσβεστον καὶ τὰς (199)
νύκτας καὶ τὰς ἡμέρας. ἄγαλμα δ' οὐκ ἔστιν
5 οὐδ' ἀνάθημα τὸ παράπαν οὐδὲ φύτευμα παντελῶς
οὐδέν, οἷον ἀλσῶδες ἤ τι τοιοῦτον. διατρίβουσι
δ' ἐν αὐτῷ καὶ τὰς νύκτας καὶ τὰς ἡμέρας ἱερεῖς
ἀγνείας τινὰς ἁγνεύοντες καὶ τὸ παράπαν οἶνον οὐ
πίνοντες ἐν τῷ ἱερῷ." (200) ἔτι γε μὴν ὅτι καὶ (200)
10 Ἀλεξάνδρῳ τῷ βασιλεῖ συνεστρατεύσαντο καὶ μετὰ
ταῦτα τοῖς διαδόχοις αὐτοῦ μεμαρτύρηκεν· οἷς δ'
αὐτὸς παρατυχεῖν φησιν ὑπ' ἀνδρὸς Ἰουδαίου κατὰ   408d
τὴν στρατείαν γενομένοις, τοῦτο παραθήσομαι.
(201) λέγει δ' οὕτως· "ἐμοῦ γοῦν ἐπὶ   τὴν (201)
15 Ἐρυθρὰν θάλασσαν βαδίζοντος συνηκολούθει τις
μετὰ τῶν ἄλλων τῶν παραπεμπόντων ἡμᾶς ἱππέων
Ἰουδαίων ὄνομα Μοσόλλαμος, ἄνθρωπος ἱκανὸς κατὰ
ψυχήν, εὔρωστος καὶ τοξότης δὴ πάντων ὁμολογου-
μένως καὶ τῶν Ἑλλήνων καὶ τῶν βαρβάρων ἄριστος.

A̲g̲. A̲p̲. - L Lat.

3-4 καὶ -- ἡμέρας: *noctibus et diebus* Lat. | 7 καὶ[1] --
ἡμέρας: *et noctibus et diebus* Lat. | 10-11 Ἀλεξάνδρῳ --
αὐτοῦ: *cum alexandri regis successoribus postea castra
metati sunt* Lat. | 10 συνεστρατεύσαντο Lat.: συνεστρα-
τεύομεν L | καὶ om. L | 11 δ' om. L Lat. |
12 φησιν: *dicens* Lat. | 16 ἡμῖν L | 17 Ἰουδαῖος
cj. Nie. | ἱκανὸς L Lat.: ἱκανῶς Nie. | κατά: καὶ
cj. Nie. | 18-19 ὁμολογουμένως cj. Nie. | ὁμολογού-
μενοσ L: *indubitanter* Lat. |

P̲.E̲. - BION

2 λυχνίον BI: λυχνία ON | 3 ἐπὶ δὲ BION Mras |
3-4 καὶ -- ἡμέρας IO[1]: del. O[z]: νυκτὸς καὶ ἡμέρας
BO[z](ἡμέρας mut.)GN | 6 οὐδέν: οὐδὲ BION Mras |
τοιοῦτο ON | 7 καὶ -- ἡμέρας IO: καὶ νυκτὸς καὶ
ἡμέρας B: νυκτὸς καὶ ἡμέρας N | 9 ἔτι γε μὴν: Ταῦτα
εἰπὼν ὑποβὰς BION Mras | 10 συνεστρατεύσατο B| 10-13
καὶ -- παραθήσομαι om. B | 13 στρατιὰν ON | 17 Μοσόλ-
λαμος Mras: Μοσόμαμος BION | ἱκανὸς BON: ἱκανῶς I Nie. |
κατὰ τὴν I | 18 ὑπὸ δὴ BION Mras | 18-19 ὁμολογούμενος
BION Mras | 19 καὶ τῶν βαρβ. καὶ τ. Ἑλλ. B |

(199)

Beside it stands a great edifice, containing
an altar and a lampstand, both made of gold,
and weighing two talents;[41] (199) upon these
is a light which is never extinguished by
night or day.[42] There is not a single statue
or votive offering, no trace of a plant, in
the form of a sacred grove or the like.[43]
Here priests pass their nights and days
performing certain rites of purification,
and abstaining altogether from wine while
in the temple."[44]

(200)

(200) The author further attests the share which
the Jews took[45] in the campaigns both of King Alexander and of his successors.[46] One incident on the
march, in which a Jewish soldier was concerned, he
states that he witnessed himself.[47] I will give the
story[48] in his own words:

(201)

(201) "When I was on the march towards the
Red Sea, among the escort of Jewish cavalry[49]
which accompanied us was one named Mosollamus,[50]
a very intelligent man, robust, and by common
consent, the very best of bowmen, whether Greek

(202)   οὗτος οὖν ὁ ἄνθρωπος διαβαδιζόντων πολλῶν (202)
κατὰ τὴν ὁδὸν καὶ μάντεώς τινος ὀρνιθευομένου
καὶ πάντας ἐπισχεῖν ἀξιοῦντος ἠρώτησε, διὰ τί
προσμένουσι. (203) δείξαντος δὲ τοῦ μάντεως (203)
5   αὐτῷ τὸν ὄρνιθα καὶ φήσαντος, ἐὰν μὲν αὐτοῦ μένῃ
προσμένειν | συμφέρειν πᾶσιν, ἐὰν δ' ἀναστὰς 409a
εἰς τοὔμπροσθεν πέτηται προάγειν, ἐὰν δ' εἰς
τοὔπισθεν ἀναχωρεῖν αὖθις, σιωπήσας καὶ παρελ-
κύσας τὸ τόξον ἔβαλε καὶ τὸν ὄρνιθα πατάξας
10   ἀπέκτεινεν. (204) ἀγανακτούντων δὲ τοῦ μάντεως (204)
καὶ τινων ἄλλων καὶ καταρωμένων αὐτῷ, "τί
μαίνεσθε," ἔφη, "κακοδαίμονες;" εἶτα τὸν ὄρνιθα
λαβὼν εἰς τὰς χεῖρας, "πῶς γάρ," ἔφη, "οὗτος τὴν
αὐτοῦ σωτηρίαν οὐ προϊδὼν περὶ τῆς   ἡμετέρας
15   πορείας ἡμῖν ἄν τι ὑγιὲς ἀπήγγελλεν; εἰ γὰρ
ἠδύνατο προγιγνώσκειν τὸ μέλλον, εἰς τὸν τόπον
τοῦτον οὐκ ἂν ἦλθε, φοβούμενος μὴ τοξεύσας αὐτὸν
ἀποκτείνῃ Μοσόλλαμος ὁ Ἰουδαῖος."   409b

Ag. Ap. - L Lat.

1 διαβαδιζόντων: *properantibus* Lat. | 5 τὴν ὄρνιθα L |
μὲν: μὲν οὖν L | 6 συμφέρῃ L | ἐὰν: ἂν L Nie. |
ἀναστᾶσ L¹ | 9 τὴν ὄρνιθα L | 12 κακοδαίμονες· εἶτα
τὸν: κακοδαιμονέστατον L Lat. | 13 λαβὼν: λαβόντεσ
L Lat. | ἔφη om. L Lat. | 18 μοσόλαμοσ L: *a mosol-
lamo* Lat. | ὁ om. L | Ἰουδαῖος: fin. Euseb., P.E.
9.4.9 |

P.E. - BION

1 βαδιζόντων BION Mras | 5 τὸν ὄρνιθα BION Mras |
6 συμφέρειν ON: συμφέρει BI | 6 ἐὰν BION Mras |
8 τοὔπισθεν BON: τὸ ὄπισθεν I | 8-9 ἑλκύσας BION Mras|
9 ἔβαλλε ON | τὸν ὄρνιθα BION Mras | 10 δὲ: τε BON |
13 ἔφη, οὗτος BON: οὗτος ἔφη I | 14 αὐτοῦ Gais.:
αὐτοῦ BION | προειδώς I | 15 ἀνήγγειλεν BION Mras |
16 ἐδύνατο I | προγινώσκειν BION Mras | 18 Μοσόλ-
λαμος Mras: Μοσόμαμος BION |

(202)   or barbarian. (202) This man, observing
that a number of men were going to and fro
on the route and that the whole force was
being held up by a seer who was taking the
auspices, inquired why they were halting.[51]

(203)   (203) The seer pointed out to him the bird
he was observing, and told him that if it
stayed in that spot it was expedient for
them all to halt; if it stirred and flew
forward, to advance; if backward, then to
retire. The Jew, without saying a word,
drew his bow, shot and struck the bird, and

(204)   killed it. (204) The seer and some others
were indignant and heaped curses upon him.
'Why so mad, you poor wretches?' he retorted;
and then, taking the bird in his hands,
continued, 'Pray, how could any sound information about our march be given by this
creature, which could not provide for its
own safety? Had it been gifted with divina-
tion, it would not have come to this spot,
for fear of being killed by an arrow of
Mosollamus the Jew.'"[52]

Pseudo-Hecataeus, On the Jews

FRAGMENT TWO (Josephus, Ag. Ap. 2.4, ¶ 42-43)

(42)   . . . Οὐ γὰρ ἀπορίᾳ γε τῶν οἰκησόντων τὴν   (42)
μετὰ σπουδῆς ὑπ' αὐτοῦ πόλιν κτιζομένην 'Αλέξαν-
δρος τῶν ἡμετέρων τινὰς ἐκεῖ συνήθροισεν, ἀλλὰ
πάντας δοκιμάζων ἐπιμελῶς ἀρετῆς καὶ πίστεως
5 τοῦτο τοῖς ἡμετέροις τὸ γέρας ἔδωκεν. (43) ἐτίμα   (43)
γὰρ ἡμῶν τὸ ἔθνος, ὡς καὶ φησιν 'Εκαταῖος περὶ
ἡμῶν, ὅτι διὰ τὴν ἐπιείκειαν καὶ πίστιν, ἣν αὐτῷ
παρέσχον 'Ιουδαῖοι, τὴν Σαμαρεῖτιν χώραν προσέ-
θηκεν ἔχειν αὐτοῖς ἀφορολόγητον.

L Lat.

4 ἀρετῆς καὶ πίστεως: *et virtute ac fide dignos inveniens*
Lat. |

Pseudo-Hecataeus, <u>On the Jews</u>

FRAGMENT TWO[53]

(42)   (42) ... For it was not lack of inhabitants to
people the city, whose foundation he had so much
at heart, that led Alexander to assemble in it a
colony of our nation.[54] This privilege he conferred
on our people, after careful and thorough scrutiny,

(43)   as a reward of valour and fidelity. (43) The
honour in which he held our nation may be illustrated
by the statement of Hecataeus that, in recognition
of the consideration and loyalty shown to him by
the Jews, he added to their territory the district
of Samaria free of tribute.[55]

Pseudo-Hecataeus, <u>On Abraham</u> (and the Egyptians ?)

FRAGMENT THREE   (Clement of Alexandria, <u>Stromata</u>
     5.14.112.4-113.1-2 = Eusebius, <u>P.E.</u> 13.13.40)

(112.4) Ναὶ μὴν καὶ ἡ τραγῳδία ἀπὸ τῶν εἰδώ- (4)
λων ἀποσπῶσα εἰς τὸν οὐρανὸν ἀναβλέπειν διδάσκει.

(113.1) ῾Ο μὲν Σοφοκλῆς, ὥς φησιν ῾Εκαταῖος (1)
ὁ τὰς ἱστορίας συνταξάμενος ἐν τῷ Κατ᾽ ῎Αβραμον
5 καὶ τοὺς Αἰγυπτίους, ἄντικρυς ἐπὶ τῆς σκηνῆς ἐκ-
βοᾷ·

(2) εἷς ταῖς ἀληθείαισιν, εἷς ἐστι<ν> θεός, (2)
ὃς οὐρανόν τε ἔτευξε καὶ γαῖαν μακρὴν
πόντου τε χαροπὸν οἶδμα καὶ ἀνέμων βίαν.
10 θνητοὶ δὲ πολλοὶ καρδίαν πλανώμενοι,
ἱδρυσάμεσθα πημάτων παραψυχὴν
θεῶν ἀγάλματα ἐκ λίθων, ἢ χαλκέων
ἢ χρυσοτεύκτων ἢ ἐλεφαντίνων τύπους·
θυσίας τε τούτοις καὶ κακὰς πανηγύρεις
15 στέφοντες, οὕτως εὐσεβεῖν νομίζομεν.

L
Clement of Alexandria, <u>Protrepticus</u> 7.74.2 (Stählin-Treu,
GCS 56, p. 56, lines 4-12); Pseudo-Justin, <u>De Monarchia</u> 2
(<u>PG</u> [6], col. 316 A-B); Pseudo-Justin, <u>Cohortatio ad</u>
<u>Graecos</u> 18 (<u>PG</u> [6], col. 273D - 276A); Eusebius, <u>P.E.</u> 13.
13.40 (Mras, <u>GCS</u> [43,2] 8.2, p. 214, line 17 - p. 215,
line 7); Cyril of Alexandria, <u>Contra Julianum</u> 1.32 (<u>PG</u>
[76], col. 549D); Theodoret, <u>Graecarum Affectionum Curatio</u>
7.46 (Raeder [Teubner], p. 193, lines 11-17).

3 μὲν: μὲν γὰρ Eus. | 4 Κατ᾽: κατὰ Eus. | ῎Αβραμον:
῎Αβραμον Eus. | 7 ἐστι: ἐστὶν Clem., <u>Protr.</u> Ps.-Justin,
<u>Mon.</u>, <u>Coh.</u> Eus. Cyr. Thdrt. | 8 τε ἔτευξε: τε ἔτευχε
Ps.-Justin, <u>Mon.</u> F et var. EC apud Denis, 162: τ᾽ ἔτευξε
Clem., <u>Protr.</u> Ps.-Justin, <u>Mon.</u> Eus. Cyr. Thdrt.: τέτευχε
Ps.-Justin, <u>Coh.</u> | μακρὴν: μακρὰν Ps.-Justin, <u>Mon.</u>, <u>Coh.</u>
Cyr. | 9 χαροπὸν Clem., <u>Protr.</u> Ps.-Justin, <u>Mon.</u>, <u>Coh.</u> Eus.
Cyr. Thdrt.: χαροποιὸν L | καὶ ἀνέμων: κἀνέμων Ps.-
Justin, <u>Mon.</u>, <u>Coh.</u> Cyr. Thdrt. | βίαν: βίας Clem., <u>Protr.</u>
Ps.-Justin, <u>Mon.</u>, <u>Coh.</u> Eus. Cyr. Thdrt.| 10 καρδίαν:
καρδίᾳ Clem., <u>Protr.</u> Ps.-Justin, <u>Coh.</u> Cyr.| 11 πημάτων:
πεμάτων Ps.-Justin, <u>Mon.</u> F apud Denis, 162: πεμμάτων Ps.-
Justin, <u>Coh.</u> F apud Denis, 162 | 11 παραψυχὴν:

cont. →

Pseudo-Hecataeus, <u>On Abraham (and the Egyptians ?)</u>
FRAGMENT THREE[56]

(4)   (112.4) Nay, indeed, Tragedy, in recoiling
from idols, teaches us to look up to heaven.

(1)   (113.1) In fact, as Hecataeus, the composer
of histories[57] reports in his book <u>According to</u>
<u>Abraham and the Egyptians</u>,[58] Sophocles exclaims
plainly on the stage:[59]

(2)   (2) One, in truth indeed, God is one,
             Who made both the heaven and the far-stretching
                  earth,
             The Deep's blue billow, and the might of winds.
             But as most mortals, having erred in heart,
             We have established, as solace for our woes,
             Images[60] of gods -- of stone, or of brass,
             Or statues wrought of gold or ivory;
             And to these, sacrifices and immoral festivals
             Appointing, we thus reckon ourselves religious.

παρὰ ψυχὴν L: παραψυχὰς Ps.-Justin, <u>Mon.</u> |
12 ἀγάλματα: ἀγάλματ' Clem., <u>Protr</u>. Ps.-Justin, <u>Mon</u>.,
<u>Coh</u>. Eus. Cyr. Thdrt. | λίϑων: λιϑίνων Clem., <u>Protr</u>.
P apud Stählin-Treu | ἢ χαλκέων: Clem., <u>Protr</u>. P apud
Stählin-Treu: τε καὶ ξύλων Ps.-Justin, <u>Coh</u>. |
13 ἐλεφαντίνων: 'λεφαντίνων Cyr. |

TESTIMONIA

Ep. Arist. 31 (= Josephus, Ant. 12.38; Eusebius, P.E.
    8.3.3)

(31) ... διὸ πόρρω γεγόνασιν οἵ τε συγγραφεῖς
καὶ ποιηταὶ καὶ τὸ τῶν ἱστορικῶν πλῆθος τῆς
ἐπιμνήσεως τῶν προειρημένων βιβλίων, καὶ τῶν
κατ’ αὐτὰ πεπολιτευμένων {καὶ πολιτευομένων }
5   ἀνδρῶν, διὰ τὸ ἀγνήν τινα καὶ σεμνὴν εἶναι τὴν
ἐν αὐτοῖς θεωρίαν, ὥς φησιν ῾Εκαταῖος ὁ ᾿Αβδηρί-
της.

Josephus, Ant. 1.7.2, par. 158-59 (cf. Clement of
    Alexandria, Strom. 5.14.113.1-2; Eusebius,
    P.E. 9.16.3; also 13.13.40)

(158) Μνημονεύει δὲ τοῦ πατρὸς ἡμῶν ᾿Αβράμου
Βηρωσσός ... (159) ῾Εκαταῖος δὲ καὶ τοῦ μνησ-
10 θῆναι πλεῖον τι πεποίηκε· βιβλίον γὰρ περὶ
αὐτοῦ συνταξάμενος κατέλιπε.

Josephus, Ag.Ap. 1.23, par. 213-14

(213) ῞Οτι δὲ οὐκ ἀγνοοῦντες ἔνιοι τῶν συγγραφέων τὸ ἔθνος ἡμῶν, ἀλλ’ ὑπὸ φθόνου τινὸς ἢ δι’
ἄλλας αἰτίας οὐχ ὑγιεῖς τὴν μνήμην παρέλιπον,
15 τεκμήριον οἶμαι παρέξειν. ῾Ιερώνυμος γὰρ ὁ τὴν
περὶ τῶν διαδόχων ἱστορίαν συγγεγραφὼς κατὰ τὸν
αὐτὸν μὲν ἦν ῾Εκαταίῳ χρόνον, φίλος δ’ ὢν ᾿Αντι-
γόνου τοῦ βασιλέως τὴν Συρίαν ἐπετρόπευεν. (214)
ἀλλ’ ὅμως ῾Εκαταῖος μὲν καὶ βιβλίον ἔγραψε περὶ
20 ἡμῶν, ῾Ιερώνυμος δ’ οὐδαμοῦ κατὰ τὴν ἱστορίαν
ἐμνημόνευσε, καίτοι σχεδὸν ἐν τοῖς τόποις δια-
τετριφώς. τοσοῦτον αἱ προαιρέσεις τῶν ἀνθρώπων
διήνεγκαν· τῷ μὲν γὰρ ἐδόξαμεν καὶ σπουδαίας
εἶναι μνήμης ἄξιοι, τῷ δὲ πρὸς τὴν ἀλήθειαν πάν-
25 τως τι πάθος οὐκ εὔγνωμον ἐπεσκότησεν.

Ep. Arist. 31[61]

(31)   ... It is for this reason that authors and
poets and the mass of historians have abstained from
mentioning these aforesaid books, and the men who
have lived and are living in accordance with them,
because the views set forth in them have a certain
holiness and sanctity, as Hecataeus of Abdera says.

Josephus, Ant. 1.58-59

(158)   And Berossus also mentions our father
Abraham ...   (159)   But Hecataeus does more than
merely mention him; indeed, he has left an entire
book written about him.

Josephus, Ag.Ap. 1.213-14[62]

(213)   That the omission of some historians to mention
our nation was due, not to ignorance, but to envy or
some other disingenuous reason, I think I am in a
position to prove.   Hieronymus, who wrote the history
of Alexander's successors, was a contemporary of
Hecataeus, and, owing to his friendship with King
Antigonus, became governor of Syria.   (214)   Yet,
whereas Hecataeus devoted a whole book to us, Hieronymus, although he had lived almost within our borders,
has nowhere mentioned us in his history.   So widely
different were the views of these two men.   One
thought us deserving of serious notice; the eyes of
the other, through an ill-natured disposition, were
totally blind to the truth.

Origen, <u>Contra Celsum</u> 1.15

(15)   καὶ ῾Εκαταίου δὲ τοῦ ἱστορικοῦ φέρεται περὶ
῾Ιουδαίων   βιβλίον,   ἐν ᾧ προστίθεται   μᾶλλόν πως
ὡς   σοφῷ τῷ ἔθνει ἐπὶ τοσοῦτον,   ὡς καὶ ῾Ερέννιον
Φίλωνα ἐν τῷ περὶ ῾Ιουδαίων συγγράμματι πρῶτον
5   μὲν ἀμφιβάλλειν, εἰ   τοῦ   ἱστορικοῦ   ἔστι τὸ σύγ-
γραμμα· δεύτερον δὲ λέγειν ὅτι, εἴπερ ἐστὶν αὐτοῦ,
εἰκὸς αὐτὸν συνηρπάσθαι ἀπὸ τῆς παρὰ ῾Ιουδαίοις
πιθανότητος καὶ συγκατατεθεῖσθαι αὐτῶν τῷ λόγῳ.

Origen, <u>Contra</u> <u>Celsum</u> 1.15 [63]

(15) Moreover, a book about the Jews is attributed
to Hecataeus the historian, in which the wisdom of
the nation is emphasized even more strongly -- so
much so that Herennius Philo in his treatise about
the Jews even doubts in the first place whether it
is a genuine work of the historian, and says in
the second place that if it is authentic, he had
probably been carried away by the Jews' powers of
persuasion and accepted their doctrine.

ANNOTATIONS

1. In Ag.Ap. 1.161-218, after having cited Egyptian,
Phoenician, and Chaldean witnesses attesting the antiquity
of the Jews, Josephus gives several examples of favorable
testimony by Greek authors, including Pythagoras, Theo-
prhastus, Herodotus, Choerilus, Clearchus and Agatharchides.
This fragment, attributed to Hecataeus of Abdera (4th -
3rd cent. B.C.E.), occurs between the testimony of Clearchus and Agatharchides.   The translation is that of H. St.
J. Thackeray, Against Apion (LCL; Cambridge, Mass.: Harvard
University Press/London: Heinemann, 1961) 1.236-46.

2. Cf. Ag.Ap. 1.161; also Ant. 1.108, where Josephus
includes Hecataeus among οἱ παρ' Ἕλλησι καὶ βαρβάροις
συγγραφάμενοι τὰς ἀρχαιολογίας. Similarly, included in
Ag.Ap. 1.215 among τοσοῦτοι τῶν Ἑλλήνων συγγραφεῖς.
His pagan status is elsewhere assumed by Josephus. Cf.
Ant. 1.159; 12.38; Ag.Ap. 1.213-14; 2.43. Also, by Clement
of Alexandria, Strom. 5.14.113.1-2, and Eusebius, P.E.
8.3.3; 9.4.1; 16.3; 13.13.40.   Note also that Ag.Ap. 1.
183b = Eusebius, P.E. 9.4.1: Ἑκαταῖος δὲ ὁ Ἀβδηρίτης,
ἀνὴρ φιλόσοφος ἅμα καὶ περὶ τὰς πράξεις ἱκανώτατος, ἰδίαν
βίβλον ἀναθεὶς τῇ περὶ Ἰουδαίων ἱστορίᾳ, πλεῖστα περὶ
αὐτῶν διέξεισιν, ἀφ' ὧν ἐπὶ τοῦ παρόντος ἀρκέσει παρα-
τεθέντα ταῦτα.

3. Cf. Suda-Life (p. 417 West): Ἑκαταῖος Ἀβδηρίτης,
φιλόσοφος ὃς ἐπεκλήθη καὶ κριτικὸς γραμματικός, οἷα
γραμματικὴν ἔχων παρασκευήν.   Cf. Diogenes Laertius 9.69;
Diodorus Siculus 1.46.8.

4. I.e., Ptolemy I Soter, satrap of Egypt (323-305 B.C.E.)
and king (305-283 B.C.E.).

5. Thus, to be distinguished from the excursus on the Jews
in his On the Egyptians apud Diodorus Siculus 40.3.1-8.
That it was a separate work devoted entirely to the Jews
is also stated in Ag.Ap. 1.214(cf. Greek text, p. 320);
also Origen, C. Cel. 1.15 (cf. Greek text, p. 322); cf.
also Eusebius, P.E. 9.4.1 (Greek text in note 2 above).
On the relationship of this work   to   On Abraham, also
attributed to Hecataeus in Ant. 1.159; Clement, Strom.
5.14.113.1-2, cf. Introduction.   Whether Περὶ Ἰουδαίων
was a technical title is problematic; still, the work is
generally designated On the Jews.

6. What follows are excerpts from the work, with breaks
clearly signalled, e.g. πάλιν (186, 190), εἶτα ... πάλιν
(190), ἔτι γε (193, 200), ἀλλὰ μὴν (196). In spite of the
breaks, the excerpts may preserve, or at least point to
the skeletal structure of the larger work.   Jacoby, FGrH
3a.66-67 notes the "eyewitness" flavor of the sections at
the beginning and end (186-89 and 200-204), whereas the
internal sections (190-99) exhibit the features and

interests typical of ethnographic works. The actual
content consists of the following topics (κεφάλαια):
κατοίκησις καὶ πολιτεία (189), πῶς ἔχομεν πρὸς τοὺς
νόμους--τεκμήρια τῆς ἰσχυρογνωμοσυνης τῆς περὶ τῶν
νόμων (190-93), πολυανθρωπία (194), τὸ μέγεθος καὶ
τὸ κάλλος τῆς χώρας (195), Ἱεροσόλυμα (197), the
temple and the cult (βωμός κ.τ.λ., 198-99), μαντεία ?
(200-204).   Cf. Jacoby, FGrH 3a.67; Conzelmann, HJC,
170.

7. I.e., Castor of Rhodes, 1st cent.-B.C.E. rhetorician
and author of Χρόνικα. Cf. FGrH 2B, No. 250, Frg. 12.
Also, Kubitschek, "Kastor von Rhodos (8)," PW 10 (1919)
cols. 2347-57; Schmid-Stählin, Geschichte, 2,1.398.
Cf. Ag.Ap. 2.84.

8. The Olympiads began with the year 776 B.C.E. Thus,
776 - (116 X 4) = 312 B.C.E. + 11 =   323 B.C.E. for the
death of Alexander the Great.

9. Thus, a response to pagan charges of the "late origin
of our constitution" (Ag.Ap. 1.58-59; also 1.2). On the
use of chronology in establishing antiquity, cf.
Wacholder, "Biblical Chronology."

10. This flattering portrait of Ptolemy I Soter contrasts
markedly with Ep. Arist. 12-13, where his actions in the
Syrian campaign are depicted as severely harsh (φόβῳ πάντα
ὑποχείρια ποιούμενος). Also, in Josephus, Ant. 12.3-10 his
hostility is stressed (3-4), though in a statement reminiscent of Pseudo-Hecataeus, Josephus says that the subju-
gated Jews were attracted to Egypt because of his "liber-
ality" (φιλοτιμία, 9; cf. LCL 2.6-7, n. b). Similarly,
Agatharchides, apud Ag.Ap. 1.209-11, describes him as
δεσπότης πικρός. For a more positive assessment of his
character, cf. Diodorus Siculus 18.14.1; 19.55.5; 86.3.
Cf. Stern, GLAJJ, 40; Hadas, Aristeas, 98-99; APOT, 2.95,
n. 12; Jacoby, FGrH 3a.69-70. It should also be noted
that the Jews' emigration is here depicted as voluntary
whereas in Ep. Arist. 12-13 it is a forced resettlement.

11. The existence of this Jewish chief priest Ezechias,
who is not mentioned in the standard lists of high priests
(1 Chr. 6:16-30; 50-53; Josephus, Ant. 10.151-53; 20.224-
51; cf. however, J.W. 2.429; also Willrich, Juden und
Griechen, 107-15) or in other literary sources, was for
a long time doubted. So, Müller, gegen Apion, 172; Willrich, Juden und Griechen, 31-32, who saw in Ezechias "only
a mask for the high priest Onias;" Jacoby, FGrH 3a.62;
Lewy, 122. However, the discovery at Beth-Zur of a
Philisto-Arabian coin dated in the early Hellenistic
period bearing the Hebrew names יהו and יחקיה has
reopened the question. Cf. Sellers, Citadel, 73-74;
Olmstead, 243-44; Gager, "Pseudo-Hecataeus," 138-39. This
numismatic evidence has not only convinced some scholars

11. (cont.) that Ezechias was an historical figure, but
has enhanced the credibility of Pseudo-Hecataeus' account
of the Jews' resettlement of Egypt. Cf. esp. Olmstead,
244: "With this unexpected proof that Hecataeus knew more
than his critics, we are constrained to accept his other
statements, that Jewish soldiers were taken to Egypt by
Ptolemy I, given some sort of modified citizenship, and
granted lands under military tenure." For Gager, "Pseudo-
Hecataeus," 138-39, the numismatic evidence is decisive
enough to reinforce Lewy's contention that the excerpts
in Ag.Ap. 1.183-204 attributed to Hecataeus of Abdera
are genuine. Cf. Stern, GLAJJ, 40-41, n. on 187;
Wacholder, Eupolemus, 268; LaFargue-Collins, 9-11;
Tcherikover, 425-26, n. 46; Walter, JS (1,2) 146, n. 15.

12.   ἀρχιερεύς, without the article, need not refer to
"the high priest" (cf. Ag.Ap., LCL, 238, n. a). Stern,
GLAJJ, 40, n. on 187: "We know that, at least in the last
generations of the Second Temple, the terms ἀρχιερεύς
and ἀρχιερεῖς were used loosely to denote different mem-
bers of the high priestly oligarchy and the chief digni-
taries of the Temple of Jerusalem. In any case, the
titles were not confined to actual high priests or ex-
high priests." Besides the literature cited in Stern, cf.
Schrenck, TDNT 3 (1965) 221-83, esp. 265-82.

13. This reference to the Jewish priests' reception of
tithes from the populace has figured centrally in the
authenticity debate. Schaller, "Hekataios," 22-26, regards
the practice described here as unquestionably anachronistic, on the grounds that it became common only during the
Hasmonean period. Prior to this time, the established
practice, dating at least to the period of the exile, was
rather that the tithes were given to the Levites, who in
turn gave a tenth of their proceeds to the priests. So,
Num 18:21, 24; 2 Chr 31:2-10; Neh 10:38-39; 12:44; 13:5,
10. After the Maccabean revolt, however, the situation
was different. Cf. Ant. 20.206; also 181; Life 80, also
63; Ant. 4.68, 205; Heb 7:5; Philo, Virt. 95, though cf.
Spec. Leg. 1.156. Thus, the earlier period, i.e. the
4th-3rd cent. B.C.E., represented by Neh 10:38-39 and
Tobit 1:7, is sharply contrasted with the later period,
i.e. the mid-second century B.C.E., represented by Jub.
32:15 and Jdt 11:13. Schaller's analysis cannot be
easily dismissed, as does Gager, "Pseudo-Hecataeus," 137-
38, by noting that a pagan author is unlikely to have
distinguished between priests and Levites. After all,
his point is that the practice itself described in the
fragment is demonstrably late, and that a Jewish forger,
in an incidental remark, betrays his actual historical
setting. So, Walter, JS (1,2) 148. Cf. full discussion in
Stern, GLAJJ, 41-42, n. on 188.

14.   According to Stern, GLAJJ, 42, n. on 188, the
number 1,500 for all the priests in the whole country
is too small. Cf. Ezra 2:36-9(4,280); Neh 11:10-36 (1,192
priests in Jerusalem); 1 Chr 9:13 (1,760); Ep. Arist. 95
(700 priests in the temple service); Josephus, Ag.Ap.
2.108 (20,000).   On their role as "administering public
affairs" (τὰ κοινὰ διοικοῦσι), cf. Hecataeus apud Diodorus
Siculus 40.3.4-5.

15.   Perhaps the high priesthood, or some other distinction
granted him by Ptolemy I. So, Reinach, Contre Apion, 36,
n. 3.

16.   Note the first person plural, an indication of the
eyewitness posture adopted by Pseudo-Hecataeus, obviously
serving to enhance the credibility of his report. Also,
cf. par. 194 (ἡμῶν), 200 (οἷς δ' αὐτὸς παρατυχεῖν φησιν
κ.τ.λ.), 201 (ἐμοῦ).

17.   The meaning is unclear, and is probably due to a
textual corruption. Literally, "having gathered some of
his associates, read to them every advantage (τὴν
διαφοράν ... πᾶσαν). Lewy, "Hekataios," 123, emends the
text to διφθέρα, "book," thus "he read to them the entire
(Torah) scroll." Similar cases of confusion between
διαφορά and διφθέρα: Ep. Arist. 176; Galen 17.1; 18.2,
cited by Lewy, 123, n. 3. Given the description in Hecataeus apud Diodorus Siculus 40.3.3: καὶ τὰ κατὰ τὴν πολιτείαν ἐνομοθέτησε τε καὶ διέταξε, Lewy's emendation appears more defensible. Reinach, Contre Apion, 36, n. 4,
refers to J. Février, La date, la composition et les
sources de la lettre d'Aristée, 70, who suggests that
διαφοράν was a rare word meaning "book," i.e. Pentateuch.
Cf. Willrich, Judaica, 91; Wendland, Review of Willrich,
1200; Engers, 236; Jacoby, FGrH 3a.71; Stern, GLAJJ, 42,
n. on 189, and additional literature; Conzelmann, HJC,
169-70, who states the various options.

18.   On the civic rights of Alexandrian Jews as bestowed
by Alexander and Ptolemy I Soter, and evidenced in docu-
mentary form, cf. Josephus, J.W. 2.487-88; Ant. 12.8;
Ag.Ap. 2.35-37.   The existence of such documents is also
mentioned in Claudius' edict, apud Ant. 19.278-81 (on
which cf. extended discussion in Feldman, LCL 9.343-51):
ἐπιγνοὺς ἀνέκαθεν τοὺς ἐν ᾿Αλεξανδρείᾳ ᾿Ιουδαίους ᾿Αλεξ-
ανδρεῖς λεγομένους συγκατοικισθέντας τοῖς πρώτοις εὐθὺ
καιροῖς ᾿Αλεξανδρεῦσι καὶ ἴσης πολιτείας παρὰ τῶν βασιλέων τετευχότας, καθὼς φανερὸν ἐγένετο ἐκ τῶν γραμμάτων
τῶν παρ' αὐτοῖς καὶ τῶν διαταγμάτων ...   On the vast
literature on the question of Jewish Alexandrian citizenship, cf. Josephus, LCL 9.583-5; also Smallwood, Jews,
224-55, esp. 225, n. 22 on Hecataeus; also 229, n. 40;
also, cf. Tcherikover, CPJ 7, n. 18.   If, as Jacoby, FGrH
3a.67 suggests, κατοίκησις καὶ πολιτεία served as a major
division (κεφάλαια) in Pseudo-Hecataeus' work, it is
even more likely to have been a standard apologetic topos.

19. The language used here (and in par. 191) is remarkably similar to that of the Maccabean period: 1 Macc 2:
42 (πᾶς ὁ ἐκουσιαζόμενος τῷ νόμῳ); 2:50 (ζηλώσατε τῷ
νόμῳ καὶ δότε τὰς ψυχὰς ὑμῶν ὑπὲρ διαθήκης πατέρων ἡμῶν);
2 Macc 6:1-31, esp. 28 (καὶ γενναίως ὑπὲρ τῶν σεμνῶν καὶ
ἁγίων νόμων ἀπευθανατίζειν); 7:2 (ἕτοιμοι γὰρ ἀποθνήσκειν
ἐσμὲν ἢ παραβαίνειν τοὺς πατρίους νόμους); 7:11 (καὶ διὰ
τοὺς αὐτοῦ νόμους ὑπερορῶ ταῦτα); 7:37 (ἐγὼ δὲ ... καὶ
σῶμα καὶ ψυχὴν προδίδωμι περὶ τῶν πατρίων νόμων); cf.
also 7:30; also cf. Dan 6:6 (εἰ μὴ ἐν νομίμοις θεοῦ αὐτοῦ).
Consequently, in the debate concerning the authenticity of
the fragments, the passage has been adduced as another
historical anachronism. E.g., Willrich, Juden und Griechen,
21; Judaica, 92-94; Jacoby, FGrH 3a.62,72. In response,
those favoring authenticity (Lewy, 124-25; Stern, GLAJJ,
42, n. on 191), or at least a much earlier dating (e.g.,
Wacholder, Eupolemus, 268-69) argue for the probability
of Persian excesses, even in the absence of hard evidence. Cf. Ant. 11. 297-301; Esth 3:8; Ant. 12.45; Sib.
Or. 3.599; 5.93-109; Ep. Arist. 13. On fidelity to
the ancestral laws as an apologetic motif, cf. Josephus,
Ag.Ap. 2.232-35, 271-80.

20. This is perhaps a reference to actions taken against
the Jews by Bagoses, a general under Artaxerxes II Mnemon
(404-359 B.C.E.), or Artaxerxes III Ochus (359-338 B.C.E.)
as reported in Ant. 11.297-303. The text, however, is
disputed. Cf. Marcus's note in LCL 6.456-61, and his
discussion in Appendix B, 498-511. Also, cf. Dan 6:7
οἱ τακτικοὶ καὶ οἱ σατράπαι; also 6:9, 13, 16.

21. γεγυμνωμένως: on adverbs formed from participles,
cf. Blass-Debrunner-Funk, Greek Grammar, par. 102 (6);
Ant. 18.22; 1 Clem. 37; 1 Tim 3:16. Cf. Müller, gegen
Apion, 173. Also, cf. 4 Macc 6:2; 9:11.

22. On repudiating the ancestral faith, cf. 4 Macc 8:7
(ἀρχὰς ἐπὶ τῶν ἐμῶν πραγμάτων ἡγεμονικὰς λήμψεσθε ἀρνησά-
μενοι τὸν πάτριον ὑμῶν τῆς πολιτείας θεσμόν); also in
general 4 Macc 8-12, esp. 9:1, 29; also 2 Macc 7:2;
1 Macc 2:19-21.

23. ἡ ἰσχυρογνωμοσύνη ... περὶ τῶν νόμων: probably
one of the main divisions of the work. So, Jacoby, FGrH
3a.67-68, who also notes that "law" in Pseudo-Hecataeus
is much more sharply defined than in Hecataeus apud
Diodorus Siculus 40.3. Radical monotheism appears to
be the crucial issue in Pseudo-Hecataeus (cf. Frg. 3),
i.e. the "cult of the one God." So, also Conzelmann, HJC,
170, n. 165. This also points to a date during the
2nd cent. B.C.E. when the issue of fidelity was more
sharply defined. On ἰσχυρογνωμοσύνη, cf. Philo, Som.
1.218.

24. On Alexander's rebuilding the temple of Bel, cf. Arrian, An. 7.171; Strabo 16.1.5 [C 738]. On his tolerance for the ancestral customs (τὰ πάτρια) of his subjects, cf. Strabo 15.1.63 [C 715]; Curtius Rufus 4.7.5. Cf. LaFargue-Collins, 15-16; Stern, GLAJJ, 42-43, n. on 192; Müller, gegen Apion, 173. Also, cf. Ant. 13.250-51. On ἱερὸν ἀνακαθᾶραι, cf. 1 Macc 4:36.

25. The historical basis, if any, for this incident is unclear, but the razing of pagan altars also fits well into a Maccabean setting. Cf. 1 Macc 2:25, 45; 5:44, 68; 11:84; 13:47-48; 2 Macc 10:1-2. As to Hecataeus' express-ing admiration for their deeds, cf. 1 Macc 5:63-64.

26. The populousness of the Jews is remarkable to Heca-taeus apud Diodorus Siculus 40.3.8, and subsequently be-comes a standard topos. Cf. Stern, GLAJJ, No. 11, par. 8. On the populousness of the Jews, cf. Philo, Leg. ad Gaium 281-84; Flacc. 45-47; Josephus, J.W. 2.398-99; 7:43; Ag.Ap. 2.282; Strabo 16.2.28 apud Josephus, Ant. 14.114-18; Sib. Or. 3.271; also 1 Macc 15:15-24. On their numbers in Palestine (Josephus, J.W. 2.280; 3.41-43; 5.248-50; 6.40, 420-34; Life 233-35); Syria and Asia (Philo, Leg. ad Gaium 245; Josephus, J.W. 7.43); Egypt (Philo, Leg. ad Gaium 214-15; Flacc. 43; V. Mos. 2.27); Rome (Josephus, J.W. 2.80; Ant. 17.299-300; 18.81-83); Cyrene (Josephus, J.W. 7.445). On population estimates for the Hellenistic-Roman period, cf. Safrai and Stern, Jewish People, 1.119-22; and standard treatments in Juster, 1. 210; Harnack, Mission and Expansion, 1-9; Baron, History, 1.170-71. Also, cf. Tacitus, His. 5.5. Cf. Jacoby, FGrH 3a.67-68; Conzelmann, HJC, 170, esp. n. 168 and 170.

27. "Persians," rather than Chaldeans, is commonly re-garded as Pseudo-Hecataeus' error. Müller, gegen Apion, 175, sees this as a slip, understandable for a pagan, and thus proof of the authenticity of the fragments. However, cf. 2 Macc 1:19 where the Babylonian captivity is said to be εἰς τὴν Περσικήν. Cf. Reinach, Contre Apion, 36, n. 2. Similar confusion between Persians and Assyrians occurs in Propertius 3.11.21. On the resettle-ment of captives by the Persians, cf. Herodotus 4.204; 5.16; 6.9, 32, 119.

28. On the Jews' settlement in Egypt, cf. Ant. 19.278-85; J.W. 2.487; in Syria, Ant. 12.119-24. On the "myriads" of deportees and migrants: after the fall of Jerusalem in 597 B.C.E., the number of captives deported to Babylon is variously given:10,000 (2 Kgs 24:14; cf. v. 16); 3,023 (Jer 52:28). After the destruction of the temple in 587 B.C.E. (cf. 2 Kgs 24:18-25:21; 2 Chr 36:11-21; Jer 39:1-10; 52:1-34), 832 captives are mentioned in Jer 52:29. After the overthrow of Babylon by Cyrus in 538 B.C.E., and the decree to return (Ezra 1:1-4; cf.

28. (cont.) 6:1-5; Neh 7:6-73), the number of returnees
given in Ezra 2:64-65 and Neh 7:66 is 42,360, less 7,337
slaves. Ep. Arist. 12-13 reports that 100,000 Jewish
slaves were transported from Judaea to Egypt by Ptolemy
I Soter, 30,000 of which were garrisoned. Cf. 1 Macc
5:20; 12:41. On the deportation of Jews by Artaxerxes
III Ochus, cf. Eusebius, Chronicle (ed. Schöne), 2.112;
Orosius 3.7.6; Syncellus (ed. Dindorf) 1.486, which
refer to their removal to Hyrcania on the Caspian Sea.
So, Stern, GLAJJ, 43, n. on 194. On military resettlement
as a chief cause of the Diaspora, cf. Safrai and Stern,
Jewish People, 1.117.

29. τὸ μέγεθος τῆς χώρας ... τὸ κάλλος probably marks
the beginning of the geographical section of the work
(cf. Fraser, Ptolemaic Alexandria, 1.497). Cf. Diodorus
Siculus 1.30-41, esp. 1.30.1 which opens by describing
the extent and beauty of the landscape (κεῖται ... κατὰ
μεσημβρίαν ... κάλλει). Cf. also Ep. Arist. 83-120 for
a utopian description of Judaea, Jerusalem and the temple,
on which cf. Hadas, Aristeas, 49-50, and ad loc.

30. I.e., approximately 2,400 square miles which, according to Wacholder, Eupolemus, 271, was a "fair estimate of
Judaea's area." An aroura was a section of land measuring
100 Egyptian cubits (52.5 meters) square, i.e., ca. 2750
square meters. Cf. Herodotus 2.168. Cf. Hadas, Aristeas,
147, n. on 116; IDB 4.838; Thackeray, Ag.Ap. 1.86 (LCL,
197, note c); LaFargue-Collins, 17. An area 20 times (!)
as large is given in Ep. Arist. 116: "originally the
country comprised no less than sixty million arourae"
(ἑξακισχιλίων μυριάδων ἀρουρῶν), though Hadas, Aristeas,
147, translates "six million aroura."

31. The reading of L: πλῆθος, "extent," is preferred to
Hudson's πλάτος, "width," though Josephus earlier (Ag.Ap.
1.86) takes the aroura as a measure of width. Cf. LCL,
197, note e.

32. A comparison of Pseudo-Hecataeus' description of
Judaea, Jerusalem, etc. in par. 197-99 with the mythical
portrait of the land of Hiera in Diodorus Siculus 5.42-46,
as noted by Lewy, 127, is especially illuminating. Among
the common motifs: the antiquity of the temple (5.42.6),
although Josephus notes the antiquity of the city (Ag.Ap.
1.196, the splendor and beautiful setting of the temple
(5.42.6), the materials of its construction (5.44.1-5),
its dimensions (5.44.1-5), the presence of statues and
votive offerings (5.44.1), and gardens (5.42.6). Also,
cf. the description of Babylon and the temple of Bel in
Diodorus Siculus 2.7.2-10.6.

33. ἐκ παλαιοτάτου κατοικοῦμεν: another echo of the
antiquity topos, perhaps apologetically motivated. Cf.
Acts 15:21.

34.   At this point, Eusebius, P.E. 9.4.2-9 begins excerpt-
ing Hecataeus from Josephus. This fragment, attributed
by Eusebius to the pagan Hecataeus, is one of a series
of testimonies by "illustrious Greek authors" who mentioned the Jews. It occurs in Eusebius after a fragment
from Porphyry about the Essenes and precedes a fragment
from Clearchus. Both it and the Clearchus fragment
appear to have been taken directly from Josephus, Ag.Ap.

35.   Josephus, Life, 235: 204 cities and villages in
Galilee. Reinach, Contre Apion, 37, n. 4, regards the
reference to "fortresses" as anachronistic. Cf. 1 Macc
9:50-53.

36.   I.e., slightly less than six miles, assuming that a
stade was 200 yards. Cf. IDB 4.838. This is larger than
other estimates of the city's circumference: 40 stades
(Timochares, apud P.E. 9.35.1 = FGrH 2B, No. 165, Frg. 1
= Stern, GLAJJ, No. 41; Ep. Arist. 105); 33 stades (Josephus, J.W. 5.159, ca. 70 C.E.; 39 furlongs in J.W.
5.508); 27 stades ("The Metrical Survey of Syria," apud
Eusebius, P.E. 9.36.1 = FGrH 3C.935, No. 849, Frg. 1 =
Stern, GLAJJ, 137-8, No. 42). Cf. Thackeray, Ag.Ap.,
LCL, 242, note c; Giff., 4.321; Stern, GLAJJ, 43, n. on
197, noting Avi-Yonah's estimate of the circumference of
the First Wall as ca. 3,800 meters, and that of the city
after the building of the Third Wall as 5,500 meters.
Cf. Rev 21:16.

37.   The number appears high. Jeremias, Jerusalem, 27, 84,
252, calculates the population of Jerusalem in the time
of Jesus as ca. 25-30,000 (though, p. 83: 55,000). Cf. J.
Jeremias, "Die Einwohnerzahl Jerusalems zur Zeit Jesu,"
ZDPV 66 (1943) 24-31, repr. in Abba (Göttingen: Vandenhoeck & Ruprecht, 1966) 335-41. Cf. Lam. Rab. 1.2 on
1.1 [Soncino 70-71]: nine and one-half billion (!), apud
Jeremias, Jerusalem, 83, n. 24. Josephus, J.W. 6.423-27:
2,700,000 participants in the Passover feast (!).

38.   Pseudo-Hecataeus' location of the temple in the
center of the city has figured in the authenticity debate.
According to Lewy, 128, 131, this is one of several indications that the author was ill-informed on Jewish matters,
hence likely a pagan writing from a distance. Followed
by Gager, "Pseudo-Hecataeus," 135. Walter, JS (1,2) 156,
n. 198a, suggests that the author does not know Jerusalem
from his own observation. Note, however, that he says
"nearly" (μάλιστα) in the center. Cf. Wacholder, Eupolemus,
270, n. 47.

39.   I.e., approximately 500 feet long and 150 feet wide,
assuming the plethron was ca. 100 feet (Cf. OCD^2, 659) and
the cubit was ca. 1½ feet (cf. IDB 4.837), thus considerably larger than the description in Ezra 6:3: "height 60
cubits ... breadth 60 cubits." Cf. Ep. Arist. 84: the three
walls enclosing the temple were ca. 70 cubits high.

40. The dimensions of the altar of burnt offering given
here (20 X 20 X 10) conform to those of the bronze altar
in 2 Chr 4:1. Cf. Eupolemus, Frg. 2B, par. 34.10:
25 X 20 X 12. On the construction from "unhewn stones,"
cf. Exod 20:25; Deut 27:6; 1 Macc 4:47; Philo, Spec. Leg.
1.274; Josephus, Ant. 4.200.

41. The language used of the temple (οἴκημα μέγα) and
its furnishings (βωμός) is remarkably unlike the usual
language of the LXX: ναός, οἶκος, ἱερόν and θυσιαστήριον; also cf. Ep. Arist. 87. Cf. 2 Chr 6. λυχνίον is
closer. This probably suggests Pseudo-Hecataeus' un-
familiarity with the Greek Bible. The amount of gold
here surpasses the biblical prescription of one talent
for the construction of the lampstand (cf. Exod 25:39),
though modest compared with Eupolemus, Frg. 2B, par. 34.7:
10 golden lampstands weighing 10 talents each. Cf.
1 Macc 1:21-23 for a more detailed inventory of the temple
contents; also Josephus, J.W. 1.152-53. Also, cf. 1 Kgs
7:48-50.

42. Cf. Exod 27:20; Lev 24:1-3.

43. Noting the absence of images is reminiscent of
Hecataeus apud Diodorus Siculus 40.3.4; cf. Diogenes
Laertius 1.10. Here, Pseudo-Hecataeus effectively feigns
the perspective of a pagan author for whom these would
have been especially conspicuous differences. Cf. Lewy,
126-27. On the other hand, they are precisely the
differences a discerning Jewish apologist would point out.
On the description of the sacred precinct of Apollo, cf.
Hecataeus, apud Diodorus Siculus 2.47.2-3; also Aelian,
NA 11.10. All of these items are standard features in
descriptions of pagan temples, real and mythical. Cf.,
e.g., Diodorus Siculus 2.7.2-10.6; 5.42-46. On the
prohibition of plants near the altar, cf. Deut 16:21;
cf. Philo, Spec. Leg. 1.74-75. Cf. also the polemic
against images in Pseudo-Hecataeus, Frg. 3.

44. On priestly abstinence from wine, cf. Lev 10:9-10;
Ezek 44:21; Josephus, J.W. 5.229; Ant. 3.279; Philo,
Spec. Leg. 1.98-100. Also, in pagan traditions, Plutarch,
De Is. et Osir. 353B; Diodorus Siculus 1.70.11; Iamblichus,
Pythag. 97-98. Cf. Lewy, 127.

45. The translation here follows the Latin textual
tradition of Josephus in reading συνεστρατεύσαντο   (also
BIO in P.E.; N reads -σατο), rather than -ομεν, as in L
of the Josephus MS tradition. The latter is preferred by
Walter (or, perhaps -σαμεν), who translates accordingly:
"dass wir ..." ἔτι γε μήν marks another break.

46.   Cf. Josephus, Ant. 11.339; also 11.321-45.   There is
reason to suspect Pseudo-Hecataeus' claim that Jews served
as mercenaries under Alexander, since this is elsewhere
one of the bases Josephus uses to argue for their
Alexandrian citizenship. Cf. Ag.Ap. 2.35, 42, 71-72;
J.W. 2.487-88. Thus, Tcherikover, Hellenistic Civilization,
272-73, doubts it. Reinach, Contre Apion, 38, n. 7:
"Mensonge évident." Hengel, Judaism and Hellenism, 1.15,
however, regards it as likely. That they served under
the Diadochi seems certain. Cf. Ep. Arist. 13, 36;
CPJ, Nos. 18-32; also Josephus, Ant. 12.149; 2 Macc 8:20;
cf. 1 Macc 10:36-37. On Jewish mercenaries, cf. Tcherikover, CPJ, 1.11-15, who treats the well-known case of
the Jewish garrison at Elephantine, ca. 6th cent. B.C.E.
Also, Hengel, Judaism and Hellenism, 1.15-18; cf. also
Stern, GLAJJ, 43, n. on 200.

47.   On the "eyewitness" perspective of the author, cf.
above, note 16.

48.   According to Jacoby, FGrH 3a.66, 74, this anecdote
probably did not occur in the section on the land and
people, but belongs to a separate section containing a
miscellaneous collection of stories.

49.   Niese conjectures Ἰουδαῖος for Ἰουδαίων, i.e.
"a Jew whose name was Mosollamus." Followed by Walter,
JS (1,2) 156. On Jewish cavalrymen, cf. 2 Macc 12:35;
1 Macc 16:4. References in Stern, GLAJJ, 43, n. on 201.

50.   The Greek transliterated form of משולם. Cf. 2 Kgs
22:3; 2 Chr 34:12; Ezra 10:29; Neh 3:4; also 1 Esdr 8:44;
9:14. Also, Josephus, Ant. 13.75 (Μεσσάλαμος). Note v.l.
in P.E.: BION Μοσόμαμος. References in Stern, GLAJJ,
43, n. on 201.

51.   The scene depicted here has an air of verisimilitude
given the well-established pagan practice of augury,
especially in military matters. Cf. Homer, Il. 12.195-
250, esp. 238; also 1.68-84; Sophocles, Ant. 998-1011;
Xenophon, An. 6.1.17-24. Cf. Josephus, Ant. 18.195; 19.
346.   The pagan critique of the practice was also well-
established. Cf. Vergil, Aen. 9.327; Cicero, Div. 2.33.
70-41.85; and in general Plutarch, Superstit. = Moralia
164E - 171F, on which cf. S. Dill, Roman Society from
Nero to Marcus Aurelius (New York: Meridian, 1964)
443-83; also M. P. Nilsson, Greek Folk Religion (New York:
Harper, 1940), 121-39 on "Seers and Oracles." The critique,
in anecdotal form, is illustrated in the confrontation
between Diogenes and the diviner in Diogenes, Epistle 38,
par. 2. Cf. A. J. Malherbe, The Cynic Epistles (SBL Source
for Biblical Study, 12; Missoula: Scholars Press, 1977)
161; also cf. Diogenes Laertius 6.24. References noted
in Lewy, 129, n. 4, who adduces another anecdote without
citation of source. Cf. Ag.Ap. 1.258.

52. The diatribal style of the anecdote should be
noted. Cf. Diogenes, Epistle 18, in Malherbe, Cynic
Epistles (note 51 above). This triumph of Jewish faith --
and markmanship ! -- over pagan superstition should be
seen in the context of the pagan critique of popular
religion, traceable to the pre-Socratics.

53. This fragment from Hecataeus is used by Josephus
in defending Alexandrian citizenship of the Jews. The
translation is that of H. St. J. Thackeray, Against Apion
(LCL, 9; Cambridge, Mass.: Harvard University Press/
London: Heinemann, 1961) 309. The limits of this fragment
are often extended to include par. 44-47. So, Jacoby,
FGrH 3A, No. 264, Frg. 22; Wacholder, Eupolemus, 263-65.
Walter, JS (1,2) 148, n. 25 and 157, n. 43a, rightly
objects, noting that par. 44-47 appear to be dependent
on Ep. Arist. 13-16. Wacholder, Eupolemus, 265, stresses
the substantial differences between the outlook and content of this fragment, over against Frg. 1, noting that
(a) it was not an eyewitness account, as was Frg. 1;
(b) the central concern is Alexandria, not Judaea, as
was the case in Frg. 1; and (c) the portrait of Ptolemy is
unfavorable (in par. 44), as opposed to the kindly
treatment of him in Frg. 1, par. 186. Accordingly, he
attributes it to a different author writing at a later
period (after Ep. Arist. and before Josephus).

54. On Jewish citizenship in Alexandria as bestowed
by Alexander himself, cf. above, note 18.

55. The incident referred to here is uncertain. Perhaps,
it is a reference to Demetrius II Nicator's grant in 145
B.C.E. of three Samaritan districts to the Jews for their
support of the Seleucids. Cf. 1 Macc 10:30-38; 11:34.
If so, it is another historical anachronism, pointing to
a Maccabean provenance for Pseudo-Hecataeus. So, Willrich,
Juden und Griechen, 21-22; Walter, JS (1,2) 147-48. In
contrast, Gager, "Pseudo-Hecataeus," 135-36, sees behind
it a reference to the Samaritan revolt against Alexander
in 331 B.C.E. (Q. Curtius Rufus 4.8.9-11 = Stern, GLAJJ,
No. 197; Eusebius, Chron. 123d [GCS, 47]), when the Jews
sided with Alexander. The language of 1 Macc 11:34 is
then taken to refer to a reaffirmation of a situation
that existed much earlier. This position is also favored
by LaFargue-Collins, 18-19. Cf. Stern, GLAJJ, 44, n. on
13, who suggests that as early as the time of Alexander
"some territorial changes, which preceded the incorporation of southern Samaria within Judaea in the forties
of the second century B.C.E. were made in favor of
Judaea." So 1 Macc 10:38; 11:34. Cf. Josephus, Ant.
11.304-307.

56. In chapter 14 of the Stromata, Clement cites several
Greek authors to show how they plagiarized from the
Hebrews. His numerous citations from pagan authors are
now widely regarded as Christian forgeries. Following
this passage attributing nine lines of poetry to Sophocles
and cited from Hecataeus, there occur quotations from
other authors including Euripides, Aeschylus, and Plato.
It is conceivable that these too were excerpted from
Pseudo-Hecataeus, but Clement does not explicitly state
this. Cf. Introduction; also Schaller, 25, n. 57.
The translation here is based on that of Wilson in ANF
2.470-71.

57. ὁ τὰς ἱστορίας συνταξάμενος: cf. Eusebius, P.E.
9.4.1: ἰδίαν βίβλον ἀναθεὶς τῇ περὶ ᾿Ιουδαίων ἱστορίᾳ
πλεῖστα περὶ αὐτῶν διέξεισιν. Possibly, Clement's
description derives from Diodorus Siculus 1.46.8, which
includes Hecataeus of Abdera as one of those who
composed histories of Egypt: συνταξαμένων δὲ τὰς
Αἰγυπτιακὰς ἱστορίας.

58. The title appears to be a conflation, recalling the
work of the genuine Hecataeus On the Egyptians, and the
work on Abraham, perhaps dependent on Josephus, Ant. 1.
159, but there is no clear evidence for this. Freudenthal,
165-66, suggested that Pseudo-Hecataeus was to be equated
with the author of Pseudo-Aristeas and Artapanus. The
title of this work does betray similar interests as
those reflected in these two works. Cf. Schaller, 16.

59. The passage is nowhere found among the genuine
works of Sophocles. Cf. Freudenthal, 166.

60. Cf. Frg. 1, par. 199. As Conzelmann, HJC, 170,n. 165,
notes, the stress in Pseudo-Hecataeus is on the law
as it relates to the cult of the one God. This passage
is similar in outlook in this respect, and in this
instance recalls the description of the cult in Frg. 1,
par. 199, as being "without images." Similarly, the
story of Mosollamus would be seen to reflect this
outlook. Cf. Frg. 1, par. 200-204.

61. The translation is that of M. Hadas, Aristeas to
Philocrates (New York: Harper, 1951), 111.

62. The translation is that of H. St. J. Thackeray,
Against Apion (LCL, 1; Cambridge, Mass.: Harvard
University Press/London: Heinemann, 1961) 249, 251.

63. The translation is that of H. Chadwick, Origen:
Contra Celsum (Cambridge: Cambridge University Press,
1953; repr. 1965, 1980) 17.

THEOPHILUS

Theophilus is included by Josephus among the Greek historians who attest the antiquity of the Jews and who "have made more than a passing allusion to us."[1] Whether this is the same Theophilus excerpted by Eusebius from Alexander Polyhistor is unclear, but it is quite possible.

No specific work of his is mentioned by Josephus, nor does Eusebius mention a title. This single extant fragment, however, suggests that Theophilus, in whatever form he dealt extensively with the Jews, discussed Solomon's temple. More than that cannot be said.

Because the fragment deals with a Jewish theme, Theophilus has been regarded as a Hellenistic Jewish or Samaritan author,[2] though it is more likely that he was a pagan.[3]

As to his date, it is only known that he antedated Alexander Polyhistor (first century B.C.E.) from whom Eusebius quoted him.

NOTES

1. Josephus, _Ag.Ap._ 1.215-16.

2. So, Reinach, _Textes_, 51-52, followed by Walter, _JS_ (1,2), 109.

3. So, Stern, _GLAJJ_, 126-27.

Bibliography

Freudenthal, 117-18.

Laqueur, R. "Theophilus (11)," PW 5.A (1934) 2137-38.

Reinach, Textes, 51-52, 216.

Stern, GLAJJ, 126-27.

Wacholder, Eupolemus, 7, 15, 243, 289.

Walter, JS (1,2) 109-110.

_____, Untersuchungen, 93-96, 222-23.

Index to Editions and Translations

Fragment One

    Source: Eusebius, P.E. 9.34.19.

    Reference Number in P.E.:   Steph., 265; Vig. 452a.

    Greek Text Used: Mras, GCS (43,1) 8.1, p. 544, lines 17-20.

    Editions: Steph., 265; Vig., 452a; Hein. 2.53; Gais., 2.433; Müll., FHG 3.228 (= No. 19); Migne, PG (21), col. 753 D; Dind. 1.521; Freu. (om.); Giff., 1.563 (notes, 4.321); Stearns (om.); Mras, GCS (43,1) 8.1, p. 544; Jac., FGrH 3.694-95 (= No. 733, Frg. 1) Denis (om.); Stern, GLAJJ, 126-27 (= No. 37).

    Translations:

        English: Giff., 3.480.

        French: Reinach, Textes, 51.

        German: Walter (JS 1.2) 111.

FRAGMENT ONE (Eusebius, P.E. 9.34.19)

ΘΕΟΦΙΛΟΥ ΠΕΡΙ ΣΟΛΟΜΩΝΟΣ

(19)   "Θεόφιλος δέ φησι τὸν περισσεύσαντα   (19)
χρυσὸν τὸν Σολομῶνα τῷ Τυρίων βασιλεῖ πέμψαι·   452a
τὸν δὲ εἰκόνα τῆς θυγατρὸς ζῷον ὁλοσώματον
5 κατασκευάσαι, καὶ ἔλυτρον τῷ ἀνδριάντι τὸν χρυσοῦν κίονα περιθεῖναι."

BION

1 ΘΕΟΦ. -- ΣΟΛ   BION | Σολομῶντος ON |
2 περιττεύσαντα   B | 3 τὸν Σολομῶνα I: τὸν Σολο-
μῶντα B: τω Σολομῶντι ON | Τυρίων BI: Τύρωνι ON |
4 ζῷον om. B |

FRAGMENT ONE[1]

Theophilus' Remarks Concerning Solomon

(19)   (19) "Theophilus says that Solomon sent to
the king of the Tyrians the gold that was left
over,[2] and that the latter made a life-like,
full-length[3] statue of his daughter[4] and used
the golden pillar to make a covering for it."[5]

ANNOTATIONS

1.   This fragment occurs at the end of the long fragment
excerpted from Eupolemus (= Frg. 2) in which Eusebius
described Solomon's building of the temple.   Immediately
before, Eupolemus had noted that Solomon sent to Hiram
the golden pillar "which is dedicated in the temple of
Zeus at Tyre."   Like the Eupolemus fragment, this fragment
from Theophilus is also taken by Eusebius from Alexander
Polyhistor.

2.   Cf. 1 Kgs 9:11-14.   Cf. also Eupolemus, Frg. 2, and
Annotations, No. 101.

3.   So, Mras, GCS (43,1) 8.1, p. 544: ζῷον ὁλοσώματον
"eine Statue mit ganger Körper" (nicht bloss Büste).

4.   I.e., the daughter given in marriage to Solomon.
Cf. Laetus apud Tatian, Oratio ad Graecos 37 = Stern,
GLAJJ, No. 29, 128-30.

5.   The syntax is unclear. Cf. Walter, JS (1,2), 111,
n. 19 b.

THALLUS

Possibly to be included among the Hellenistic Jewish authors is the historian Thallus[1] to whom Eusebius ascribes a three-volume chronological work encompassing the period from the Trojan war to the 167th Olympiad, i.e., 112-109 B.C.E.[2] However, the extant fragments of Thallus' work, which are presumably from the same book[3] and are preserved only by Christian writers,[4] indicate that the work was broader in scope, reaching from approximately 300 years prior to the Trojan war until the first century C.E.[5] Thus, either the testimonium from Eusebius' Chronicle is corrupt,[6] or the work was later extended.[7]

The work was doubtless written in Greek and appears to have been entitled The Histories.[8] Ancient writers, at least, regarded the work as history,[9] as Thallus is consistently included in the company of Polybius, Diodorus Siculus, Castor, and Herodotus.[10] The assessment of the medieval chronographers is even more glowing: George Syncellus and John Malala include him among the "wisest" and "most distinguished" historians.[11]

Date. His flourit has been put as late as the mid- to late first century C.E.[12] The terminus post quem is either 112-109 B.C.E., if the testimonium from Eusebius' Chronicle is correct, or 29 C.E., if Frg. 1 is reliable. The terminus ante quem is ca. 220/221 C.E., when his history was used by the Christian chronographer Julius Sextus Africanus, who is the earliest author to mention him.[13]

Identity. He has been identified as Augustus' secretary who is mentioned by Suetonius (Aug. 67.2),[14] but also as "the man of Samaritan origin ... (and) freed- man of the emperor Tiberius" (Josephus, Ant. 18.167), who in 36 C.E. loaned Agrippa a million drachmas.[15] Although Thallus is not explicitly identified elsewhere as a

Samaritan, Africanus describes him as one of the historians,
along with Castor, who treated "Syrian matters."[16]
Freudenthal argued strongly for his Samaritan identity,[17]
noting (a) that he is said to be among those historians
"who mentioned Moses as a very ancient and time-honored
prince of the Jews;"[18]   (b) that the contents of Frg. 1
reflect interest in Palestine and events that occurred
there; and (c) that the euhemeristic tendencies of the
work are similar to those of the anonymous Samaritan
historian, Pseudo-Eupolemus. However, the case for his
Samaritan identity is by no means certain.[19]   It is
difficult to decide, with respect to (a) and (b), whether
they reflect the interests of Thallus or the authors who
were quoting him (Pseudo-Justin and Africanus). As to
(c), euhemerism per se need not point to a Samaritan
identity, although in this respect he would be similar
to Pseudo-Eupolemus.[20]   As a rule, he is included by
ancient writers with other Greek historians.[21]   Whether
he should be classified as a pagan,[22] Hellenistic Jewish,[23]
or Samaritan[24] historian remains uncertain.

Importance. Among the more intriguing features of
the fragments is Thallus' mention of an eclipse which
occurred in the year 29 C.E., i.e., the fifteenth year of
the reign of Tiberius.[25]   For this reason, he has been
counted among the earliest non-Christian writers who,
at the most, reflect knowledge of Jesus and the synoptic
tradition,[26] or, at the least, a version of the Christian
story of the crucifixion.[27]   Because of the indirect
nature of the evidence, however, this connection is very
tenuous, and should be used cautiously. If Thallus belongs
among the Samaritan authors, his interest in pagan traditions is strikingly similar to those of Pseudo-Eupolemus,
and this would further reinforce the picture of Samaritans
in the first century C.E. as open to syncretistic
influences. His central interest in chronicles would
place him in the same tradition with Demetrius the
Chronographer, and he would thus become another example

of the use of chronography for apologetic purposes.
Because of the indirect and fragmentary nature of the
material from Thallus, it is impossible to know how,
if at all, he treats Jewish history and events, except
that his strong euhemeristic outlook is well-documented,
and this doubtless accounts for his popularity among
Christian chronographers.[28] If, on the other hand, he
was a pagan, he belongs among those pagan authors who
mentioned Moses, albeit only briefly.[29]

NOTES

1. Testimonia: Eusebius, Chronicle (= FGrH 2B.1156
[= No. 256, T 1]; Africanus in Eusebius, P.E. 10.10.8;
Tertullian, Apol. 19.5-6.

2. Eusebius, Chronicle, ed. J. Karst (GCS, 20), p. 125,
lines 22-23: "aus des Thallos drei Büchern; in welche er
abrissweise zusammengefasst hat von der Einnahme Ilions
bis zur 167. Olympiade." The Chronicle survives only
in Armenian. Cf. FGrH 2B.1156 (= No. 256, T 1).

3. So, Jacoby, FGrH 2D.835.

4. Thallus has also been regarded as a source for Velleius
(Christ) and Pseudo-Lucian, Macrobioi (Rühl), but this is
doubted by Jacoby, FGrH 2D.835, who also notes that it is
not at all clear from Tertullian, Apol. 19.5-6, that
Josephus knew, much less responded, to Thallus, as argued
by Gutschmid, Kleine Schriften, 4.212. Cf. Jacoby, FGrH
2D.836, on T 3.

5. In Frg. 2, Thallus says that Belos "antedated the
Trojan war by 322 years," i.e. ca. 1515 B.C.E. According
to Frg. 1, Thallus mentioned an eclipse which Africanus
equated with the darkness accompanying the crucifixion of
Christ. Africanus dated the crucifixion in 29 C.E., and
thus the chronicle of Thallus appears to have extended
at least this far. Cf. Pfeiffer, History, 203.

6. So, Jacoby, FGrH 2D.835; Rigg, 113.

7. So, Müller, FHG 3.517; OCD^2, 1050; against Jacoby,
FGrH 2D.835.

8. Cf. Frg. 1, which indicates that the book had a title
and numbered book divisions. So, Jacoby, FGrH 2D.835.

9. Africanus = Frg. 1: ἐν τριτῇ τῶν Ἱστοριῶν; Theophilus
= Frg. 2: κατὰ ... τὴν Θάλλου ἱστορίαν; Africanus,
apud Eusebius, P.E. 10.10.4 = Frg. 4, par. 4: καὶ τῶν
Θαλλοῦ καὶ Κάστορος ἱστοριῶν.

10. Cf. Tertullian, Apol. 10 = Frg. 3; also Minucius
Felix, Oct. 21.4; Lactantius, Div. Inst. 1.13; Eusebius,
P.E. 10.10.4 & 7-8 = Frg. 4.

11. On Syncellus, cf. K. Krumbacher, Geschichte der
byzantinischen Litteratur von Justinian bis zum Ende des
oströmischen Reiches (527-1453) (HAW 9.1; 2nd ed.;
München: C. H. Beck, 1897) 339-42; and now, W. Adler,
George Syncellus and His Predecessors: Ante-Diluvian
History in the Chronicle of Syncellus and His Acknowledged
Authorities (Unpublished Ph.D. Dissertation. University
of Pennsylvania, 1982).

11. (cont.) Syncellus = Frg. 5: πολλοὶ τῶν ἐπισήμων
ἱστορικῶν; Malala = Frg. 6: οἱ σοφώτατοι Θαλλος κ.τ.λ.
Though, cf. Jacoby, FGrH 2D.835.

12. Eusebius, Chron. (FGrH 2B.1156), extends the limit
to the 167th Olympiad, in Greek presumably ρξλ, i.e.
112-109 B.C.E. Müller, FHG 3.517 emends the text to σζ,
the 207th Olympiad, i.e. 49-52 C.E. Gutschmid, Kleine
Schriften, 4.412, emends the text to read the 217th
Olympiad, i.e. 89-92 C.E. Cf. Jacoby, FGrH 2B.1156,
app. crit.

13. On Africanus, cf. Gelzer, Sextus.

14. So, Täubler in Rhein. Museum 71 (1916) 572, apud
Laqueur, PW, 1226; though, doubted by Stein, "Thallos (4),"
PW, 1226. Cf. OCD², 1050.

15. So, Müller, FHG 3.517; Freudenthal, Alexander Polyhistor, 100; Gelzer, Sextus, 2.96; cf. Stein, "Thallos (5),"
PW, 1226-27. Josephus, Ant. 18.167: καὶ γὰρ ἦν ἄλλος
(Hudson: Θάλλος) Σαμαρεὺς γένος Καίσαρος δὲ ἀπελεύθερος·
παρὰ τούτου δάνεισμα μυριάδας ἑκατὸν εὑρόμενος τῇ τε
Ἀντωνίᾳ καταβάλλει τὸ ὀφειληθὲν χρέος κ.τ.λ. (LCL).
As early as the 17th century, ἄλλος was seen as problematic
and difficult to render. Accordingly, J. Hudson emended
the text to read Θάλλος, and thus identified the otherwise
unnamed Samaritan as the historian of the Augustan age.
The emendation was rejected by Niese, also Schmid-Stählin,
Geschichte, 2,1.415-16, n. 3 ("falsche Lesung von Jos."),
though accepted by Naber; also Schürer, Geschichte 3.495,
but doubted by Jacoby, FGrH 2D.836. Also, cf. L. Feldman,
ad loc., LCL 9.107, n. f, who, following Rigg, however,
finds meaningful alternatives for translating ἄλλος. Cf.
Rigg, 119. Also, cf. Miéris, Rev. Belge de Philol. et
d'hist. 13 (1934) 733 ff., apud LCL 9.106. Note the
inscription mentioned by Laqueur, PW, 1226: Tiberius
Cladius Thallus; cf. Denis, 267. The name frequently
appears in Greek inscriptions from the 4th cent. B.C.E.
onwards. Cf. Jacoby, FGrH 2D.836.

16. Africanus, apud Eusebius, P.E. 10.10.8 = Frg. 4, par.
8: οἵ τε τὰ Σύρια Κάστωρ καὶ Θάλλος. Jacoby, FGrH 2D.835:
(Ἀσ)συριακά.

17. Freudenthal, Alexander Polyhistor, 100-101.

18. So, Pseudo-Justin, Coh. ad Gen. 9; cf. text included
after Frg. 4. Clearly, Pseudo-Justin is dependent on
Africanus, apud Eusebius, P.E. 10.10.7-8. Cf. Jacoby,
FGrH 2B.1158, Frg. 5.

19.   Jacoby, FGrH, 2D.837, e.g., stresses the differences
between Thallus and Pseudo-Eupolemus, and sees greater
similarity between Thallus and Castor, esp. FGrH, No.
250, Frg. 1, noting that Castor was probably Thallus'
Vorlage. The differences in their chronographical
calculations are acknowledged, however.

20.   Especially questioned by Jacoby, FGrH 2D.836.

21.   Cf. esp. Lactantius, Div. Inst. 1.13: *Gracei Diodorus
et Thallus*; also Minucius Felix, Oct. 2.14; Tertullian,
Apol. 10 = Frg. 3; Africanus, apud Eusebius, P.E. 10.10.8=
Frg. 4, par. 8; cf. Frgs. 5 & 6.

22.   Jacoby, FGrH 2D.835: "... war er vermutlich weder
jude (oder Samaritaner) noch Christ" (because he was
excerpted by Porphyry); Rigg, 111-19; Pfeiffer, 202,
following Rigg: "... no compelling reason ... to consider
Thallus a Samaritan," Denis, 268: "l'historien de la
Syrie;" Wacholder, EncJud, 1045: "probably heathen."

23.   Schmid-Stählin, Geschichte, 2,1.415: "vermutlich
hellenisierter Jude (Samaritaner ?)."

24.   Müller, FHG 3.517; Gelzer, Sextus, 2.97; Wachsmuth,
Einleitung, 146; Täubler, Rh. Museum 71 (1916) 572, apud
Jacoby, FGrH 2B.836; Stearns, Fragments, 62: "a Syrian --
probably a Samaritan .. a Grecizing Samaritan;" Goguel,
Jesus, 91; A. H. McDonald, OCD², 1050: "... may perhaps
be the Samaritan Thallus, Augustus' secretary or
Tiberius' freedman;" Hengel, Judaism and Hellenism, 1.89:
"Thallus ... who was possibly a countryman of the
anonymous Samaritan, and at least a Syrian;" Charlesworth,
PAMR, 209: "apparently ... a Samaritan."

25.   Cf. Frg. 1.

26.   So, Goguel, Jesus, 91: "... the first non-Christian
author who, so far as we know, has alluded, if not to
Jesus, at least to the Gospel tradition," in the chapter
on "Non-Christian Sources for the Gospel story." Also,
cf. Goguel, RHR, following Eisler, 2.140-41. Conceivably,
Thallus merely mentioned the eclipse of 29 C.E., without
any knowledge of or reference to the events described in
the Gospel tradition. It is Africanus, after all, who says
"this darkness" (τοῦτο σκότος), not Thallus. On the other
hand, he is not cited by Christian authors as an independent pagan witness to the eclipse. He is rather censured
for seeing it merely as a natural phenomenon. From this
it has been deduced that he knew the Gospel tradition
but in keeping with his euhemeristic outlook interpreted
it rationalistically, and it is this to which Africanus
takes exception. Cf. Rigg, 112, n. 7, and 113.

27.   So, Guignebert, <u>Jesus</u>, 13, n. 1, who is only willing
to concede that Thallus "was acquainted with the account
of the crucifixion given by the Christians of his time,"
noting that Goguel and Eisler over-argue their case.
The more modest position is also argued by F. F. Bruce,
<u>Jesus and Christian Origins Outside the New Testament</u>
(Grand Rapids: Eerdmans, 1974) 29-30, esp. 30.

28.   So, Jacoby, <u>FGrH</u> 2B.835.

29.   Unmentioned by Gager, <u>Moses</u>.

Bibliography

Bruce, F. F. Jesus and Christian Origins Outside the New
    Testament (Grand Rapids: Eerdmans, 1974) 29-30.

Charlesworth, PAMRS, 209-10.

Denis, Introduction, 267-68.

Eisler, R. 'Ιησοῦς Βασιλεὺς οὐ βασιλεύσας (2 vols.;
    Heidelberg: C. Winter, 1929-30) 2.140-41.

Freudenthal, Alexander Polyhistor, 100-101.

Gelzer, Sextus, 2.96-97.

Goguel, M. "Un nouveau témoignage non-chrétien sur la
    tradition évangélique d'apres M. Eisler," RHR
    98 (1928) 1-12.

_____, The Life of Jesus (New York: Macmillan, 1944)
    91-93.

Guignebert, Ch. Jesus (London: Kegan Paul, 1935) 13.

Hengel, Judaism and Hellenism, 1.89; 2.60-61, notes 247
    and 249.

Jacoby, F. FGrH 2D.835-37 (commentary on FGrH 2B.1156-58,
    No. 256, Frg. 1-8); also FGrH 3b [Supplement], vol.
    1, pp. 380-89 (commentary on FGrH 3B, No. 328, Frg.
    92 = Philochorus), and notes in FGrH 3b [Supplement],
    vol. 2, pp. 278-84, on No. 328, Frg. 92.

Müller, FHG 3.517-19.

Laqueur, R. "Thallos (1)," PW, second series 5 (1934)
    1225-26.

Pfeiffer, History, 202-203.

Rigg, H. A. "Thallus: The Samaritan?" HTR 34 (1941) 111-19.

Sanders, B. "Θάλλος, the Samaritan?" Unpublished Seminar
    Paper. Harvard New Testament Seminar. April 10, 1970.
    7 pp.

Schmid-Stählin, Geschichte, 2,1.415-16.

Schürer, Geschichte, 3.368-69.

Stearns, Fragments, 62-66.

Stein, A. "Thallos (4 & 5)," PW, second series 5 (1934)
    1226-27.

Wacholder, "Biblical Chronology," 463, 466, n. 60, 471,
    476, n. 101.

_____, Eupolemus, 116-23.

_____, "Thallus," EncJud 15 (1971) 1045.

Wachsmuth, K. Einleitung in das Studium der alten
    Geschichte (Leipzig: S. Hirzel, 1895) 146.

Index to Editions and Translations

Fragment One

Source: Julius Sextus Africanus, Χρονογραφίαι 18.1,
apud Georgius Syncellus 'Εκλογὴ Χρονογραφίας

Greek Text Used: G. Dindorf, Georgius Syncellus et
Nicephorus   (Corpus Scriptorum Historiae
Byzantinae, 12 [microfiche]; Bonn: E. Weber,
1829) vol. 1, p. 609, line 21 - p. 610, line 16.

Editions: Routh, Reliquiae Sacrae 2.297-98; Müll.,
FHG 3.519 (= Frg. 8); Migne, PG (10) col. 89
A-B; Stearns, 66 (= Frg. 6); Jac., FGrH 2B.1157
(= No. 256, Frg. 1; commentary FGrH 2D.836-37).

Translations:

English: ANF 6.136-37.

French:

German:

Fragment Two

Source: Theophilus, Ad Autolycum 3.29.

Later Citations: Lactantius, Div. Inst. 1.23.2.

Greek Text Used: R. M. Grant, Theophilus of Antioch:
Ad Autolycum (Oxford: Clarendon Press, 1970)
144.

Editions: Müll. FHG 3.517 (= Frg. 2); Stearns, 63-
64 (= Frgs. 2 & 4); Jac., FGrH 2B.1157 (= No.
256, Frgs. 2 & 3); Grant, 144.

Translations:

English: M. Dods, ANF 2.120; Grant, 145.

French:

German:

Fragment Three

Source: Tertullian, Apologeticus 10.

Later Citations: Cf. Tertullian, Ad nat. 2.12;
Lactantius, Div. Inst. 1.13; Minucius Felix,
Oct.   21.4.

Latin Text Used: Oehler as printed in J. E. B.
Mayor, Q. Septimi Florentis Tertulliani Apologeticus (Cambridge: Cambridge University Press,
1917) p. 36, line 33 - p. 38, line 6.

Editions: Migne, PL (1) col. 383A; T. H. Bindley,
Tertulliani Apologeticus (Oxford: Clarendon,
1889) 40; Müll. FHG 3.517 (= Frg. 1); Stearns
(om.);   Jacoby, FGrH 2B.1158 (= No. 256, Frg. 4).

Translations:

English: A. Souter, in Mayor, Apologeticus,
37 & 39; T. R. Glover in Tertullian,
Apology, De Spectaculis (LCL), 57;
S. Thelwall, ANF 3.26.

French:

German:

Fragment Four

Source: Julius Sextus Africanus in Eusebius, P.E.
10.10.4 & 7-8.

Later Citations: Pseudo-Justin, Coh. ad Gent. 9.

Reference Number in P.E.:   Steph., 286-87; Vig. 488b-
489a.

Greek Text Used: Mras, GCS (43,1) 8.1, p. 591, line
21 - p. 592, line 2; p. 592, lines 9-18.

Editions: Steph. 286-287; Vig. 488b-489a; Routh,
Reliquiae Sacrae 2.271-72; Gais., 2.508-509;
Müll., FHG 3.518 (= Frg. 6 [P.E. 10.10.4] &
Frg. 3 [P.E. 10.10.7-8]; Migne, PG (10) 73 C -
76 A; PG (21) 812 C - 813 A; Dind., 1.565-66;
Freudenthal (om.); Giff., 2.38-39 (notes 4.354-
55); Stearns, 63 & 65 (= Frg. 3 [P.E. 10.10.4]
& Frg. 5 [P.E. 10.10.7-8]); Jacoby, FGrH 2B.1158
(= No. 256, Frg. 7 [P.E. 10.10.4] & Frg. 5 [P.E.
10.10.7-8]; commentary FGrH 2D.835-37; Mras,
GCS (43,1) 8.1, 591-92; Denis (om.).

Translations:

English: Giff., 3.523; ANF 6.133.

French:

German:

Fragment Five

Source: Georgius Syncellus, 'Εκλογὴ Χρονογραφίας

Greek Text Used: G. Dindorf, Georgius Syncellus et
    Nicephorus (Corpus Scriptorum Historiae Byzan-
    tinae, 12 [microfiche]; Bonn: E. Weber, 1829)
    vol. 1, p. 172, lines 17-23.

Editions: Müll., FHG   3.518 (= Frg. 4); Stearns,
    62 (= Frg. 1); Jac., FGrH 2B.1158 (= No. 256,
    Frg. 6).

Translations:

    English:

    French:

    German: Weissbach, PW second series 1.A
                  (1920) 2453-54.

Fragment Six

Source: John Malala, Chronographia

Greek Text Used: L. Dindorf, Ioannis Malala:
    Chronographia (Corpus Scriptorum Historiae
    Byzantinae, 15 [microfiche]; Bonn: E. Weber,
    1831) Book 6, p. 157, lines 18-21.

Editions: Migne, PG (97) col. 260 A; Müll. FHG 3.
    519 (= Frg. 7); Stearns (om.); Jacoby, FGrH
    2B.1158 (= No. 256, Frg. 8).

Translations:

    English:

    French:

    German:

FRAGMENT ONE (Julius Sextus Africanus, Χρονογραφίαι
    18.1, apud Georgius Syncellus Ἐκλογὴ Χρονογρα-
    φίας)

(1) καθ' ὅλου τοῦ κόσμου σκότος ἐπήγετο φοβερώ-   (1)
τατον, σεισμῷ τε αἱ πέτραι διερρήγνυντο καὶ τὰ
πολλὰ Ἰουδαίας καὶ τῆς λοιπῆς γῆς κατερρίφθη.
τοῦτο τὸ σκότος ἔκλειψιν τοῦ ἡλίου Θάλλος ἀποκα-
5   λεῖ ἐν τρίτῃ τῶν Ἱστοριῶν· ὡς ἐμοὶ δοκεῖ, ἀλό-
γως. Ἑβραῖοι γὰρ ἄγουσι τὸ πάσχα κατὰ σελήνην
ιδ', πρὸ δὲ μιᾶς τοῦ πάσχα τὰ περὶ τὸν σωτῆρα
συμβαίνει. ἔκλειψις δὲ ἡλίου σελήνης ὑπελθούσης
τὸν ἥλιον γίνεται· ἀδύνατον δὲ ἐν ἄλλῳ χρόνῳ,
10   πλὴν ἐν τῷ μεταξὺ μιᾶς καὶ τῆς πρὸ αὐτῆς κατὰ
τὴν σύνοδον αὐτὴν ἀποβῆναι. πῶς οὖν ἔκλειψις
νομισθείη κατὰ διάμετρον σχεδὸν ὑπαρχούσης τῆς
σελήνης ἡλίῳ; ἔστω δή, συναρπαζέτω τοὺς πολλοὺς
τὸ γεγενημένον καὶ τὸ κοσμικὸν τέρας ἡλίου ἔκλει-
15   ψις ὑπονοείσθω ἐν τῇ κατὰ τὴν ὄψιν. Φλέγων
ἱστορεῖ ἐπὶ Τιβερίου Καίσαρος ἐν πανσελήνῳ
ἔκλειψιν ἡλίου γεγονέναι τελείαν ἀπὸ ὥρας ἕκτης
μέχρις ἐνάτης, δηλῶν ὡς ταύτην. τίς δ' ἡ
κοινωνία σεισμῷ καὶ ἐκλείψει, πέτραις ῥηγνυ-
20   μέναις καὶ ἀναστάσει νεκρῶν, τοσαύτη τε κινήσει
κοσμικῇ; *(reek ?*

AB

1 ἐπήγετο Dindorf: ἐπείγετο vulg. apud Dindorf:
ἐπεγένετο Scaliger apud Dindorf | 2 τε B: δὲ Goar
apud Dindorf | 3 τῆς Ἰουδαίας Goar apud Dindorf |
κατερρίφθη B: κατερρίφη Goar apud Dindorf | 6 σελήνης
Routh | 7 δὲ τῆς Routh | 8 συνέβη Routh | 10 μιᾶς:
νουμηνίας Routh | 15 ἐν τῇ B: ἔν τι Goar apud Dindorf:
ἔκ γε τῆς Routh | post ὄψιν add. πλάνης Routh |
17 τελεία A | 18 ἐννάτης Routh | δῆλον Goar et
Scaliger apud Dindorf | 20 τοσαύτη B | 20-21 κινήσει
κοσμικῇ Dindorf: κίνησις κοσμική AB |

FRAGMENT ONE[1]

(1)   (1) On the whole world there pressed a most fearful
darkness; and the rocks were rent by an earthquake,
and many places in Judaea and other districts were
thrown down. In the third book of his History,[2]
Thallus calls this darkness[3] an eclipse of the sun[4]--
in my opinion, wrongly. For the Hebrews celebrate
the Passover on the 14th day according to the moon,
and the passion of our Savior falls on the day
before the Passover; but an eclipse of the sun takes
place only when the moon comes under the sun. And
it cannot happen at any other time but in the interval
between the first day of the new moon and the last
of the old, that is, at their junction. How then
should an eclipse be supposed to happen when the moon
is almost diametrically opposite the sun? Let that
opinion pass however; let it carry the majority with
it; and let this portent of the world be deemed an
eclipse of the sun, like others a portent only to the
eye. Phlegon records that, in the time of Tiberius
Caesar, at full moon, there was a full eclipse of the
sun from the sixth hour to the ninth -- manifestly
that one of which we speak.[5] But what has an eclipse
in common with an earthquake, the rending rocks, and
the resurrection of the dead, and so great a pertur-
bation throughout the universe? Surely no such event
as this is recorded for a long period. But it was a
darkness induced by God, because the Lord happened
then to suffer.

FRAGMENT TWO (Theophilus, <u>Ad Autolycum</u> 3.29)

(29)   Καὶ γὰρ Βήλου τοῦ ʼΑσσυρίων βασιλεύσαντος   (29)
καὶ Κρόνου τοῦ Τιτᾶνος Θάλλος μέμνηται, φάσκων
τὸν Βῆλον πεπολεμηκέναι σὺν τοῖς Τιτᾶσι πρὸς
τὸν Δία καὶ τοὺς σὺν αὐτῷ θεοὺς λεγομένους, ἔνθα
5   φησίν, "Καὶ "Ωγυγος ἡττηθεὶς ἔφυγεν εἰς Ταρτησ-
σόν, τότε μὲν τῆς χώρας ἐκείνης ʼΑκτῆς κληθείσης,
νυνὶ δὲ ʼΑττικῆς προσαγορευομένης, ἧς "Ωγυγος
τότε ἦρξεν." καὶ τὰς λοιπὰς δὲ χώρας καὶ πόλεις
ἀφ' ὧν τὰς προσωνυμίας ἔσχον, οὐκ ἀναγκαῖον ἡγού-
10   μεθα καταλέγειν, μάλιστα πρὸς σὲ τὸν ἐπιστάμενον
τὰς ἱστορίας. ὅτι μὲν οὖν ἀρχαιότερος ὁ Μωσῆς
δείκνυται ἀπάντων συγγραφέων (οὐκ αὐτὸς δὲ μόνος
ἀλλὰ καὶ οἱ πλείους μετ' αὐτὸν προφῆται γενόμενοι) καὶ Κρόνου καὶ Βήλου καὶ τοῦ ʼΙλιακοῦ
15   πολέμου, δῆλόν ἐστιν. κατὰ γὰρ τὴν Θάλλου ἱστορίαν ὁ Βῆλος προγενέστερος εὑρίσκεται τοῦ
ʼΙλιακοῦ πολέμου ἔτεσι τκβ'. ὅτι δὲ πρὸς που
ἔτεσι λ' ἢ καὶ ,α προάγει ὁ Μωσῆς τῆς τοῦ ʼΙλίου
ἀλώσεως, ἐν τοῖς ἐπάνω δεδηλώκαμεν.

= Lactantius, <u>Div</u>. <u>Inst</u>. 1.23.2

20   (2) κατὰ γὰρ τὴν Θάλλου ἱστορίαν ὁ Βῆλος προγε-   (2)
νέστερος εὑρίσκεται τοῦ ʼΙλιακοῦ πολέμου ἔτεσι
,τκβ'.

VBP

2 τοῦ Τιτᾶνος Θάλλος edd.: του τιτανωσθαλλος V |
5 "Ωγυγος Niebuhr: ὁ Γύγος V | 5-6 καὶ -- Ταρτησσόν:
Κρόνος ἡττηθεὶς ἔφυγεν εἰς Ταρτησσὸν, "Ωγυγος δὲ εἰς τὴν
ἀπ' αὐτοῦ ὀνομασθεῖσαν ʼΩγυγίαν Müll. <u>FHG</u> 3.518 |
6 ἐκείνης ʼΑκτῆς: ἐκείνης <Ταρτάρου λεγομένης, ὥσπερ>
ʼΑκτῆς Niebuhr apud Müll. <u>FHG</u> 3.518 | 7 "Ωγυγος Wolf
apud Grant: ὁ Γύγος V |

FRAGMENT TWO[6]

(29)   (29)   In fact, Thallus mentioned Belos,[7] who reigned
over the Assyrians, and the Titan Kronos, and said
that with the Titans Belos waged war against Zeus
and the so-called gods on his side.   Then he says:

> "And Ogygos[8] in defeat fled to Tartessus;
> the country which Ogygos then ruled was at
> that time named Akte and is now called
> Attica."[9]

We do not consider it necessary to list the other
lands and cities and the persons from whom they
received their names, especially for you who know
the history.   But it is obvious that Moses proves
to be more ancient than all writers (not only he, but
also most of the prophets after him) and Kronos and
Belos and the Trojan war; for according to the
history of Thallus, Belos antedated the Trojan war
by 322 years,[10] while we have already shown that
Moses antedates the capture of Troy by 900 or 1,000
years.

Lactantius, Div. Inst. 1.23.2

(2)   (2)   (Theophilus says that) Thallus relates in his
history, that Belus ... is found to have lived 322
years before the Trojan war.

FRAGMENT THREE (Tertullian, _Apologeticus_ 10)

(10) *Saturnum itaque, si quantum litterae docent,* (10)
neque Diodorus Graecus aut Thallus neque Cassius
Seuerus aut Cornelius Nepos neque ullus commenta-
tor eiusmodi antiquitatum aliud quam hominem
5 *promulgauerunt, si quantum rerum argumenta, nus-*
quam inuenio fideliora quam apud ipsam Italiam,
in qua Saturnus post multas expeditiones postque
Attica hospitia consedit, exceptus a Iano, uel
Iane, ut Salii uolunt.

= Minucius Felix, _Oct_. 21.4:

10 (4) *Saturnum enim, principem huius generis et* (4)
examinis, omnes scriptores vetustatis Graeci
Romanique hominem tradiderunt. Scit hoc Nepos et
Cassius in historia, et Thallus ac Diodorus
hoc loquuntur.

= Lactantius, _Div_. _Inst_. 1.13:

15 (13) ... *omnes ergo non tantum poetae, sed his-* (13)
toricarum quoque ac rerum antiquarum scriptores
hominem fuisse consentiunt, qui res eius in
Italia gestae memoriae prodiderunt: Graeci
Diodorus et Thallus, Latini Nepos et Cassius et
20 *Varro.*

FRAGMENT THREE[11]

(10)   (10) With regard to Saturn therefore, if we make
       appeal to what we can learn from literature, neither
       the Greek Diodorus[12] nor Thallus[13] nor Cassius
       Severus[14] nor Cornelius Nepos,[15] nor any other
       recorded of such ancient beliefs, has proclaimed him
       anything but a man;[16] if to proof from facts, I find
       nowhere more reliable proofs han in Italy itself,
       in which Saturn after many expeditions and after
       a residence in Attica took up his abode, having been
       welcomed by Janus, or Janes, as the Salii prefer to
       call him.

       Minucius Felix, Oct. 21:4[17]

(4)   (4) Saturn, the fountainhead of this family and
       clan, all antiquarians, Greek and Roman, treat as
       a man. So Nepos, and Cassius in his history, and
       Thallus and Diodorus say the same.

       Lactantius, Div. Inst. 1.13[18]

(13)   (13) Not only therefore all the poets, but the
       writers also of ancient histories and events, agree
       that he was a man, inasmuch as they handed down
       to memory his actions in Italy: of Greek writers,
       Diodorus and Thallus; of Latin writers, Nepos,
       Cassius, and Varro.

FRAGMENT FOUR (Eusebius, P.E. 10.10.4 & 7-8)

(4) μετὰ δὲ τὰ ο᾽ τῆς αἰχμαλωσίας ἔτη Κῦρος   (4)
Περσῶν ἐβασίλευσεν, ᾧ ἔτει ᾽Ολυμπιὰς ἤχθη νε᾽,   488c
ὡς ἐκ τῶν Βιβλιοθηκῶν Διοδώρου καὶ τῶν Θαλλοῦ
καὶ Κάστορος ἱστοριῶν, ἔτι δὲ Πολυβίου καὶ
5   Φλέγοντος ἔστιν εὑρεῖν, ἀλλὰ καὶ ἑτέρων, οἷς
ἐμέλησεν ᾽Ολυμπιάδων· ἅπασι γὰρ συνεφώνησεν ὁ
χρόνος.

* * * * *

(7) τὰς δὲ πρὸ τούτων ὡδί πως τῆς ᾽Αττικῆς   (7)
χρονογραφίας ἀριθμουμένης, ἀπὸ Ὠγύγου τοῦ παρ᾽
10 ἐκείνοις αὐτόχθονος πιστευθέντος, ἐφ᾽ οὗ γέγονεν
ὁ μέγας καὶ πρῶτος ἐν τῇ ᾽Αττικῇ κατακλυσμός,
Φορωνέως ᾽Αργείων βασιλεύοντος, ὡς ᾽Ακουσίλαος
ἱστορεῖ, μέχρι πρώτης ᾽Ολυμπιάδος, ὁπόθεν
῞Ελληνες ἀκριβοῦν τοὺς | χρόνους ἐνόμισαν, ἔτη   489a
15 συνάγεται χίλια εἴκοσιν, ὡς καὶ τοῖς προειρη-
μένοις συμφωνεῖ καὶ τοῖς ἐξῆς δειχθήσεται. (8)   (8)
ταῦτα γὰρ <οἱ τὰ> ᾽Αθηναίων ἱστοροῦντες, ῾Ελ-
λάνικός τε καὶ Φιλόχορος οἱ τὰς ᾽Ατθίδας, οἵ
τε τὰ Σύρια Κάστωρ καὶ Θαλλὸς καὶ <ὁ> τὰ πάντων
20 Διόδωρος ὁ τὰς Βιβλιοθήκας ᾽Αλέξανδρός τε ὁ
Πολυΐστωρ καὶ τινες, <οἳ> τῶν καθ᾽ ἡμᾶς ἀκρι-
βέστερον ἐμνήσθησαν καὶ τῶν ᾽Αττικῶν ἁπάντων.

BIGN(D)

1 δὲ τὰ om. ND¹ (add. D⁴) | 2 πεντεκοστῇ πέμπτη N:
πεντηκοστῇ D¹ | 3 Βιβλ. Διοδ. I: Διοδ. Βιβλ. GN |
Θαλοῦ IGN | 4 ἔτι δὲ: καὶ ND¹(corr. D⁴) | 5-6 ἔστιν--
᾽Ολυμπιάδων: καὶ ἑτέρων ἐστὶν εὑρεῖν ND¹ (corr. D⁴) |
8 τὰς: τὰ ? Routh, Reliquiae Sacrae 2.271 | 15 συνάγε-
ται IG: συνάγονται BN | χίλια εἴκοσιν I: ,ακ᾽ GN:
,αη B | ὡς: ὃ ? Routh, Reliquiae Sacrae 2.272 |
17 <οἱ τὰ> ? Routh, Reliquiae Sacrae 2.273 | 18 οἱ: ὁ ?
Routh, Reliquiae Sacrae 2.272 | 18-22 οἵ -- ἁπάντων om. B |
19 Θαλλὸς I: Θαλὸς GN | <ὁ> ? Routh, Reliquiae Sacrae
2.272 | 20 ὁ τῶν Βιβλιοθηκῶν ND | 21 καὶ τινες <οἳ>
Mras: καὶ τινες MSS: οἵτινες ? Routh, Reliquiae Sacrae
2.272.

FRAGMENT FOUR[19]

(4)   (4) "After the seventy years of the Captivity,[20]
Cyrus became king of Persia, in the year in which
the fifty-fifth Olympic festival was held,[21] as one
may learn from the <u>Bibliotheca</u> of Diodorus,[22] and
the histories of Thallus and Castor,[23] also from
Polybius[24] and Phlegon,[25] and from others too who
were careful about Olympiads: for the time agreed
in all of them."

                    *   *   *   *   *

(7)   (7) "And the Athenian chronology computes the
earlier events in the following way; from Ogyges,[26]
who was believed among them to be an aboriginal, in
whose time that great and first flood occurred in
Attica,[27] when Phoroneus was king of Argos, as
Acusilaus relates, down to the first Olympiad from
which the Greeks considered that they calculated
their dates correctly, a thousand and twenty years
are computed,[28] which agrees with what has been stated
before, and will be shown to agree also with what
(8)   comes after. (8) For both the historians of Athens,
Hellanicus[29] and Philochorus[30] who wrote <u>The Attic
Histories</u>,[31] and the writers on Syrian history,[32]
Castor[33] and Thallus, and the writer on universal
history, Diodorus the author of the <u>Bibliotheca</u>,
and Alexander Polyhistor,[34] and some of our own
historians recorded these events more accurately
even than all the Attic writers."

FRAGMENT FOUR

= Pseudo-Justin, Cohortatio ad Gentiles 9

(9) Ἄρξομαι τοίνυν ἀπὸ τοῦ πρώτου παρ' ἡμῖν   (9)
προφήτου τε καὶ νομοθέτου Μωυσέως, πρότερον
τοὺς χρόνους, καθ' οὓς γέγονε, μετὰ πάσης
ἀξιοπίστου παρ' ὑμῖν μαρτυρίας ἐκθέμενος· οὐ
5 γὰρ ἀπὸ τῶν θείων καὶ παρ' ἡμῖν ἱστοριῶν μόνον
ταῦτα ἀποδεῖξαι πειρῶμαι, αἷς ὑμεῖς οὐδέπω
διὰ τὴν παλαιὰν τῶν προγόνων ὑμῶν πλάνην
πιστεύειν βούλεσθε, ἀλλ' ἀπὸ τῶν ὑμετέρων καὶ
μηδὲν τῇ ἡμετέρᾳ θρησκείᾳ διαφερουσῶν ἱστορι-
10 ῶν, ἵνα γνῶτε ὅτι πάντων τῶν παρ' ὑμῖν εἴτε
σοφῶν εἴτε ποιητῶν εἴτε ἱστοριογράφων ἢ φιλο-
σόφων ἢ νομοθετῶν πολλῷ πρεσβύτατος γέγονεν ὁ
πρῶτος τῆς θεοσεβείας διδάσκαλος ἡμῶν Μωυσῆς
γεγονώς, ὡς δηλοῦσιν ἡμῖν αἱ τῶν Ἑλλήνων
15 ἱστορίαι. Ἐν γὰρ τοῖς χρόνοις Ὠγύγου τε καὶ
Ἰνάχου, οὓς καὶ γηγενεῖς τινες τῶν παρ' ὑμῖν
ὑπειλήφασι γεγενῆσθαι, Μωυσέως μέμνηνται ὡς
ἡγεμόνος τε καὶ ἄρχοντος τοῦ τῶν Ἰουδαίων
γένους.   Οὕτω γὰρ Πολέμων τε ἐν τῇ πρώτῃ τῶν
20 ἑλληνικῶν ἱστοριῶν μέμνηται, καὶ Ἀππίων ὁ
Ποσειδωνίου ἐν τῇ κατὰ Ἰουδαίων βίβλῳ καὶ ἐν
τῇ τετάρτῃ τῶν ἱστοριῶν, λέγων κατὰ Ἴναχον
Ἄργους βασιλέα Ἀμάσιδος Αἰγυπτίων βασιλεύοντος ἀποστῆναι Ἰουδαίους, ὧν ἡγεῖσθαι Μωυσέα.
25 Καὶ Πτολεμαῖος δὲ ὁ Μενδήσιος, τὰ Αἰγυπτίων
ἱστορῶν, ἅπασι τούτοις συντρέχει. Καὶ οἱ τὰ
Ἀθηναίων δὲ ἱστοροῦντες, Ἑλλανικός τε καὶ
Φιλόχορος ὁ τὰς Ἀτθίδας, Κάστωρ τε καὶ Θαλλὸς
καὶ Ἀλέξανδρος ὁ πολυΐστωρ, ἔτι δὲ καὶ οἱ
30 σοφώτατοι Φίλων τε καὶ Ἰώσηπος, οἱ τὰ κατὰ
Ἰουδαίους ἱστορήσαντες, ὡς σφόδρα ἀρχαίου
καὶ παλαιοῦ τῶν Ἰουδαίων ἄρχοντος Μωυσέως μέμνηνται.

FRAGMENT FOUR[35]
Pseudo-Justin, <u>Coh. ad Gent</u>. 9

(9)   (9) I will begin, then, with our first prophet and
        lawgiver, Moses; first explaining the times in which
        he lived, on authorities which among you are worthy
        of all credit. For I do not propose to prove these
        things only from our own divine histories, which as
        yet you are unwilling to credit on account of the
        inveterate error of your forefathers, but also from
        your own histories, and such, too, as have no refer-
        ence to our worship, that you may know that, of all
        your teachers, whether sages, poets, historians,
        philosophers, or lawgivers, by far the oldest, as
        the Greek histories show us, was Moses, who was our
        first religious teacher. For in the time of Ogyges
        and Inachus, whom some of your poets suppose to have
        been earth-born, Moses is mentioned as the leader
        and ruler of the Jewish nation. For in this way he
        is mentioned both by Polemon in the first book of
        his <u>Hellenics</u>, and by Apion son of Posidonius in his
        book against the Jews, and in the fourth book of his
        history, where he says that during the reign of
        Inachus over Argos the Jews revolted from Amasis king
        of the Egyptians, and that Moses led them. And
        Ptolemaeus the Mendesian, in relating the history of
        Egypt, concurs in all this. And those who write
        the Athenian history, Hellanicus and Philochorus
        (the author of <u>The Attic History</u>), Castor and Thallus,
        and Alexander Polyhistor, and also the very well
        informed writers on Jewish affairs, Philo and
        Josephus, have mentioned Moses as a very ancient
        and time-honoured prince of the Jews.

FRAGMENT FIVE (Georgius Syncellus, Ἐκλογὴ Χρονο-
    γραφίας)

ταύτην Ἀσσυριων μα' διεδέξαντο βασιλεῖς, οἳ
καὶ ἀρξάμενοι ἀπὸ τοῦ ,γσις' καθολικοῦ ἔτους
κόσμου ἔληξαν εἰς τὸ ,δχοε' ἔτος τοῦ κόσμου,
διαρκέσαντες ἔτη ὅλα ,αυξ' ἀπὸ τοῦ πρώτου
5   αὐτῶν Βήλου ἕως τοῦ μα' Μακοσκολέρου τοῦ καὶ
Σαρδαναπάλλου, ὡς συμφωνοῦσι πολλοὶ τῶν ἐπισήμων ἱστορικῶν, Πολύβιος καὶ Διόδωρος, Κεφαλίων
τε καὶ Κάστωρ καὶ Θάλλος καὶ ἕτεροι.

FRAGMENT SIX (John Malala, Chronographia)

ταῦτα δὲ ἱστόρησαν οἱ σοφώτατοι Θάλλος καὶ
10 Κάστωρ καὶ Πολύβιος συγγραψάμενου καὶ μετ'
αὐτοὺς Ἡρόδοτος ὁ ἱστοριογράφος· ἅτινα καὶ
ὁ σοφὸς Θεόφιλος ἐχρονογράφησεν.

---

5 Θωνοσκονκολέρου mg apud Dind. | σαρδαναπαλου Bm. ?
apud Dind. | Κεφαλλίων Goar apud Dind. | 8 Θάλλως
Goar apud Dind. | 9 Θάλλος vulg: Θάλης Bentley apud
L. Dindorf |

FRAGMENT FIVE[36]

This one (i.e., the kingdom of the Arabs) succeeded
the forty-one Assyrian kings who, having begun in
the 3216th general year of the world (2286/85),
ended in the 4675th year of the world (927/26),
lasting in all 1460 years, from Bel their first,
until their forty-first Makoskoleros,[37] who is also
called Sardanapallus,[38] as all the distinguished
historians agree -- Polybius,   Didorus, Kephalia,[39]
and Castor,   and Thallus, and others.

FRAGMENT SIX[40]

And these things the wisest of the historians
reported -- Thallus and Castor and Polybius, and
with them Herodotus the historian; such things also
the wise Theophilus chronicled.[41]

ANNOTATIONS

1. Of the surviving fragments from Africanus' chronography,
No. 18 treats the chronological details pertaining to the
death and resurrection of Christ. This reference to
Thallus occurs at the beginning of Frg. No. 18, where
Africanus discusses the darkness accompanying the death
of Christ. The translation is that of ANF 6.136-37, with
slight modification.

2. αἱ ἱστορίαι, perhaps the title. The work was apparently titled and divided into numbered sections.

3. τοῦτο τὸ σκότος: It is not clear from the text whether
"this darkness" of the crucifixion story is mentioned by
Thallus, or whether he merely mentions an eclipse which
Africanus has connected with the Gospel story. Jacoby,
FGrH 2D.836, doubts whether Thallus mentioned the eclipse
in connection with Jewish history. Cf. Mark 15:33; Luke
23:44; Matt 27:45. Cf. also V. Taylor, The Gospel According
to St. Mark (New York: St. Martin's Press, 1966) 592-93.
Goguel, Jesus, 91, thinks Thallus knew the Gospel tradition
but gave it a rationalistic interpretation.

4. On the solar eclipse reported on Nov. 24, 29 C.E.,
cf. Phlegon, FGrH 2B.1159-94 (= No. 260), esp. Frg. 16;
also Boll, "Finsternisse," PW 6 (1909) 2329-2364, esp.
2360. Also, cf. E. Bickerman, Chronology of the Ancient
World (London: Thames and Hudson, 1968) 105, n. 69, and
literature cited therein.

5. Phlegon, cf. FGrH 2B.1159-94 (= No. 260).

6. In Ad Autolycum 3.16, Theophilus turns to the question
of chronology, seeking to demonstrate the antiquity of
Christianity. This passage occurs at the end of the
"chronological epilogue." Thallus is cited by Theophilus
to clinch his point that Moses was far older than the
Greek accounts of the Trojan war. The translation is that
of R. M. Grant, Theophilus of Antioch: Ad Autolycum
(Oxford: Clarendon Press, 1970) 145.

7. On Belos as king of the Assyrians, cf. John of
Antioch, FHG 4.541-42 (= Frg. 4, par. 1-6), who notes that
Belos was the son of Zeus and Hera, and came to rule in
Assyria. Cf. also Nonnus, Dionys. 18.302; 40.382. Cf.
Tümpel, "Belos (3)," PW 3 (1899) 259-64, esp. 263,
section k.

8.   Ogygos - mythical king, originally associated with
Boeotia (Pausanias 9.5.1), later (by the 8th cent. B.C.E.)
with Attica, as father/founder of Eleusis (Pausanias 1.
38.7; Africanus apud Eusebius, P.E. 10.10.10). The
Athenian connection is doubted by Jacoby, FGrH 3b (Suppl.)
vol. 2, p. 282, n. 44 (commentary on No. 328, Frg. 92);
also cf. FGrH 3b (Suppl.), vol. 1, p. 387, and generally
pp. 380-87. In Christian chronography the reign of
Ogygos in Attica serves as a terminus a quo for establish-
ing Athenian chronology. Cf. Africanus apud Eusebius, P.E.
10.10.4 & 7-8 = Frg. 4. Cf. J. Miller, "Ogygos (1),"
PW 17 (1937) 2076-78, esp. 2078; also Wacholder, Eupolemus,
115-24. According to Castor of Rhodes, FGrH 2B.1132
(= No. 250, Frg. 1), Ogygos was a king of the Titans.
Note the app. crit.: the MSS tradition reads ὁ Γύγος.
Thallus possibly confused Ogygos, king of Thebes in
Boeotia, with Gyges, king of Lydia ca. 680 B.C.E. So,
Stearns, 64.

9.   Or, according to Müller's emendation: "Having been
defeated, Kronos fled into Tartessus, but Ogygos fled into
the region of Ogygia which was named for him." Cf. app.
crit. Thus, Kronos would have fled to the west (Tartessus=
Tarshish, near Gibraltar) where he then ruled (cf. Diodorus
Sic. 5.66.5; Cicero, de nat. deor. 3.17; Pindar, Ol. 2.70).
Ogygos, however, would have fled to Ogygia, later named
Attica. Cf. Müll., FHG 3.518; Pfeiffer, History, 203.

10.   I.e., 1515 B.C.E. (1193 B.C.E. + 322). As Jacoby,
FGrH 2D.837, notes, Thallus is cited to document the dates
of Greek chronology, not to prove the high antiquity of
the Jews; the latter is Theophilus' agenda.

11.   In defending the Christian refusal to worship pagan
gods, Tertullian turns to pagan authors themselves to
demonstrate that the Greek and Roman gods of mythology
were originally human beings, later deified, and therefore
not worthy as objects of veneration. Thallus is cited
as a pagan author who attests the original humanity of
Saturn. Similarly, cf. Ad nat. 2.12, although Thallus
is not mentioned. The same argument is repeated by
Minucius Felix and Lactantius. Cf. also Tertullian,
Apol., Frg. to ch. 19, cited in Bindley, 65-68: *Secundum
enim historiam Thalli, qua relatum est bellum Assyriorum
et Saturnum Titanorum regem cum Jove dimicasse* ...
The translation of Frg. 3 is that of A. Souter in Mayor,
Tertulliani Apologeticus (Cambridge: Cambridge University
Press, 1917) 37 & 39.

12.   Cf. Diodorus Siculus 5.66.4-6; 68.1; 69.4-5; 70.1-6;
esp. Frgs. of 6.1.1-3; 8-10; 2.1.

13.   Making the same point in Ad nat. 2.12, Tertullian
adduces a similar list of pagan authors, omitting however
Thallus, and substituting instead Tacitus. Cf. Hist. 5.2.4.

14.   Perhaps Cassius Hemina or Cassius Longinus. Cf.
Müller, FHG 3.517. Bindley, Tertulliani Apologeticus,
40: "Not Cassius Severus, the satirist and orator, who
was banished by Augustus and died A.D. 33, but Lucius
Cassius Hemina, a Roman annalist (ca. B.C. 140), who
wrote a history of Rome from the earliest times to the
end of the third Punic War."

15.   Died ca. 24 B.C.E.

16.   On the use of euhemerism by Christian apologists,
cf. Minucius Felix, Oct. 21; Theophilus, Ad Autolycum
1.9; Clement, Cohort. 1.9; Lactantius, Div. Inst. 1.11;
Augustine, de civ. Dei 6.7; 7.26; cf. Cicero, de nat.
deor. 2.42. References cited by Bindley, 40.

17.   The translation is that of G. H. Rendall, Minucius
Felix (LCL; London: Heinemann/New York: Putnam's, 1931)
375.

18.   The translation is that of W. Fletcher in ANF 7.25.

19.   Towards the end of Book 10, Eusebius turns to a
demonstration of the antiquity of Moses and the prophets
(10.9-14), by citing pagan (Porphyry), Christian (Africanus, Tatian, Clement), and Jewish (Josephus) authors.
This fragment, excerpted from Africanus' Chronographia,
is derived from a section where he sought to synchronize
Hebrew history with that of other peoples. The translation
is that of E. H. Gifford, 2.523-24. It should be noted
that the value of the following fragments (Frgs. 4-6)
is seriously doubted by Jacoby, FGrH 2D.835.

20.   Having previously mentioned the Babylonian captivity,
Africanus noted that Nebuchadnezzar is also mentioned
by the Babylonian historian/ethnographer Berossus.

21.   I.e., ca. 560 B.C.E. (776 B.C.E. - (54 X 4) = 560-
559 B.C.E.). Cyrus' defeat of Astyages did not occur,
however, until ca. 550 B.C.E. Cf. Giff., 4.354; IDB 1.754.

22.   Cf. Diodorus Siculus 2.34.6; 9.20.4; 9.21.1, which =
P.E. 10.10.4.

23.   Cf. FGrH 2B.1130-45 (= No. 250), esp. Frg. 6.

24.   Cf. FGrH 2B.1153 (= No. 254), Frg. 4.

25.   Cf. FGrH 2B.1159-94 (= No. 257), Frg. 8.

26.   Cf. Frg. 2, and above note 8. On the use of Ogygos in
chronology, cf. Jacoby, FGrH 3b (Supplement), vol. 1,
pp. 380-89, and notes in 3b (Supplement), vol. 2, pp.
278-84.

27.   On the flood in the time of Ogygos, cf. Eusebius,
P.E. 10.9.20; 11.20 (Tatian); 12.9 (Clement). On the
flood traditions, cf. Jacoby, FGrH 3b (Supplement), vol.
2, p. 282, n. 50 on Frg. 328, Frg. 92.

28.   I.e., 1796 B.C.E. (776 B.C.E. + 1020).   Also, cf.
P.E. 10.10.21 (Africanus).   Elsewhere, Ogygos is cited as
contemporary with the Exodus. Cf. Eusebius, P.E. 10.10.
9-11 (Africanus).   Africanus, apud Eusebius, P.E. 10.10.
14-15, computes the time from Ogygos until the time of
Cyrus as 1237 years.

29.   Cf. FGrH 1A.104-52 (= No. 4), Frg. 47.

30.   Cf. FGrH 3b (Supplement), vol. 1, pp. 280-395, esp.
383-85 (= No. 328, Frg. 92). Also, texts in FGrH 3B.97-160
(= No. 328), Frg. 92, and commentary in FGrH 3b (Supplement), vol. 2, pp. 380-89.

31.   Pseudo-Justin, Coh. ad Gen. 9, gives the title as
ὁ τὰς 'Ατθίδας. Cf. Thucydides 1.97.

32.   τὰ Σύρια: Hengel, Judaism and Hellenism, 1.89, concludes, apparently on the basis of this text, that
Thallus was "at least a Syrian."

33.   Cf. FGrH 2B.1130-45 (= No. 250), Frg. 7.

34.   Cf. FGrH 3A.96-126 (= No. 273).

35.   This fragment from Pseudo-Justin appears to be
directly dependent on Africanus = Frg. 4. The translation
is that of M. Dods in ANF 1.277.

36.   This fragment occurs in the section of Syncellus'
chronology treating the 18th generation, anno mundi,
specifically the Arabian kings who succeeded the
Chaldean rulers.

37.   Μακοσκολέρου: perhaps a conflation of μαλακός and
χαλαρός = Μα(λα)κοσχαλαρος. On the effeminacy of Sardanapallus, cf. Diodorus Siculus 2.23.1-4. So, Stearns,
63.   Note app. crit.: Θωνοσκονκολέρου. Also, Syncellus
1.312 apud Weissbach (cf. next note), 2454: Θῶνος ὁ
λεγόμενος Κονκόλερος Ἑλληνιστὶ Σαρδανάπαλλος.

38.   Sardanapallus is perhaps a conflation of Ashurbanipal
(668-627 ?) and Shamashshumukin.   On Sardanapallus, cf.
Weissbach, "Sardanapal," PW second series 1.A (1920)
2436-75, esp. 2453-54, par. 19.

39.   Cf. FGrH 2A.436-46 (= No. 93), Frg. 2.

40.   This fragment occurs in a section of Malala's chronicle which treats Croesus and Cyrus.

41.   Cf. above, Frg. 2.

Justus of Tiberias,[1] who flourished in the late first
century C.E., is known primarily through the unflattering
portrait of him in Josephus' _Life_. Like Josephus, he
played an active role as a leader of the resistance forces
in Galilee in the Jewish revolt against the Romans in
66-70 C.E., though he eventually left his native city of
Tiberias and went over to Agrippa II.[2] Although Josephus
assails his character, impugns his motives, and casts him
in the role of political agitator and extremist,[3] most
likely he was a man with far more moderate views who was
forced into the war unavoidably and lived to regret it.[4]
The exact nature of his role in the Galilean campaign and
his motives for opposing Josephus' military efforts in
Tiberias are still debated, lost in Josephus' heated
polemic.[5]

Ironically enough, however, it was Josephus, his
literary and political rival, who immortalized Justus since
he is largely unknown from any other source. In spite of
its polemical nature, Josephus' account makes several
things clear. First, Justus, and his father, Pistus,[6]
were prominent Tiberians well enough reputed to assume
positions of leadership in the early stages of the war.[7]
For all his disparaging remarks, Josephus nevertheless
attests Justus' cultural achievements and social standing,
asserting that he was "not unversed in Greek culture."[8]
Josephus also openly admits his oratorical ability.[9]
Further evidence of his Hellenization is seen in his Greek
name, as well as that of his father.[10] He was doubtless
fluent in Greek as seen by his later elevation as the
private secretary of Agrippa II, a position from which he
was later dismissed.[11]

371

The fragments, though scant, with their citation of
an anecdote about the young Plato,[12] and their clear
interest in history in the form of world chronicle,[13]
reinforce this portrait of a Jewish man of affairs,
directly involved in war and politics, thoroughly at home
in the Hellenistic-Roman world. Though his career after
the war was checkered with setbacks, imprisonments, and
banishments from his native city, to which he returned
after the war, he managed to fend for himself rather
well in court politics.[14] The year of his death is
unknown, but he is mentioned as late as the reign of
Nerva,[15] and lived at least until after the death of
Agrippa II.[16]

Works. Three separate works, all apparently written
in Greek, are attributed to Justus: (1) A Chronicle of
the Jewish Kings. The title is attested by Photius (9th
cent.) who describes it as "very scanty in detail" and
as having "passed over very many necessary items."[17] It
appears to have extended from the time of Moses until the
death of Agrippa II,[18] and may in fact have been a comprehensive world chronicle.[19] The work was most certainly
used as a source by Julius Africanus,[20] from whom Eusebius
in his Chronicon[21] and Syncellus[22] probably cited it.
The work was possibly used by the Arian historian
Philostorgius (d. ca. 429 C.E.),[23] and may have had even
wider influence among later Christian chronographers.[24]
(2) A History of the Jewish War. Although sometimes
identified with the Chronicle, this was most likely a
separate work.[25] This work was the object of Josephus'
scorn in his Life, and was mentioned by later writers
including Eusebius, Jerome, Photius, the Suda, and
Stephanus of Byzantium,[26] all of whom appear to be
directly dependent on Josephus for their information.
Josephus' Life was written largely as a refutation of
the work.[27] Once again, Josephus' remarks about the work
in his Life provide unintended historical information
about the work. The work apparently concentrated on the

Galilean campaign prior to the arrival of Vespasian,
and directly attacked Josephus for his punitive actions
against the city of Tiberias.[28] Josephus assails Justus
for describing events he had not witnessed, e.g., certain
events in Galilee, the siege of Jotapata, and the siege
of Jerusalem,[29] and for writing long after the fact.
Though he worked on the History during a twenty-year
period,[30] Justus did not publish it until after Vespasian,
Titus, and Agrippa II were dead.[31] It is also clear from
Josephus' remarks that Justus' account of the war was
both comprehensive and detailed.[32] The impact of the work
was apparently negligible.[33] (3) Jerome attributes a
third work to Justus, a scriptural commentary, but the
work is nowhere else attested, and its existence is
generally doubted.[34]

Importance. In many respects, Justus resembles
Eupolemus: both were Greek-speaking Jewish historians
from Palestine who were actively involved in war and
politics during a turbulent period of Jewish history.
Obviously, Josephus belongs to the same historiographical
tradition. Justus also represents the tradition of Jewish
chronography that was seen as early as Demetrius and
continued in other Hellenistic-Jewish writers such as
Eupolemus and Pseudo-Eupolemus. He becomes another
valuable witness to the degree of Hellenization within
Palestine. He continues to remain central to the discussion of Jewish historiography in first century Palestine,
and a valuable source, albeit indirectly through Josephus'
Life, for reconstructing the events in Galilee in the
early stages of the Jewish revolt.

The Fragments and Their Arrangement. Strictly
speaking, no fragments of Justus' works survive. The
remaining evidence is more in the nature of testimonia.
Nevertheless, the materials have been included and
arranged as "fragments," following Jacoby's arrangement
in FGrH 734. A sixth "doubtful" fragment is mentioned by
Jacoby, but is not included here. Cf. Note 23.

NOTES

1. Testimonia: Josephus, Life 32, 36-42, 65, 87-88, 174-78, 276-78, 336-44, 349-50, 355-60, 390-93, 410 = FGrH 734, T 3 & 6; Eusebius, H.E. 3.10.8; Chronicle ad ann. Abrah. 2113 = FGrH 734 T 5; Jerome, De viris illustribus 14 = PL (23) col. 631 = TU 14.1 (1896) p. 16 = FGrH 734 T 1; Pseudo-Sophronius = TU 14.2 (1896) p. 17 = Suda s.v. Ἰουστος Τιβερεύς; Stephanus of Byzantium s.v. Τιβεριάς = FGrH 734 T 4; Photius, Bibliotheca 33 = FGrH 734 T 2; Syncellus, ed. Dindorf 116,18; 122,9; 655,7.

2. Josephus, Life 354, 357, 390-97.

3. Josephus, Life 36-42, 344, 391.

4. So, Schürer (Vermes-Millar) 1.34-35; also Schalit, EncJud, 480; against Krauss, 398-99, who is more sympathetic to Josephus' interpretation of Justus' actions. Cf., esp. Josephus, Life 36: ὑπεκρίνετο μὲν ἐνδοιάζειν πρὸς τὸν πόλεμον ...

5. For a recent treatment, cf. Cohen, 114-43.

6. Cf. Josephus, Life 34; Photius, Bibliotheca 33.

7. Cf. Josephus, Life 32-34. Pistus belonged to the group of ἄνδρες εὐσχήμονες.

8. Josephus, Life 40: οὐδ᾽ ἄπειρος ἦν παιδείας τῆς παρ᾽ Ἕλλησιν.

9. Josephus, Life 40, 279.

10. The name Justus is well attested in the period, and most likely his Hebrew name was Zadok, or possibly Joseph. Cf. Krauss, 399; Cohen, 141, who notes the inscriptional evidence for Justi of Tiberias in Frey, CIJ 1. No. 502; Vincent, RB 30 (1922) 121 (as noted by Rajak, 351); also IG 5.1, No. 1256. Cf. Acts 1:23; 18:7; Rom 16:23; Col 4:11.

11. Josephus, Life 356.

12. Cf. Frg. 1. As Cohen, 143, n. 147, notes, "Historical or not, the story is a good sign of Justus' Greek education."

13. Cf. Frgs. 2-3.

14. Krauss, 399, raises the possibility that he, like Josephus, spent his last years in Rome.

15. Cf. Eusebius, Chron. = Karst, GCS (20), p. 218,
where Justus of Tiberias is mentioned as a Jewish author
during the reign of Nerva (96-98 C.E.).

16. This is according to the testimony of Photius, Bib.
33, who places the death of Agrippa II in the third year
of the reign of Trajan (98-117 C.E.), that is, ca. 100
C.E. Cohen, 170-80, however, notes that the testimony
from Photius is the primary evidence for this, and argues
for putting the death of Agrippa ca. 92-93 C.E.

17. Photius, Bibliotheca 33, p. 6 b 23-7 a 5, = ed. R.
Henry, Paris (1959) 1 = FGrH 734 T 2: 'Ανεγνώσθη 'Ιούστου
Τιβεριέως χρονικόν, οὗ ἡ ἐπιγραφὴ ''Ιούστου Τιβεριέως
'Ιουδαίων Βασιλέων τῶν ἐν τοῖς στέμμασιν.' (2) οὗτός ἀπὸ
πόλεως τῆς ἐν Γαλιλαίᾳ Τιβεριάδος ὡρμᾶτο.(3) ἄρχεται δὲ τῆς
ἱστορίας ἀπὸ Μωϋσέως, καταλήγει δὲ ἕως τελευτῆς 'Αγρίππα
τοῦ ἑβδόμου μὲν τῶν ἀπὸ τῆς οἰκίας 'Ηρῴδου, ὑστάτου δὲ ἐν
τοῖς 'Ιουδαίων βασιλεῦσιν, ὃς παρέλαβε μὲν τὴν ἀρχὴν ἐπὶ
Κλαυδίου, ηὐξήθη δὲ ἐπὶ Νέρωνος καὶ ἔτι μᾶλλον ὑπὸ Οὐεσπασιανοῦ, τελευτᾷ δὲ ἔτει τρίτῳ Τραϊανοῦ, οὗ καὶ ἡ ἱστορία
κατέληξεν. (4) ἔστι δὲ τὴν φράσιν συντομώτατός τε καὶ τὰ
πλεῖστα τῶν ἀναγκαιοτάτων παρατρέχων. ὡς δὲ τὰ 'Ιουδαίων
νοσῶν, 'Ιουδαῖος καὶ αὐτὸς ὑπάρχων τὸ γένος, τῆς Χριστοῦ
παρουσίας καὶ τῶν περὶ αὐτὸν τελεσθέντων καὶ τῶν ὑπ' αὐτοῦ
τερατουργηθέντων οὐδὲν ὅλως μνήμην ἐποιήσατο. (5) οὗτος
παῖς μὲν ἦν 'Ιουδαίου τινὸς ὄνομα Πίστου, ἀνθρώπων δέ, ὡς
φησι 'Ιώσηπος, κακουργότατος, χρημάτων τε καὶ ἡδονῶν ἥττων.
ἀντεπολιτεύετο δὲ 'Ιωσήπῳ, καὶ πολλὰς κατ' ἐκείνου λέγεται
ἐπιβουλὰς ῥάψαι, ἀλλὰ τόν γε 'Ιώσηπον, καίτοι ὑπὸ χεῖρα
πολλάκις λαβόντα τὸν ἐχθρόν, λόγοις μόνον ὀνειδίσαντα
ἀπαθῆ κακῶν ἀφεῖναι. (6) καὶ τὴν ἱστορίαν δὲ ἣν ἐκεῖνος
ἔγραψε, πεπλασμένην τὰ πλεῖστά φησι τυγχάνειν, καὶ μάλιστα
οἷς τὸν 'Ρωμαϊκὸν πρὸς 'Ιουδαίους διέξεισι πόλεμον καὶ τὴν
'Ιεροσολύμων ἅλωσιν. Full translation in Cohen, 142;
also cf. Collins, 49.

18. I.e., ca. 100 C.E., though cf. above note 16.

19. Frg. 1 suggests that it also treated Greek events.

20. So, Gelzer, Sextus, 246-65.

21. Cf. Frg. 2.

22. Cf. Frg. 3.

23. Suda s.v. Φλέγων: τούτου τοῦ Φλέγοντος, ὡς φησι
Φιλοστόργιος, † ὅσον † τὰ κατὰ τοὺς 'Ιουδαίους συμπεσόντα
διὰ πλείονος ἐπεξελθεῖν τοῦ πλάτους ... = FGrH 737, Frg.
3. Valckenaer apud Jacoby emended the text to read:
<περὶ> τούτου τοῦ Φλέγοντος {ὡς} φησι Φιλοστόργιος,
'Ιοῦστον (or perhaps 'Ιώσηπον) ... As Schürer (Vermes-
Millar) 1.37, note, "It is possible that the original
reading was 'Ιοῦστον, but more likely in fact that it was
'Ιώσηπον, for Josephus is explicitly referred to a few
lines lower down."

24.   Cf. Gutschmid, Kleine Schriften, 2.203.

25.   Cf. Schürer (Vermes-Millar) 1.35.

26.   Cf. references in note 1 above. The title is given
by Stephanus of Byzantium: ὁ Ἰουδαϊκὸς πόλεμος ὁ κατὰ
Οὐεσπασιανοῦ.

27.   Laqueur also suggested that Ag.Ap. 1.46-56 was
directed against Justus. Cf. Cohen, 116, esp. n. 64.

28.   Cf. Cohen, 116.

29.   Cf. Frg. 4.

30.   Cf. Cohen, 115.

31.   Josephus, Life 359-60; cf. Frg. 4.

32.   Josephus, Life 40, 336, 338.

33.   Cohen, 143, remarks the greater success of Justus'
Chronicle: "While the Chronicle had some influence, the
History of the War disappeared without a trace. Josephus
so dominated Christian historiography that Justus was
ignored. There is no sign that any pagan author even
read Justus' History."

34.   Jerome, De viris illustribus 14 = FGrH 734 T 1 =
PL (23) col. 63: Iustus Tiberiensis de provincia Galileae
conatus est et ipse Iudaicarum rerum historiam texere et
quosdam commentariolos de scripturis; sed hunc Iosephus
arguit mendacii. constat autem illum eo tempore scripsisse
quo et Iosephum.

Bibliography

Baerwald, A. _Josephus in Galiläa. Sein Verhältniss zu den Parteien, insbesondere zu Justus von Tiberias und Agrippa II_ (Breslau: Koebner, 1877).

Cohen, S. J. D. _Josephus in Galilee and Rome. His VITA and Development as a Historian_ (Columbia Studies in the Classical Tradition, 8; Leiden: Brill, 1979) 15-16, 17, 21, 75, 79, 114-43, 159, 167-69, 172, 218, 238-39.

Collins, _Athens and Jerusalem_, 48-49.

Denis, _Introduction_, 267.

Drexler, H. "Untersuchungen zu Josephus und zur Geschichte des jüdischen Aufstandes 66-70," _Klio_ 19 (1925) 277-312, esp. 293-306.

Frankfort, T. "La date de l'autobiographie de Flavius Josèphe et des oeuvres de Justus de Tibériade," _Revue Belge de philologie et d'histoire_ 39 (1961) 52-58.

Gelzer, _Sextus_, 1.4, 20, 118, 207, 265.

Gelzer, M. "Die Vita des Josephos," _Hermes_ 80 (1952) 67-90.

Graetz, _History_ 2 (1893; repr. 1946) 274, 319-20, 390.

_____, "Das Lebensende des Königs Agrippa II, des Justus von Tiberias und des Flavius Josephus und die Agrippa-Münzen," _MGWJ_ 26 (1877) 337-59.

Gutschmid, _Kleine Schriften_ 2.196-203.

Hegermann, _Umwelt_, 1.321.

Hengel, _Judaism and Hellenism_, 1.99, 105.

Jacoby, F. "Iustus (9)," _PW_ 10 (1919) 1341-46.

Krauss, S. "Justus of Tiberias," _JE_ 7 (1904) 398-99.

Laqueur, R. _Der jüdische Historiker Flavius Josephus. Ein biographischer Versuch auf neuer quellen- kritischer Grundlage._ (Giessen, 1920) 6-23.

Landman, I (ed.), "Justus of Tiberias," _UJE_ 6 (1942) 272.

Lohse, E. "Justus von Tiberias," _RGG_[3] 3 (1959) 1077.

Luther, H.   Josephus und Justus von Tiberias. Ein Beitrag
    zur Geschichte des jüdischen Aufstandes (Doctoral
    dissertation, Halle. 1910).

Müller, FHG 3.523.

Niese, B. "Der jüdische Historiker Josephus," Historische
    Zeitschrift 40 (1896) 193-237, esp. 227-29.

Pelletier, A. Flavius Josèphe. Autobiographie. Texte établi
    et traduit. (Paris, 1959) xiv.

Pfeiffer, History, 210.

Rajak, T. "Justus of Tiberias," CQ n.s. 23 (1973) 345-68.

Rühl, F.   "Justus von Tiberias," Rheinisches Museum
    71 (1916) 289-308.

Schalit, A.   "Josephus und Justus. Studien zur Vita des
    Josephus," Klio   26 (1933) 67-95.

_____, "Justus of Tiberias," EncJud   10 (1971) 479-80.

Schlatter, A.   "Der Chronograph aus dem zehnten Jahre
    Antonins," TU 12,1 (1894) 37-47.

_____, Geschichte, 17, 329, 342-44, 367.

Schmid-Stählin, Geschichte, 2,1.601-603.

Schürer (Vermes-Millar), 1.34-37.

_____, Geschichte, 1.58-63; 3.496-97.

_____, Literature, 222.

Wacholder, Eupolemus, 43, 56, 60, 63-64, 67, 123-27, 243,
    260, 298-306.

Wachsmuth, Einleitung, 438.

Index to Editions and Translations

Kings of the Jews Who Are in the Genealogical Lists

Fragment One

Source: Diogenes Laertius 2.41.

Greek Text Used: R. D. Hicks, Diogenes Laertius
    (LCL; New York: Putnams / London: Heinemann,
    1925), vol. 1, p. 170, lines 17-21.

Editions: Jac., FGrH 3C.699 (= No. 734, Frg. 1).

Translations:

    English: R. D. Hicks, Diogenes Laertius
                    (LCL), vol. 1, p. 171.

    French:

    German:

Fragment Two

Source: Eusebius, Chronicon.

Later Citations: Eustathius, In Hexaemeron
    commentarius = PG (18) col. 707A/708A;
    Georgius Syncellus, Ἐκλογὴ Χρονογραφίας.

Greek Text Used: G. Dindorf, Georgius Syncellus et
    Nicephorus (Corpus Scriptorum Historiae
    Byzantinae, 12 [microfiche]; Bonn: E. Weber,
    1829), vol. 1, p. 122, lines 3-10.

Editions: Migne, PG (19) cols. 315A - 317A;
    R. Helm, Eusebius Werke: Die Chronik des
    Hieronymus (GCS, 47 [24 & 34], p. 7, lines
    11-17 (Latin); also, cf. p. 279, line 7;
    Jac., FGrH 3C.699 (= No. 734, *Frg. 2).

Translations:

    English:

    French:

    German:

Kings of the Jews (cont.)

Fragment Three

    Source: Julius Africanus

    Later Citations: Georgius Syncellus, Ἐκλογή
    Χρονογραφίας.

    Greek Text Used: G. Dindorf, Georgius Syncellus
    et Nicephorus (Corpus Scriptorum Historiae
    Byzantinae, 12 [microfiche]; Bonn: E. Weber,
    1829), vol. 1, p. 116, line 17 - p. 117, line 3.

    Editions: Jac., FGrH 3C.699 (= No. 734, *Frg. 3);
    cf. Migne PG (10), col. 77B; Routh, Reliquiae
    Sacrae 2.276.

    Translations:

        English:

        French:

        German:

The Jewish War Against Vespasian

Fragment Four

    Source: Josephus, Life 357-60.

    Greek Text Used: H. St. J. Thackeray, Josephus
    (LCL; Cambridge, Mass.: Harvard University
    Press / London: Heinemann, 1961), vol. 1, pp.
    130 & 132.

    Editions: Niese, 4.378-79; Jac., FGrH 3C.699 (= No.
    734, Frg. 4; cf. T 3c; 6g).

    Translations:

        English: Thackeray, LCL, vol. 1, pp. 131 & 133.

        French: A. Pelletier, Flavius Josèphe. Auto-
                  biographie (Paris: Société d'edition
                  "Les Belles Lettres," 1959), pp. 57-
                  58.

        German: Heinrich Clementz, Des Flavius
                  Josephus. Kleinere Schriften (Halle:
                  Hendel, 1901), p. 63.

Jewish War (cont.)

Fragment Five

Source: Josephus, Life 340.

Greek Text Used: H. St. J. Thackeray (LCL; Cambridge,
    Mass.: Harvard University Press / London:
    Heinemann, 1961), vol. 1, p. 124.

Editions: Niese 4.376; Jac., FGrH 3C.699 (No. 734,
    Frg. 5).

Translations:

    English: Thackeray, LCL, vol. 1, p. 125.

    French: A. Pelletier, Flavius Josèphe. Auto-
                 biographie (Paris: Société d'edition
                 "Les Belles Lettres," 1959), p. 55.

    German: H. Clementz, Des Flavius Josephus.
                 Kleinere Schriften (Halle: Hendel,
                 1901), p. 60.

1. ΙΟΥΔΑΙΩΝ ΒΑΣΙΛΕΙΣ ΟΙ ΕΝ ΤΟΙΣ ΣΤΕΜΜΑΣΙΝ

FRAGMENT ONE (Diogenes Laertius 2.41)

(41) Κρινομένου δ' αὐτοῦ φησιν 'Ιοῦστος ὁ Τιβε-   (41)
ριεὺς ἐν τῷ Στέμματι Πλάτωνα ἀναβῆναι ἐπὶ τὸ βῆμα,
καὶ εἰπεῖν 'νεώτατος ὤν, ὦ ἄνδρες 'Αθηναῖοι, τῶν
ἐπὶ τὸ βῆμα ἀναβάντων,' τοὺς δὲ δικαστὰς ἐκβοῆσαι
5 'κατάβα, κατάβα.'

FRAGMENT TWO (Eusebius, Chronicon apud Georgius
      Syncellus 'Εκλογὴ Χρονογραφίας, p. 122,3-10
      Dindorf)

Μωϋσέα γένος 'Εβραῖον, προφητῶν ἁπάντων πρῶτον,
ἀμφὶ τοῦ σωτῆρος ἡμῶν, λέγω δὲ τοῦ Χριστοῦ, ἀμφί
τε τῆς τῶν ἐθνῶν δι' αὐτοῦ θεογνωσίας χρησμοὺς
καὶ λόγια θείᾳ γραφῇ παραδεδωκότα, τοῖς χρόνοις
10 ἀκμάσαι κατὰ ῏Ιναχον εἰρήκασιν ἄνδρες ἐν παιδεύσει
γνώριμοι, Κλήμης, 'Αφρικανός, Τατιανὸς τοῦ καθ'
ἡμᾶς λόγου τῶν τε ἐκ περιτομῆς 'Ιώσηπος καὶ
'Ιοῦστος, ἰδίως ἕκαστος τὴν ἀπόδειξιν ἐκ παλαιᾶς
ὑποσχὼν ἱστορίας.

FRAGMENT THREE (Julius Africanus apud Georgius
      Syncellus 'Εκλογὴ Χρονογραφίας, p. 116,17 -
      p. 117,3 Dindorf)

15 οἵ τε γὰρ ἐκ περιτομῆς πάντες, 'Ιώσηππός τε καὶ
'Ιοῦστος, οἵ τε ἐξ 'Ελλήνων, Πολέμων φημὶ καὶ
'Απίων Ποσειδώνιος καὶ 'Ηρόδοτος τὴν ἐξ Αἰγύπτου
πορείαν τοῦ 'Ισραὴλ κατὰ Φορωνέα καὶ ῏Απιδα τοὺς
'Αργείων βασιλεῖς συνέγραψαν, 'Αμώσεως Αἰγυπτίων
20 βασιλεύοντος .....

---

6 γένος 'Εβραῖον Scaliger apud Dindorf: γένος 'Εβραίων
Sync.: κατὰ γένος 'Εβραῖον mg apud Dindorf: *gentis
hebraeae* Hieron. | 9 θεῖα A: θεία B: θείᾳ Goar apud
Dindorf: *sacris (litteris)* Hieron. | παραδεδωκότας Goar
apud Dindorf | 16 Πολέμῳ B | 17 Ποσιδώνιος B:
Ποσειδωνίου mg apud Dindorf |

1. Kings of the Jews Who Are in the Genealogical Lists[1]

FRAGMENT ONE[2]

(41)   (41)   And while he[3] was being tried, Justus of
Tiberias says in his book The Genealogy,[4] that Plato
ascended to the platform and said, "O men of Athens,
since I am the youngest to have ascended the platform
....," but the judges cried out, "Get down! Get
down!"

FRAGMENT TWO[5]

Men of distinguished learning -- Clement, Africanus,
and Tatian from our persuasion, and from among those
of the circumcision Josephus and Justus -- have said
that Moses, by race a Hebrew,[6] preeminent among all
the prophets, who transmitted oracles and utterances
in sacred scripture[7] for the sake of our Savior,
I mean Christ, and for the sake of the nations'
knowledge of God through him, flourished in the time
of Inachus,[8] each in his own way claiming that he
belonged to a period of remote history.

FRAGMENT THREE[9]

For indeed all those of the circumcision -- Josephus
and Justus -- as well as those of the Greeks --
I also include Polemo, Apion, the son of Posidonius,[10]
and Herodotus -- described the journey of Israel from
Egypt (as occurring) at the time of Phoroneus and
Apis,[11] kings of Argos, while Amosis reigned over
the Egyptians ....

2. ΙΟΥΔΑΙΚΟΣ ΠΟΛΕΜΟΣ (Ο ΚΑΤΑ ΟΥΕΣΠΑΣΙΑΝΟΥ)

FRAGMENT FOUR (Josephus, Life 357-60)

(357) Θαυμάζειν δ᾽ ἔπεισί μοι τὴν σὴν ἀναίδειαν, (357)
ὅτι τολμᾷς λέγειν ἁπάντων τῶν τὴν πραγματείαν
ταύτην γεγραφότων αὐτὸς ἄμεινον ἐξηγγελκέναι,
μήτε τὰ πραχθέντα κατὰ τὴν Γαλιλαίαν ἐπιστάμενος,
5 ἧς γὰρ ἐν Βηρυτῷ τότε παρὰ βασιλεῖ, μήθ᾽ ὅσα
ἔπαθον Ῥωμαῖοι ἐπὶ τῆς Ἰωταπάτων πολιορκίας ἢ
ἔδρασαν ἡμᾶς παρακολουθήσας, μήθ᾽ ὅσα κατ᾽ ἐμαυτὸν
ἔπραξα πολιορκούμενος δυνηθεὶς πυθέσθαι· πάντες
γὰρ οἱ ἀπαγγείλαντες ἂν διεφθάρησαν ἐπὶ τῆς παρα-
10 τάξεως ἐκείνης. (358) ἀλλ᾽ ἴσως τὰ κατὰ τὴν (358)
Ἱεροσολυμιτῶν πραχθέντα μετὰ ἀκριβείας φήσεις
συγγεγραφέναι. καὶ πῶς οἷόν τε; οὔτε γὰρ τῷ
πολέμῳ παρέτυχες οὔτε τὰ Καίσαρος ἀνέγνως ὑπομνήματα. μέγιστον δὲ τεκμήριον· τοῖς {γὰρ} Καίσαρος
15 ὑπομνήμασιν ἐναντίαν πεποίησαι τὴν γραφήν. (359) (359)
εἰ δὲ θαρρεῖς ἄμεινον ἁπάντων συγγεγραφέναι, διὰ
τί ζώντων Οὐεσπασιανοῦ καὶ Τίτου τῶν αὐτοκρατό-
ρων τοῦ πολέμου γενομένων καὶ βασιλέως Ἀγρίππα
περιόντος ἔτι καὶ τῶν ἐκ γένους αὐτοῦ πάντων,
20 ἀνδρῶν τῆς Ἑλληνικῆς παιδείας ἐπὶ πλεῖστον
ἡκόντων, τὴν ἱστορίαν οὐκ ἔφερες εἰς μέσον; (360) (360)
πρὸ γὰρ εἴκοσιν ἐτῶν εἶχες γεγραμμένην καὶ παρ᾽
εἰδότων ἔμελλες τῆς ἀκριβείας τὴν μαρτυρίαν ἀπο-
φέρεσθαι. νῦν δ᾽, ὅτ᾽ ἐκεῖνοι μὲν οὐκέτ᾽ εἰσὶν
25 μεθ᾽ ἡμῶν, ἐλεγχθῆναι δ᾽ οὐ νομίζεις, τεθάρρηκας.

PRAMW

1 δέ μοι ἔπεισι MW | ἀναίδιαν P | 3 γεγραφηκότων MW |
5 μήτε MW | 6 ἰωταπατῶν P: ἰωταπάντων A | 7 μήτε MW |
8 ἔπραξα: ἔδρασα P | 9 ἂν om. R | 10 τὴν: τὰ R |
11 ἱεροσολυμιτῶν AMW: Ἱεροσόλυμα Niese | μετ᾽ R |
13 ἀνέγνως: ἀναγνοῦσ PRMW | 14 δὲ om. P: ὃν MW | {γὰρ}
Thackeray: γὰρ Niese: om. PAMW | 18 τοῦ πολέμου γενομένων
(γενομένου M) PAMW: τῶν τὸν πόλεμον κατεργασαμένων Niese |
ἀγρίππα^υ A | 19 περιόντος: ε ex α corr. R | ἐκ: ἐκ τοῦ W|
ἁπάντων MW | 22 εἴκοσιν RAM: εἴκοσι Niese | 24 δὲ MW |
ὅτε AMW | οὐκ ἔτι AMW | 25 δὲ MW |

2. The Jewish War (Against Vespasian)[12]

FRAGMENT FOUR [13]

(357) (357) I cannot, however, but wonder at your impudence in daring to assert that your narrative is to be preferred to that of all who have written on this subject, when you neither knew what happened in Galilee -- for you were then at Berytus with the king -- nor acquainted yourself with all that the Romans endured or inflicted upon us at the siege of Jotapata; nor was it in your power to ascertain the part which I myself played in the siege, since all possible informants perished in that conflict.

(358) (358) Perhaps, however, you will say that you have accurately narrated the events which took place at Jerusalem. How, pray, can that be, seeing that neither were you a combatant nor had you perused the Commentaries of Caesar, as is abundantly proved

(359) by your contradictory account? (359) But, if you are so confident that your history excels all others, why did you not publish it in the lifetime of the Emperors Vespasian and Titus, who conducted the war, and while Agrippa and all his family, persons thoroughly conversant with Hellenic culture, were

(360) still among us? (360) You had it written twenty years ago, and might then have obtained the evidence of eyewitnesses to your accuracy. But not until now, when those persons are no longer with us and you think you cannot be confuted, have you ventured to publish it.

FRAGMENT FIVE (Josephus, <u>Life</u> 340)

(340) Πῶς οὖν, ἵνα φῶ πρὸς αὐτὸν ὡς παρόντα,   (340)
'Ιοῦστε, δεινότατε συγγραφέων, τοῦτο γὰρ αὐχεῖς
περὶ σεαυτοῦ, αἴτιοι γεγόναμεν ἐγώ τε καὶ Γαλι-
λαῖοι τῇ πατρίδι σου τῆς πρὸς 'Ρωμαίους καὶ πρὸς
5 τὸν βασιλέα στάσεως;

PRAMW

4 τῆς: τῇ PR | 5 στάσει R |

FRAGMENT FIVE[14]

(340)   (340)   How, then, Justus -- if I may address him
as though he were present -- how, most clever of
historians, as you boast yourself to be, can I and
the Galileans be held responsible for the insurrection
of your native city against the Romans and against
the king?

ANNOTATIONS

1. The title is supplied by Photius, Bibliotheca 33 =
FGrH 734 T2. Cf. Introduction, Notes, no. 17.

2. The fragment occurs in Diogenes Laertius' treatment
of Socrates (2.18-47).

3. I.e., Socrates.

4. Hicks, LCL, renders τῷ στέμματι "The Wreath," a fully
justified rendering in its own right. However, other
sources suggest that Justus' work was genealogical, in
some form. Cf. Schürer (Vermes-Millar), 1.37, who suggests
that the anecdote in Diogenes Laertius is taken from
another genealogical list (στέμμα) belonging "to another
part of the complete work" other than the στέμμα of the
Jewish kings known to Photius. On the difficulty of the
title ἐν τῷ στέμματι, cf. Cohen, 143, n. 145, and the
literature cited there.

5. This fragment occurs in the foreword to the second
book of the Chronicle which contains chronological tables
arranged synchronistically. Cf. Adler, Syncellus, 89, n. 1.
Syncellus uses, or refers to this fragment, several times.
Cf. Dindorf 1.118, 228, 280. It should be noted that
Jacoby marks this fragment with an asterisk (*), thus as
defective.

6. Several variations of this phrase occur in the textual
tradition. Cf. app. crit.

7. Or, "sacred utterances in Scripture" (λόγια θεῖα
γραφῇ). In his text, Dindorf reads λόγια θεῖα. The text
here follows Jacoby. Cf. app. crit.

8. Inachus was the first king of Argos, ca. 1976 B.C.E.,
with whom both Jewish and Christian chronographers syn-
chronized Moses and the Exodus. The synchronization ill
fits that of the following fragment where Moses is placed
in the time of Phoroneus. Cf. Wacholder, Eupolemus 119,
124.

9. This fragment is marked by Jacoby with an asterisk
(*), thus as defective.

10. The translation here follows the marginal reading
reported by Dindorf: Ποσειδωνίου. Cf. also PG (10) 77B;
Routh, Reliquiae Sacrae 2.276: Ἀπίων δὲ ὁ Ποσειδωνίου.

11. In an older chronographical tradition, Phoroneus
was the first king of Argos. Cf. Wacholder, Eupolemus,
124. On the synchronization of Moses with Amosis, cf.
Thallus, Frg. 4, par. 7.

12. The title is supplied by Stephanus of Byzantium
(ed. Meineke) s.v. Τιβεριάς = FGrH 734 T 4: ἐκ ταύτης
ἦν ᾿Ιοῦστος ὁ τὸν ᾿Ιουδαϊκὸν πόλεμον τὸν κατὰ Οὐεσπασιανοῦ
ἱστορήσας.

13. This fragment occurs after Josephus describes Justus'
relationship with Agrippa, and is included here because
in it Josephus directly discusses Justus' historical
work itself. The translation is that of H. St. J.
Thackeray, Josephus (LCL), vol. 9, pp. 131 & 133.

14. This fragment occurs at the beginning of Josephus'
long digression of Justus, beginning with par. 65. The
translation is that of H. St. J. Thackeray, Josephus (LCL),
vol. 9, p. 125.